Desktop Publishing Secrets

Desktop Publishing Secrets

The best desktop publishing tips,
tricks, techniques, and solutions from
the pages of Publish *magazine*

by

Robert C. Eckhardt,
Bob Weibel, and Ted Nace

Peachpit Press
Berkeley, California

DESKTOP PUBLISHING SECRETS

Peachpit Press
2414 Sixth Street
Berkeley, CA 94710
510/548-4393

ISBN 0-938151-74-6
Printed and bound in the United States of America.

PRINTED ON RECYCLED PAPER

❧ This book is dedicated to those who have plied us with questions, to those who have shared their tips with us, and to those who have benefited from reading the "Q&A" and "Tips" columns in Publish *magazine. ❧*

Overview

Contents

Chapter 6   **Hardware**

Foreword

❧ Throughout *Publish*'s five year history, its monthly "Q&A" columns and "Tips" sections have always been among the most popular parts of the magazine. These are the places where readers go to learn the things their manuals never tell them—the secrets, the shortcuts, the workarounds. Now, I'm happy to report, the same people who answered even the toughest questions and tested and refined every tip have put together this easy-to-use, all-in-one-place compilation of more than 500 of their most useful and popular shortcuts, tricks, answers, and solutions. *Desktop Publishing Secrets* is no mere rehash of old, familiar material, however. Much of what appears here is new, and everything that has appeared previously in *Publish* has been retested, reworked, expanded, updated, and illustrated with helpful examples and screen shots.

There's a tremendous amount of information on these pages for both PC and Mac owners. And no matter what software you work with, *Desktop Publishing Secrets* will increase your efficiency, give you fresh ideas, and quite possibly show you how to do things you thought were impossible. This is an encyclopedia of publishing, an important reference for anyone who uses a personal computer to produce newsletters, display ads, software and hardware manuals, magazines, marketing materials...well, you get the idea. *Desktop*

Publishing Secrets is so comprehensive, all you need to do is add hardware and software, and, voilá, you're an expert.

If you want to understand your publishing hardware and software inside-out, if you want to become more efficient so you can generate more work in the same number of hours, if you want to rediscover the fun and fascination of putting out publications on a computer, here's my most valuable tip: buy this book. It will be one of the best investments you've ever made.

James A. Martin, Executive Editor, *Publish* magazine

Acknowledgments

🐝 This book would not have been possible without the participation of dozens and dozens of our fellow desktop publishers. Their queries, insights, tips, comments, corrections, inspiration, experience, and overall collective wisdom make *Desktop Publishing Secrets* possible. In particular, we would like to thank the following people and organizations for their contributions, large and small:

Aldus Technical Support, Carol Alloway, Rick Altman,
Leroy Anderson, Carl Aron, Lenny Bailes, Keith Baumann,
Mike Benhup, Jerri Bionda, Dave Blake, Doug Boltson,
Ginny Boswinkle, Tony Bove, Richard Briggs, Carl Brightman,
M. Travis Brown, Diane Burns, Rick Burress, Fred Caprilli,
Bruce Charonnat, Tom Colandrea, Caleb Coleman,
Alyssa Connolly, Corporate Presentations, Gary Cosimini,
Patti Cragg, Bill Crider, Steve Cummings, Aaron Davis,
Design North, N. Donahoe, David Doty, John Drummond,
Ed Eitelman, Adam E. Ek, Electronic Directions, Electronic Ink,
Bob Elmer, Mike Fanara, James Felici, Roger Fidler,
Finnie/CVC Graphics, Shawn Freeman, Nikki Nahmens Gage,
Jacqueline Landman Gay, Lenn George, Danny Goodman,
Michael Gorman, Linda Gould, Dave Haber, Dorothy Hadfield,
Vincent Hao, Warren W. Hardy, Jeff Harmon, Geoff Hart,
Hawkey & Associates, H. John Henry, Jonathan Hoefler,
Richard E. Howland-Bolton, Ross Hunter, Tim Hutchison,
John M. Irwin, Richard Jantz, James Kaplan, Elizabeth Keyes,
Bill Kimmel, Felix Kramer, Olav Martin Kvern, Chuck Lazar,
Frank Lee, Jonathan Lehrer, Bartholemew Logue, Maggie Lovaas,

Mark Mandel, Aaron Marcus, Tom Marshall, Sam Mattes,
Deke McClelland, Steve McKinstry, Mark Monlux, Bert Monroy,
Pamela Montgomery, Paul A. Moreira, Brian Patrick Mucha,
Thomas J. Nagorski, NewType, Don Nissen, Brian O'Dea,
R. Steven O'Neal, Clayton L. Olson, Dave Peters, Eugene Peterson,
Dennis Peterson, Bobby Potter, Jack Powers, Printz, Dick Pruitt,
Cherie Pyron, Quark Creative Services Department,
Mel Ramaswamy, Louise Rausch, James Restle, Cheryl Rhodes,
Ruth Rhodes, Becky Riegler, Bruce Robinson, Helen Ross,
Steve Roth, Philip C. Russell, Janusz Rychter, Sanjay Sakhuja,
Sue Ann Sanders, Phil Sasso, Seiko Sato, Peggy Sattler, Kim Schive,
John N. Serio, Brian Shaw, Kennon Showen, Barry Simon,
Teresa Singleton, Richard Sleigh, Robert Smallman, Stat Store,
Mark H. Suggs, Jim Suhre (KNVB), Michael Sullivan,
Margaret Swart, John Taylor, TechArt, Carol Terrizzi, Rudy Teseo,
Sivasailam Thiagarajan, Michael Utvitch, Betsy Valentine,
S. Venit, Ventura Software Technical Support, Kris Versdahl,
Leslie Vincent, Paul Volk, Waldman Graphics, Jeff Walker,
Linda Wallace, Suzanne Walzman, Lynn Watson,
Watzman + Keyes, Howard Wiener, Laurie Wigham,
Daniel Will-Harris, David Williams, Matthew Williams,
Howard A. Wright, Judy Zatz, Tanya Zumach.

On the Macintosh side, Erfert Fenton and Danny Goodman patiently
responded to what must have seemed a never-ending stream of major
and minor requests. Other Macintosh colleagues who have been
especially helpful include Steve Roth, Lon Poole, and Jim Heid. On
the PC side, Daniel Will-Harris and Richard Jantz patiently offered
their time and expertise. Margaret Swart and Amy Ecclesine assisted
in locating and compiling "Tips" and "Q&A" columns from the *Publish* archives. Olav Martin Kvern designed the layout and gave valuable advice and criticism as the pages progressed toward final form
David Smith created the Mac and PC icons that help organize the
contents of the book. Our copy editor, Nancy Hackleman of the
Southern Oregon State College English department, provided polish
and clarity to our technically complex manuscript. And vendors too
numerous to mention generously helped us in our attempts to better
understand their products.

🐦 We offer particular thanks to a few special friends and colleagues: Susan Gubernat, *Publish*'s first Editor-in-Chief, has always been supportive and encouraging—and was instrumental in germinating the seeds that became this book. Jim Felici, *Publish*'s first Technical Editor, brought several of us to the magazine and was in large part responsible for the early and unflagging popularity of the "Tips" and "Q&A" sections. Sandra Rosenzweig, *Publish*'s Editor-in-Chief during the creation of this book, gave us encouragement and has been an important partner in resolving the legal matters that always entangle a book like this one. And Jake Widman, *Publish*'s current Senior Technical Editor, edits our work at the magazine and is currently the unsung hero of the "Tips" and "Q&A" sections.

While all of this assistance is gratefully acknowledged, we are, of course, solely responsible for any errors which may have found their way onto these pages. If you locate an error and would like to see your name in the Acknowledgments to the next edition of this book, please send us a correction at the address that appears at the end of the introduction.

Introduction

☞ While we were putting this book together, we were often asked by friends and colleagues to give a quick, one-sentence description of our current project. Invariably, we would say that we were compiling more than four years of desktop publishing tips and techniques from the pages of *Publish*. But this facile answer is at best imprecise—and at worst flat-out wrong.

True, there are hundreds of tips on the following pages that have their origin in our "Q&A" and "Tips" columns in *Publish* and in the magazine's annual "101 Tips" issues. But virtually every one of these tips has been extensively rewritten, researched, enlarged, and re-checked against the current version of the software involved. We've also transformed many hopelessly out-of-date tips into entirely new techniques, similar in general concept but entirely different in the details. And many tips that appear here were written specifically for *Desktop Publishing Secrets*. This book may be based on four years' worth of tips and A's (our "word" for the answers in the "Q&A" column), but it's no simple regurgitation.

To help our questioners grasp our enthusiasm for the project, we would also tell them that the "Q&A" and "Tips" columns in *Publish* are consistently rated as the most frequently read and most popular parts of the magazine. Although we have revised or rewritten most pre-existing material specifically for this collection, we have made every attempt to preserve those qualities that our *Publish* readers prize most: an easy-to-read style, a wide range of subject matter, and an emphasis on techniques useful to beginners and power-users alike. As a result, we believe you'll find *Desktop Publishing Secrets* at least as stimulating, helpful, and informative as the tips and A's which are its inspiration.

Desktop Publishing Secrets is intended for desktop publishers of all kinds and levels of expertise. We enjoyed writing it, and learned a lot in the process. We hope you enjoy reading it, and whether you use a Mac or a PC, whether you consider yourself a novice or an old hand, we think you'll learn a lot, too. The tips and techniques in this book have made us better desktop publishers, and we're sure they'll do the same for you.

. . . .

How to use this book

Although we call it *Desktop Publishing Secrets*, we like to think of it as a book of solutions. Every tip in this book solves a problem. The problem may be a simple one (how to accomplish a straightforward task more efficiently) or a difficult one (accomplishing a task which to many seems impossible). But big or small, the problems posed in this book are ones desktop publishers face every day, and many of the shortcuts, techniques, and tips on these pages will likely work their way into your daily routine, saving you time, effort, and money.

To bring some order out of chaos, we have divided the hundreds of tips in this book into nine chapters according to subject matter; we have further subdivided each chapter into a number of subordinate topics. (A brief scan of the overview at the beginning of the book should give you a good idea of the chapter topics and subtopics.) You could, we suppose, read this book chapter by chapter, topic by topic, from beginning to end, but we'd like to suggest several alternatives.

One useful way to read *Desktop Publishing Secrets* is to consult the overview, the table of contents, or the index to locate the topic most relevant to what your work involves now—this minute—and then read the tips under that topic. This "directed" method almost always reaps significant rewards since there's usually a high degree of over- lap between the issues you're turning over in your mind and the solutions described in the book. Another way to use this book is to flip through it in spare moments (while you're waiting for the printer to spit out a page, or while you're uploading or downloading a file) and read the tips that catch your eye. This "serendipitous" method often yields insights which you would not hit upon in a more purposeful search.

No matter how you read this book, you'll find that each tip is marked with one or two icons. A Mac icon appears in the margin next to tips relating to Macintosh hardware and software. A PC icon appears in the margin next to tips regarding PC hardware and software. And both PC and Mac icons appear in the margin next to tips relevant to both Mac and PC hardware and software. We've marked the tips in this way so that readers in need of immediate help can quickly locate techniques and solutions written specifically for their computer and software. Nevertheless, we hope that these icons do not deter Mac owners from browsing PC tips, or PC owners from browsing Mac tips. Time and again, *Publish* readers tell us that they learn almost as much from tips for "the other computer" as they do from tips for their own hardware set-up. That, in fact, is precisely why we have combined both kinds of tips in one book and refrained from creating separate sections for Mac and PC tips. We hope you will take some time to peruse the tips for "the other computer"; we think you'll be surprised at how rewarding those tips can be.

Finally, we'd like to draw your attention to the last chapter. Unlike the other chapters, Chapter 10 isn't a list of tips. Instead, it's a brief description of how we created this book: How we wrote it and edited it; how three authors collaborated and divided up the various tasks; how we worked together when we were as much as 3,000 miles apart; and how we produced the final pages you're reading right now. The last section of Chapter 10 describes in detail some of the more intricate techniques we used. We thought you'd like to know how we did it, and we hope that the retelling of our experiences in publishing this book will give you some insight into large and complex projects, we perhaps giving you the courage to try one yourself.

The major software covered

In the chapters that follow, we write about many different hardware and software products. In terms of software, we tested virtually every tip or technique described here on the version of the application current when this book went to press. For those applications which we mention frequently, we note the current versions here, rather than repeatedly throughout the text.

On the Macintosh side, we cover these major programs and versions:

Adobe Illustrator 3.0.1
Adobe PhotoShop 1.0.7
Aldus FreeHand 3.0
Aldus PageMaker 4.0a
FullWrite Professional 1.5s
MacDraw II 1.0v4
MacroMind Director 2.0.1
Microsoft Word 4.00D
QuarkXPress 3.0
Ventura Publisher 3.0
WordPerfect 2.0

On the PC side, we cover these major programs and versions:

Aldus PageMaker 4.0
Arts and Letters 3.1
CorelDRAW 2.0
Harvard Graphics 3.0
Micrografx Designer 3.02
Microsoft Windows 3.0
Microsoft Word for Windows 1.1a
Microsoft Word for DOS 5.5
WordPerfect 5.1
Ventura Publisher 3.0 GEM Edition
Ventura Publisher 3.0 Windows Edition

Mac and PC software is, of course, constantly upgraded, so by the time you read this, tips or techniques for some programs may be based on a version which is no longer current. In most instances, we doubt that this will significantly detract from the usefulness of the tips, but you may find that options, commands, or other items are no longer where we say they are. Your new manual or upgrade documentation should be able to direct you to the right location; if not, a brief search through the program itself should do the trick and introduce you to many of the other changes in the new version as well.

Conventions used in this book

While we were putting this book together, we worked hard to find a set of terms and typographic conventions which would help readers quickly identify the many menu titles, command names, and other computer terms which are, alas, unavoidable. Given that we write about such a wide variety of computing environments, the task has not been an easy one. Ultimately, we had to make a few compromises, but we think both Mac and PC owners will readily understand our standard terms and conventions.

Nomenclature

PC owners usually call the arrow controlled by the mouse the cursor, while Mac owners call it the pointer. PC owners also use *cursor* for the flashing bar where text will be inserted, while Mac owners call the flashing bar the insertion point. To avoid cursor confusion, we've decided to call the mouse arrow the pointer and the flashing bar the insertion point, regardless of whether you're using a Mac or a PC. Keep in mind that the pointer sometimes changes shape; when this occurs, and when we can find the right words, we modify the term *pointer* so it describes what you see on the screen. For example, when you press the Help key in Microsoft Word, the pointer turns into a bold question mark; not too surprisingly, we call this the question mark pointer.

Dialog box options in both the Mac and PC come in a variety of shapes and sizes. We use the term *option* to refer to any dialog box choice, including those specified with a radio button, a check box, a pop-up menu, a scrolling list, or a text box. (A text box is a small rectangle in which you can enter text or numbers, such as the width of a margin or the character to use as a tab leader.) In DOS programs without graphical interfaces, such entries are made at what we refer to as a *prompt*, a line of text which indicates the entry that's required. We also use *option* to refer to choices in the screens of many non-Windows PC programs.

Finally, when we use the term *button*, we refer to a term or phrase (such as OK or Cancel or Print) surrounded by a button-shaped outline. Buttons are most often found in a dialog boxes, and clicking a button initiates an action of some sort. A button may open another dialog box, save or cancel your option settings, print a document, and so on.

Typographic conventions

In addition to a standard terminology, we also use certain typographic conventions throughout this book. Their purpose is to make instructions easier to follow and the text, in general, easier to understand:

- At their first occurrence in each technique description, the names of the major programs discussed appear in boldface, as in **FreeHand** and **CorelDRAW**. We do this to help readers quickly find information about specific programs. You can, of course, use the index to locate each mention of a specific program. But if you're browsing through a section on a topic of special interest and want to read carefully all the information on PageMaker, for example, simply keep an eye peeled for **PageMaker**.

- Menu titles, button names, and dialog box titles are indicated by initial caps, as in the Save As dialog box, the File menu, and the Print PostScript button.

- The names of menu commands appear in small caps, as in ADD/REMOVE FONTS and OPEN HEADER. On the Macintosh, a menu command which leads to a dialog box always ends in an ellipsis on the menu; for clarity's sake, however, all such ellipses are omitted in this book. For example, although it appears as PRINT MERGE... on the menu, we would render this command simply as PRINT MERGE.

- All dialog box options and PC menu selection prompts appear in italics, as in *Encapsulated PostScript File* and *Odd Pages Only*.

- Text and/or numbers which you should enter verbatim from the keyboard are set in Courier, like this:

```
softfont1=c:\psfonts\pfm\morg____.pfm.
```

- The names of the keys on the keyboard are spelled out and appear in initial caps, except when the appropriate numbers or symbols are easily understood. For example: the S Key, the Shift Key, the Page Down Key, the Comma Key, the 2 Key, and the / Key. Note that the letters in letter keys, such as the S in the S Key, are rendered in uppercase for clarity only; the fact that a letter key name is in uppercase does not mean that you should press both the Shift Key and a letter key. If and when you need to press the Shift Key, we'll let you know.

- Key combinations you should press simultaneously, rather than sequentially, are written as a string of key names separated by plus signs. If we ask you to press Shift + Command + S, for example, press the Shift Key, the Command Key, and the S Key all at the same time.

Do the right environmental thing

As much as possible while writing this book, we tried to give concrete form to our environmental concerns. We traded files and edited each other's work almost entirely in electronic form in an effort to save paper. When printed versions were required, we used recycled paper (Weyerhaeuser Recycled Laser Copy). We recycle our toner cartridges and soda cans, turn out the lights whenever we leave the room (and not just because mother always told us to), and lower the thermostat at night. And we are publishing with Peachpit Press in part because of its commitment to print its books on recycled paper. We try, in short, to minimize the demands we place on the earth's renewable and nonrenewable resources. We strongly encourage you to do the same.

In general, the computer industry does not tread lightly on this earth; Silicon Valley has one of the most serious toxic waste problems in the country, and most hardware and software vendors still generate plastic-wrapped, unnecessarily bulky packaging like there was no tomorrow. Thus it's doubly important that computer users do everything they can to minimize their environmental impact—and that they take every opportunity to put pressure on hardware and software companies to clean up their act.

Scattered throughout this book you'll find a variety of suggestions on ways to minimize waste, reuse or recycle materials, reduce energy consumption, and so on. But because it's so important, we'd like to offer much, much more in this vein, both in *Publish* itself and in the next edition of this book. Therefore, if you are currently using or are aware of effective environmental strategies appropriate for desktop publishers, we'd like to hear about them so we can pass them along.

How to contact us

If you have a question you'd like to ask us or a tip you'd like to tell us about, we would enjoy hearing from you. *Publish* pays a modest (but not insignificant) sum for every tip that appears in the magazine, and although we can't respond personally to every question, we try to answer as many as we can. In addition, if your tip or our response to your question appears in the next edition of *Desktop Publishing Secrets*, you'll have the satisfaction of seeing your name listed in the Acknowledgments. So keep those postcards and letters coming, folks, and address them to

Editor, Tips and Q&A
Publish Magazine
201 Second Street
San Francisco, CA 94107.

Type and Typography

Correct characters

The dotless i?

One of the basic characters in PostScript fonts is the dotless i. Created originally for use with accents, this character is also useful in display type, where the dot can get in the way when your text is tightly leaded or kerned (Figure 1-1). On the Mac, you can enter a dotless i using the Shift + Option + B key combination. According to Adobe, there's no way to enter a dotless i in Windows-based and other PC programs short of major hacking. For display type, you can, however, use **CorelDRAW** or Micrografx **Designer** to convert the text containing the offending i to editable graphics and then remove the dot on the i.

FIGURE 1-1 *When the dot on the i gets in the way, try using the dotless i.*

PostScript primes

The only proper primes (used to indicate feet, inches, minutes, and seconds) in PostScript fonts are found in the Symbol font (Alt + 0233 for ′, Alt + 0198 for ″ in Windows; Option + comma and Option + 4, respectively, on the Mac). But you can create equally professional-looking primes simply by italicizing the standard typewriter-style quotes found in all PostScript fonts (Figure 1-2).

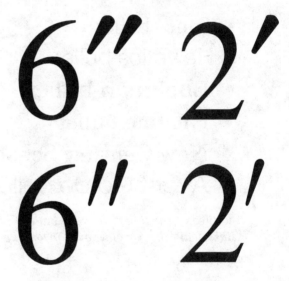

FIGURE 1-2 *You can use italicized typewriter-style quotes (bottom) as a quick substitute for the Symbol font's prime characters (top).*

 ## Budget bullets

If your PC word processor or layout program doesn't give you easy access to or adequate control over a bullet character, create your own from a period. Provided your program has the necessary functions, enter a period for your bullet, set it as bold text, and then at least double its point-size. Use a superscript function to raise it from the baseline.

Large-caliber bullets

The bullets in the basic laser printer fonts (Helvetica, Times, and Courier) tend to look dinky. If you're using a laser printer with an extended font set, you'll get heftier bullets if you use those in Avant Garde, New Century Schoolbook, Bookman, or Palatino instead (see Figure 1-3). For the best effect, always add some space between the bullet and the word that follows it.

- Times bullet
- Helvetica bullet
- Bookman bullet
- Palatino bullet
- New Century Schoolbook bullet
- Avant Garde bullet

FIGURE 1-3 *The bullets in some built-in laser printer fonts are pretty dinky, while those in other built-in fonts are more substantial.*

 ### Typing special characters

Many Macintosh fonts have special characters which are not assigned a standard key combination and are thus not accessible from the keyboard. Zapf Dingbats, for example, contains three arrows which cannot be entered with a key combination. Despite their inaccessibility, there are several ways you can insert these characters in your documents.

If you are working in **Microsoft Word** for the Mac and you know the ASCII code of the special character you need, you can use the PASTE SPECIAL CHARACTER command to insert it in your document. For example, the three special arrows in Zapf Dingbats are assigned ASCII codes 252, 253, and 254. To enter the first of these, you'd press Option + Command + Q (the keyboard command for PASTE SPECIAL CHARACTER), then type 252, then press Return. Of course, you'll need to change the resulting character's font format to Zapf Dingbats to display the arrow.

Another way to insert inaccessible characters is to use Page Studio Graphics' **FindPIXymbols** desk accessory or **WriteFontSize,** a shareware desk accessory by Jeffrey S. Shulman. To enter one of the Zapf Dingbats arrows using WriteFontSize, for example, you'd open the desk accessory, select Zapf Dingbats from the pop-up Font menu at the bottom of the main window, and click on the Grid button to display the font's entire character set (Figure 1-4). You can then select the desired arrow (the special arrows are the three at the end of the last column) and paste it into your document.

WriteFontSize and FindPIXymbols can also be used to determine a character's ASCII code for use with Word's PASTE SPECIAL CHARACTER command. For any character in WriteFontSize's character grid, for example, simply add the numbers at the beginning of that character's column and row; the sum of these two numbers is the

Zapf Dingbats

	0	16	32	48	64	80	96	112	128	144	160	176	192	208	224	240
0																
1																
2																
3																
4																
5																
6																
7																
8																
9																
10																
11																
12																
13																
14																
15																

Click mouse to continue. Option-click to select and continue.

FIGURE 1-4 *WriteFontSize's grid displays the entire character set for the selected font.*

character's ASCII code. WriteFontSize is a particularly useful alternative to Apple's Key Caps utility since it displays a font's entire character set in one large grid instead of a clutch of different keyboard maps.

 ## Entering open and closed quotes

When you place text in **PageMaker** for the Mac with the *Convert Quotes* option turned on, typewriter-style quotation marks are automatically converted to true open and closed quotation marks. But if you enter text directly in PageMaker, either directly on the page or in the story editor, you must enter true quotation marks yourself with the appropriate key combinations:

To enter	Press this key command on a Mac	on a PC
Open single quote (')	Option +]	Control + [
Close single quote (')	Shift + Option +]	Control +]
Open double quote (")	Option + [	Shift + Control + [
Close double quote (")	Shift + Option + [	Shift + Control +]

We know very few people who can correctly recite all four of these key combinations; most people (and that includes us) either experiment until they hit the right combination, or they keep a list like the one above close at hand. An easy way to remedy this sad state of affairs is to assign **QuicKeys 2**'s QuickQuotes and Double Quick-Quotes to the Quote/Apostrophe Key (Figure 1-5). Thereafter, the correct single or double quotation mark is automatically entered; you no longer have to think about whether an open or closed quote is required or what the proper key combination is. Note, however, that if you use another program with a built-in "smart quotes" feature—such as **Microsoft Word**—you should add the QuickQuotes keystrokes to the PageMaker keyset, not the Universal keyset. Adding the QuickQuotes keystrokes to the Universal keyset may interfere with the other program's built-in "smart quotes" function.

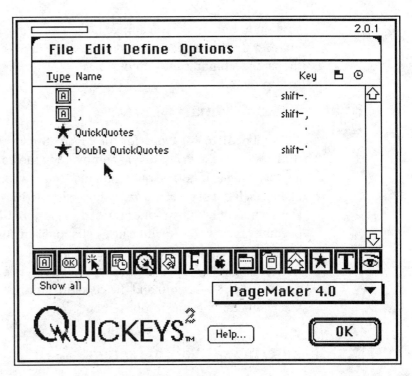

FIGURE 1-5 *Assign QuickQuotes and Double QuickQuotes to the Quote/Apostrophe Key in QuicKeys 2 to make it easier to enter true quotation marks.*

Open and closed quote substitutes

If you're using PC fonts that don't include true open and closed quotation marks, **WordPerfect** for the PC provides characters which you can use instead. Here's how to enter them:

1. Place the cursor where you'd like to enter the quotation mark, and then type Ctrl + V.

2. At the *Key* = prompt, enter 4,32 (type the comma) for an opening quotation mark, or 4,31 for a closing quotation mark, and then press Return.

Your quotation marks will appear on screen as small square boxes, but they'll print O.K. You can also enter the illusive em dash using the same technique and entering 4,34.

 ## Tricking "Smart Quotes"

Normally, **Microsoft Word** for the Mac's "Smart" Quotes feature (turned on via the PREFERENCES command in the Edit menu) enters an open single or double quotation mark after a space and in front of the first letter of a word. It's easy, however, to trick Word into giving you a typesetter's apostrophe (a closed single quotation mark) at the beginning of a word—to indicate a colloquialism, for example, as in " 'neath the starry sky." To enter the apostrophe, type any character, followed by a single quotation mark (Word enters a closed quote—an apostrophe—for you) and the colloquial term. Then delete that first character; the apostrophe remains.

 ## Entering special characters

If you've switched from a typewriter to a PC word processing or page layout program, you may have noticed that you have more type characters to contend with. Typographically correct characters such as open and closed quotation marks, em dashes, copyright symbols, foreign characters, and many others are *de rigueur* these days. A few PC programs, like **PageMaker** for Windows, let you access these characters via special key combinations, but most programs are not so kind. Nevertheless, in most PC word processing and page layout programs, you can enter and print characters that aren't on your keyboard by holding down the Alt Key while you type the appropriate character codes on the numeric pad.

Unlike the decimal codes for common PC character sets like Ventura International, Roman-8, or PC-8, the ANSI character codes used by Windows always start with a zero. For example, to enter a double open quotation mark in **Word** for Windows (which lacks a keyboard shortcut for the character), hold down the Alt Key and enter 0147; for the double closed quote, enter 0148.

Character reference charts

For any Macintosh font package that lacks an accompanying character chart, keyboard map, or type sample, there are several ways to create your own. One method, of course, is to generate a chart from scratch in your graphics or page layout program. This is the most effort-intensive solution, to be sure, but it's one that allows you to customize your reference chart to your particular needs.

Another inexpensive solution is to call Adobe customer service and ask for the **Character Set Sample Page** disk. The disk is free and contains a character set sample page in PostScript format and instructions for printing it. The sample page it produces, however, contains nothing more than one complete character set in roman style (no keyboard map or keystroke chart; see Figure 1-6 on page 10), and producing pages for large numbers of fonts can be a laborious process.

A much more elegant, and expensive, solution to the lack of a font reference chart is Omega Systems' **SPECtacular**. This utility program can produce sample pages for all your installed fonts in a single step, and it offers a wide variety of beautifully designed sample pages (see Figure 1-7 on page 11), ranging from character sets in four style variants to sample paragraphs (your choice of text) in different sizes and leadings, keyboard maps, and character lists sorted by key strokes. SPECtacular can also print a pica ruler and a list of all your fonts, each in its own face. If font families have been compressed or harmonized with **Suitcase II** or **MasterJuggler**, the font list can include information on how each style is created; it will tell you, for example, that Bauhaus Light formatted in boldface produces Bauhaus Demi.

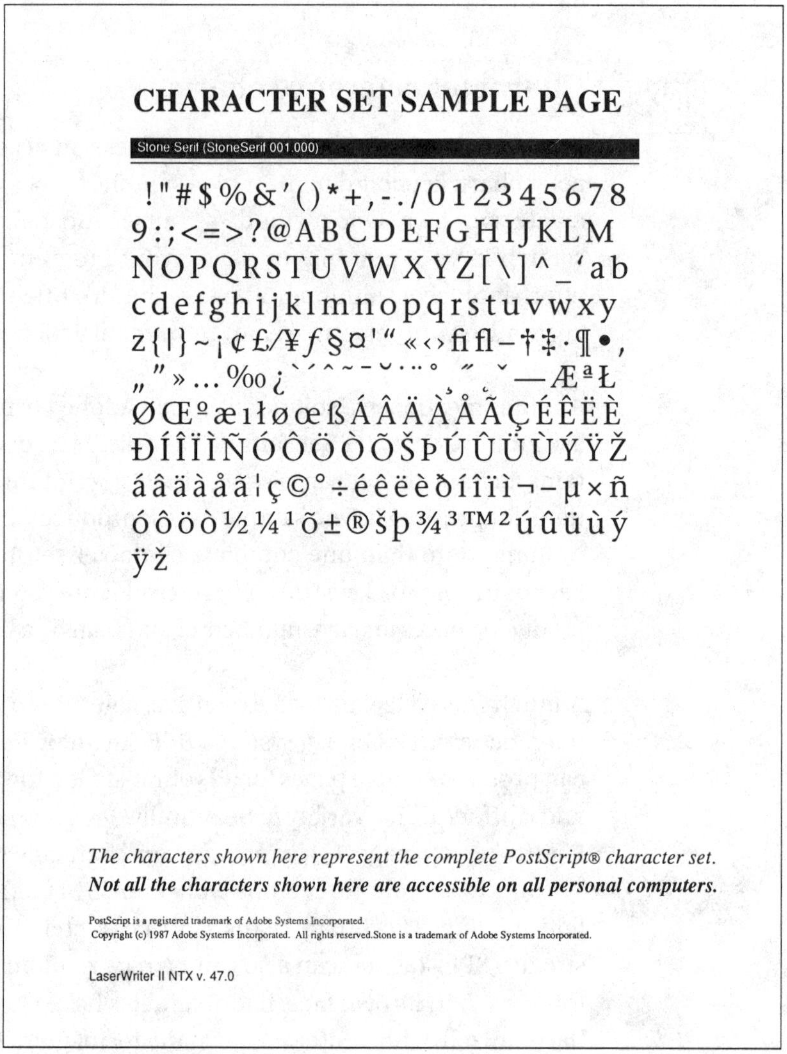

CHARACTER SET SAMPLE PAGE

Stone Serif (StoneSerif 001.000)

!"#$%&'()*+,-./012345678
9:;<=>?@ABCDEFGHIJKLM
NOPQRSTUVWXYZ[\]^_‘ab
cdefghijklmnopqrstuvwxy
z{|}~¡¢£⁄¥ƒ§¤'“«‹›ﬁﬂ–†‡·¶•,
„”»…‰¿`´ˆ˜¯˘˙¨˚¸˝˛ˇ—Æª Ł
ØŒºæıłøœßÁÂÄÀÅÃÇÉÊËÈ
ÐÍÎÏÌÑÓÔÖÒÕŠÞÚÛÜÙÝŸŽ
áâäàåã¦ç©°÷éêëèðíîïì¬−µ×ñ
óôöò½¼¹õ±®šþ¾³™²úûüùý
ÿž

The characters shown here represent the complete PostScript® character set.
Not all the characters shown here are accessible on all personal computers.

PostScript is a registered trademark of Adobe Systems Incorporated.
Copyright (c) 1987 Adobe Systems Incorporated. All rights reserved.Stone is a trademark of Adobe Systems Incorporated.

LaserWriter II NTX v. 47.0

FIGURE 1-6 *A page produced with Adobe's Character Set Sample Page file.*

StoneSerif

StoneSerif Italic

StoneSerif Semibold

StoneSerif Semibold Italic

Aa1Aa1Aa1 Aa1 Aa1 Aa1 Aa1 Aa1 Aa1

Aa1Aa1Aa1 Aa1 Aa1 Aa1 Aa1 Aa1 Aa1

ABCDEFGHIJKLMNOPQRSTUVWXYZ
abcdefghijklmnopqrstuvwxyz
1234567890"!@#$%^&*(){}[]<>\.,;:?"

ABCDEFGHIJKLMNOPQRSTUVWXYZ
abcdefghijklmnopqrstuvwxyz
1234567890"!@#$%^&(){}[]<>\.,;:?"*

ABCDEFGHIJKLMNOPQRSTUVWXYZ
abcdefghijklmnopqrstuvwxyz
1234567890"!@#$%^&*(){}[]<>\.,;:?"

ABCDEFGHIJKLMNOPQRSTUVWXYZ
abcdefghijklmnopqrstuvwxyz
1234567890"!@#$%^&*(){}[]<>\.,;:?"

Excellence in typography is the result of nothing more than an attitude. Its appeal comes from the understanding used in its planning; the designer must care. In contemporary advertising the perfect integration of design elements often demands unorthodox typography. It may require the use of compact spacing, minus leading, unusual sizes and weights. Excellence in typography is the result of nothing more than an attitude. Its appeal comes from the understanding used in its planning; the designer must care. In

14866**A**

FIGURE 1-7 *One of the many different kinds of specimen pages which SPECtacular is capable of producing.*

Typing special menu symbols

There are several ways you can insert the special characters found in many Macintosh menus—the Command Key symbol (⌘), the Apple menu apple (), or the menu check mark (✓)—in a document. If you you can use TrueType fonts, you'll find these characters—plus the diamond (◆)which sometimes appears in list boxes—in Chicago, one of the three system fonts found in all Macintoshes. The Control Key is part of the required key combination for each of these four characters; thus you must have an Apple standard or extended keyboard, or a third-party equivalent, to be able to type them:

To enter	Press
⌘	Control + Q
	Control + T
✓	Control + R
◆	Control + S

If a PostScript font is what you want, you can use the shareware Post-Script font **ChicagoSymbols** by Bradley Poulson. The four characters are assigned to the number keys 1 through 4 and therefore are accessible from any keyboard. These symbols are also found in several commercial PostScript fonts. **PIXymbols 2000** from Page Studio Graphics contains the ⌘ symbol rendered in several different sizes and weights and hollow and filled versions of the symbol, as well as a wide variety of familiar (and not so familiar) Macintosh icons (Figure 1-8, top). All four characters also appear in Chicago Laser, one of six fonts in **Key Caps**, Volume 29 of Fluent Laser Fonts by Casady & Greene. As the name implies, Chicago Laser is a PostScript rendition of the entire Chicago font (Figure 1-8, bottom); to type the four special characters in Chicago Laser, use the same Control-key combinations listed above for Chicago. Key Caps is also available in PC format.

abcdefghijklmnopqrstuvwxyz
ABCDEFGHIJKLMNOPQRSTUVWXY
1234567890!@#$%&*(){}

FIGURE 1-8 *PIXymbols 2000 (top) contains a variety of well-known Mac-intosh icons and objects. Chicago Laser (bottom) is a PostScript copy of the Chicago system font.*

A dash for the LaserJet

Many PC fonts for the Hewlett-Packard LaserJets don't include an em dash. To approximate an em dash with **Ventura Publisher**, type three fixed spaces using Ctrl + spacebar, highlight the three spaces, then select Strike-Thru from the Set Font menu of the DOS/GEM Edition's sidebar. In the Windows Edition, select STRIKETHRU from the Text menu.

Finding graphic characters

Finding a particular character in a graphical (non-alphabetic) character font can be a real headache on a Mac. If the characters are large or the only screen fonts are in large point-sizes, the keyboard map in Apple's Key Caps desk accessory is almost incomprehensible. A far better alternative is **FindPIXymbols**, a desk accessory created specifically for owners of PIXymbols fonts, but which is quite handy with any graphics font.

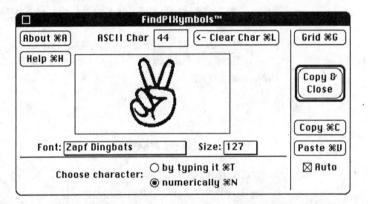

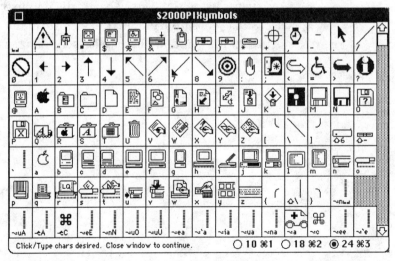

FIGURE 1-9 *FindPIXymbols' main window (top) and character grid window (bottom).*

FindPIXymbols's main window displays one character at a time (Figure 1-9, top); specify the desired character either by typing its key combination or entering its ASCII code. With ATM and a Type 1 PostScript font, FindPIXymbols can display impressively smooth and detailed characters in any size up to 127 points. When the desired character is displayed, you can copy it to the Clipboard and paste it into your document.

If you don't know a character's key combination or ASCII code, use the program's character grid window (Figure 1-9, bottom). There, FindPIXymbols displays the full character set for the selected font in either 10, 18, or 24 points (your choice), together with a shorthand code for the keystrokes required to type each character. You can select any number of characters in the grid simply by Shift + clicking on them, and can then copy them all to the Clipboard for pasting into your document.

Remapping the WordPerfect keyboard

WordPerfect 4.2 for the PC's Ctrl/Alt Keys Screen (obtained by pressing Ctrl + F3) easily allowed you to remap your keyboard—to add Spanish language characters, for example. WordPerfect 5.1's new Keyboard Definitions/Layout feature is more versatile but not as straightforward. Here's an example of how you would use the new Keyboard Definitions/Layout feature to make the Spanish ñ available from a key combination:

1. From the Setup menu (opened by pressing Shift + F1) choose option 5, *Keyboard Layout.*

2. In the resulting Keyboard/Layout screen you'll see a list of alternative keyboard layouts (ALTRNAT, ENHANCED, EQUATION, etc.) which are added during the standard WordPerfect installation (unless you opt not to install them). Ignore these; simply choose 4, the *Create* option, to define a new keyboard layout. Enter SPANISH at the Keyboard Filename prompt to give your new layout a name, and then press Return.

3. With SPANISH highlighted, select 7, the *Edit* option, to redefine a key character.

4. At the top of the Keyboard Edit menu you'll see three headings: Key, Action, and Description. At the moment, there are no entries below the headings since no new key definitions have been assigned yet. To add an entry for the ñ character, first select 4, the *Create* option.

5. The Key: prompt now appears; type the combination to which you want to assign a new character. In this case, press the Alt and N keys simultaneously.

6. At the Description prompt that now follows, type in "n tilde" or another apt description; then press Return.

7. A box now appears on the screen with the code {ALT N} in the upper left corner. Press the delete key to get rid of the code; then, while holding down the Alt Key, enter the PC-8 symbol set code for ñ (164) on your keyboard's numeric key pad. At this point, ñ should be the only character in the window.

8. Press F7 and you'll be back at the Keyboard Edit menu, where your new key assignment is listed under the Key, Action, and Description headings. You're now ready to select 4, the *Create* option, and enter the next key assignment.

When you finish your key assignments, select your new keyboard layout; then type F7 and go to work. You'll be able to enter special characters quickly, using your newly defined Alt Key key combinations, which certainly beats having to remember the PC 8 character code each time you need to enter a special character.

Here are some PC-8 character codes for Spanish and other foreign language characters you may want to add to your new keyboard layout. Check a LaserJet manual for a complete listing:

Character	Code	Character	Code
á	160	ú	163
é	130	ü	129
É	144	Ü	154
í	161	¿	168
ñ	164	¡	173
Ñ	165	«	174
ó	162	»	175

If you're using WordPerfect for the Mac, most foreign language characters are already accessible, either via standard Option + Key and Option + Shift + Key commands or by means of special sequences of key commands (such as Option + N, then N, for the Spanish ñ). You can use the Keyboard Management dialog box, however, to reassign often-used characters so they're easier to remember and type. Here's how, using the Spanish ñ as an example:

1. Select the KEYBOARDS command from the Preferences submenu (in the File menu) to open the Keyboard Management dialog box.

2. If it is not already selected, select the Default Keyboard from the Keyboard pop-up menu at the bottom of the dialog box.

3. Create a new keyboard based on the default key assignments by clicking the Copy Keyboard button. Give the new keyboard a name, such as Spanish Keyboard, in the ensuing dialog box. Make sure the new keyboard is now the selected keyboard in the Keyboard pop-up menu.

4. Select Characters from the Type pop-up menu at the top of the dialog box. A scrolling list of standard and special characters now appears below the pop-up menu.

5. Scroll the character list until you locate the accented characters and click on the ñ to select it. Note that no key combinations are currently listed in the Keystrokes list for the ñ. (This is because the ñ normally requires not one but two key combinations in sequence, as described above.)

6. Click the Assign button to open the Assign Keystroke dialog box. Press Option + N to assign the ñ to that key combination (and replace the tilde, the default assignment for Option + N). Click the Assign button.

7. Back in the Keyboard Management dialog box with the ñ character selected, you'll see the new key combination displayed in the Keystrokes list (Figure 1-10). Add other key assignments as desired; click the Done button when you're finished.

Don't forget that Spanish Keyboard (or whatever you call your new keyboard layout) must be selected in the Keyboard Management dialog box whenever you want to use your new key assignments.

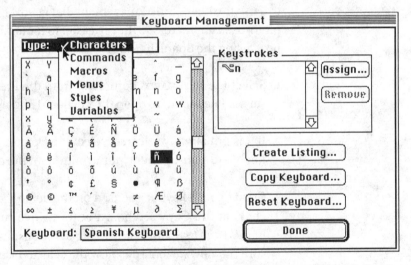

FIGURE 1-10 *To assign the ñ to a new key combination in WordPerfect for the Mac's Keyboard Management dialog box, first select Characters from the Type pop-up menu, and then select the ñ in the scrolling list.*

Drawing true outlines

Because the width of a stroke in **Illustrator** or **FreeHand** falls equally on both sides of the line being stroked, outlining an object or letter by stroking it subtly changes the shape (Figure 1-11). To maintain the integrity of the shape you want to outline, try this instead:

1. Stroke the object with twice the outline you want: for a 1-point outline, give it a 2-point stroke.

2. Create a copy of the object directly on top of the original. Use the COPY and PASTE IN FRONT commands for this in Illustrator, or the CLONE command in FreeHand.

3. Fill the new top copy with white and change the stroke to None.

The result is an outline that extends only to the outside of the object.

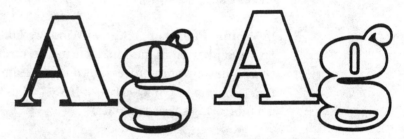

FIGURE 1-11 *Outlining a type character in FreeHand or Illustrator by simply stroking it (left) subtly changes its shape; for a true outline, layer a white, unstroked copy on top of a stroked one (right).*

Do-it-yourself characters

Making a ballot box

In most PostScript fonts, including Zapf Dingbats (which contains a variety of different boxes), there's no ordinary, unfilled ballot box (☐). You can make one quite easily, however. To do so, first type a lower-case n, select it, and choose Zapf Dingbats from the Font menu; what you'll see is a solid black box (■). Now format the solid box in Outline style. The result is a standard, empty ballot box.

A better ellipsis

Compared to those in traditional ellipses, the dots in the ellipsis character (...) in most PostScript fonts are too close together. For a better looking ellipsis, build one of your own. Use three periods (four if the ellipsis ends a sentence) and separate one period from the next with a single space. Use nonbreaking spaces (Option + Spacebar or Command + Spacebar in most Macintosh programs, Ctrl + Spacebar in many PC programs) to keep the ellipsis from splitting apart at the end of a line.

In **Ventura Publisher** GEM and Windows Editions, use the Ctrl + Space Bar key combination, as usual, to create the nonbreaking spaces. In your word processor, you can create the ellipsis for Ventura Publisher by typing <N>.<N>.<N>. (<N>is the Ventura code for a nonbreaking space character).

Faster slash fractions

Here's a quick and easy way to make a slash fraction in **PageMaker:**

1. Type the fraction as standard text, making sure to use the real fraction bar rather than the standard slash (top fraction, Figure 1-12). On the Mac, press Shift + Option + 1 to enter the fraction bar. On the PC, use the fraction bar from the PostScript Symbol font (Alt + 0164 on the numeric keypad), or just / (slash) if you're using an Adobe Expert Set, or the nonbreaking slash (Ctrl + Shift + /) if all else fails.

2. Select the numerator, choose the TYPE SPECS command, and select the *Superscript* option in the Position pop-up menu.

3. Select the denominator, choose the TYPE SPECS command, and select the *Subscript* option in the Position pop-up menu.

4. The fraction as it now stands falls well below the baseline (as in the center fraction, Figure 1-12); a better-looking fraction sits on

the baseline. Move it by selecting the entire fraction and choosing the TYPE SPECS command. Click the Options button to open the Type Options dialog box and change the last three size and position options to 55, 35, and 0.

The fraction should now sit comfortably on the baseline, as illustrated by the bottom fraction in Figure 1-12.

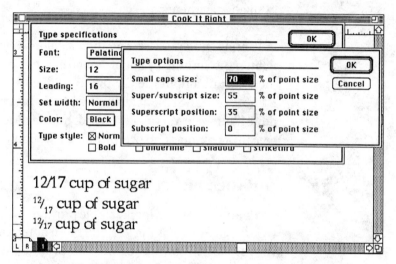

FIGURE 1-12 *Use PageMaker's Type Options dialog box to adjust the position of numerator and denominator and make a good-looking slash fraction.*

  ## A better division sign

The dots of the division sign character (÷) in most PostScript fonts tend to crowd the cross bar when printed on 300-dpi laser printers. You can avoid this problem by creating your own easier-to-read division sign. This is easily accomplished by kerning a colon and an en dash so that the two characters overlap. (An en dash is obtained by pressing Option + dash in all Macintosh programs. In **PageMaker** for the PC, press Control + = for an en dash; in **Ventura Publisher** DOS/GEM Edition, hold down the Alt Key while you type 196 on the numeric key pad; in the Windows Edition of Ventura use the Alt + 0151 key combination.)

In **QuarkXPress**, for example, type an en dash and then a colon, place the insertion point between them, and set the Kern amount (under the Style menu) to about -70. In PageMaker, place the insertion point between the two characters and kern them manually, using Command + Delete on the Mac (Ctrl + Backspace on the PC) to increase the kerning amount in large increments and Option + Delete on the Mac (Shift + Ctrl + Backspace on the PC) to increase it in small increments.

In Ventura, enter a dash and then a colon, highlight the dash, and tighten the kerning by about .4 ems in the Type Specs dialog box in the Mac Edition, in the Change Font dialog box in the DOS/GEM Edition, or with Set font attributes under the Text menu in the Windows Edition. In **Microsoft Word** for the Macintosh, use the Displace formula command to overprint the two characters.

Outline type tricks

The standard PostScript preamble provided with **Ventura Publisher** DOS/GEM Edition is the PS2.PRE file; it automatically downloads to your PostScript printer before you print a job. This preamble file (also known as a PostScript header file) has special routines for handling the Ventura documents you print. One of the things it can't do, unfortunately, is print outline style type. An alternate preamble file is provided, though, that does allow you to print outline type and other special effects. You simply need to install the alternate preamble. Here's how:

1. Copy the file PS2.EFF from the POSTSCPT directory of the Ventura Utilities disk into the Ventura subdirectory of your hard disk.

2. From the DOS prompt, type REN PS2.PRE PS2.REG and then type COPY PS2.EFF PS2.PRE to replace the regular PostScript preamble with the special-effects preamble.

With this new preamble installed, you can print any font in outline style by selecting magenta as the color, using either the *Set Font* option from the sidebar or the Font command under Paragraph menu.

The other colors are also associated with special effects: green produces gray type, red results in a very dark shade of gray, and blue creates a slightly less dark gray shade (green is the most useful of the three. Cyan rotates the text so that it runs vertically up the page—yellow rotates it to run down the page.

Though you'd normally be better off using the text-rotation control in the Paragraph Alignment menu (since that also lets you preview the rotation on screen), you might want to use the special effects rotation feature to rotate a Zapf Dingbats character that you're employing as a bullet via Ventura's Special Effects dialog box. To do so, use the *Set Font Properties* option of the Special Effects dialog box (where the bullet font definition is located) under the Paragraph menu. Simply choose the ASCII character code number, the font (Zapf Dingbats), and set the color as cyan or yellow. You won't see the effect on screen, but it will appear when printed.

If you're using a LaserJet printer, use the **Font Special Effects** utility from SoftCraft to create outline type. This utility can convert any LaserJet bit-mapped soft font into an outline form; it can create other bit-mapped font variations as well. You can also use Micrologic Software's **More Fonts** utility which generates a wide range of printer fonts from their proprietary outlines, including bit-mapped fonts for the LaserJets. You can also generate these with special effects such as starburst textured characters and outline characters.

Black, white, or gray type

White text on black

In the GEM and Windows Editions of **Ventura Publisher**, creating a narrow bar of reversed type against a darker background, such as white on black (Figure 1-13), is easy if you use Ventura's paragraph rules feature to create the background. Here's how:

1. Select the text and set the font color to White.

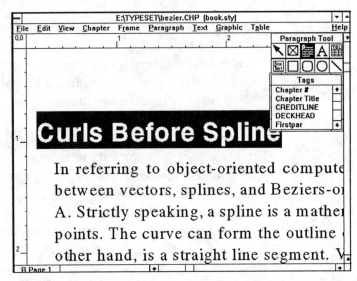

FIGURE 1-13 *In this example of reversed text in Ventura, the black rule draws from the baseline up over the white type.*

2. Using the RULING LINE ABOVE command in the GEM Edition's Paragraph menu, set the Height of Rule 1 to the desired rule thickness, which should be at least the point-size of your type. In the Windows Edition you'll need to click the *User-Defined* option in the Ruling Line Above dialog box in order to access the more detailed User-Defined Ruling Style dialog box, which is comparable to that of the GEM version.

3. For the GEM Edition, in the Space Below Rule 3 text box, enter the same value you entered for Height of Rule 1 in step 2 above, plus about half the point-size of the type; then click on the boxed minus sign to give the bar a negative value. This will move it down, over the text. In the Windows Edition, enter the same value, but manually enter a minus sign in front of your Space Below Rule 3 entry, to make it a negative number.

You should now see the white text appear against the black rule. Since the text's background is actually part of the paragraph, it moves with the text as you edit your layout. If you want to create a reversed-out (white on black) headline that doesn't flow with the text, you can use Ventura's Box Text to create the text against a darker frame background:

1. Enter the text as Box Text, a graphics option in the GEM Edition, or a tool palette choice for the Windows Edition.

2. Select the text and set its color to White in the Set Font Attributes section of the Text menu in the Windows Edition, or in the Set Font dialog box in the GEM Edition.

3. Select a solid background for the text box using the FILL ATTRI-BUTES command under the Graphics menu.

As a variation of the above technique, you can anchor the frame to a paragraph if you create the Box Text within a Ventura frame or paste in the text box after creating the frame. This will link the text box so that it will flow with your text. Here's how to do it:

1. Select the frame containing the box text.

2. In the Anchors & Captions dialog box, enter a name of your choosing in the Anchor: box.

3. Using the Text tool, place the insertion point at the paragraph where you want to attach the box text frame.

4. Select INSERT SPECIAL ITEM from the Edit menu in the Ventura GEM Edition or from the Text menu in the Windows Edition. Choose the *Frame Anchor* option, and, at the Frame's Anchor Name prompt, enter the anchor name that you gave the frame in step two, above. If you want the box text to appear right at the anchor point, not above or below it, select *Relative, Automatically At Anchor* as the Frame's New Location option.

Keeping track of white text

When working on a white background in **PageMaker** and other programs, it's easy to lose track of a text block in reverse type. To keep track of reversed text, put a special symbol, such as < , at the end of the text block and set it as black type. The special character will appear black when the text is on a light background, so you can easily locate the block, but it will disappear when the reverse type is placed on a black box.

 Gray type in PageMaker

Here's a quick way to create gray type in **PageMaker**:

1. Choose the DEFINE COLORS command in the Element menu and click the New button in the Define Colors dialog box.

2. In the Edit Color dialog box, turn on on the *CMYK* option if it is not already on.

3. Enter zero percent in the three color text boxes (Figure 1-14) and the desired percentage of gray in the Black text box. (You can also click on the *Pantone* option and select a gray from the Pantone library.)

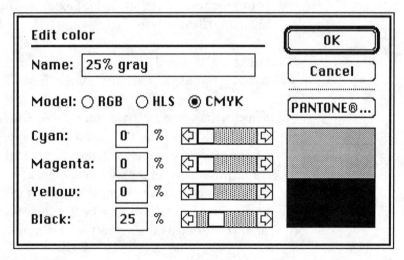

FIGURE 1-14 *To create gray type in PageMaker, first define a shade of gray in the Edit Color dialog box.*

4. Enter a descriptive name (such as 25% gray) in the Name text box. Click the OK buttons of the Edit Color and Define Colors dialog box. Your new gray shade should now appear in the color palette. (Press Command + K on the Mac, or Ctrl + K on the PC, or select the COLOR PALETTE command from the Windows menu to open the color palette if it's not yet open.)

5. Back in the document window, highlight the desired text with the Text tool (not the Pointer tool).

6. Apply the newly defined gray shade either by clicking on its name in the color palette or by opening the Type Specs dialog box and selecting the shade from the Color pop-up menu.

The text will appear in the designated gray shade both onscreen (if you have a color monitor) and on paper.

. . . .

The right font for the job

. . . .

 ### Free and shareware PostScript fonts

If you're short on cash, there's a wealth of free and shareware PostScript fonts available for the Macintosh—if you know where to find them. Most free and shareware fonts are display fonts, many are a bit eccentric, and all vary widely in quality. But if you find a font that meets your needs, you can't beat the price.

Most Macintosh bulletin boards and information services maintain on-line software libraries, and most of these include free and shareware PostScript fonts among their offerings. Some of the best on-line sources of fonts that we know of are CompuServe (try Data Library 5 in the Macintosh Productivity Forum [GO MACPRO] and Data Library 9 in the Desktop Publishing Forum [GO DTPFORUM]), America On-Line, and GEnie.

Other good sources of free and shareware PostScript fonts include user group software libraries. The Berkeley Macintosh Users Group (BMUG) and the Boston Computer Society (BCS) maintain remarkably comprehensive ones. Educorp Computer Services is also an excellent source of free and shareware software. In addition to font-filled floppy disks, Educorp sells two CD ROM collections—the Desktop Publishing CD ROM and the Educorp CD ROM (a two-disk set)—containing large numbers of PostScript fonts (Figure 1-15), not to mention clip art, utilities, templates, and more.

A two-volume type specimen catalog of 200 free and shareware PostScript fonts, HyperActive Software's *The Font Catalog*, can help you determine which fonts are of interest before you download them or purchase a disk from a software library. Each volume is sold separately and contains 100 unbound, loose-leaf pages; each page illustrates a single font and includes the name of the author, the shareware fee (if any), a complete character set, roman, bold and italic faces (the last two computer-generated if none are supplied), text blocks in three sizes and leadings, and a scaled letter E. Sources for individual fonts are not listed, but most fonts in the catalog can be obtained from the on-line services and software libraries mentioned above.

  ## Pick a more appropriate default font

It's easy to change the default font in **PageMaker**; the font you choose will be selected automatically each time you open a new document. First, if you have a document open, save it and close it. Then choose the desired default font from the Font submenu. That's all there is to it. You can use this same technique to change the default type size, justification, leading, type style, line weight, shades, and other settings as well.

 ## Convert your handwriting into a font

For that personal touch, consider converting your own hand lettering into a Macintosh PostScript font. With PostScript font editors such as **Fontographer** and **FontStudio**, this is not as daunting a task

There is a sumptuous variety about the New England weather that compells the stranger's admiration -- and regret.

I WAS GRATIFIED TO BE ABLE TO ANSWER PROMPTLY, AND I DID. I SAID I DIDN'T KNOW.

WEATHER IS A LITERARY SPECIALTY, AND NO UN-TRAINED HAND CAN...

WHEN I'M PLAYFUL I USE THE MERIDIANS OF LONGI-TUDE AND PARALLELS OF LATITUDE FOR A SEINE, AND DRAG THE ATLANTIC OCEAN FOR WHALES.

The widder eats by a bell; she goes to bed by a bell;—everything's so awful reg'lar a body can't stand it.

PROBABLE NOR'EAST TO SOU'WEST WINDS, VARYING TO THE SOUTHARD AND WESTARD AND EASTARD AND POINTS BETWEEN; HIGH AND LOW...

FIGURE 1-15 *A selection of fonts found on Educorp's Desktop Publishing CD ROM (from top): Alison Script, Caveman, Library, Theater, Urban-Scrawl, Zirkle. (Words courtesy of Mark Twain.)*

as it sounds. Start by drawing the complete character set for your font on one or more sheets of paper. To convert your pen art to computer art, scan your lettering and save it in TIFF format. (You might also consider scanning your company logo so you can make it a character in your new font as well.)

Now launch your font editor and open a new font file. With a graphics program like **DeskPaint**, open the file of scanned letters, copy a single character, and then paste that letter into the background of the appropriate character window; the scanned image can be resized or moved within the window as required. Then use the font editor's autotrace function to trace a smooth outline around the character's scanned image. Tweak the outline to improve on the trace or to improve your handwriting.

Repeat this process for each character. Once you've finished a character, you may want to delete the scanned image; an accumulation of background templates can take up a lot of disk space. When everything is the way you want it, generate PostScript and screen font files. Note that this is also a good way to convert otherwise unavailable printed alphabets (such as those found in the typeface specimen collections published by Dover Publications) into a much more convenient electronic form.

PC character set on a Mac

If you need to print characters from the IBM PC extended ASCII character set in a Macintosh document, Page Studio Graphics has two font packages that solve the problem. **PIXymbols 2107/09** contains three Type 3 PostScript fonts, each one containing the complete IBM PC character set. The three fonts differ only in their key assignments; you use the one that best fits your needs. (One font is designed for use with SoftPC screen dumps, for example, another for ease of access from the Mac keyboard.) **PIXymbols 2110** contains one Type 1 PostScript font (Figure 1-16) which works with Adobe Type Manager. Because Type 1 fonts cannot render gray-scale, the shaded character in the PC character set is missing in this font.

```
┌─────────────────────────────────────────────┐
│             PIXymbols 2110                    │
├─────────────────────────────────────────────┤
│                                               │
│   ! " @ # $ % ' ^ & * ( ) _ - + /             │
│   0 1 2 3 4 5 6 7 8 9 ; < = > ?               │
│   A B C D E F G H I J K L M N O               │
│   P Q R S T U V W X Y Z [ \ ] {               │
│   a b c d e f g h i j k l m n o               │
│   p q r s t u v w x y z ~ { ¿ }               │
│   Ç ç ê Ä Å ┘ ┌ │ ┤ ╡ ╖ ╕ ╣                    │
│   ╗ ╝ ╜ ╛ ┐ └ ┴ ┬ ├ ─ ┼ ╞ ╟ ╚ ╔                │
│   ╩ ╦ ╠ ═ ╬ ╧ ╨ ╤ ╥ ╙ ╘ ╒ ╓ ╫ ╪               │
│                                               │
└─────────────────────────────────────────────┘
```

FIGURE 1-16 *With PIXymbols 2110, you can recreate an entire PC screen on a Macintosh.*

Working with italics

Since lengthy italicized text can be difficult to read on screen, don't hesitate to temporarily change it to non-italic while editing. In most programs you can create a separate style or tag with larger, more readable text attributes to make reading and editing easier. Keep in mind, however, that very long stretches of italicized text make slow going for your readers as well; editing will be easier—and you may attract and keep your readers more effectively—if you use italics sparingly in your publications.

Gray fonts in the font menu

From time to time you may encounter fonts which are displayed in gray type in **PageMaker** for the Mac's Font menu (Figure 1-17) or are preceded by a question mark in PageMaker for Windows' Font menu. These are fonts which are used in the document you're working on but which aren't currently installed. On the Mac, if you use a font/DA utility such as **Suitcase II** or **MasterJuggler** to organize and install your fonts, grayed font names usually mean that the suitcases containing the needed fonts are closed. If you're working on a document prepared by someone else, you'll get grayed or questioned font names if the document's creator used fonts that you haven't installed. In either case, the remedy is to install the missing fonts.

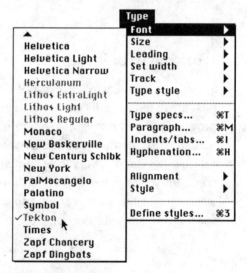

FIGURE 1-17 *Fonts used in a document but not currently installed are grayed-out in PageMaker for the Mac's Font menu.*

 ## Pick a font that's easy on the eyes

If you find yourself squinting at your Macintosh monitor while drafting a document, try switching to a font that's larger and bolder, such as 12- or 14-point New York. It's easier on the eyes, and you can change back to the appropriate PostScript font and size later when you're ready to lay out your document.

Fonts designed for low-res printers

If you print camera-ready copy on a LaserWriter or other 300-dpi laser printer, you might want to consider PostScript or TrueType fonts designed specifically for low-resolution printers. The Lucida family, designed by digital type expert Charles Bigelow, is a good example. Its simple, open letterforms were carefully crafted for good legibility at lower resolutions. Hairlines and serifs are relatively thick, the serifs are kept short, and the x-height is large. Lucida, a PostScript font, is available from several vendors and includes serif, sans serif (each in roman, italic, bold, and bold italic), and special mathematics fonts.

Among PostScript fonts, we also like Stone, Prospera, Bitstream Charter, and Bitstream Amerigo (Figure 1-18 on page 34). Adobe's director of typography, Sumner Stone, created the Stone family of typefaces as a kind of safety net for nondesigners—a solution to the problem of combining two or three different yet compatible typefaces in a single document. The Stone family is sold in three packages: Stone Serif, Stone Sans, and Stone Informal (each in roman, italic, semibold, bold, semibold italic, and bold italic). Peter Fraterdeus's Prospera, available from Alphabets, Inc., is a classic-looking typeface with pronounced serifs and large, open counters (the enclosed spaces in letters like o and B). It is available in roman and italic versions.

Bitstream Charter is a serif face with clear letterforms and relatively thick serifs. It's packaged in four weights: regular, italic, black, and black italic. Although the letterforms are distinctly modern, Bitstream Amerigo has tapered strokes that give it a classical appearance. This package includes regular, italic, bold, and bold italic.

If you're printing with TrueType fonts, consider using the TrueType versions of New York, Geneva, and Monaco that are included in the Macintosh System 7 package. When converted to TrueType outlines by Bigelow & Holmes, these Macintosh old-timers were given a serious face-lift and optimized for printing on low-resolution laser and ink-jet printers.

Four score and seven years ago our fathers brought forth on this continent, a new nation...

Now we are engaged in a great Civil War, testing whether that nation or any nation so conceived and so...

We are met on a great battlefield of that war. We have come to dedicate a portion of that field, as a final...

It is altogether fitting and proper that we should do this. But, in a larger sense, we can not dedicate, we can...

The brave men, living and dead, who struggled here, have consecrated it, far above our poor power to add or detract.

FIGURE 1-18 *Samples of (from top) Lucida, Stone Informal, Prospera, Bitstream Charter, and Bitstream Amerigo. (Words courtesy of Abraham Lincoln.)*

Ventura fonts by number

If you want to kill two birds with one stone, you can insert **Ventura Publisher** (GEM or Windows editions) font changes in your word processing document as you compose the text. Entering the code <F51M> in your word processor, for example, tells Ventura to switch to Avant Garde Demi, whose Ventura font ID is 51. As you can see, however, if you want to enter font codes as you write, you need to know the font ID numbers of the fonts you are working with.

One way to ascertain the font ID numbers of your installed fonts is to use Ventura's WIDTOVFM utility. Although WIDTOVFM is included only with the GEM edition (you'll find it on the utilities disk), Windows edition owners can use it as well if they can locate a copy. Whether you own the Windows or GEM editions of Ventura, here's how WIDTOVFM can determine font ID numbers for you:

1. Copy the WIDTOVFM.EXE file to your Ventura subdirectory.

2 Check your Ventura subdirectory to determine the name of the currently installed Ventura font width table. (Font width tables end with extension WID.)

3. Type WIDTOVFM *filename*.WID (where *filename* is the name of your actual .WID file). Wait a few moments while WIDTOVFM generates a Ventura font metric (VFM) file for each font included in the font width table.

4. Within each of the new VFM files is the name of a font and its corresponding font ID number. Since VFM files are in ASCII (plain text) format, you can read these files in your word processor or text editor, or view them from the DOS prompt by typing TYPE *filename*.VFM | MORE, where *filename* is the name of an individual VFM file. This latter method will print the VFM file on your screen, one screen-full at a time.

Open each VFM file created by WIDTOVFM and copy the requisite information to compile a complete list of font ID numbers for your installed fonts. The name of the font and its font ID number are listed near the top of the VFM file. In the sample portion of the VFM file below, for example, the font name is on the second line and that font's ID number is on the third line:

```
DEVICE POSTSCRIPT
TYPEFACE Minion Expert
FACEID 1030
SIZES  255
ATTRTYPE 1
UFACEID 1030
USTYLE  28
SFACEID 1030
```

Once you have your list of fonts and their ID numbers, it's easy to convert these to font change codes: Simply bracket each ID number with <F on the left and M>, B>, I>, or BI> on the right (depending on whether you want the medium, bold, italic, or bold italic version of the font.

Another way to determine font change codes is to create a Ventura chapter with a number of snipets of text, and to then format each snippet with a font whose code is unknown. Format the text using Ventura's SET FONT command in the GEM Edition, or the SET FONT ATTRIBUTES command (under the Text menu) in the Windows Edition. Then save the chapter and open the text file in your word processing program to see the codes with which Ventura itself has marked each piece of text.

 ## Easy bar codes

Although you can create bar codes on a Macintosh by drawing them by hand in a graphics program, there are several products that make the process less painful. Bear Rock Technologies' **PrintBar 3.0** is one. It's a collection of fonts divided into four volumes for Code 39; Interleaved 2 of 5; PostNET (including FIM codes); and UPC, ISBN, and

EAN (European Article Numbering). Volumes are sold separately and may be purchased for ImageWriters, PostScript laser printers, or PostScript imagesetters. Each package contains a utility that translates the desired code digits into the required text string for the selected bar code font and adds any necessary checksum or start or stop characters.

ElseWare Corporation's **BarCode Kit** is intended for those who would rather not have to attend to the details themselves. It contains PostScript fonts for Code 39, UPC, Interleaved 2 of 5, and PostNET (including FIM) codes which can be used, like PrintBar fonts, within any application. BarCode Kit also contains easy-to-use HyperCard stacks which automatically compute the correct code and generate the final bar code art in EPS format, plus business reply envelope templates (Figure 1-19) for use with Microsoft Word, MacWrite, Freehand, Illustrator, PageMaker, and Quark XPress.

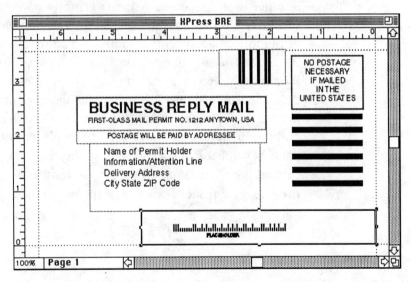

FIGURE 1-19 *This is one of a number of business reply templates included in BarCode Kit. The selected EPS graphic in the lower right corner is a PostNet bar code created with the kit's HyperCard ZIP Stack. The bar code graphic includes the clear zone required by the Postal Service.*

Catalogs of fonts

With new PostScript fonts appearing daily, it's difficult to keep track of what's available and who's selling it. There are, however, some books and catalogs which can help. The most comprehensive one we know of is the *MacTography PostScript Type Sampler*. This multi-volume, constantly updated (and expensive) work lists more than 5000 fonts from over 40 different manufacturers for both the Macintosh and the PC. It packs six fonts to a page, and each font is illustrated with a complete character set and a sample of 14-point text (Figure 1-20). The whole thing is printed on a Linotronic phototypesetter at 1,270 dpi. For those who have difficulty finding a particular font locally, the publisher is also a mail-order source for many of the fonts listed in the *Sampler*.

Another useful resource is Erfert Fenton's *Macintosh Font Book*, second edition. It contains over 250 typeface samples from a variety of vendors, a list of vendor names and addresses, and a wealth of useful font information for Macintosh owners, from resolving font ID conflicts to creating custom fonts. Font catalogs from type vendors, especially Adobe, Bitstream, and Agfa Compugraphic, can be helpful, too. The two volume *Adobe Type Guide* from Adobe, for example, includes full character sets, sample text, and the character per pica value for all Adobe fonts. Adobe also publishes a quarterly catalog, *Font & Function*, which contains an up-to-the-minute index to all Adobe typefaces as well as samples (often extensive) of recent releases.

MacTography™ Type Sampler Update

Continued From Previous Page **ITC Berkeley Oldstyle Black Italic**	!"#$%&'()*./0123456789:;<=>?@ABCDEFGHIJKLMNOPQRST UVWXYZ[\]^_`abcdefghijklmnopqrstuvwxyz{|}~ÄÅÇÉÑÖÜáàâ ãåçéèêëíìîïñóòôõöúùûü†°¢£§•¶ß®©™´¨≠ÆØ∞±≤≥¥µ∂∑∏ªºΩæ ø¿¡√ƒ≈∆«»…ÀÃÕŒœ––""''÷◊ÿ⁄¤‹›fifl‡·‚„‰ÂÊÁËÈÍÎÏÌÓÔÒÚÛ Ùıˆ˜¯˘˙˚¸˝˛ˇ *My time is unfortunately too short to stay and give to this truth the*
Package #107 List Price $185.00 Macintosh & IBM **Antique Olive® Bold Condensed**	!"#$%&'()*+,-./0123456789:;<=>?@ABCDEFGHIJKLMNOPQRSTUVWXYZ[\]^ _`abcdefghijklmnopqrstuvwxyz{|}~ÄÅÇÉÑÖÜáàâãåçéèêëíìîïñóòôõöúùûü†° ¢£§•¶ß®©™´¨≠ÆØ∞±≤≥¥µ∂∑∏ªºΩæøø¿¡√ƒ≈∆«»…ÀÃÕŒœ––""'' ÷◊ÿ⁄¤‹›fifl‡·‚„‰ÂÊÁËÈÍÎÏÌÓÔÒÚÛÙıˆ˜¯˘˙˚¸˝˛ˇ **My time is unfortunately too short to stay and give to this truth the parley,**
Antique Olive Compact	!"#$%&'()*+,-./0123456789:;<=>?@ABCDEFGHIJ KLMNOPQRSTUVWXYZ[\]^_`abcdefghijklmnop qrstuvwxyz{|}~ÄÅÇÉÑÖÜáàâãåçéèêëíìîïñóòô õöúùûü†°¢£§•¶ß®©™¨≠ÆØ∞±≤≥¥µ∂∑∏ªºΩæøø¿¡ √ƒ≈∆«»…ÀÃÕŒœ––""''÷◊ÿ⁄¤‹›fifl‡·\‰ÂÊÁËÈÍÎÏÌÓ ÔÒÚÛÙıˆ˜¯˘˙˚ **My time is unfortunately too short to stay**
Antique Olive Nord	!"#$%&'()*+,-.0123456789:;<=>?@ABCDEF GHIJKLMNOPQRSTUVWXYZ[\]^_`abcde fghijklmnopqrstuvwxyz{|}~ÄÅÇÉÑÖÜ áàâãåçéèêëíìîïñóòôõöúùûü†°¢£§•¶ ß®©™´≠ÆØ∞±≤≥¥µ∂∑∏ªºΩæøø¿¡√ƒ≈«»ÀÃÕ Œœ––""''÷◊ÿ⁄¤‹›fifl‡·‚„\‰ÈÁËÈÍÎÏÌÓÔÒÚÛÙ ı **My time is unfortunately too short**
Antique Olive Nord Italic	!"#$%&'()*+,-./0123456789:;<=>?@ABCDEF GHIJKLMNOPQRSTUVWXYZ[\]^_`abcdefgh ijklmnopqrstuvwxyz{|}~ÄÅÇÉÑÖÜáàâãåâ çéèêëíìîïñóòôõöúùûü†°¢£§•¶ß®©™´¨ÆØ∞ ±≤≥¥µ∂∑∏ªºΩæøø¿¡√ƒ≈∆«»…ÀÃÕŒœ––""''÷ ◊ÿ⁄¤‹›fifl‡·‚„\‰ÂÊÁËÈÍÎÏÌÓÔÒÚÛÙıˆ˜¯˘˙˚ **My time is unfortunately too short to**
Package #108 List Price $145.00 Macintosh & IBM **Parisian™** *Continued on Next Page*	!"#$%&'()*+,-./0123456789:;<=>?@ABCDEFGHIJKLMNOPQRSTU VWXYZ[\]^_`abcdefghijklmnopqrstuvwxyz{|}~ÄÅÇÉÑÖÜáàâãåçéèêëíìîïñóòôõöú ùûü†°¢£§•¶ß®©™´¨≠ÆØ∞±≤≥¥µ∂∑∏ªºΩæøø¿¡√ƒ≈∆«»…ÀÃÕŒœ–– ""''÷◊ÿ⁄¤‹›fifl‡·‚„‰ÂÊÁËÈÍÎÏÌÓÔÒÚÛÙıˆ˜¯˘˙˚¸˝˛ˇ My time is unfortunately too short to stay and give to this truth the development it deserves;

Adobe Systems, Inc. (Update)-28

FIGURE 1-20 *A page from the MacTography PostScript Type Sampler.*

Custom font list order

Tired of scrolling through CorelDRAW's alphabetical list of 150 fonts every time you want to select Vogue, Zurich Calligraphic, or other end-of-the-alphabet fonts? To put the program's font list in any order you like, edit the CORELDRW.INI file. Here's how:

1. Using Windows Notepad accessory, open the CORELDRW.INI file
    (in the CORELDRW subdirectory) and go to the first section, titled
    [CorelDrwFonts], where the fonts are listed alphabetically in sin-
    gle lines, such as *Avalon=15 avalon.wfn 3.*

2. Rearrange the order of the fonts in the list by cutting a line (be sure
    to cut the entire line) and pasting it elsewhere in the same section
    (Figure 1-21).

When you close the CORELDRW.INI file, you'll find that the fonts in
the font selection window are now in the same order as the fonts in
the newly edited *[CorelDrwFonts]* section.

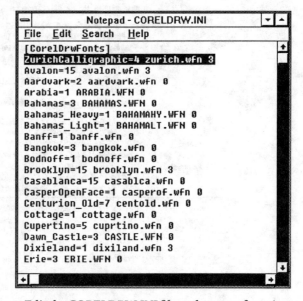

FIGURE 1-21 *Edit the CORELDRW.INI file so that your favorite end-of-the-
alphabet fonts show at the top of CorelDRAW's font selection window.*

 ## Keyboard keys in a font

If you write instruction sheets or training manuals, there are several
Macintosh PostScript fonts that allow you to replace phrases like
"the H Key" and "the Page Down Key" with graphic representations
of actual keyboard keys. **PIXymbols 2011** and **PIXymbols 2012** are a

complementary pair of fonts in which the key symbols are drawn in a shadowed, three-dimensional style. Both cover keys for Mac and PC keyboards. PIXymbols 2011 contains uppercase letter keys only and spells out the names of function keys (such as Return and Shift). PIXymbols 2012 contains lower- and uppercase letter keys and uses symbols for many function keys. **PIXymbols 2013** (Figure 1-22, top) and **PIXymbols 2113** are thinner, outline versions of PIXymbols 2011 and 2012. All four fonts are designed to be used with 10- and 12-point body text. **Key Caps** by Casady & Greene offers yet another variation on the same theme (Figure 1-22, middle).

If you want to render part or all of a keyboard in an illustration, Page Studio Graphics also makes fonts which can make this task easier. These fonts require several keystrokes to generate a single key, and

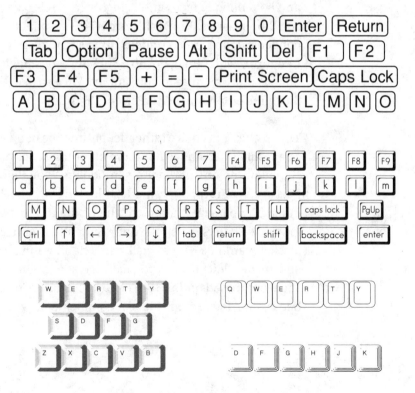

FIGURE 1-22 *Use PIXymbols 2013 (top) or Key Caps (center) to replace terms like "the Shift Key" in body text. Use PIXymbols 2005 (bottom) to produce a realistic drawing of a keyboard or part thereof.*

the realistic-looking keys they create can be arranged in groups that mimic the layout of almost any part (or all) of the keyboard. **PIXymbols 2005** (Figure 1-22, previous page, bottom) includes all the keys on Macintosh keyboards, while **PIXymbols 2008** covers the keys on IBM PC, AT, and PS/2 keyboards.

 ## Fonts for architects and other hand letterers

If you're looking for PostScript fonts that resemble the hand lettering —for architectural drawings, for example— there are several that we recommend (Figures 1-23, and 1-24 on page 44). One, Adobe's **Tekton**, is based on the hand lettering of author and architect Francis D. K. Ching. Characterized by straight verticals, slanted horizontals, and tilted elliptical shapes, Tekton includes roman, oblique, bold, and bold oblique faces and is highly readable, even in body text at small point-sizes. EmDash's **ArchiText** (available in roman, bold, condensed, and bold condensed) is slightly less formal and more free form, while Image Club's **Surf Style** (available in roman and bold) is more angular in appearance. We also like the look of Judith Sutcliffe's **Lutahline**, LetterPerfect's **TomBoy**.

Three other fonts delve rather deeply into the handwritten past and, as a result, offer somewhat more eccentric styles of hand lettering. **Herculanum**, one of the fonts in Adobe's **Type Before Gutenberg I** package, is a surprisingly modern-looking face that works well even in lengthy passages (although the distinction between upper and lower case letters is a subtle one). Suttcliffe's **Leonardo Hand** recreates Leonardo da Vinci's backwards handwriting, cleaned up a bit and turned left-to-right for easier reading. On the same disk is **Tagliente**, based on the 16th century Italian writing master's copybooks, and **Tagliente Initials**, a complementary set of ornamental caps.

I went to the woods because I wished to live deliberately, to front only the essential **facts of life, and see if I could not learn...**

I did not wish to live what was not life, living is so dear; nor did I wish to practise resignation, unless it was quite necessary.

I wanted to live deep and suck out all the marrow of life, to live so sturdily and Spartan-like as to put to rout all that...

Our life is frittered away by detail. An honest man has hardly need to count more than his ten fingers...

Simplicity, simplicity, simplicity! I say, let your affairs be as two or three, and not a hundred or a thousand; instead of a million count half...

WHY SHOULD WE LIVE WITH SUCH HURRY AND WASTE OF LIFE? WE ARE DETERMINED TO BE STARVED BEFORE WE ARE HUNGRY. MEN SAY THAT...

FIGURE 1-23 *Samples of (from top) Tekton (roman, italic, and bold), ArchiText, SurfStyle, Lutahline, TomBoy, and Herculanum. (Words courtesy of Henry David Thoreau.)*

I long ago lost a hound, a bay horse, and a turtledove, and am still on their trail.

For many years I was the self-appointed inspector of snow storms and rain storms... and rain storms...

A B C M P S

FIGURE 1-24 *Samples of Leonardo Hand (top) and Tagliente and Tagliente Initials (bottom). (Words courtesy of Henry David Thoreau.)*

. . . .

Large, small, and drop caps

. . . .

  ### Better display type

When creating display type using drastically different point-sizes of the same face, use a bolder version of the small letters to better match the weight of the larger type. Although the proportion varies from face to face, when the small type is about ⅔ the size of the larger, a semibold in the smaller type will generally match the weight of the larger (Figure 1-25). When the small type is about half the size of the larger characters, try using a full bold.

FIGURE 1-25 *A semibold weight for the small type (lower sample) matches the initial cap better than the regular weight (upper sample).*

Better small caps

Like most programs, **PageMaker, Microsoft Word,** and **XPress** create Small Caps style by replacing all lowercase letters with capital letters in a smaller point-size (existing uppercase letters remain unchanged). One disadvantage of this method, however, is that the smaller capital letters appear lighter than the standard-size capital letters. For text of a more uniform color, use a heavier-weight version of the font for the smaller capital letters (Figure 1-26). The keyboard shortcut, by the way, for Small Caps text in PageMaker for the Mac, Word for the Mac, and QuarkXPress, is Shift + Command + H. In the Windows version of PageMaker, it's Ctrl + Shift + H; in Word for Windows, it's Ctrl + K.

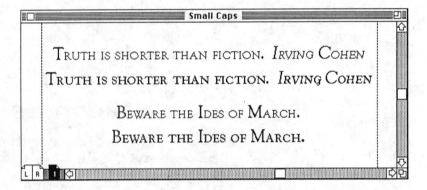

FIGURE 1-26 *The upper version of each pair of sayings is in standard Small Caps style. In the lower version, the smaller capital letters are formatted in boldface.*

Quick drop caps

The standard technique for creating drop caps in **PageMaker** (as described in the manual) involves creating and carefully aligning three separate text blocks for the paragraph containing the drop cap. If that seems unwieldy, try one of the following alternative techniques:

- In PageMaker for the Mac, a quick way to create a drop cap is to convert the initial letter into a graphic:

  1. Create a text block containing the letter you wish to be the drop cap and nothing more; format the letter in a size and weight close to what the drop cap should have.

  2. Select the text block with the pointer tool (not the text tool), copy or cut it, and paste it into the Scrapbook.

  3. Choose the PLACE command and select the Scrapbook file in the System folder. The pointer that appears will have a number on it, indicating the number of images in the Scrapbook. Click once and the last item in the Scrapbook—the letter you just pasted in—appears on the page as a graphic. Click on any tool in the toolbox to unload the pointer (so you don't place any more images from the Scrapbook).

  4. Resize or distort the drop cap if desired. For instance, you can scale the drop cap in your page layout program to adjust its size to better fit your design. But for a consistent appearance, scale all drop caps within the same story uniformly.

  5. Drag the drop cap into position at the beginning of the paragraph, lining up the left edge of the drop cap with the left margin.

  6. Select the drop cap with the pointer tool and apply text-wrap to it with the TEXT WRAP command in the Element menu.

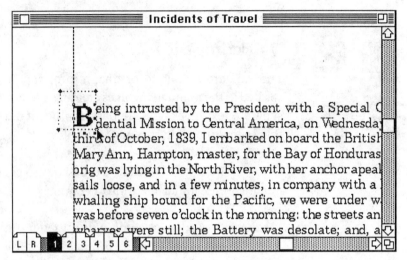

FIGURE 1-27 *After placing and positioning the drop cap, apply text-wrap to it and adjust the surrounding text.*

Adjust the text around the drop cap using the text-wrap handles (Figure 1-27).

Continue to make minor adjustments in the size of the drop cap and the position of the text-wrap surrounding it until you're satisfied. Oh, and don't forget to delete the first character of the first word in the paragraph, which the drop cap now replaces.

- In Windows, you can't convert text to a graphic as easily as you can on the Mac. This next technique, which works on both Mac and Windows versions of PageMaker, involves creating an EPS graphics version of the cap before placing it in your page layout program:

  1. Create the necessary large-size cap in a drawing program like Aldus FreeHand or Adobe Illustrator on the Mac, or Corel-DRAW or Micrografx Designer on the PC, and save it as an EPS graphic..

  2. Place the EPS version of the letter on the PageMaker page.

3. Select the letter (a graphic object, not text), and, from the Text Wrap options under the Elements menu, choose the option that wraps your text around the drop cap.

Just as you did previously, you can manipulate the text-wrap border to wrap text to the irregular outline of the drop cap—under the eaves of a W or T, for instance.

- If you don't have a drawing program that allows you to create a graphical drop cap, try this next technique. It works with drop caps entered as text, not placed as graphics, and it works on both Mac and PC versions of PageMaker:

  1. After placing your main text, drag one of the handles on the left side of the text block toward the right, beyond the point where the drop cap will extend; this keeps the text from constantly rewrapping as you perform the steps that follow.

  2. Create a separate text block, enter and format the drop cap, and move it into position. Make the cap's text box as narrow as possible, so you can bring the text-wrap border of a hidden rule you'll create in the next step as close as you need to the drop cap.

  3. Using the straight line tool, draw a vertical rule through the center of the drop cap.

  4. With the rule still selected, select the TEXT WRAP command (from the Element menu) and specify that text wrap around both sides. Set a stand-off of about half the cap's width left and right, and zero top and bottom.

  5. With the rule still selected, manually adjust the text-wrap border so the border's left side sits on the left column guide and the right side falls where you want the body text to begin.

  6. Hide the vertical rule by setting its line width to None, using the LINE command under the Element menu.

7. Drag the left border of the body text block back to the left column guide; the text will wrap around the drop cap.

If the drop cap keeps popping out of the text-wrap border, adjust the drop cap's text block handles so that they stay within the text-wrap border, as we've done for the illustration in Figure 1-28. If the window shade extends too far below the drop cap, decrease the cap's leading and use the Spacing options dialog box in the Paragraph dialog box (available from the Type menu) to set the leading method to *Top of caps.*

On the Mac, you may find that the cap pops out the text-wrap border if you try to manipulate the border too close to the cap. If that's the case, try specifying a fairly (but not very) tight stand-off in the Text wrap dialog box and don't make any manual adjustments afterward.

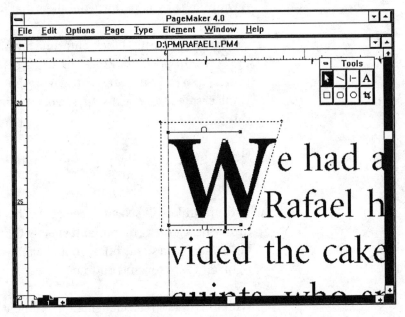

FIGURE 1-28 *A rule through the center of a drop cap text block in Page-Maker lets you control the text-wrap. Even when you make the rule invisible, the wrap remains.*

- This last technique for laying out drop caps in PageMaker doesn't involve using any graphic elements nor does it require breaking your text into separate blocks. Assuming, for example, that you need a drop cap extending up from the baseline of the second line, here's what you do:

1. Set the Leading method to *Proportional* in the Spacing Attributes dialog box, reached via the Spacing button in the Paragraph dialog box (which is opened with the PARAGRAPH command under the Type menu).

2. Specify a precise amount of leading, not Autoleading, from the Type specs dialog box.

3. Highlight the first character of the paragraph, and increase its point-size. Make the cap large enough so that, were you to place the cap on the second line, the top of the cap would align with the top of the paragraph.

4. Select the enlarged character and copy it to the clipboard.

5. With the initial cap in the first line still selected, set the enlarged capital's type style to Reverse to make it invisible. There is now a gap in the first line that is the width of the enlarged cap.

6. Paste the capital from the Clipboard into the beginning of the second line (Figure 1-29 on page 52). If you sized it correctly, the cap should extend from the second baseline to the top of the Wrst line. Text on the second line moves left to accommodate the pasted letter; the necessary space should already exist on the first line.

The hidden large capital extending above the first line may print white over the normal text preceding the drop cap. If it does, and the paragraph above the drop cap is in a separate text block, select the drop cap paragraph's text block with the pointer tool; then select Send to Back from the Element menu. If the paragraph above is in the same text block, you'll need to use the PARAGRAPH command under the Type menu and increase the *Before Para-graph* space option for the drop cap paragraph so the hidden cap doesn't overlap the paragraph above it.

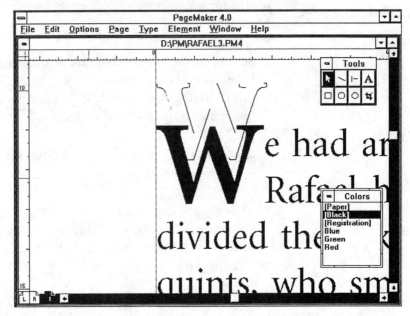

FIGURE 1-29 *A reversed (invisible) large cap placed on the first line makes visual space for the drop cap that shows. In this illustration we've ghosted the reversed cap so you can see its position.*

 ## Quick change to lowercase

To quickly change a lot of all-caps text to upper- and lowercase, copy the text and paste it into **MacDraw II** (in several sections, if there's a lot of it). In MacDraw, click on the text with the pointer and select the LOWERCASE command from the Style menu to convert all the text to lowercase letters (Figure 1-30). Then select the text with the text tool, copy it, and paste it back into your word processor or page layout program. All that remains is to add initial caps to those words that require them.

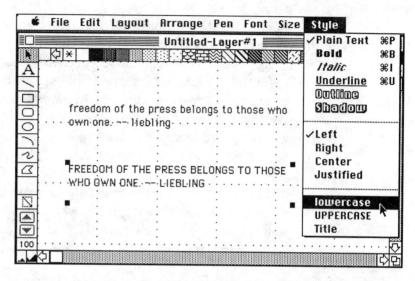

FIGURE 1-30 *MacDraw II's Lowercase command converts a selected block of all-caps text (lower text block) to all-lowercase text (upper text block).*

Easily lowered uppercase text

Should you need a length of text in uppercase characters, enter it in normal upper- and lowercase first, and then apply an All Caps or similarly labeled text attribute (if your word processor or layout program has this feature) which makes the text appear in all uppercase. This way, if you decide not to use all capital letters later on, you can easily convert the text back to standard upper- and lowercase without having to retype it.

En-spaced headlines

If a line of text in a headline or other line of text set in all caps looks too crowded, replace standard spaces with en spaces between each word in the headline. Here's an example:

CHRONICLE OF THE CENTURY (with standard spaces)

CHRONICLE OF THE CENTURY (with en spaces)

Note: Normally, the width of an en space is half an em space, and the width of an em space is equal to the point-size of your type. (If you're using 12-point type, for example, an en space would be 6 points in width.). One important exception to the standard em space (and by extension, en space) defiinition, however, is Ventura Publisher . Ventura's Reference Guide states that an em space is, quite literally, the width of the current typeface's letter m; in the program itself, on the other hand, the em space is based on the width of the @ character.

Adding en spaces is simpler than trying to make fancy adjustments to the character and word spacing, which, depending on the software you're using, may adversely affect other lines in the text. Check your manual for how to enter an en space or an em space.

Large-type headline workaround

If you're using **WordPerfect** for DOS and a printer that can't access large fonts, you can still create large-type headlines using WordPerfect's equation feature. When you create an equation, Word-Perfect uses its own built-in scalable outline fonts which are Times Roman, Helvetica, and Courier equivalents. Thus a headline disguised as an equation can overcome your printer's limitations. These are the steps:

1. In WordPerfect, press Alt + F9, then 6 (the *Equation* option), followed by 1 (the *Create* option), then 9 (the *Edit* option) to enter the equation Editing and Display windows screen.

2. In the Editing window at the lower portion of the screen (Figure 1-31), type the headline. You must enter a tilde (~) or an accent grave (`) character in place of a space character; a tilde is four times as wide as an accent. Certain words require special treatment— Acute, Bar, Check, Circle, Dot, Grave, Hat, Bold, From, Left, Matrix, Over, Phantom, Right, Stack, Sub, To, and Underline— all must be preceded by a backslash (\). If they aren't, Word-Perfect will assume they're commands. The default typeface is italic; if you want roman you need to start the headline with FUNC{ and end it with }.

3. Set the exact point-size you want by pressing Shift + F1 for the Equation Options screen, press 2 to select the *Graphical Font Size* option, press 2 again (the *Set Point Size* option), and then enter the point-size.

4. WordPerfect will select its own outline font for the equation, whichever is closest in appearance to the font used in the text preceding the equation. To change the headline from WordPerfect's serif-faced equation font to WordPerfect's sans serif equation font, for example, place the cursor before the equation box marker on your page, and change the base font from Times (serif) to Helvetica (san serif). To do that, type Shift + F8, then 3, then 3 again, and make the font selection.

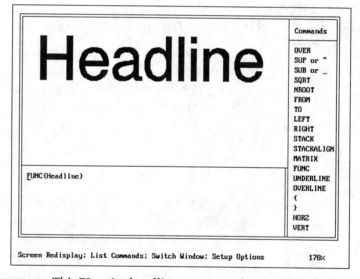

FIGURE 1-31 *This 72-point headline was created with WordPerfect's equation editor, using its Helvetica-like font—a handy trick if your printer doesn't provide for large-size type.*

Word and letter spacing

One space, not two

Although you may have learned to type two spaces between senten-ces way back in typing class, this convention is inappropriate for today's laser- or image-set documents. Thus, to save time and proof-reading hassles later on, search for all pairs of consecutive spaces and replace them with single spaces before placing files in your page makeup program.

Help with manual kerning

When kerning characters manually on screen, especially when **Adobe Type Manager** is in use, highlight the text you're working on so that it appears reversed (white on black, instead of black on white). You'll find that letter pairs not properly kerned are often eas-ier to see.

Spread the word

It's often interesting typographically to space out a word or line of text to fill a column width or other measure. There are a couple of easy ways to do this in **Ventura Publisher**. If you want to spread out two or more words, make the text a separate paragraph and then use Ventura's interactive on-screen kerning/tracking to move the char-acters apart. Here's how:

1. On the PC, set the paragraph's alignment, under the Paragraph menu, to Center. On the Mac, select Center alignment via the ALIGNMENT command in the Tags menu.

2. On the PC, switch to the text tool and highlight all but the last letter in the line. Then hold down the Shift Key and press the Right Arrow Key repeatedly to spread out the text to fit the projected

width (Figure 1-32). If you go too far, use the Shift-left Arrow key combination to tighten the kerning.

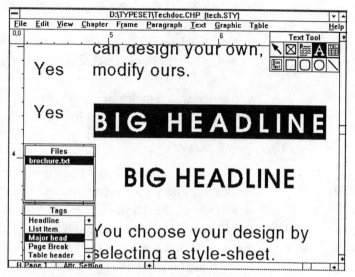

FIGURE 1-32 *Use Ventura's interactive kerning feature to force selected text, as in the first subhead above, to justify across a column.*

On the Mac, use the tag tool to select the paragraph, and then choose the PARAGRAPH TYPOGRAPHY command from the Tags menu. Select the *Looser* option in the Tracking pop-up menu and enter a small tracking amount in the Ems text box. Click the Apply button to see how your setting looks, adjust the amount in the Ems text box accordingly, click Apply again, and continue making adjustments until your text looks the way you want it.

If you want to fill a column with a single word, like this:

E   N   C   Y   C   L   O   P   E   D   I   A

use Ventura's justified text alignment to force Ventura to justify the word across the full width of the line. Here's how:

1. On the PC, under the Paragraph menu, set the Alignment to *Justified* and the In/Outdent Width to zero. On the Mac, set the *Justified* option using the ALIGNMENT command in the Tags menu.

2. Next, click on the Text icon and type the word you want justified, with a space after each character, including the last one.

3. Finally, type a series of nonbreaking spaces (Control-space bar) until the spaces wrap, as a block, onto the next line. At this point your spaced-out word should be justified.

If your spaced-out word is within (but not the last line of) a paragraph, Ventura conveniently ignores the nonbreaking spaces that wrap onto the next line, so they won't indent the text that follows. If your line is a separate paragraph or the last line in a paragraph, the paragraph that follows is pushed down a line by the nonbreaking spaces; so you'll need to make allowances for that. (This technique also works in PageMaker, Word for Windows, and many other programs.)

Caution: horizontal scaling

When you scale type horizontally in **QuarkXPress** or **PageMaker** (both Mac and PC versions), keep in mind that the width of vertical strokes changes along with the overall width of a character, while the width of horizontal strokes remains essentially unchanged. Scaling more than 30 percent in either direction will therefore significantly distort the relationship between vertical and horizontal strokes. This may produce the effect you want, or it may simply look bizarre. Horizontal scaling often seems to work better with bold, blocky faces, and less well with subtly modulated faces (Figure 1-33). You might also want to try it with type that has a calligraphic look.

Condensed typefaces

Condensed versions of a typeface have letters of standard height but narrower than usual width. There are at least three ways you can obtain a condensed version of a PostScript typeface:

Franklin Gothic Not Scaled
Franklin Gothic 70% Scaled

Garamond Not Scaled
Garamond 70% Scaled

Zapf Chancery Not Scaled
Zapf Chancery 70% Scaled

FIGURE 1-33 *Boldfaces like Franklin Gothic Heavy often fare better than more subtle faces, such as Garamond, when you scale them horizontally (like these examples from QuarkXPress). Calligraphy fonts such as Zapf Chancery often scale well, too.*

- One option is to buy the condensed version of the typeface as a standard PostScript font. Adobe, Linotype, and other vendors sell Univers Condensed, Futura Condensed, and Helvetica Condensed, for example. Casadyware markets Bodoni Ultra Condensed and Sans Serif Bold and Extra Bold Condensed. Because the characters in these fonts are all designed by hand, they almost always look better than those obtained by the other two methods.

- Font modification programs, such as **ParaFont** and **FontMonger** on the Macintosh, allow you to generate your own condensed typeface font by horizontally scaling all the characters in an existing font. You can scale all characters by the same amount, or you can subtly adjust the degree of scaling from character to character.

- Many drawing and page layout programs (including **Illustrator**, **Freehand**, **Designer**, **CorelDraw**, **PageMaker**, and **QuarkXPress**) allow you to condense text by scaling it horizontally. Although this is the least expensive and most convenient way to obtain condensed type, the results are usually not quite as good as those provided by the other two alternatives.

Make a tracking chart

Try experimenting with different tracking values in **QuarkXPress** for the various fonts you use regularly. Start with a value of -2 for 10-point text and increase the value of the negative number as the point-size increases. Once you've come up with the tracking values you prefer for each font, make up a spacing chart, like the one below, that you can keep in a handy location and refer to easily.

Font name	10-point	12-point	14-point	18-point
Palatino	-1	-3	-4	-5
Palatino italic	-2	-3	-5	-7
Palatino bold	-2	-3	-5	-8
Palatino bold italic	-3	-5	-7	-8
Garamond	-2	-3	-5	-6
Garamond italic	-1	-2	-4	-6
Garamond bold	-2	-3	-3	-4

Kerning the number one

In most fonts, the numerals 0 through 9 have equal character widths so that they line up when you use them in tables. Because the numeral 1 is much narrower than the others, its character width is wider than is necessary in standard text. To close the gaps that result, you might want to add some kerning pairs that include 1 to your fonts' kerning tables—when 1 appears next to other numerals, a period, a dollar sign, and so on. Just make sure you turn kerning off for all tabular matter; this will ensure that you obtain the correct alignment that the equal character widths were meant to produce.

Widows, orphans, and what to do with them

Widow or orphan?

We thought we knew what widow and orphan meant until we read a summary (by Kathleen Tinkel in one of our favorite desktop design newsletters, *Step-by-Step Electronic Design*) of the definitions that appear in the standard trade references. A slim majority define a widow as a short line at the end of a paragraph and an orphan as a single line, usually the last of a paragraph, at the top of a column. But some reverse the definitions, and others use the term widow for both. We suggest that you follow the majority opinion, but, to be on the safe side, it's probably a good idea to define your terms whenever you use them so the reader doesn't get confused.

Widow control

Publish readers, writers, and editors have had more to say about how to eliminate a pesky widow—a stray word or syllable dangling alone in the last line of a paragraph—than just about anything else. Here's a rundown of the most useful suggestions:

- Edit the paragraph. Take the advice of E. B. White (*Elements of Style*) and "omit unnecessary words." Substituting a shorter word for a longer one may make a widow disappear and might improve your writing, too.

- E. B. White, were he alive today, would probably be less pleased to hear this suggestion: Add a few words somewhere in the paragraph to give your widow some company.

- Try tightening the spacing of any loosely set lines. You can do this in any program that allows you to adjust the spacing of selected text via tracking or track kerning. Reduce the tracking gradually until the widow moves up to the previous line. If that doesn't work, try kerning individual pairs of characters. Look for combinations of characters with extra visual space, such as any punctuation followed by a space, a capital Y or T followed by a short lowercase character, or a lowercase r or y followed by a comma or period.

- A trick that sometimes works with ragged-right text is to move the paragraph containing the widow into a separate text block. Then adjust the right-hand margin rightward just enough to bring the widow up to the previous line. With luck, the margin change won't be noticeable.

- You can often bring the straggler into the fold by justifying the last full line. First, place a hard return just before the last full line to make it and the widow a separate paragraph. Be sure to remove formats such as first-line indents or between-paragraph spacing from the new paragraph; then format it as fully justified text. This will often tighten the spacing enough to pull up the dangling word.

- If all else fails, manually rebreak lines above the widow to force another word or two onto the last line.

Leading, alignment, and the like

Aligning footnoted numbers

Right-aligning a column of numbers can be a problem if some of those numbers are marked with footnote references (see Figure 1-34, top numeral). A good solution to the problem is to align the numbers with a decimal tab stop, instead of a right-aligned tab stop. If the number contains decimal points, the digits will line up correctly and the footnote markers will fall to the side of the column (Figure 1-34, bottom numeral).

In **Microsoft Word** for the Macintosh, Word for Windows, and some other programs, the numbers will align properly even if they don't contain decimal points. In other programs, you'll need to place an invisible decimal point (a period formatted as reverse or hidden type) after each number's final digit, in front of any footnote markers. In **Ventura Publisher**, a thin space will work as well as a period set to white.

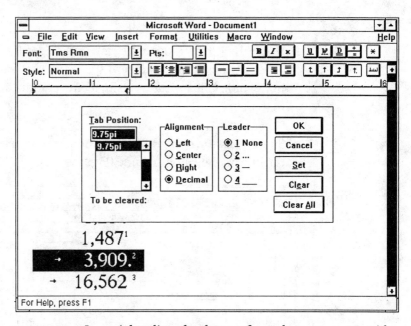

FIGURE 1-34 *In a right-aligned column of numbers, an entry with a footnote marker will appear misaligned (top numeral). A decimal tab stop at the right margin solves the problem (bottom numeral).*

  Fixing centered text that's off-center

If centered text in your page layout program appears to be off-center, check to make sure that its paragraph indents are set correctly. In **PageMaker**, for example, if lines centered using the ALIGN CENTER command don't look right, select the PARAGRAPH command under the Type menu to open the Paragraph Specifications dialog box. If a left- or first-line indent has been set, PageMaker will count that as part of the line and place your text too far to the right. If a right indent has been set, PageMaker will place your text too far to the left. Set all three indents to zero and your text should center properly.

Centering graphics

You can use **PageMaker**'s column guides to center text or graphics between page margins, even on pages with uneven side margins. Here's how:

1. Using the COLUMN GUIDES command under the Options menu, specify two columns and zero space between columns; the column guide will appear as a single line equidistant from the side margins.

2. Simply place text or graphics elements with their center handles directly on the column guide (Figure 1-35).

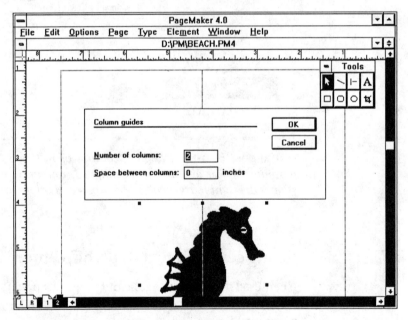

FIGURE 1-35 *You can center a graphic or text block on a PageMaker page by aligning the center handles on a center guide for a two-column layout with no space between columns.*

Since the center handles mark the horizontal center of the block irrespective of the visual center of the text or graphic, make sure the right and left boundaries of the text block or graphic don't extend beyond the actual text or image. If they do, the text or graphics will appear off-center. Adjust the text block corner handles or crop the graphic if you need to remove any unnecessary space.

Clean ragged right

To achieve a "tight" or "clean" rag, keep to a specific range of distances between line endings (usually 1, 1.5, or 2 picas). Staying within the chosen range is often difficult in word processing programs with minimal hyphenation controls, but selective manual hyphenation and manual line breaks (Shift + Return in most programs), added to what your program can accomplish automatically, will create a highly professional look. As you check each line, focus on the difference from line to line, not on the variation from the top of the paragraph to the bottom.

Well-centered text

To get an attractive rag in centered text, it's common practice to manually enter returns or end-of-line marks to break lines at desired points. This often creates lines that begin or end with word spaces, and these extra spaces can make your lines appear off-center. Needless to say, the remedy is to remove the unnecessary spaces. Many word processor and page-layout programs have a feature that displays spaces as small dots, carriage returns as paragraph symbols, and so on, making it easy to spot the errant beginning or end-of-line spaces (Figure 1-36).

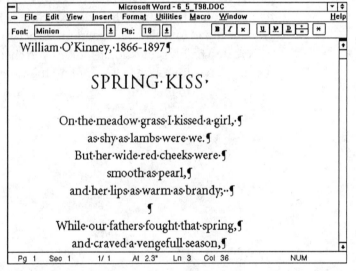

FIGURE 1-36 *Be sure to remove extra space characters from the beginnings and ends of centered lines (some of which still remain in the stanza in this illustration).*

  ## Precise visual alignment

When you center the lines of a headline with **PageMaker's** ALIGN CENTER command in the Alignment submenu of the Type menu (or with the equivalent feature in other page layout programs), lines that end in periods or commas can appear off-center to the eye. That's because the software includes in its calculations the full width of the punctuation mark's character space, but ignores the visual effect. As far as PageMaker is concerned, for example, a comma takes up as much space as a letter even though it doesn't have the same presence on the page (Figure 1-37).

You can compensate for the visual imbalance by adding the same punctuation mark to the beginning of the line, then changing its attribute to Reverse (via the Style submenu under the Type menu) so that it won't display or print. The hidden opening punctuation will push the line slightly to the right and visually compensate for the ending punctuation. Beware though, that this technique can backfire in some cases. A character with a visual overhang at the beginning of a centered line, like a capital T, is already enough visual compensation for the ending comma. A hidden comma placed before the T would actually make things worse.

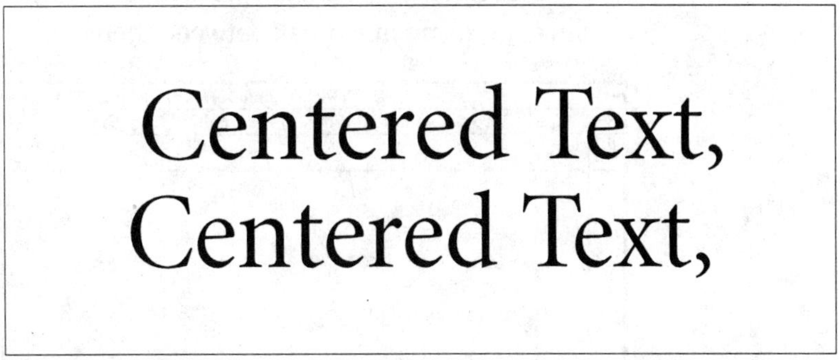

Centered Text,
Centered Text,

FIGURE 1-37 *A second, invisible, comma before a centered headline ending in a comma makes centered text appear more balanced (top). Without the hidden comma, the centered text appears to be too far to the left (bottom)*

Variable Ventura indents

In some page designs the paragraph following a short subhead begins on the same line and is indented in relation to the width of the subhead (Figure 1-38). If you take advantage of its *Relative Indent* and *Line Break* options, **Ventura Publisher** makes this easy. Here's how :

1. When defining the subhead style tag, choose the BREAKS command under the Paragraph menu on the PC and specify Line Break as *Before*. On the Mac, choose the BREAKS command from the tags menu and turn on the *Beside Last Line of Previous Paragraph* option in the Breaks dialog box.

2. In the style tag for the indented paragraph of text, specify Line Break as *After*. This way, the paragraphs will start on the same line since there's no line break between them.

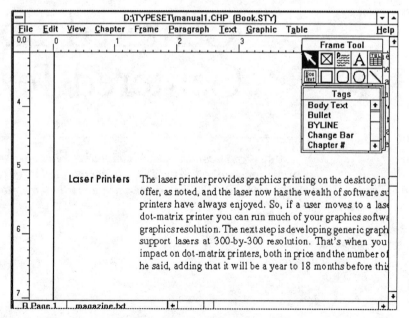

FIGURE 1-38 *By manipulating Ventura's relative indent settings, you can indent a paragraph by an amount dependent on the length of the previous paragraph's last line.*

3. To automatically indent the second paragraph from the end of the subhead, select Relative Indent using the ALIGNMENT command under the Paragraph menu on the PC. On the Mac, select the ALIGNMENT command from the Tags menu and turn on the *Relative to Previous Paragraph* option.

4. To define how much space should separate the end of the subhead from the beginning of the indented paragraph, enter the value in the In/Outdent Width text box on the PC, or in the Width text box on the Mac.

5. To maintain this hanging point for all the lines of the paragraph, enter a large number for In/Outdent Height on the PC or in the Height text box on the Mac; this specifies the number of lines that follow the indent.

Doing dotted leaders

If you enter dotted leaders—the strings of periods that connect items in a table—by hand, it will be a rare day when the individual dots in one line are aligned with those of the lines above and below (Figure 1-39). To generate neatly aligned leader dots, use tabs and specify a

Manually Entered Leaders

Chapter 16 21
Section 1 32
Section 2 55
Chapter 17 67

Leadered Tabs

Chapter 16 21
Section 1 32
Section 2 55
Chapter 17 67

FIGURE 1-39 *Leader dots rarely align when typed in (top sample). Instead, use your program's leadered tabs feature for automatic alignment (lower sample). (Use the dotted vertical line to check the two samples.)*

dotted leader. Check out your page layout or word processing program's manual to get the skinny on generating leadered tabs. Also, make sure all the leaders are in the same font and style.

Creating hung quotation marks

You may have noticed that call outs or pull quotes in publications often use "hung" quotation marks, where the opening and closing quotation marks hang outside the text margin. In the Style dialog box in **Illustrator** for the Mac, you'll find a *Hanging Punctuation* option. Turn it on for selected text, and only actual text will fall within the text rectangle; beginning punctuation marks (and if they fall at the end of a line, internal and ending marks, too) will automatically extend beyond it. Use this option for display type, call outs, or pull quotes (Figure 1-40) that call for hanging punctuation.

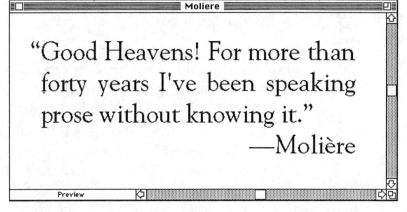

FIGURE 1-40 *Illustrator's* Hanging Punctuation *option places punctuation at the beginning or end of a line outside the text rectangle.*

Most desktop publishing programs, however, don't offer a hanging punctuation option, so you'll have to hang the punctuation marks manually. Here are a couple of techniques for **PageMaker**:

- If you have only two or three lines of quoted text, simply type the opening quotation marks in front of the second and third lines, and change their style to Reverse, so they don't show up. The reversed quotation marks will create the necessary indent. The

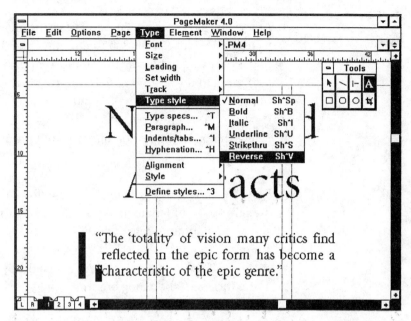

FIGURE 1-41 *For quick and dirty hung quotation marks, start the second and succeeding lines with a hidden (reverse type style) quotation mark to create the correct indent.*

second line of the pull quote in Figure 1-41, for example, starts with a reversed (hidden) quotation mark. The quotation mark for the third line is in the process of being reversed.

The invisible quotation marks may get moved out of position should any lines rewrap when you edit the text—a minor drawback with this technique. You'll have to delete them and add new ones if this happens. If the quotation mark is included in any custom automatic kern pair combinations (created using third-party font utilities), you'll need to turn off automatic pair kerning for that paragraph.

• A slicker approach, if you use hung quotes frequently or you're dealing with larger sections of text, is to use PageMaker's IN-DENTS / TABS command under the Type menu to create an "out-dent" for the opening quote. The trick is to set a left indent that's the width of the quotation mark while leaving the first line indent at zero. Here's how:

1. As a visual aid, work in 200-percent view and line up a vertical ruler guide with the first character after the initial quotation mark. As an aid to placing the guide, temporarily add a quotation mark to the second and third lines so; this give you more points with which to visually align the guide.

2. Select the paragraph or paragraphs that require hung quotation marks.

3. From the Indents/tabs dialog box, hold down the Shift Key and drag the lower indent icon to the right, using the ruler guide to gauge the quotation mark width. Then click OK. The left margin of the indented text should fall along the guide created in step one. If not, select the text and adjust the lower indent icon in the Indents/tabs dialog box.

You can build this setting into a paragraph style so that you can easily use it on other paragraphs. Keep in mind, however, that the amount of indent needed to compensate for the quotation marks will vary depending on the typeface and point-size of the text.

Using soft returns

Many programs, including **QuarkXPress**, **PageMaker**, and **Microsoft Word** for the Mac and for Windows, allow you to start a new line of text within the same paragraph, rather than as a new paragraph, with the key combination Shift + Return. One important use of "soft returns," as they are often called, is to specify line breaks in headlines that are more than one line long (Figure 1-42). Because the lines on each side of the soft return are part of the same paragraph, paragraph formats such as extra space above or extra space below appear only above the first line or below the last line of the headline, not between the lines of the headline. Soft returns are also useful when creating tables. If you end each line in the table with a soft return, the entire table is a single paragraph, making it easy to adjust margins or tab stops for the entire table all at once.

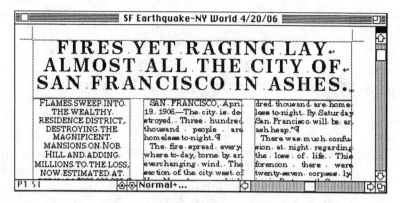

FIGURE 1-42 *With the* Show ¶ *option turned on in Word, you can see the soft returns (bent arrows) at the ends of the first two lines of this document's headline.*

  ## Autoleading in Word

In **Microsoft Word**, autoleading automatically applies the appropriate line spacing as you change font sizes. In Word for the Mac, text is automatically formatted with autoleading (unless you alter the definition of the Normal style so that it specifies fixed leading). In Word for the PC or Word for Windows, text is automatically formatted with fixed leading, but you can easily apply autoleading to all the text in your document. Here's how:

1. Select the entire document by pressing Shift + F10 in the DOS version; in Word for Windows, either press Ctrl + 5 (using the 5 on the numeric keypad) or, with the cursor in the selection bar in the left margin, click while holding the Ctrl Key.

2. In the Format Paragraph dialog box of the Windows version, tab over to the Line Spacing text box or click on the box using the mouse, and enter the word Auto. In the DOS version you can either press the down arrow, or click on the arrow to the right of the Line Spacing text box, and *Auto* should appear as a choice. Press Enter to activate the option.

Now, whenever you change the size of a font, Word adjusts the line spacing automatically.

Slanting a text margin in Ventura

Here's how to set text on a slanted left margin in **Ventura Publisher**:

1. Select the Graphics mode and the line-drawing tool in the GEM Edition, or simply select the line-drawing tool from the Toolbox Window in the Windows Editions; then draw a diagonal line to define the slanted margin.

2. Next, change to the Frame function and select *Turn Line Snap On* in the Options menu in the GEM Edition. For the Windows Edition select Line Snap under the View menu.

3. Using the diagonal line you've drawn as a guide, create a stairway of separate frames, each a line space in height, from the left margin to the diagonal line (Figure 1-43). The Line Snap will make this

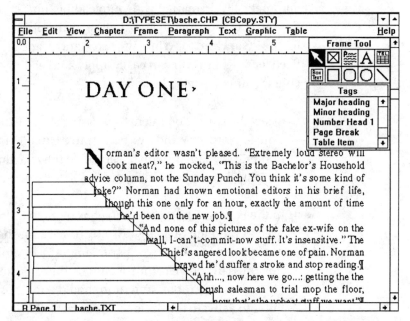

FIGURE 1-43 *A staircase of line-height frames in Ventura creates text with an angled left margin.*

relatively easy. Make sure that for each frame, *Flow Text Around*, under the Sizing and Scaling dialog box of the Frame menu, is set to *On*. The frames will show on screen when selected but will otherwise remain hidden.

When you place text in the frame containing your staircase of added frames, text will pushed to the right, creating a slanted margin.

 ## Aligning the bottoms of columns

In multi-column layouts containing lengthy stories with numerous internal heads and subheads, it can be difficult to get the bottoms of all the columns on a page to line up exactly. Here's one way to get your columns into alignment in a page layout program:

1. Move the ruler's zero point to the baseline of the last line of the longest column on the page.

2. For each shorter column, place a guideline at the baseline of the column and note the distance (in points) between the zero point and the guideline (Figure 1-44). If necessary, change the ruler's unit of measurement to points and picas in order to do this.

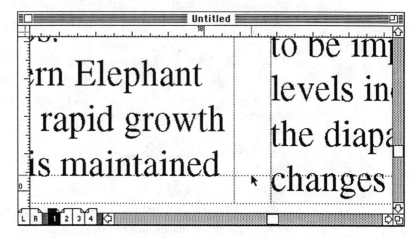

FIGURE 1-44 *Measure the difference in length between the longest column on the page and a shorter column; add that amount of space above any headings in the shorter column to properly align the two column endings.*

3. For each shorter column, insert the measured distance as blank space within the column: Either add it above headlines and sub-heads (never below), or evenly distribute it between all the paragraphs in the column with your program's *Space Above* option.

For example, in the **PageMaker** document in Figure 1-44 on page 75, the difference between the longest column (on the right, and on which the ruler's zero point is fixed) and the shorter column to the left is five points according to the guideline we've pulled down. To align these two columns, we would carefully add a total of five points of extra space above headings or between paragraphs in the shorter column. Note that to read the ruler accurately, we're in an enlarged, 400-percent view.

Aligning text across columns

Here's a technique which makes it easy to align body text across a spread (or throughout a publication, such as a newsletter) in **Page-Maker**:

1. Open the Preferences dialog box, select the *Custom* option from the Vertical Ruler pop-up menu, and enter the body text's leading in the Points text box opposite the pop-up menu. Make sure Snap to rulers (under the Options menu) is selected.

2. Turn on the rulers with the Ruler command (or press Command + R on the Mac or Ctrl + R on the PC) if they are not already displayed along the window borders. The major divisions on the vertical ruler should now equal the leading of your text.

3. Move the zero point of the ruler so that it is aligned with the baseline of any line of existing, correctly positioned body text. Do this by clicking in the open square at the intersection of the horizontal and vertical rulers and dragging the resulting horizontal guideline under the line of text. Each major division on the vertical ruler should now correspond to the baseline of a properly positioned line of body text.

4. To align other body text (or anything else) in the document, pull down additional ruler guides, always making sure to position them on the major divisions of the vertical ruler (Figure 1-45).

Although this technique makes it easy to align anything you want with the baselines of your body text, don't be a slave to the major divisions on the vertical ruler. Some (perhaps many) parts of your design may not align with body text. In Figure 1-45, for example, body text baselines and illustrations are all in alignment, but the baselines of the one-column headlines fall midway in between the major ruler divisions.

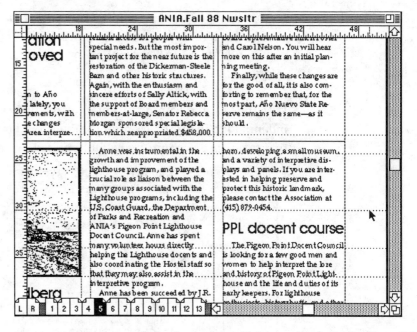

FIGURE 1-45 *Custom rulers whose major divisions match the leading of your body text make it easy to align text, graphics, and other items anywhere in a document.*

Easy Ventura outdents

To produce outdented numbers in **Ventura Publisher** (Figure 1-46), make the number a separate paragraph with its own tag, followed by the paragraph of text with a different tag. This way, you can easily set (and reset) the numeral in a different font from that of the text since it uses a different tag. Plus, with Ventura's Auto-Numbering feature, you can easily renumber the paragraphs if you decide to change the order in which they appear. This technique works in any version of Ventura. These are the steps for the GEM and Windows Editions:

1. Format the body text as a nonbreaking paragraph. To do that, select the Paragraph tool and click on the text. Using the BREAKS command under the Paragraph menu, set the Line Break option to *After*.

2. With the SPACING command, enter the the body text paragraph's indent at the In From Left prompt. You should enter an amount that takes into account the width required by your numbering

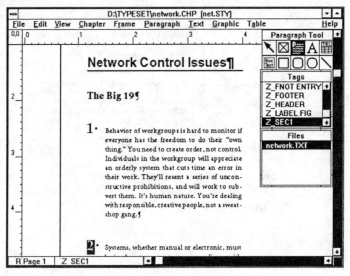

FIGURE 1-46 *By making hanging numbers separate paragraphs with their own tag, you can easily reformat all paragraph or section numbers in a single step, instead of one at a time.*

style (roman numerals, hyphenated numerals, etc.). Make your best estimate for now since you can easily adjust it later.

3. Select the number paragraph preceding the text, and set the Line Break option in the Breaks dialog box to *Before*.

4. If you intend to include several indented paragraphs under a single numbered heading, make the indent of all the following paragraphs is the same as that for the first text paragraph. But under Breaks, the Line Break option for all the following paragraphs should be set to *Before*; otherwise the following paragraphs will overwrite the first.

In the illustration (Figure 1-46), notice that we use an automatic section number as the numbered paragraph and have formatted the generated tag (Z_SEC1) as described above.

Hyphenation

Lines of comfortable length

Here's a good rule of thumb for typesetting text: Strive to have between 45 and 75 characters per line. Columns of text much narrower than this often have awkward line breaks and hyphenation, while longer lines are difficult for your readers to follow.

Keeping word combinations from breaking

In **PageMaker**, letter or word combinations employing a slash, such as PS/2, have an annoying tendency to break at the slash when at the end of a line. In PageMaker for Windows, avoid the problem by replacing the slash with a nonbreaking slash (Ctrl + Shift + /). On the Mac, replace the slash with a fraction bar by typing Option + Shift + 1. The fraction bar is not identical to the slash, but few, if any, of your readers will notice the difference. In **QuarkXPress**, by the way, the standard slash is a nonbreaking character and this change is not needed.

Preventing unwanted hyphenation

To prevent a word from hyphenating in **Microsoft Word**, **PageMaker**, or **QuarkXPress**, or to "unhyphenate" quickly an already hyphenated word, insert a "soft hyphen" (obtained by pressing Command + hyphen on the Mac or Ctrl + hyphen on the PC) directly in front of the first character of the word. You won't see the soft hyphen, but it is a signal to all of these programs that the word that follows must not be broken. Don't forget that a soft hyphen, when inserted within a word, indicates an acceptable hyphenation point; the hyphen is invisible except when it is necessary to break the word at the end of a line.

Adding hyphenation points to the dictionary

When you add a word to **PageMaker's** user dictionary, you can indicate hyphenation points as well as the correct spelling. At each acceptable hyphenation location, insert a tilde (~) within the word in the Add Word To User Dictionary dialog box (reached via the SPELLING command under the Edit menu when you're working from the Story Editor). You can enter one, two, or three tildes at each break point to indicate your preferences; one tilde indicates the most desirable position, three tildes the least. Insert a tilde in front of a word to prevent hyphenation no matter what the circumstances.

Grab bag

Entering text that frequently changes format

When you have to type in a simple mathematical expression with many subscripted and superscripted characters, such as $ax_4{}^4 + bx_3{}^3 + cx_2{}^2 + dx = 0$, first type all of the characters, ignoring sub- and superscripts. Then go back and sub- or superscript all the appropriate characters all at once. This is, in fact, a time-saver for any text that frequently changes formats—from roman to italic, from one font to another, and so on.

The secret lives of AFM files

Did you ever wonder what to do with the AFM (Adobe Font Metrics) files that come with Linotype, Adobe, and other Type 1 PostScript fonts? An AFM file contains information related to the corresponding font's style, weight, character widths, and automatic kerning. Generally speaking, however, you can safely ignore Macintosh and PC AFM files, since most Macintosh programs don't use them (they obtain the same information elsewhere) and most PC font installation utilities extract needed information from AFM files automatically.

Under Windows, for example, PFM (Printer Font Metric) files are generated from the corresponding AFM files when you run the font installer for Adobe licensed fonts. PageMaker for Windows and many other Windows programs use these PFM files, rather than the AFM files, for font information. Similarly, under DOS, the Adobe Font Foundry utility included with each PC font package generates application-specific font metric files with information obtained from the AFM files. Programs such as WordPerfect, Microsoft Word 5, or Ventura Publisher GEM Edition, use these application-specific font metric files, rather than the AFM files. In both cases, once the font installer or utiltiy program has read the required AFM files, the AFM files can be discarded.

Only rarely on a PC do you need to keep a font's AFM file on hand for day-to-day use. CorelDRAW is perhaps the most widely used exception to this rule; its WFN BOSS utility (which converts Type 1 and other font formats to CorelDRAW font format, and vice versa) looks in the AFM files of Type 1 fonts to find information about automatic kerning pairs. Fortunately, the utility alerts you if the AFM files are missing.

For PostScript fonts on the Mac, all essential AFM information is stored in the screen font suitcase; thus, in most cases, AFM files may be left safely on your font's master disk. PostScript font editing programs such as Fontographer are among the rare programs that use the information in AFM files. In any event, should the AFM file be missing, Fontographer and the few other programs that require them will ask you to provide the AFM files.

A little bigger is lots better

For cleaner type when printing at 300-dpi resolution, use 11-point type for body text as opposed to the standard 10-point. That seemingly small increase is actually a full 10 percent bigger, and fonts appear much sharper at 11 points on 300-dpi laser printers. Make sure to use at least 2 points of leading (11 on 13) to complete the improvement.

Printing Kanji characters in English programs

If you have Apple's KanjiTalk Macintosh System software, you can print Japanese characters even if you don't have software that's designed to handle them. You can run the English version of programs such as PageMaker or QuarkXPress in KanjiTalk, and, since the screen fonts for Japanese are available under KanjiTalk, EPS files containing Kanji characters print correctly. Your printer, of course, must also have access to the Kanji printer font outlines.

Selecting text from the keyboard

Tired of always reaching for the mouse to select text? You don't have to take your hands off the Mac keyboard if you don't want to. Just hold the Shift Key down as you move the insertion point through the text with the arrow keys. The left and right arrow keys allow you to select character by character; the up and down arrows let you select line by line. In many programs, holding down Command + Shift causes the left and right arrow keys to select word by word, the up and down arrow keys paragraph by paragraph.

CHAPTER 2

Word Processing

....

Shortcuts

....

Word table tips

If you've created a table at the very top of a document in **Microsoft Word** for the Mac and you want to add text—such as a headline—above it, place the insertion point anywhere in the first row of the table and press Command + Option + Spacebar. This creates a paragraph mark (a blank line) immediately above the table. In **Word for Windows**, position the cursor as above, and then press Ctrl + Enter. This will insert a hard page break and paragraph mark; press the Delete Key just once to get rid of the page break, and you'll be left with a blank paragraph above the table.

You can use the same technique to insert a paragraph mark between two rows in a table and thereby split the table in two (Figure 2-1). This allows you to enter standard text in the space between the two halves of the newly divided table.

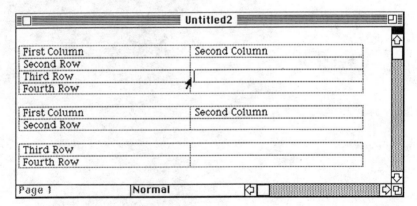

FIGURE 2-1 *To split a Microsoft Word for the Mac table in two, place the insertion point anywhere in the row below the desired division (top table) and press Command + Option + Spacebar (bottom two tables).*

Recovering typed-over text

If you accidentally type over something in **WordPerfect** for the PC because you have the *Typeover* option turned on, you can restore the text using the following technique:

1. Press F1.

2. At the Undelete: prompt, select *Restore*.

Since *Typeover* is actually a form of Delete that puts text into the Delete buffer, Undelete inserts it back into the text.

Reorganizing a Word table

For people whose work includes fill-in-the-blank forms or in-text tables, **Microsoft Word** for the Mac's table feature is a godsend. There's one drawback, however: reorganizing the rows in a Word table is slow and tedious if you use the traditional cut and paste method. Here are some techniques which make rearranging Word table rows quick and easy:

• To sort a Word table alphanumerically by the first item in each row (by the contents of the first column, in other words), simply select the entire table and select the SORT command from the Utilities menu. To sort in descending instead of ascending order, press the Shift Key when you choose SORT.

• To sort rows according to the contents of a column other than the first row (the zip codes in the last column, for example), select that column only and then choose the SORT command. Although only one column is selected, the whole table is sorted.

- To reorganize rows by hand, turn on outline view (by pressing Command + U). Each table row is now an outline paragraph which can be quickly and easily dragged to a new location (Figure 2-2) in standard outline editing fashion. Turn outline view off by pressing Command + U again to resume text entering and editing.

	English	Bouton	Salayer	Sian	Cajeli	Tidore
	ant	osea	kalihara	kiaso	mosisin	bifi
	body	karoko	kaleh	badan	batum	rohi
	box	bueti	puti	bantali	bueti	barua
	day	heo	allo	rokadi	gawak	wellusita
	dog	muntoa	asu	kapuna	aso	kaso
	feather	owhu	bulu	dokoi	bolon	gogo
	gold	hulawa	bulain	mas	blawan	gurachi
	hair	bulwa	uhu	utan	buloni	hutu
	husband	obawinena	burani	kapopungi	umlanei	nau
	island	liwuto	pulo	toadi	nusa	gurumo
	monkey	roke	dare	babah	kessi	mia
	moon	bula	bulan	buran	bulani	o'ra
	post	otuko	palayaran	dihi	ateoni	ngasu
	rain	wao	bosi	tahiti	bessar	u'lani
	salt	gara	sela	asing	sasi	gasi
	sea	andal	laut	laudi	olat	nolo
	sun	soremo	mata-alo	kaliha	lehei	wangi
	sweet	mameko	tuni	mawangi	emminei	mani
	wood	okao	kaju	kalu	aow	luto

Malay Database — Page 1 — Normal

FIGURE 2-2 *If you switch to outline view, the rows in a Word table can be reorganized quickly and easily by dragging them up or down in standard outline editing fashion.*

Centering a text column

Centering a single, narrow column of text on a **FullWrite Professional** page can be a complex affair, especially if you don't want to do so by altering the document's page margins. If your right and left page margins are equal (page margins are established in the Set Margins dialog box, which is reached via the Page Setup dialog box), here is a quick and relatively easy column centering technique: Open the Layout dialog box for the chapter containing the text column and drag the Column Offset control as far to the right as it will go (Figure 2-3). (The Column Offset control is the left triangle at the bottom of the miniature page.) Make note of the figure in the Offset Columns By text box and then replace it with a number which is exactly half that amount. If the Offset Columns By text box contains 2.5, for example, delete it and enter 1.25. When you click on the OK button, the column should be centered correctly on the page.

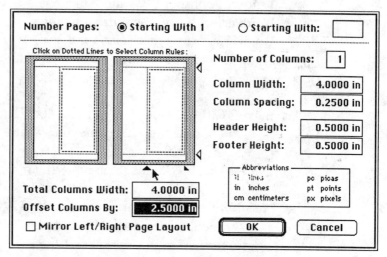

FIGURE 2-3 *To center a column on a FullWrite page, first drag the Column offset control all the way to the right.*

· ·

From word processor to page layout program

· ·

 ## Avoiding unwanted blank lines

If you place a multisection **Microsoft Word** for the Mac document in **PageMaker**, Word's section breaks will appear as blank lines. To avoid these unwanted blank lines, delete the section breaks prior to placing the Word file. A quick and easy way to do this in a document with many sections is to open the Change dialog box, enter ^d in the Find What text box, leave the Change To text box empty, and click the Change All button.

. . . .

Moving WordPerfect footnotes to Ventura

Ventura Publisher GEM and Windows editions ordinarily ignores **WordPerfect** footnotes, but you can create a macro that uses WordPerfect's Extended Search and Block Move features to convert WordPerfect footnotes to a format that Ventura won't ignore. Here's how:

1. Press Ctrl + F10 to define a macro. At the Define macro: prompt, enter `foot`, or any other name you want to give the macro.

2. Press Home + F2 (the EXTENDED SEARCH command), and search for the [Note Num] code. In order to enter the [Note Num] code at the Extended srch: prompt, press Ctrl + F7 to bring up the Foot-note/Endnote menu, and choose 1, the Footnote submenu, and from the next submenu choose 2, the *Edit* option. Then press F2 to begin the extended search. The first footnote encountered in the search should appear on screen with the footnote number highlighted.

3. Highlight the entire footnote by pressing Alt + F4, then the End Key.

4. Copy the highlighted footnote text by pressing Ctrl + F4 and then 1 for the Block submenu, and then 2 for the *Copy* option. Then exit the footnote window by pressing F7.

5. At the text cursor, type Ventura's end code bracket (>).

6. Press the left arrow to move to the left of the bracket and then backspace over WordPerfect's footnote reference to delete it.

7. Press Enter to paste in the footnote text you copied.

8. Type in Ventura's start footnote code (<$F). Since the insertion point was already positioned to the left of the footnote text, the start footnote code will be properly positioned.

9. Invoke the "foot" macro again (Alt + F10) before completing the macro (Ctrl + F10), so it will repeat until all footnotes are tagged.

When you run the macro, all WordPerfect footnotes will become coded as Ventura Publisher footnotes, as you'll see when you load the text file into Ventura. To convert the Ventura footnotes back to WordPerfect footnotes, you'll need to build a new macro that works in similar but reverse fashion to the one above: It should search for Ventura footnotes, specify them as WordPerfect footnotes, and delete the Ventura footnote codes.

Transferring Word tables and equations

Equations created in **Microsoft Word** for the Mac using the program's formula commands don't survive the transfer to a page layout program. The same is true for tables created with Word's special table function. If you first convert a Word equation or table into a graphic, however, it will appear in your page layout program without a hitch.

To convert either a table or an equation, first make sure the *Show ¶* and *Page View* options are both turned off; then select the table or equation (Figure 2-4). Next press Command + Option + D; this copies the table or equation to the Clipboard and turns it into a PICT graphic. Finally, insert the graphic version into your Word document

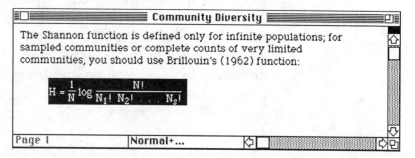

The Shannon function is defined only for infinite populations; for sampled communities or complete counts of very limited communities, you should use Brillouin's (1962) function:

$$H = \frac{1}{N} \log \frac{N!}{N_1! \; N_2! \; \ldots \; N_s!}$$

FIGURE 2-4 *Select a Word equation as shown here and convert it to a graphic if you want it to appear correctly when placed in your page layout program.*

with the PASTE command and delete the original. Make sure that the table or equation is exactly the way you want it before you convert it; once converted into a graphic, you can't edit it. You can scale it, however, using Word's standard graphic scaling techniques.

- -

 ## Easier editing of tagged text

When editing a Ventura document's **WordPerfect** text file on a PC, **Ventura Publisher** tag and formatting codes can be a real distraction. WordPerfect lacks a hidden-text format per se, but if you convert Ventura tags and other codes to comments in your text file, you can then hide the the distracting codes temporarily while you work on the file. Hiding the codes makes it easier to edit the file, of course, and makes it less likely that the codes will be altered accidentally.

In the paragraphs below, we first show how to convert a Ventura code manually into comment text in WordPerfect. We then show how to create WordPerfect macros that accomplish this conversion automatically for an entire document. First, here's the manual procedure:

1. Select a Ventura code with the mouse, or press Alt + F4, the BLOCK command, and highlight the text using cursor keys.

2. Press Ctrl + F5. At the Create a comment? prompt that appears, select *Y*, for Yes. The text will appear on screen surrounded by a double-ruled box.

You'll need to repeat this procedure for each occurrence of Ventura coding in your document. At the moment, the comments/codes are still visible. To hide the comments (or redisplay them later), use the WordPerfect SETUP command:

1. Press Shift + F1; then select 2 for the Setup: Display submenu.

2. Select 6 for the Edit-Screen submenu.

3. Select option 2, *Comments Display*, to toggle between *Yes* or *No*.

Now let's see how to create macros to turn Ventura tags and format codes into hidden comments and then turn comments back into tags and codes. The first macro converts tags and codes into comments. It starts by turning off the display of Comment text. It then searches for the @ character that begins all Ventura paragraph tags. When it finds the first @ character, it starts a text block, then searches for the = (space + equal sign + space) combination (the other end of the tag) in order to complete the text block. It then changes the block to a comment. Here's how to create this macro:

1. Press Ctrl + F10 and enter a macro name at the Define macro: prompt.

2. Press Shift + F1; then select 2 for the Setup: Display submenu. Select 6 for the Edit-Screen submenu, select option 2, *Comments Display*, and then select the *No* option

3. Press F2, and then enter @ at the Search: prompt; then press F2.

4. When the first @ character is found, press Alt + F4.

5. Press F2; then enter Space + Equal sign + Space (=).

6. Press Ctrl + F5, then Y.

7. Stop recording the macro (Ctrl + F10).

8. Load the macro into the macro editor to add some additional commands to control how the macro functions. To do that, press Ctrl + F10, and, at the Macro Define: prompt, enter the name of the macro you just recorded. At the Already Exists: prompt, enter 2, the *Edit* option. In the macro editor, add the commands listed in boldface in the macro below; the others should already appear on screen. You needn't add the macro comments, which are preceded by {;} characters.

```
{DISPLAY OFF}{Home}{Home}{Up}
{;} hides Comment text~
```

```
{Setup}262n000
{;} runs second macro after first is finished.~
{CHAIN}bracket~
{;} loop repeats until all paragraph~
{;} tags are converted to comments.~
{ON NOT FOUND}{RETURN}~
{LABEL}tag~
{Search}@{Search}{Left}{Block}{Search}.=.{Search}
{Text In/Out}y
{GO}tag~
```

When you run this macro, all paragraph tags will become hidden comments, but other Ventura text formatting, like <BI> for bold italic, will still show. The next macro converts most of the codes missed by the first macro. It works much like the first, except that it searches for the < and > characters which bracket many Ventura text formatting codes. Follow the previous procejure to record this macro as well, changing step 3 and step 5 to search for < and > respectively. Then edit the macro to add the commands listed in boldface. Here's the listing of the second macro:

```
DISPLAY OFF}{Home}{Home}{Up}
{ON NOT FOUND}{RETURN}~
{LABEL}tag~
{Search}<{Search}{Left}{Block}{Search}>{Search}
{Text In/Out}y
{GO}tag~
```

Note that the second macro is "chained" to the first (via the {CHAIN} command code you added to the first macro) so that both will run from the first macro. Be aware as well that Ventura table and equation codes will still be visible after running the macro, so take care not to alter them inadvertently in WordPerfect.

Finally, you'll need to convert all WordPerfect comments back to text before opening your document again in Ventura. Here's how to create a macro that finds each comment and reformats it as regular text:

1. Press F10 to begin recording the macro and to give it a name.

2. Press F2, and at the Search: prompt press Ctrl + 5. Then press 1, which will enter the [Comment] code in the search field. Press F2 to begin the search.

3. When the first [Comment] code is found, press Ctrl + F5, then 4 for the Comment submenu, then 3 for the *Convert to Text* option.

4. Stop recording the macro (Ctrl + F10).

5. As described above, load the macro into the macro editor. Then add thecommands that appear in boldface) so that the completed macro listing reads like this:

```
DISPLAY OFF}{Home}{Home}{Up}
{ON NOT FOUND}{RETURN}~
{LABEL}comment~
{Search}{Text In/Out}1{Search}{Left}
{Text In/Out}43
{GO}comment~
```

Now you're read to roll. To hide the Ventura tags and formatting codes in WordPerfect, use the first macro. Before loading the text in Ventura use the second macro to redisplay the tags.

Moving styles between PageMaker and QuarkXpress

Whether or not you own a copy of **Microsoft Word** for the Mac, you can use Word's file format to transfer style sheets between **PageMaker** and **QuarkXPress**. The transfer isn't always perfect, but it sure beats reentering everything by hand. Here's what to do:

1.   In PageMaker, place the insertion point within a story that uses the style sheet you want to move, and choose the EXPORT command under the File menu.

2. In the Export dialog box, select the *Microsoft Word 3.0/4.0 Format* option and make sure that the *Export Tags* option is turned off. Give the story file a name and click on OK to save it.

3. In QuarkXPress, open the file you just created using the GET TEXT command; make sure that the *Include Style Sheets* option is turned on before you click on the Open button.

To transfer QuarkXPress style sheets into Pagemaker, use XPress's SAVE TEXT command to save the formatted text in Word file format; place the saved file in PageMaker with the *Retain Format* option turned on. When either transfer is complete you'll find the new styles listed in the receiving program's style list.

Too many spaces

If you use **WordPerfect** for the PC and work with files created by colleagues in other word processing programs, you may have received text files in which space characters are used to indent or center text. This may occur because your colleague is not well versed in text formatting, more likely because his or her word processor substitutes spaces for indented, centered, and flush-right text lines when the file is saved in plain ASCII text format. Whatever the cause, these extra spaces will wreak havoc with your layout when you load the file into Ventura Publisher or other layout programs. There are several solutions to this problem:

- Ask your colleagues to save their files in a word processing format that WordPerfect's CONVERT utility can handle, formats such as WordStar 3.3, Microsoft Word, MultiMate Advantage II, or IBM DCA.

- If that's not possible, consider purchasing a file conversion utility like Mastersoft's Word for Word Professional (or others too numerous to mention here). A file conversion utility usually preserves most of the original document's formatting, like tabs and indents, making its preparation for Ventura Publisher much easier.

- To clean up a file without such a utility, use WordPerfect's search-and-replace feature. Search for a hard return followed by a space, and replace that combination with a hard return only; this removes a space character at the beginning of a line but not the spaces between words. To get rid of numerous spaces before lines, incorporate this search-and-replace strategy into a macro that performs the search and replace, moves the cursor back to the beginning of the document (Home + Home + up arrow), and calls itself so that it repeats. Let the macro run for a few seconds; then press F1 to interrupt it. All the padding should be gone except any in the first line. If not, run the macro a bit longer.

- A more elegant route, if you're comfortable with WordPerfect macro programming, is the following macro, which loops through the document looking for hard return/space combinations and then quits at the end:

```
{DISPLAY OFF}{Home}{Home}{Up}
{GO}loop~
{QUIT}
{LABEL}loop~
{Search}{Enter}(HitSpacebar){Search}{Left}{Del}{Left}
{ON NOTFOUND}{RETURN}~
{GO}loop~{Return}.
```

Your colleagues may also have inserted extra carriage returns to achieve vertical spacing between paragraphs, headlines, etc. In Ventura it's easy to get rid of extra carriage returns. Simply type @PARAFILTR ON = on a line by itself at the top of your word processing document. Ventura will automatically remove the extra carriage returns when it imports the file.

  ## Troublesome Word files

If you have trouble importing a file from **Microsoft Word** for the Mac or for Windows into **QuarkXPress** or **PageMaker**, use Word's SAVE AS command to convert the file to Interchange Format (RTF); then convert it back to the standard Word format. Any bugs a Word file picks up can usually be eliminated this way.

To save a file in Interchange Format, simply choose SAVE As and click the File Format button on the Mac, or the Options button in Windows; in the File Format dialog box, turn on the *Interchange Format (RTF)* or *RTF* option, and then save the file under a new name. After the Interchange Format conversion is complete, close the file and reopen it, answering Yes when you are asked if Word should convert the file. Finally, save the file again in the usual way and import this file into your page layout program.

How to

 ## Finding formats in Word

To find text in **Microsoft Word** for the Mac, you use the FIND command; to find character or paragraph formats, however, you must use the little-known FIND FORMATS command. To locate one or a combination of paragraph formats (justification, line spacing, paragraph indents, etc.), select the paragraph mark of a paragraph exhibiting the desired format. (Choose the SHOW ¶ command in the Edit menu to see paragraph marks.) Then press Command + Option + R, the key combination for FIND FORMATS, to locate the first paragraph that matches the model paragraph. Press either Command + Option + R or Command + Option + A to locate subsequent matches.

Except for font size, FIND FORMATS can also locate any of the format choices listed in the Character dialog box. The procedure is much like that for finding paragraph formats, but there are three important differences: You can select any amount of text as a model for the search, but you must not include a paragraph mark in the selection. Word will search for only one type of format at a time, even if the model text is formatted with several types (such as bold and expanded). Finally, to find all matches after the first one, you must use Option + Command + A, not Option + Command + R.

Note that if the selected model text displays a combination of character formats, FIND FORMATS will search for the format of the "highest level" only. Character format levels, in order from highest to lowest, are style (such as bold and italic), the four underline formats, superscript and subscript, expanded and condensed, color, and font. For example, to find text in a certain font—the lowest-level format—the model text must not display any other character format; if it does display some other format, such as italic, that format will take precedence and be searched for instead.

 Underlined spaces in FullWrite

None of **Fullwrite Professional**'s four underline styles draws a line beneath tabbed spaces (for a questionnaire or order blank, for example). The only way to underline a tabbed space in Fullwrite is with a tab leader. First, open the ruler regulating the text in question and double-click on the appropriate tab marker. In the Tabs dialog box that then opens (Figure 2-5), turn on the *Other* Tab Leader option and enter the underline character (Shift + Dash) in the option's text-entry box. Click on the OK button, and you'll find the tabbed space in your document is now underlined.

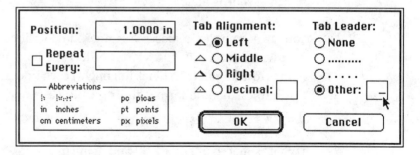

FIGURE 2-5 *Specify the underline character for a tab leader to underline tabbed spaces in FullWrite.*

 Faster printing of multiple copies

To speed up printing multiple copies of a document in **Microsoft Word for Windows**, especially when automatically downloading fonts to a laser printer, don't specify multiple copies by using the Copies text box in Word for Windows' Print dialog box. Instead, specify the number of copies you want in the Printer Setup box (choose File menu, Printer Setup, Setup). Your copies should print at least twice as fast because Windows will send the fonts and document data to the printer just once for all copies, not repeatedly for each separate copy, as it would otherwise. Leave Copies set at 1 in the Print dialog box unless you want to print multiples of the number of copies you specified in Printer Setup dialog box. When finished, be sure to change the number in the Copies text box in the Printer Setup dialog box back to 1.

 ## Replacing WordPerfect underline with italics

If you want to convert underline to italics (or bold to italics) by simply using **WordPerfect**'s search and replace feature to replace all Underline codes (appearing as [UND] in Reveal Codes) with Italics Print codes, it doesn't work. That's because the start Italics Print code [ITALC] replaces the start Underline code [UND], but the end Underline code [und] disappears and no end Italics Print [italc] code is put in its place. The result is that the entire document from the first replaced code is italic.

You can accomplish a successful underline to italic conversion, however, with a macro that uses Word Perfect's SEARCH and BLOCK commands to automatically block (highlight) each underlined section of text and change its format to italicized. Here's how to create the macro:

1. Start a macro (CTRL + F10) and name it.

2. Now that the macro is recording, use the SEARCH command to search for a start Underline code. To do that, press F2, and, at the Srch: prompt, press F8, which will enter the [UND] code. Then press F2 to initiate the search.

3. Once the first [UND] code is found, begin a text block by pressing ALT + F4.

4. Now search for the end Underline code [und]; to do that press F2 and then press the F8 Key twice, which will enter the start and end underline codes, [UND][und]. Press the Left Arrow Key to skip past the [und] search entry, and backspace over the start Underline code [UND] to delete it; this will leave only the end Underline code [und]. Now press F2 to complete the search. The underlined word or words encountered in this first search procedure should now be highlighted.

5. Set the text to italic. To do that, press CTRL + F8 to bring up the Text Attribute menu, and then select 2 for the Appearance submenu. Then from the list of appearance options that appears, select 4, the *Italic* option.

6. To get rid of the Underline codes, press the Left Arrow Key once to skip past the [italc] code just entered, and backspace once over the [und] code, which will erase both the [und] code at the end and the [UND] code at the start of the text block.

7. Force the the macro to loop so it will repeat until all underlined text is converted each time it's invoked by having it call on itself (ALT + F10). Then stop the macro recording (CTRL + F10).

To use the macro, press Alt + F10 and enter the macro name at the Macro: prompt.

Forcing footnotes to the bottom of the page

On the last page of a **Fullwrite Professional** document, footnotes normally fall immediately below the last line of text instead of at the bottom of the page (Figure 2-6). To force the footnotes to the bottom of the page, insert a page break after the last line of text. The page break adds a blank page to the end of the document so you can either discard the extra page when you print or specify a page range that excludes the last page.

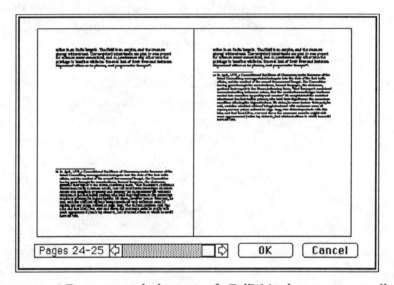

FIGURE 2-6 *Footnotes on the last page of a FullWrite document normally appear immediately below the text (right); inserting a page break forces them to the bottom of the page (left).*

Titles for contents, endnotes, and bibliography sections

Fullwrite Professional doesn't let you add titles or other text to its automatically generated endnote, bibliography, and contents sections, except via a header or footer. Using a header or a footer, however, usually causes more problems than it solves. A better method is to add the desired text or title with one of Fullwrite's posted notes.

For a table of contents section, for example, insert a posted note just before the first contents note in your document. Inside the posted note, insert a contents note, entering the title and any text you want to open the section with, and format it exactly as you want it to appear in the table of contents section (Figure 2-7). This contents-within-a-posted-note will appear at the top of the table of contents section, but, because it's placed within a posted note, FullWrite doesn't display a page reference.

The same strategy applies to Fullwrite's automatically generated endnote and bibliography sections as well. For an endnote section, you must also use the OTHER SYMBOL command from the Endnote menu to mark the endnote-within-the-posted-note with a single space (to suppress the endnote number). For a bibliography note-within-a-posted-note, enter a space in the Bibliography Reference Name text box and leave the Reference Date text box blank. Since the first lines in both of these notes will begin with a space, you may need to add a space at the beginnings of subsequent lines in order to ensure proper alignment.

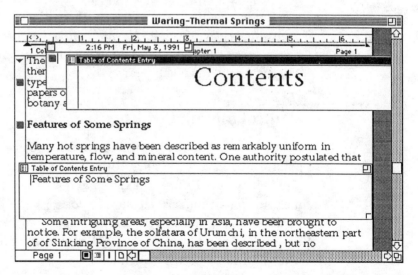

FIGURE 2-7 *The contents note within a posted note at the top of this FullWrite window is the first contents note in the document. You can use this note to insert a title and other opening text at the top of the first page of the table of contents section.*

Although this method of adding titles doesn't work for multicolumn indexes, you can use this same technique to add extra-large or decorative letters at the beginning of each alphabetical division within an index.

Preserving left/right and even/odd conventions

Whether or not it uses the default page numbering scheme or a custom scheme that you designate, **Fullwrite Professional** always starts a document with a right-hand page and alternates left and right on subsequent pages. Thus, if you specify a numbering scheme which starts with an even page number (for a continuation of another document, for example), you'll end up with even-numbered right-hand pages and odd-numbered left-hand pages, contrary to the accepted convention. In addition, right headers and footers will appear on left-hand pages and left headers and footers will appear on right-hand pages.

To avoid such confusion and counterconvention, always begin a custom page number scheme with an odd number. If circumstances require that the first page of the document be an even-numbered page, simply leave the first, odd-numbered page blank (by inserting a page break above the first line of text) and discard the first page when you print the document.

Controlling ruler width

A little-known feature in **WordPerfect** for DOS gives you complete control over the width of rules. You can specify just how thin a "thin" line is, how thick a "thick" line is, and how many dots and dashes make up dotted and dashed lines. To do so, press Shift + F8 to bring up the Format menu, select 4 for the Other submenu, and then 8 for the Border Options choice. The Border Options submenu which appears (Figure 2-8) is self-explanatory.

Since rule widths are usually specified in points, you'll probably want to use points as your unit of measure. To do that, simply type Shift + F1 for the WordPerfect Setup menu, then 3, the Environment submenu, under which you should select 8, the Units of Measure submenu. Select *p*, for points, as the unit of measure for specifying margins, tabs, rules, and other specs, and as a way of having the status line display values in points.

```
Format: Border Options

    1 - Single -      Width            0.013"
                      Shading          100%

    2 - Double -      Width            0.013"
                      Shading          100%
                      Spacing Between  0.013"

    3 - Dashed -      Width            0.013"
                      Shading          100%
                      Dash Spacing     0.013"
                      Dash Length      0.053"

    4 - Dotted -      Width            0.013"
                      Shading          100%
                      Dot Spacing      0.013"

    5 - Thick -       Width            0.063"
                      Shading          100%

    6 - Extra Thick - Width            0.125"
                      Shading          100%

Selection: 0
```

FIGURE 2-8 *WordPerfect's Border Options under the Format menu give you fine control over the width and style of rules.*

Remove old codes

If font choices made to text in **WordPerfect** for DOS don't show up (for example, when changing the base font), you probably need to delete an old font change format code that's still embedded in your text from a previous font selection. Here's how to do so:

1. Select Reveal Codes (Alt + F3).

2. In the Reveal Codes window that opens in the lower half of the screen, cursor over to the offending font call code (*[Font:Helvetica Bold 18pt]*, for example) and press the Delete Key to delete it.

You sometimes have to do this with other formatting codes as well, such as tab and indent settings.

CHAPTER 3

Graphics

. . . .

Drawing

. . . .

 ## Straight segments in freehand lines

If you're using the freehand tool in **FreeHand** and you want to draw
a straight segment within your freehand line, press the Option Key
at the point where the straight segment should begin and continue
to drag the pointer (Figure 3-1). (To constrain the straight segment
to a horizontal, vertical, or 45-degree line, press both the Option and
Shift keys.) The straight segment will stretch out like a rubber band
from the starting point; drag in any direction and release the Option
Key when you reach the ending point of the straight segment. Continue to drag the pointer to resume drawing freehand style.

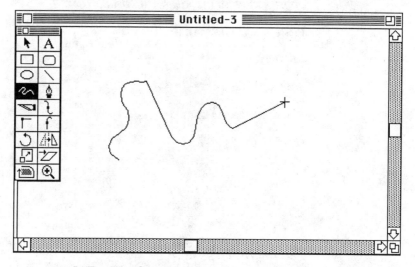

FIGURE 3-1 *In FreeHand, you can draw a straight segment within a freehand line by pressing the Option Key.*

Creating curved or diagonal guidelines

CorelDRAW has nonprinting horizontal and vertical ruler guides which you can use to align text and art. But you can also create thin diagonal or curved lines to use as guides. To create them, draw the lines and set their outline to No Outline (the X-shaped icon), using the Outline tool from the Toolbox (on the right of the CorelDRAW screen). The custom guidelines you've created will appear in the drawing window, but they won't be visible in the Preview window (Figure 3-2) and they won't appear in the final printed graphic.

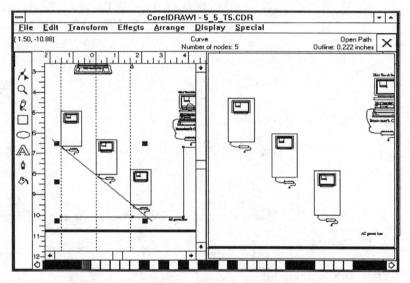

FIGURE 3-2 *You can create diagonal or curved guidelines in CorelDRAW, in addition to the standard horizontal and vertical guides (dotted lines). Give them a no outline Outline setting, and they'll appear in the drawing window (left) but not in the preview (right).*

Working in layers

Take advantage of **FreeHand**'s ability to display or hide different parts of a drawing by putting separate elements of a complex drawing in separate layers. When you're done working on a particular element, hide the layer that contains it by unchecking the layer in the

Layers palette. With the layer hidden from view, you won't have to wait for that part of the graphic to redraw every time you change something else. Position ruler guides around important hidden elements to indicate their position while you're working on other layers.

. . . .

 ## Drawing outlined rules

To make outlined rules (as in Figure 3-3) in **Illustrator** or **Freehand**, layer a white rule on top of a thicker black rule. First draw the black rule; give it a fill of *None* and a stroke of the appropriate width in Illustrator, or set the appropriate line weight in Freehand. Then use the Copy and Paste in Front (in Illustrator) or Clone (in Freehand) commands to place a duplicate directly on top of the original line. Reduce the stroke or weight of the duplicate by twice the width of the desired outlines and color the duplicate white. Now select both lines and group them. To create outlined dashed rules, use this same technique but employ a dashed thick rule and a solid thin rule (Figure 3-3).

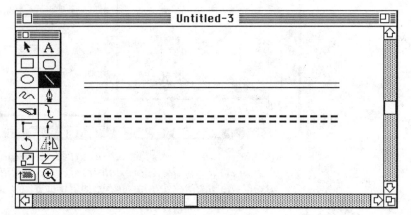

FIGURE 3-3 *Laying a thin white line atop a thicker solid (top) or dashed (bottom) black line produces an outlined rule.*

Drawing with a grid

If you don't have access to a scanner, maps and other graphics can be drawn accurately in a Mac or PC drawing program using an old-fashioned tracing grid:

1. Create evenly spaced horizontal and vertical lines on screen. The number of lines and their length depend on the size of the original map or graphic you want to trace.

2. Group the lines and gave them a medium gray stroke to lighten them.

3. Print out the grid on transparent overhead projector film—the kind designed for use with copiers.

4. Lay the transparency on the original and tape the grid down so it won't shift.

You can now use your program's drawing tools to recreate the image, square by square, on the corresponding grid on the screen. When the drawing is complete, delete the on-screen grid. This technique takes some getting used to, but, once you master the hand-eye coordination, it's fast and accurate.

 ## Avoiding premature polygons

When drawing with the Polygon tool in **MacDraw II**, hold down the Option Key to avoid ending the polygon prematurely. This is especially helpful when you want to draw line segments that end near the polygon's starting point. When you're ready to finish the polygon, release the Option Key and double-click on the end of the final line segment. (Click once if the last line segment ends at the polygon's starting point.)

. . . .

  ## Large-size tracing models

When scanning artwork to be traced in an illustration program, scan the original art larger than your final drawing size. This makes it easier to get fine detail in the tracing, and you can later scale the art back to the original size.

. . . .

 ## Quick and easy spheres

You can use **FreeHand**'s PASTE INSIDE command to create realistic spheres quickly and easily. These are the steps:

1. Draw a circle about one-third larger than the size you have in mind for the sphere.

2. Select the circle and then choose the FILL AND LINE command from the Attributes menu. In the Fill side of the Fill and Line dialog box, select the *Radial* option from the Fill pop-up menu. Choose a light-to-dark gradation by entering the appropriate colors in the

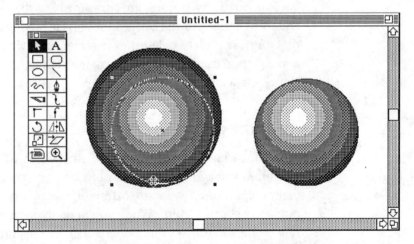

FIGURE 3-4 *To quickly create a sphere in FreeHand, first position an unfilled circle over a larger, radial-filled circle (left). Then cut the filled circle and paste it inside the unfilled one (right).*

From and To pop-up menus (light color in the From menu, dark color in the To menu).

3. Draw the circle which is to become the sphere; make sure its fill is *None*. (For the best effect, choose a thin line as well.) Drag the sphere/circle over the filled circle; position the sphere/circle so that the highlight area in the filled circle is off to one side of the sphere/circle (Figure 3-4).

4. Cut the large filled circle to the Clipboard. Select the sphere/circle and then choose the PASTE INSIDE command from the Edit menu.

Your sphere may look somewhat crude on screen, but it should print well, especially on a high-resolution printer.

New dingbats from old

To create interesting ornamental shapes, combine Zapf Dingbats characters with simple boxes and circles available in your page lay-out program. Reverse the dingbat to white, and then place it over the darker box or circle so that the shape of the Dingbat creates a white silhouette on a darker background.

Drawing a five-pointed star

Five-pointed stars are devilishly hard to draw by hand but relatively easy if you work with **FreeHand**'s or **Illustrator**'s rotation tools and perform a little mental arithmetic:

1. Start by drawing one straight vertical line (a long line in FreeHand, a shorter line in Illustrator). Then do the following:

   • In FreeHand, clone the line, select the clone, choose the Rotate tool, press the Option Key as you click on the line, and in the Rotate dialog box enter a rotation of 36° and turn on the *Center of Selection* option. After the first rotation, choose DUPLICATE from the Edit menu three times to create a symmetric set of "spokes" (Figure 3-5, top left, on page 112).

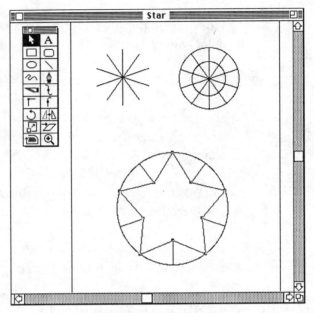

FIGURE 3-5 *The evolution of a five-pointed star, FreeHand version.*

- In Illustrator, select the line, choose the Rotate tool, press the Option Key as you click on the bottom end of the line, and in the Rotate dialog box enter a rotation of 36° and click the Copy button (not the OK button). Choose TRANSFORM AGAIN from the Arrange menu (or press Command + D) eight more times to create a symmetric set of "spokes."

2. Draw a circle which is centered on the intersection of all the spokes and whose circumference touches the end of each spoke. Draw another smaller circle inside it, also centered on the inter-section point (Figure 3-5, top right). The size of the inside circle depends on how sharp you want your star's points to be; draw a small circle for stiletto points and a not-so-small circle for blunt points. Group the spokes and the circles together.

3. Draw a line from the intersection of the first line and the outer circle to the intersection of the second line and the inner circle, and so on, all the way around the circle (Figure 3-5, bottom). Use the Corner Freeform tool in FreeHand or the Pen tool in Illustrator to make one continuous line that defines a closed shape.

4. When the star is complete, delete the grouped spokes and circles. Select your star and give it the desired fill and stroke.

An alternative method is to create a set of spokes at 72° intervals, select the spokes, copy and rotate them 36°, and scale the copy by about 40 percent. Simply connect the tips of the longer lines to the tips of the shorter ones to draw your star. As for the math, you need ten radiating lines for a five-pointed star; 360° divided by 10 lines equals the 36° we used to rotate each spoke. For a six-pointed star, you need 12 lines, and thus you would rotate each spoke by 30°, and so on.

Straightening lines in Arts & Letters

If you've drawn a freeform line in **Arts & Letters** that's at a slight angle and you need a line that's horizontal or vertical, you could redraw the line or drag the line's point handles with the *Grid* option of the SNAP TO command (under the Construct menu) turned on. But there's an easier way to force the line into vertical or horizontal alignment. Use the MAKE HORIZ/VERT command, which automatically makes lines horizontal or vertical with a click of the mouse. Here's how:

1. Select the whole line or segment of the line you want to straighten.

2. Select the MAKE HORIZ/VERT command under the Construct menu.

3. Click any point handle to straighten the line. When you click the point handle on one end of the line, the point handle on the other end remains immobile, as if stuck to the page. The clicked point snaps into position so that the line is either vertical or horizontal.

Curved labels for maps

If you're creating a map and want to add text labels at odd angles or along irregular contours like creeks and rivers, use **CorelDRAW's** FIT TEXT TO PATH command, **Illustrator's** path-type tool, or **FreeHand's**

JOIN ELEMENTS command. These options allow a string of text to follow an arbitrary path. Here, for example, is how you would create a curving text label in CorelDRAW (the process is almost identical in FreeHand):

1. Draw a line up the middle of the river, or along side it, depending on the scale.

2. Enter the text. You may want to increase the inter-character spacing using the Text Spacing options (click Spacing in the Text box).

3. Select both the text block and the line drawn in the first step. Either lasso both objects with the Pick tool (pointer), or Shift + click each one.

4. With text and line selected, click the FIT TEXT TO PATH command under the Arrange menu.

The text will then flow along the line (Figure 3-6), starting at the point where you began drawing the line.

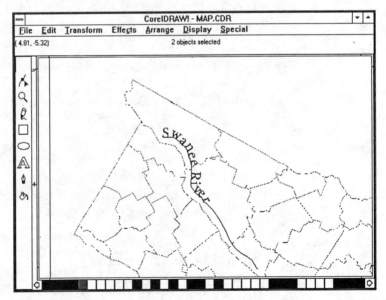

FIGURE 3-6 *Labeling irregular contours in scanned maps is easy in Corel-DRAW and other programs that snap text to a curved path.*

Erasing part of a FreeHand line

If you goof while drawing with the freehand tool in **Illustrator** or **FreeHand**, you can easily delete the faulty portion of the path and try again. Say, for example, you're fairly well along in tracing a complex image and you've messed up the last inch or so. Don't panic. While you continue to hold down the mouse button, press the Command Key. The pointer changes from black to white and, in effect, becomes an eraser. As you continue to press both the mouse button and Command Key, back up over the portion of the freehand line that you want to erase. (FreeHand requires that you retrace the line almost exactly; Illustrator is a little more forgiving.) When you've deleted your mistake, release the Command Key and resume tracing as before.

Drawing waves in FreeHand

To create smooth and even wave forms in **FreeHand**, draw a long rectangle and divide it into equal sections to serve as a guide (Figure 3-7). With the curve tool, start at one end of the rectangle and click where each vertical divider intersects the box, clicking at the top of one divider and the bottom of the next as though you were drawing a series of connected diagonal lines. Each curve in the wave will form

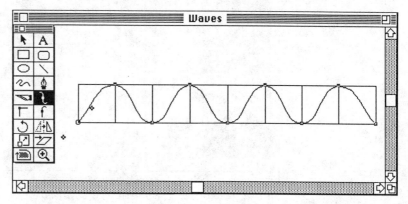

FIGURE 3-7 *An evenly partitioned rectangle serves as a guide for drawing a smooth wave form.*

automatically as soon as you create the next point in the curve. To give the outermost curve segments the same shape as the inner curves, select each endpoint and drag its handle so the handle is in line with the top or bottom of the rectangular guide. When you're all done, delete the guide.

Drawing stairstep lines

In **Ventura Publisher**, you can use the Clipboard to draw a series of perfectly connected lines for a stairstep or jagged-line effect.

1. Draw the first line and copy it to the clipboard.

2. Grab the handle at one end of the line you just drew and swing it to a new position. The other end of the line, which remains anchored, becomes the axis around which the line sweeps, like the hand of a clock (Figure 3-8).

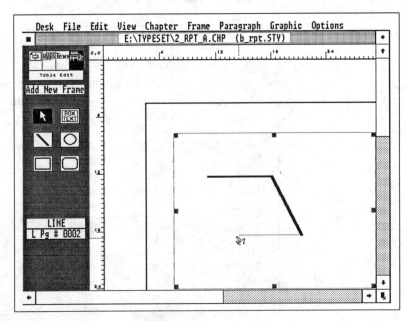

FIGURE 3-8 *You can create a series of connected lines in Ventura Publisher by using the Copy and Paste functions.*

3. After you've rotated the line, paste the copy back onto the page. Since you didn't move the anchor point of the first line, since the pasted line automatically reappears in its original position, the two lines meet at the point around which you swiveled the first line.

4. Repeat the procedure with the second line. Select the line. Copy it to the clipboard. Then drag the end point that abuts the previously pasted line you pasted, not the point at the free end, and swing it into position. It will appear that you have two disconnected lines on screen, but that gap will fill when you paste in the clipboard copy.

Repeat this technique for each segment of your segmented line. Remember that the pasted line connects to the stationery end of the copied line, so you need to drag each new segment from the end point that adjoins the previously created segment.

It's also a good idea to select rounded line endings from the Line Attributes dialog box (under the Graphics menu) when you use this technique. The rounded ends overlap to form a smoother-looking connection than the squared ends do, especially when the angle of the connection is other than 90 degrees.

Selecting two stacked objects

In **FreeHand**, there's an easy way to select two objects lying directly on top of one another, objects which also have other objects close to or underneath them that you don't want to include in the selection. First select the top object and move it to the side. While it's still selected, press the Shift Key and select the second object. Now press Command + Z; this will undo the move so that the objects are back in perfect alignment but are both still selected.

. . . .

Quick flowchart diamonds

A quick way to draw diamond shapes for flowcharts in **Ventura Publisher** is to use the grid snap feature of Ventura's graphics tools. These are the steps:

1. Under the Graphics menu, select GRID SETTINGS in the GEM and Windows Editions, or SET GRAPHICS GRID on the Mac.

2. In the dialog box that appears, turn on *Grid Snap* in the GEM or Windows Editions, or *Snap to Grid* on the Mac.

3. Set Horizontal Spacing and Vertical Spacing to a relatively large increment—about one or two picas. Then click OK.

Now any lines you draw will begin and end only at the points on the grid (Figure 3-9), so you'll find it easy to draw precisely proportioned diamonds without additional help.

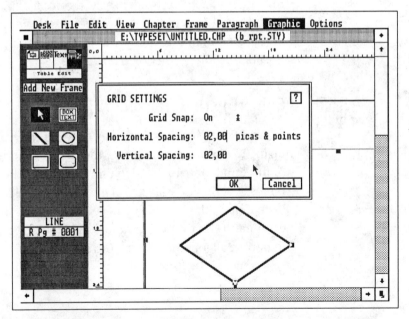

FIGURE 3-9 *Ventura's* Grid Snap *option makes it easy to draw perfectly proportioned diamonds for flowcharts.*

Strings of circles or squares

In **FreeHand** and **Illustrator** for the Mac, you can easily transform a simple line into a string of filled circles or squares for use for a border or a graphic accent. Here's how, with Illustrator:

1. Select the line you want to transform and choose the STYLE command from the Paint menu.

2. In the Paint Style dialog box, select no fill, black stroke, and either rounded caps (the second option in the Caps section) for circles or projecting caps (the third and last option) for squares.

3. Turn on the *Dashed* option in the Dash Pattern section of the dialog box. Enter zero in the first text box after the option and a relatively large number, like 14, in the second box. (The second number determines the spacing of the circles or squares that will make up the rule.)

4. Adjust the size of the circles or squares by typing a point value, such as 8, in the Weight text box. This value must be smaller than the one you entered in the second Dashed text box, or the elements will overlap.

Turn on Preview mode (Figure 3-10, next page) and you'll see that the selected line is now a string of circles or squares.

You can change a line into a string of nearly perfect circles or squares in FreeHand this way:

1. Select the line you want to transform and choose the FILL AND LINE command from the Attributes menu.

2. In the Fill and Line dialog box, make sure the *Basic Line* option is turned on. Turn on either the second option (rounded caps) for circles or the third option (projecting caps) for squares.

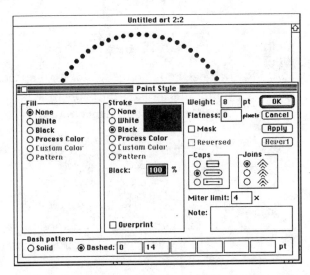

FIGURE 3-10 *Choosing a gap greater than the line width and round end caps can turn a dashed line—such as the arc shown here in Illustrator—into a string of round dots.*

3. Enter a line weight in the Weight text box appropriate for the size circles or squares you want to create. (If the line weight is thick enough, you'll barely notice that your circles or squares are slightly imperfect.)

4. Press the Option Key and choose a dashed line style from the Dash pop-up menu. In the resulting Line Pattern dialog box, enter 1 (the smallest value permitted) in the topmost On text box and a value larger than the line weight in the topmost Off text box. Leave the remaining text boxes blank.

To create a row of hollow circles or squares in either program, create an overlapping copy of the dotted line (use the CLONE command in FreeHand, COPY and PASTE IN FRONT in Illustrator). Then apply a line weight thinner than the original and a white stroke to the frontmost copy.

Sizing, measuring, aligning, moving

 ## Centering an object on the page

Here's a quick way to center an object on the page; it works in most programs that have an ALIGNMENT command, including **FreeHand**, **MacDraw II**, and **DeskDraw**. Let's say you want to horizontally center an object on a page in **FreeHand**. Here's how:

1. Draw a horizontal line across the page from edge to edge (or margin to margin).

2. Select both the object you want to align and the line you drew in the previous step.

3. Choose the ALIGNMENT command from the Element menu (or press Command + /). In the Alignment dialog box, turn on the *Horizontal* and *Center* options (Figure 3-11) and click the OK

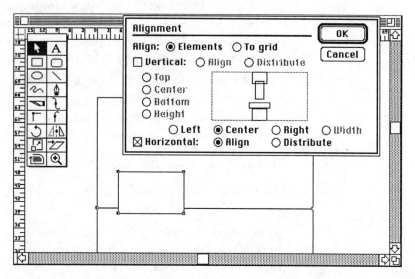

FIGURE 3-11 *To center an object on the page in FreeHand, use the Alignment command to center both the object and a line that spans the page.*

button. Both of the selected items should now be centered horizontally on the page.

To center an object vertically, draw a vertical line and proceed as above but turn on the *Vertical* and *Center* options in the Alignment dialog box. To center an object both vertically and horizontally on the page, draw vertical and horizontal lines (or a rectangle the same size as the page) and turn on the *Vertical, Horizontal,* and both *Center* options in the Alignment dialog box. Oh yes— don't forget to delete the centering line or rectangle when you're done.

Proportionally resizing imported images

To resize a placed graphic proportionally (so that it retains its original aspect ratio) in **PageMaker** for the Mac or the PC, press Shift as you click and drag one of the image's corner handles. In **QuarkXPress**, press Command + Option + Shift as you click and drag one of the image's corner handles. In **Ventura Publisher** Macintosh Edition, double-click on the graphic to open the Scaling & Cropping dialog box; in the PC Editions, click on the graphic to select its frame; then select SIZING & SCALING from the Frame menu to open the Sizing & Scaling dialog box. Make sure that the *Fit in Frame* Scaling option and *Maintained* Aspect Ratio option are turned on, and then click on OK. Back in the document window, the image's handles and frame should be highlighted in black. Click and drag any one of the handles; although the frame can be scaled to any size or shape, the image within will be resized proportionally.

Moving objects pixel-by-pixel

Moving objects short, precise distances, whether it be in a graphics program or a page layout application, can be pretty frustrating. If, like us, you tend to be all thumbs, you probably miss the mark far more often than you hit it. A simple solution to this problem is Apple's Easy Access startup document; you'll find it on one of your Macintosh System disks. To install it, simply drop a copy in the System Folder and restart your computer. These steps follow:

1. Press Command + Shift + Clear to turn on Easy Access. (The Clear Key is in the upper left corner of the keypad.)

2. Select the object you want to move and position the pointer over the object, as if you were going to drag it in the usual manner.

3. Press the 0 Key on the keypad. (Just press and release it; you don't need to hold it down.) This "locks" the mouse button and is equivalent to clicking and holding the mouse button.

4. Now use the even-numbered keys on the keypad to move the object, one pixel at a time, in any of eight directions:

   • To move the object up one pixel, press the 8 Key.

   • To move the object down one pixel, press the 2 Key.

   • To move the object left one pixel, press the 4 Key.

   • To move the object right one pixel, press the 6 Key.

   • To move the object diagonally one pixel, press the 1, 3, 7, or 9 Key.

   Press these keys as often as required to move the object to the desired location, one pixel at a time. If you find a gross position change is required, move the mouse until the object is close to the correct location; then resume precise positioning with the keypad keys.

5. When the object is where you want it, press either the 5 Key or the Decimal Point Key on the keypad to "unlock" (release) the mouse button.

6. If you want to move another object, repeat steps 2 through 5. When you're done, press Command + Shift + Clear again to turn Easy Access off.

This trick works anywhere, by the way, even on the desktop; you can use it to move windows or anything else.

Resizing a group of objects

Here's a quick and easy way to resize a group of objects in **MacDraw II**. If you haven't already, turn on the rulers with the SHOW RULERS command, making sure the ruler is in inches (change the unit of measurement with the RULERS command if it is not), and display the size box with the SHOW SIZE command. These steps follow:

1. Draw a one-inch square with the rectangle tool and drag it next to or within the area occupied by the objects you want to resize.

2. If *Autogrid* is on, turn it off now.

3. Select the square and the group of objects you want to resize.

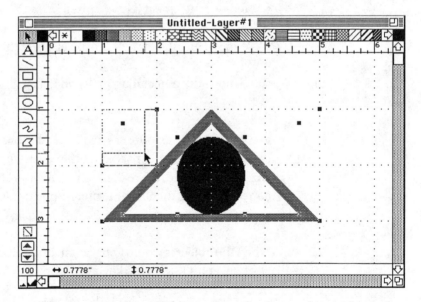

FIGURE 3-12 *As you resize the one-inch square, the numbers in the size box at the bottom of MacDraw II's window indicate the percent by which all the selected objects are scaled.*

4. Click on the lower right handle of the one-inch square, drag into the square to reduce the selected objects or outside the square to enlarge them, and keep your eyes on the size box. (Press Shift as you drag if you want to scale all objects proportionally.) Only the square changes size as you drag (Figure 3-12); all selected objects are reduced or enlarged, however, as soon as you release the mouse button.

5. Delete the square which you drew in step 1.

Note that the numbers displayed in the size box at the bottom of the window are not just the final dimensions (in inches) of the one-inch square; they also indicate the percent enlargement or reduction of all the selected objects.

Aligning object edges

To align the edges of two or more objects in **Illustrator** for the Mac, first make sure that the *Snap to Point* option in the Preferences dialog box is turned on. Then, to align a number of objects, create a ruler guide at the desired alignment position by dragging the pointer from inside a ruler out onto the image area. All objects dragged to within two pixels of the ruler guide will automatically "stick" to—and align with—the guide. Keep in mind, however, that only the edge or corner being dragged is sticky.

To align just two or three objects, it's often easier to align by anchor points. (As before, the *Snap to Point* option must be turned on for this technique to work correctly.) Here's how: Drag one object by an anchor point you want to align by and drop that anchor point on top of another object's anchor point; you'll find the two anchor points snap to each other the same way objects snap to ruler guides. Now drag the still-selected object again by the same anchor point, and press the Shift Key after you start dragging. As soon as you press Shift, the two objects remain aligned—vertically, horizontally, or 45 degrees diagonally—by the two anchor points.

Lines that stay put

To avoid accidentally pulling a straight line out of alignment in a page layout or drawing program, draw a box instead of a line. Make the box height or width equal to 0, which will give you a line the thickness of your line-width setting. The line will always remain perfectly vertical or horizontal unless you use a graphics rotation feature (if your program has one) to purposely alter it.

 ## Creating a grid for Illustrator

For reasons only Adobe knows for sure, there is no snap-to-grid option for easy alignment of objects in **Illustrator**. If a grid that lacks a snap-to capability is helpful to you, create one in a program like **Macdraw II** by drawing over Macdraw's own grid with .25-point rules. Make sure Macdraw's *Auto-grid* option (in the Layout menu) is turned on and use the DUPLICATE command to make the job easier. Save the grid in PICT format, and then open it in Illustrator as a template (Figure 3-13).

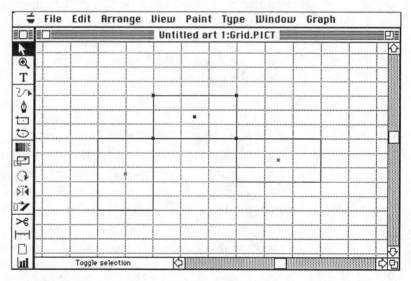

FIGURE 3-13 *Illustrator doesn't have a grid option, but you can draw one of your own in a program that does and open it as a template.*

Creating custom spacing guides

Illustrator's Measure tool is a big help if you need to maintain a consistent spacing between the objects in a drawing. If a drawing contains numerous objects all evenly spaced, however, you may be better off creating a special spacing guide. To do so:

1. Select the Oval tool and click once anywhere in the drawing.

2. In the Oval dialog box (Figure 3-14), specify a diameter (in one or both dimensions) that matches the space you want between objects.

3. Select the resulting oval (or circle), choose the STYLE command from the Paint menu, and in the Paint Style dialog box set the stroke and fill of the circle to *None*.

Now, when you need to space two objects, drag the circle to the edge of one of them; then move the second object so it abuts the opposite side of the circle. Because of its stroke and fill settings, you'll see the spacing guide while drawing but not in Preview mode or on the printed page.

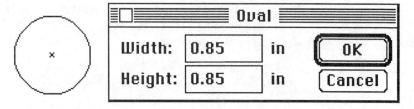

FIGURE 3-14 *You can use a circle as a tool for maintaining consistent spacing. When you create the circle in Illustrator, specify a diameter in the Oval dialog box that matches the desired space between objects.*

Moving multiple items

An easy way to reposition a number of items in **FreeHand** is to select them (either by Shift + clicking on each item, or by dragging a selection rectangle around the entire group) and drag them all at one time to the new location. When you select and move large numbers of items, however, it is not uncommon to inadvertently miss a few items and, after the rest are repositioned, find them left behind. If this happens to you, there's no need to undo the move and start all over again. Instead, simply select the items that were left behind and choose the Move command from the Edit menu (or press Command + M). Click the OK button in the Move Elements dialog box that then appears and the stragglers will automatically move into the correct position relative to the previously moved items. Keep in mind that this works only if you act quickly and round up the stragglers before moving something else; since the Move command remembers and applies the horizontal and vertical offsets of the previous move only, the previous move must be the one you want to correct.

Scaling objects in 3-D

Here's a really quick way to scale three-dimensional shapes to a vanishing point in **Illustrator**. Let's say you want to create a sequence of boxes, starting in the lower left and heading toward a vanishing point in the upper right. Here's how to do it:

1. Draw the front face of the first and largest box in the lower left corner of the Illustrator page.

2. Draw three lines from the top and lower right corners of the box face to the vanishing point. The vanishing point can be within the page's boundaries or somewhere out on the pasteboard. (Put it out on the pasteboard, as in Figure 3-15, for a more realistic effect.)

3. Convert the three vanishing point lines to guidelines with the Make Guide command in the Arrange menu.

4. Now complete the top and right face of the first box, using the guidelines to help you create the correct perspective. Stroke and fill each face to give the effect of a single light source. Group the three faces together when you're done.

5. Select the box and then choose the Scale tool. Click once on the vanishing point; then press the Shift and Option keys and drag the box toward the vanishing point. Illustrator scales the box in perspective, and, because you're holding down the Option Key, it makes a duplicate.

6. Use TRANSFORM AGAIN (Command + D) to create evenly spaced boxes in a perspective row, or repeat step 5 to create additional boxes at the desired intervals.

Choose the PREVIEW ILLUSTRATION command to see how your three-dimensional boxes stack up (Figure 3-15).

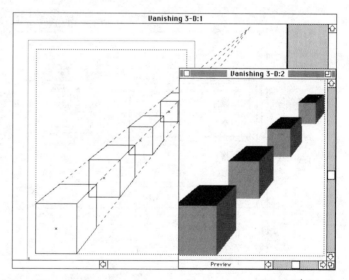

FIGURE 3-15 *With a few simple steps, you can scale images to a vanishing point in Illustrator.*

· ·

 ## Step and repeat

Here's a quick and convenient way to "step and repeat" an element in **Illustrator**:

1. First create the element.

2. While the element is still selected, press the Option Key and click on the pointer tool in the Tool palette.

3. In the Move dialog box which is now open, designate how far to offset the element in the Distance text box and in what direction in the Angle text box (Figure 3-16).

4. Click the Copy button to create and move a copy of the element according to your specifications.

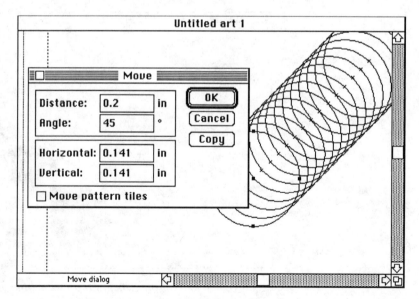

FIGURE 3-16 *To start a step and repeat in Illustrator, enter the distance between steps and the direction in the top two text boxes of the Move dialog box.*

5. Select the TRANSFORM AGAIN command from the Arrange menu or press Command + D repeatedly until you have created the desired number of stepped objects.

· ·

Patterns, blends, and fills

· ·

 ## Shifting the pattern in an object

In **Illustrator** for the Mac, repeating patterns take the ruler origin (the point where the zeros on the two rulers intersect) as their starting point. If a pattern doesn't sit well within a particular shape, you can shift it in any direction by moving the ruler origin to a more appropriate location, as illustrated in Figure 3-17. Move the ruler origin by dragging from the blank rectangle at the intersection of the two window rulers into the document window; release the mouse button when the cross hair is over the desired point of origin.

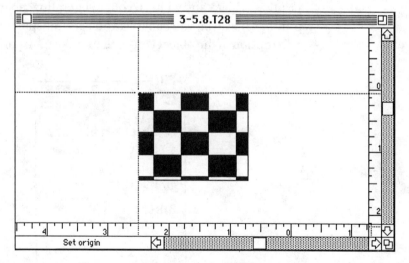

FIGURE 3-17 *You can make a pattern in Illustrator start at a certain point by dragging the ruler origin to that point. Here the ruler origin is being moved to one of the object's corners so that the squares in the fill pattern will align checkerboard-style with the object's edges.*

Note that moving the ruler origin is one of the few changes you can make in Preview mode; since fill patterns are visible only in Preview mode, you'll want to take advantage of this in order to see what you're doing. Beware of a drawing with more than one pattern-filled object, however. If you change the ruler origin, you'll affect the placement of patterns within all filled elements, and you may end up with a worse problem than before.

Resolving pattern printing difficulties

If you have trouble printing a pattern-filled object in **Illustrator**, try creating the pattern separately and then masking the pattern with the object (instead of filling the object directly). In most cases this will solve the problem.

Transparent objects in Illustrator

There's no way to create transparent objects in **Illustrator** when printing in black and white. If you're generating separations for color printing, however, you can make objects transparent with the *Overprint* option. If the object you want to make transparent is filled with

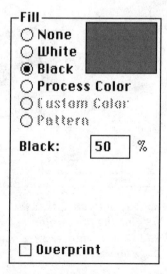

FIGURE 3-18 *The Overprint option is at the bottom of the Fill section in Illustrator's Paint dialog box.*

gray or a solid color, simply turn on *Overprint* in the Paint dialog box when specifying the fill for that object (Figure 3-18). If the object is filled with a pattern, use a pattern which has *Overprint* turned on in the pattern definition. You'll have to use your imagination when overprinting objects since Illustrator doesn't display the transparent effect on screen or in test prints. *Overprint* kicks into action only when you create color separations.

Stand-in graphics

In any graphics program, if you plan to create graduated fills in a drawing, put them in last since they tend to slow down the screen redraw. Use a solid fill as you work on the drawing; change it to a graduated fill as the last step.

Since graduated fills also print very slowly, it's a good idea to create two versions of any drawing you intend to import into a page layout program: The final version and a skeleton version showing only the outlines of the objects. Use the skeleton version for all revisions except the final one. This way, when you print intermediate proofs of your page designs, you won't have to wait for the graduated fills to process. When your layout is complete, substitute the finished art for the final printout.

Filling letters with a blend

In **Illustrator**, you can easily fill an entire word, or group of words, with a blend. Here's how:

1. Type the text you want to fill.

2. Select the text and choose the CREATE OUTLINES command from the Type menu to change the text to artwork.

3. Select the text outlines and choose the MAKE COMPOUND command from the Paint menu.

4. Select the STYLE command from the Paint menu and turn on the *Mask* option for the selected text outlines.

5. Create a blend and drag it on top of the text.

Switch to Preview Illustration view and you'll see that the blend now shows through the type outlines (Figure 3-19). One word of caution lest you become too fond of type blends: An excessive amount of blended text may result in a document that prints rather slowly.

FIGURE 3-19 *It's easy to fill words with a blend in Illustrator.*

Creating a complex reversal

In **Illustrator** and **FreeHand**, there are several ways you can "half-fill" or partially reverse an object so that it is one color or pattern on one side of an arbitrary dividing line and another pattern or color on the other. For relatively simple objects, cut the object in half with the scissors or knife tool, join the free ends of each half, and fill the two halves with different colors or patterns. For complex shapes or type, such as the text in Figure 3-20, you'll need to create two differently filled copies of the object and a mask for one of the copies.

Say you want to create the Illustrator graphic in Figure 3-20, in which the text is sliced horizontally, the upper half is filled with 80-percent gray, and the lower half is filled with 40-percent gray. These are the steps:

FIGURE 3-20 *Use two pieces of text, one masked and one not, to create a reverse out such as this one in Illustrator.*

1. Open an Illustrator document and create the text you want to reverse out. Use standard text, or, if you want to customize the lettershapes in some way, convert the text to outlines. Both work equally well for a "half-filled" graphic.

2. Select the text and specify a fill of 80-percent gray and a simple, 1-point black stroke with the STYLE command from the Paint menu.

3. With the text still selected, choose the COPY command (or press Command + C) and then the PASTE IN FRONT command (or press Command + F).

4. With the copy of the text now selected, specify a fill of 40-percent gray and the same 1-point stroke with the STYLE command.

5. Draw a rectangle over the lower half of the text. The top of the rectangle should cut across the text at the precise location where you want the reverse to occur. (If the reverse's border is to be something other than a horizontal line, create an irregular shape with the appropriate top border; make sure the shape covers all of the lower part of the text.)

6. Select the rectangle, ungroup it, and delete the rectangle's center point.

7. Select the rectangle with an Option + click and use the STYLE command again to turn on the *Mask* option. Specify a fill and stroke of None for the rectangle.

8. Select the top text copy and choose the BRING TO FRONT command (or press Command + =).

9. Select both the top text copy and the rectangle and group them with the GROUP command from the Arrange menu.

If you now select the PREVIEW command, you'll see one piece of text filled with two shades of gray (Figure 3-20 on page 135). Although the details differ, the steps are much the same in FreeHand. The major difference is that FreeHand has no *Mask* option per se. Instead, you cut the cloned copy of the text and use the PASTE INSIDE command to place it inside the overlapping rectangle (or polygon). Another difference in FreeHand is that you don't need to remove the center point of the rectangle into which the text is pasted.

Special backgrounds

For quick, organic-looking background patterns, scan the real thing on a flatbed color scanner. A good source for granite, marble, metallic, or patterned surfaces are the samples you can get at hardware stores for formica, wallpaper, and flooring. Fabric stores can provide burlap and other textured fabrics. Tape sand or soil between two pieces of glass for a cross-section of earth (but be sure you don't spill any dirt in your scanner).

Clip art

A clip art encyclopedia

If you're looking for exactly the right piece of clip art, try looking in *Canned Art: Clip Art for the Macintosh* by Erfert Fenton and Christine Morrissett. Weighing in at about six pounds, the book's 800 pages illustrate more than 15,000 images from an impressive number of disks produced by 37 clip art vendors. Images are organized by manufacturer first and then by disk. File format (such as Paint, PICT, or PostScript) and complete ordering information with prices are provided for each disk. The excellent, cross-referenced, 29-page index is the best way we know to find individual images by subject matter.

Divide sections with printer's ornaments

Printer's ornaments are a nice way to divide sections of text and add some visual interest to the page (see Figure 3-21 and 3-22 on pages 138 and 139). Many Macintosh printer's ornaments are sold in Post-Script font format. Wood Type Ornaments I and II, part of the **Adobe Wood Type** collection, volumes 1 and 2, provide a wealth of classic floral, abstract, and other flourishes. Giampa Textware's **Leaves I** consists entirely of 19th-century floral ornaments. Volume 1 of Kingsley ATF's **Classic Type** series includes QuillScript Flowers, which contains 16 ornamental leaves (but no flowers) designed to be used with Thompson Quillscript, and Cleland Border 1805, a set of eight script-style border elements which can be used as ornaments as well.

Altsys' **Printers Ornaments** package consists of three fonts containing Art Deco silhouettes of people, sketches of children, ornate fish, a few floral designs, and more. Many of the characters in Altsys' **Borders Fonts** can be used as ornaments, either alone or in groups of two or three, as well. U-Design Type Foundry is also an excellent source of font-based printer's ornaments. Their **Bill's DECOrations**

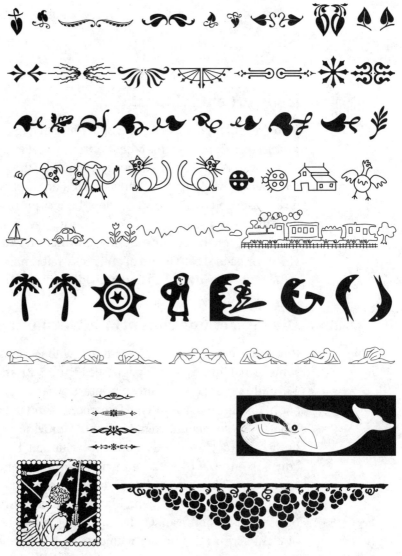

FIGURE 3-21 *Examples of printer's ornaments, by row from top: (1) Leaves I; (2) Adobe Wood Type Ornaments I; (3) QuillScript Flowers; (4) Tschichold; (5) Electric Hand I; (6) Barbara Plump; (7) Printer's Ornaments; (8) Typographer's Ornaments, EPS series; (9) Typographer's Ornaments, TIFF series.*

FIGURE 3-22 *More examples of printer's ornaments, by row from top: (1, 2) Bill's DECOrations; (3, 4) Bill's Victorian Ornaments; (5, 6) Bill's Barnhart Ornaments; (6 and below) Borders & Ornaments, DigitArt Volume 23.*

font, for example, contains Art Deco symbols (both figurative and abstract) borrowed from period posters, pinball machines, advertisements, sign painting manuals, and other sources. **Bill's Victorian Ornaments** font reflects the architecture and crafts of an earlier age with floral, gingerbread, and other ornaments. **Bill's Barnhart Ornaments** font derives from the Barnhart Brothers and Spindler specimen book of 1909 and includes many finely detailed floral ornaments. And among its many arrows and dingbats, **Bill's Box Specials** font includes several bird ornaments, a snail, a candlestick, palm trees, dragonflies, and lobsters.

Judith Sutcliffe's wonderfully original fonts usually contain a half dozen or more ornaments per font. The Barbara Sisters trio of fonts contains such Santa Barbara, California, fixtures as palm trees, a Chumash Indian sun, leaping dolphins, surfers, and even St. Barbara herself. **Electric Hand I** includes a locomotive, train cars, railroad track, planes, cars, trees, clouds, hills, water, and more for making miniature landscapes. And **Tschichold**, a Bauhaus-style font based on circles, is graced with a humorous set of barnyard animals, cats, mice, and a barn.

Richard Mitchell, publisher of the *Underground Grammarian*, offers probably the best and least-expensive set of printers' ornaments in EPS and TIFF graphic formats. Eight volumes of TIFF files are available; each contains about 40 ornaments. The volumes are organized by topic: people, plants, whimsies, animals, books and music, and so on. The ten EPS volumes each contain a mixed selection of 20 or more ornaments, from people, dogs and cats, to candles, dragons, bookshelves, and rural scenes. Also in EPS format is Image Club Graphics' **DigitArt** Volume 23, Borders & Ornaments (available separately, or as part of their ArtRoom CD ROM collection). Especially noteworthy in this collection are the classic rules and flourishes and a skillfully rendered set of floral ornaments.

Decorative caps for chapter openers

Ornamented letters and decorative caps make a nice, eye-catching beginning to a chapter (see Figure 3-23) and are available in a variety of formats . Image Club Graphics' **Drop Caps**, for example, is a PostScript font containing two complete sets of ornamented letters. In one set the letters are surrounded by a script-like filigree; in the other set the design is bold and dark. Cassady & Greene's **Troubador Initials** font (designed by Judith Sutcliffe) contains reversed (white-on-black) initials entwined with alphabetically-related California native wildflowers. A columbine sprouts from the *C*, for example, hummingbird sage from the *H*, and yerba buena from the *Y*. Another Judith Sutcliffe PostScript font, **Tagliente Initials**, is also composed of reversed, decorative initials; you'll find examples of Tagliente Initials in Figure 1-24 on page 44 .

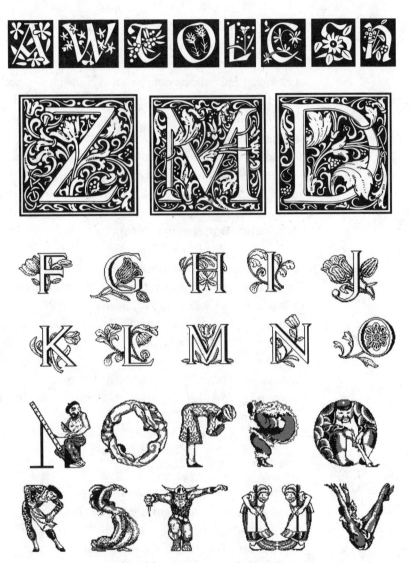

FIGURE 3-23 *Examples of decorative caps, by row from top: (1) Troubador Initials; (2) Goudy's Illuminated Initials; (3, 4) ClickArt Publications; (5,6) Mac the Knife Volume 5 (People, Places, Things).*

Clip art is another source of ornamented letters. Dubl Click's **Wet Paint: Printer's Helper** collection of images contains over 100 19th-century-style initials wrapped around or imitated by a variety of humorous caricatures, as well as an assortment of letters decorated with plants and animals. **Mac the Knife Volume 5 (People, Places,**

Things) from Miles Computing, contains a set of initials composed of people in peculiar positions, while **Mac the Knife Volume 3 (Mac the Ripper)** includes a medieval-style decorated alphabet. T/Maker's **ClickArt Publications** contains a French-style alphabet ornamented with flowers. All these collections are comprised of bitmapped images.

Image Club Graphics' Borders & Ornaments, Volume 23 of the Digit-Art series (available separately, or as part of their ArtRoom CD ROM collection), contains a nicely rendered set of Art Nouveau drop caps in EPS format. And in a class all their own are **Goudy's Illuminated Initials** from Giampa Textware, a set of incredibly ornate and elegant decorative caps, also in EPS format.

Finally, Dover Publications publishes a number of books on lettering and alphabets; you may reproduce up to ten images per publication without fee. The *Treasury of Authentic Art Nouveau Alphabets, Decorative Initials, Monograms, Frames and Ornaments* by Ludwig Petzendorfer and *Decorative Alphabets and Initials* by Alexander Nesbitt are two of many excellent—and inexpensive—sources of ornamented letters. You can scan the letters and use them as is or convert your scans into high-quality PostScript outlines with **Adobe Streamline.**

Photos from outer space

For out-of-this-world photographs, you'll find a wide variety of gray-scale and color images in the Space and Astronomy Library (DL14) of CompuServe's Graphics Corner Forum (use the GO CORNER command). The files are in CompuServe GIF format, which **Adobe Photoshop** can read directly, but which must be converted to a standard Mac format for most other Macintosh graphics programs. Most of the images are relatively small; they range from spacecraft and astronauts to the Earth, the moon, and the planets in the solar system.

One of the best Macintosh space collections we know of is **The Right Images** CD ROM by Tsunami Press (see Figure 3-24). It contains over 100 images in PICT2 format. Each image comes in three versions:

FIGURE 3-24 *Three images from The Right Images CD ROM.*

8-bit gray-scale, 8-bit color, and 24-bit color. Included are pictures
of astronauts on the moon and floating in space, shuttle launches
and landings, the planets from Mercury to Saturn, and a variety of

Earth views; in addition there are images of comets, the Sun (including a spectacular solar flare), star clusters, galaxies, and nebulae.

Crop, don't cut, your clip art

To prepare clip art that comes with multiple images per file, avoid the tedious "lasso, cut, and paste" procedure to tease out individual images in your paint or draw program. If you only want to place a few of them in **PageMaker**, don't bother trying to separate them out; just place the entire page of clip art on PageMaker's pasteboard. Then use the cropping tool to crop out what you don't need, and size the remaining graphic for final positioning.

To refine this technique, especially for longer documents with lots of clip art, use PageMaker's LINKS command, under the File menu, to maintain an external link to the clip art file. That way, the Page-Maker document itself won't become overly laden with multiple copies of large clip art files. Here's how to link a clip art file:

1. Choose the LINKS command from the File menu (after you've placed the file), and in the Links dialog box select the clip art file and click the Links Options button. Or select the LINKS OPTIONS command from the Element menu.

2. In the Links Option dialog box, turn off the *Store copy in publication* option under Graphics.

You can check the location of the linked file using the LINK INFO command in the Element menu.

Clips of the natural world

Clip art of plant and animal subjects is always popular and widely available (see Figures 3-25 and 3-26). Good all-around Macintosh clip art collections in bitmap (MacPaint) format include **WetPaint: Animal Kingdom** (3 disks) from Dubl-Click and a variety of different packages (one disk each) from Sunshine, including **Creatures of the Sea, A Treasury of Large Mammals, A Treasury of Birds**, and **The**

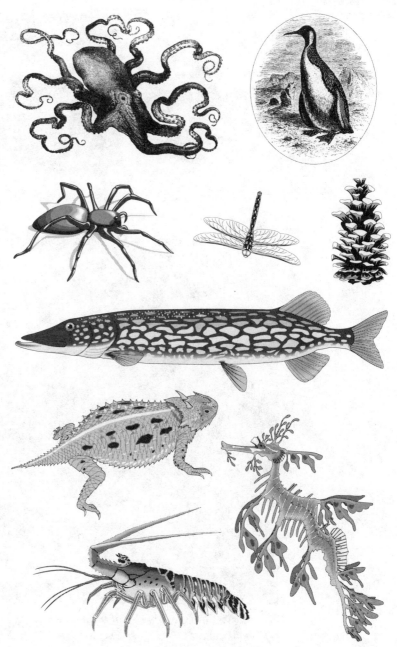

FIGURE 3-25 *Examples of natural world clip art from: (top row) Sunshine's Treasury of Birds and Creatures of the Sea volumes; (second row) ClickArt: EPS Animals & Nature; (center and below) Totem Graphics' general collections, Volumes 8 and 9.*

P. Conway /Focus Stock Photo Inc.,
For color transparency call 800-387-2758   scan by Barneyscan

FIGURE 3-26 *More examples of natural world clip art, by row from top: (1) Down to Earth CD ROM; (2) Quality Artware CD ROM; (3) Darkroom CD ROM.*

Wonderful World of Insects. (We also like Sunshine's Mayan ruins collections, but that's getting a little off the subject.)

In TIFF format, you might try the **Birds & Beasts** or **Flowers, Etc.** volumes (one disk each) from The Underground Grammarian's Typographer's Ornaments series; because they are printers' ornaments, the images on these disks are quite small. T/Maker's **ClickArt: EPS Animals & Nature** (5 disks) contains more than 150 illustrations in EPS format, all in black-and-white. For color EPS images, most of Totem Graphics' general clip art volumes, along with their **Domestic Animals, Fish,** and **Wild Animals** collections (9 to 18 disks each), are probably the best available (and are available in your choice of EPS, FreeHand, or Illustrator format).

On CD ROM, the best natural world collection we know of is Wayzata's **Down To Earth**. Created by Josepha Haveman, Down To Earth contains drawings (in Illustrator, FreeHand, and EPS format) and photographs (in PICT, TIFF, and MacPaint format) in both black-and-white and color of flowers, fruits, vegetables, foliage, landscapes, and clouds. Another Wayzata CD ROM, **Clip Art Masterpieces**, at least partly makes up for the dearth of animals in Down To Earth. Clip Art Masterpieces consists of drawings in the style of nineteenth century engravings or woodcuts. In addition to large selections of men, women, children, household objects, buildings, and vehicles, there are sizable collections of animals (ranging from bees and butterflies to tigers and zebras) and plants (from trees to morning glories).

Other CD ROMs containing plant and animal images include FM Waves' **Quality Artware** and Image Club's **Darkroom**. Quality Artware CD ROM contains a large selection of detailed drawings (in 400 dpi TIFF format) of insects, fish, frogs, dogs, farm animals, mammals, and birds (as well as political, business, fantasy, and fashion cartoons). Darkroom CD ROM, on the other hand, consists of striking black-and-white photographs, including two collections of natural subjects. The more limited Wildlife collection offers elephants, whales, owls, grizzly bears, and other birds and mammals. The larger, more diverse Nature/Scenics collection contains a broad spectrum of landscapes from national parks, coastal, and other areas, as well as clouds, waves, and a few close-ups.

Banner clip art

ClickArt Color Graphics for Presentations by T/Maker contains 48 national flags—for countries you're most likely to hear about in business discussions—in PICT or EPS format for the Macintosh or .WMF (Windows Metafile) format for the PC). But the most comprehensive collection of state and national flags that we know of is two five-disk packages of Macitosh EPS images by DiskArt (Figure 3-27). The **Flags of the U.S.A.** package contains the flags of all fifty states and U.S.

FIGURE 3-27 *Examples of EPS format flag images from Disk Art's Flags of the U.S.A. (top four) and Flags of the World (bottom four).*

territories, ten historical flags (including several Confederate banners), and, of course, the Stars and Stripes, both draped and fully extended. The "Flags of the World" package contains over 160 national flags arranged by continent, as well as a number of international flags, including the NATO, United Nations, and Olympic flags.

All the DiskArt images can be placed directly into your page layout program or modified in **Illustrator** or **Freehand**. All print in either black and white or color.

Using PostScript clip art on a LaserJet

If you'd like to use EPS clip art with **PageMaker** for Windows and an HP LaserJet printer, you don't necessarily need a PostScript cartridge for the printer, or a software-based PostScript interpreter for your computer. Instead, if the EPS clip art is in Adobe Illustrator PC format, you can use **CorelDRAW** to convert it to a non-PostScript format, such as CGM, TIFF, or PCX, before loading it into PageMaker. Like EPS, CGM (Computer Graphics Metafile) graphics are object oriented, so they look smoother than bitmapped formats such as TIFF or PCX when scaled up or printed on high-resolution printers and imagesetters. EPS and CGM are quite different formats, though, and changes in fine detail, scale, and font styles often occur during file conversion. EPS headlines or logos, for example, often appear expanded when converted to CGM, for example, but you can usually scale the graphic in your page layout program to compensate for the distortion,

Clip art the old-fashioned way

Don't be an electronic publishing purist and overlook the value of good old-fashioned clip art books. Quality disk-based clip art costs between $30 and $200 per package, from which you might only want a single image. Clip art books, sold at art supply and large book stores, cost only $4 to $12 and may contain dozens of usable images. You can scan an image in a book or simply clip it out and physically paste it onto your finished art. To resize the image before physically pasting it in, make a photocopied or photostatic enlargement or reduction first.

. . . .

Scans and scanning

. . . .

  ## Squaring up sheet-fed scans

Square up your artwork before scanning it in a sheet-fed scanner by trimming the top edge of the sheet so it's parallel to the horizontals in the drawing. Or, if your original art is irregularly shaped, tape it to a larger sheet of paper after aligning it with a T square. However you do it, precisely squaring the original prevents it from twisting as it enters the sheet-fed scanner and minimizes jagged horizontal and vertical lines in the scanned image.

. . . .

 ## Masking a scanned image

Here's a technique you can use to mask part of a scanned image in **FreeHand**:

1. Save a color scan as an EPS format file (import the file into **Photo-Shop** to convert it, if necessary) and use the PLACE command to import the EPS image into FreeHand; black-and-white scans in TIFF format can be placed without conversion.

2. Trace around the part of the image you want to remain visible, creating a closed path.

3. Select the scan and cut it with the CUT command.

4. Select the traced path and choose the PASTE INSIDE command. Only that part of the image which falls inside the path should now be visible (Figure 3-28).

You can adjust the path in the usual way (and after the scan is pasted inside) to fine-tune an imperfect trace. Select the path and change

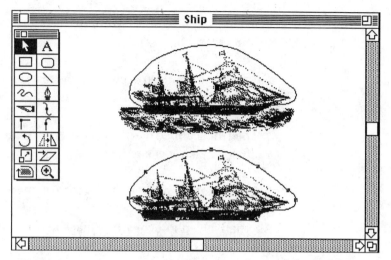

FIGURE 3-28 *You can mask an imported scan by drawing a path around it (top) and then pasting the scan inside the path (bottom). Change the path color to None to hide the mask when you're done.*

the line color to None to make the mask itself invisible. You can also scale and rotate the masked scan; the quality of the screen image won't look all that terrific, but the printed image should be fine.

  ## Scanning transparencies or negatives

To scan a slide, large-format transparency, or negative on a color flatbed scanner that doesn't have an attachment for these, buy or borrow an inexpensive, small lightbox (used to view transparencies, available from most art supplies stores). Put your transparent art face-down on the scanner; then place the light box lit-side-down on top of the art. Turn on the light box and scan away. If you're scanning a negative, use an image-editing program such as **PhotoShop** to invert the scanned negative to a positive.

  ## Scans wider than your scanner

To scan a photo that's wider than your scanner allows (to use for positioning only), you can rotate the photo 90 degrees on the scanner bed and scan it in the usual way. Then rotate it 90 degrees in an image-editing program. If you don't have an image-editing program, try this technique:

1. Rotate the photo 90 degrees on the scanner bed and scan it in the usual way.

2. Load the scanned file into a page layout or image-editing program and print it out at a reduced size.

3. Then scan the printout in the correct orientation.

Alternatively, photocopy the image at a reduced size to bring the photo down to scanning size. Either way, you'll get an image to use for positioning.

· ·

Clearer, darker scans in FreeHand

In **FreeHand** on a color monitor, scanned images placed in the background layer tend to look washed out, making details harder to see. For a clearer and darker image, place the scanned art in a layer other than the background (Figure 3-29).

· ·

Scans within PostScript graphics

A great way to add a unique background or a photorealistic image to a PostScript illustration is to incorporate a scan in your **Illustrator** or **FreeHand** document (Figure 3-30). In FreeHand, use the PLACE command (in the File menu) to insert a PICT or TIFF format scan in much the same way that you would place a graphic in a page layout program. For Illustrator, you'll need to save the scan in EPS format, either with your scanner's software or in a program like **PhotoShop**, and then open the EPS file with Illustrator's PLACE ART command. To see the imported image in both Artwork and Preview mode, make sure the *Show Placed Images* option is turned on in the Preferences dialog box. (To see the imported image on screen at all, of course, the EPS file must contain a PICT preview.)

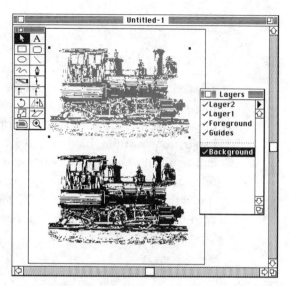

FIGURE 3-29 *Scanned images placed in FreeHand's background layer (top) look washed out; if placed in any other layer (bottom), they're clearer and darker.*

FIGURE 3-30 *You can place a scan in a PostScript document to create an interesting background (as in this FreeHand document) or an unusual effect. (Cloud photo from Down To Earth by Josepha Haveman.)*

Low-res place keepers

To speed your work on a page layout document that contains bit-mapped images such as scanned photos, turn off on-screen graphics display if you can. The GEM and Windows Editions of **Ventura Publisher**, for example, have a HIDE ALL PICTURES command which causes all graphics in your document to display as gray boxes. You'll find the command under the View menu in the Windows Edition or under the Options menu in the GEM Edition. In the Mac Edition, the command is called SHOW ALL PICTURES and you'll find it under the View menu.

If turning off on-screen graphics is not an option in your program, create a lower-resolution version of the graphic and use it as a place keeper. To do this, scan the image at low resolution in black and white to create the placeholder. Then scan at high resolution with multiple gray-scales or colors to create the image file you'll use to print. If you're working with clip art instead of scanned images, use an image-editing program to create a lower-resolution file. Either way, use the low-resolution files for position only and replace them with the high-resolution versions when you print.

 ## Use RIFF format to save space

If your scanner files are too big to manipulate easily, keep in mind that **QuarkXPress** can import RIFF files. RIFF is a more compressed format than TIFF and can save you precious disk space. If your scanning software doesn't save files in RIFF format, open the scan in **ImageStudio** and and choose the SAVE AS OTHER command from the File menu. Select the *RIFF* option from the Type pop-up menu and click the Save button to create a RIFF format file. While you're at it, other options in the SAVE AS OTHER dialog box allow you to save only a selected part of the image (and thus crop the scan) and to scale the scan up or down.

Creating a graphic keyline trap

A keyline trap marks the exact position of a graphic or image which will later be added to the page by conventional pre-press methods. Here's how to create a keyline trap for a scanned photograph for position-only placement in PageMaker:

1. Place the scanned image on the page and draw a box around it with the box tool.

2. For a precision fit, use a 400-percent view and adjust the box so that its four inner edges extend onto the photograph. In version 4.0 of PageMaker, this is easier than in earlier versions because the rule is reversed where it overlaps another object (Figure 3-31). The reversed area is easy to see on screen and serves as a good indicator that you're on the mark.

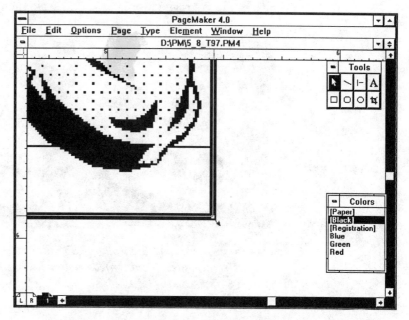

FIGURE 3-31 *Wherever a graphic overlaps a line in PageMaker, the line is reversed, making it easy to position a keyline trap around a photograph.*

Tilting a template

Illustrator doesn't allow you to rotate the image you use for a template. If you need to tilt a template, do so before opening it in Illustrator. Use **DeskPaint**, **DeskDraw**, or **PhotoShop**, for example, to rotate the image, saving it in PICT or Paint format (Illustrator will accept either for a template).

Scaling scanned artwork

Scaling a scanned image such as a company logo to fit a given design in your page layout program usually yields a poor company image. Bitmapped images such as TIFF and PCX files don't scale well because the page layout program simply enlarges individual dots as you make the image larger, and this process typically creates a blocky, jagged image (Figure 3-32, right). They look fine at the original size but get ragged-looking as you scale them up.

FIGURE 3-32 *A scanned logo placed on your page looks lumpy when enlarged (right). An object-oriented version maintains its smoothness (as in the EPS image on the left).*

If you need your logo or other image in only a few predetermined sizes, your best bet is to create a separate scanned version for each size.

A more elaborate—but more flexible—solution is to create your logo in PostScript or some other object-oriented format like PICT (on a Mac) or CGM (Computer Graphics Metafile), a commonly used format on PCs. Object-oriented formats are designed with scaling in mind; these formats describe images mathematically rather than as a pattern of discrete dots and thus look good at any size.

On the PC side, the leading candidates for creating an object-oriented version of your logo are Micrografx **Designer**, Adobe **Illustrator**, and **CorelDRAW**. On the Mac side, we recommend **Illustrator**, **FreeHand**, and **MacDraw II**. These programs, and others, will even trace the scanned image automatically, making it much easier to convert it to an object-oriented format. Some service bureaus and graphic design services can do this work for you, delivering a scalable logo in the file format of your choice.

. . . .

 ## Scans too big for FreeHand

If you have a scan that you want to use in **FreeHand**, but FreeHand complains that it's just too big, **PhotoShop** may be able to help. If possible, the scan should be at a relatively low resolution, no more than 200 dpi. If it's not in PICT format already, use your scanner software to save the image as a PICT file. Open the file in Photoshop and cut away any unneeded portions; while you're at it, straighten and clean up any scraggly lines. Then save the image as an EPS file with 1- or 4-bit preview, depending on the amount of detail you need.

Now import the image into FreeHand with the PLACE command. Once that's done, the EPS file can be thrown in the trash since the necessary image information is now stored in the FreeHand file. Finally, size or trace the image as needed or move it to FreeHand's non-printing layer for future reference.

. . . .

Photos and gray-scale images

. . . .

 ### Rotating a rectangular image

If you select a rectangular image with the marquee tool in **Photo-Shop** and then rotate it, the long ends of your rectangular image will be clipped if the ends don't fit within the narrow dimension of the image area. To rotate an entire rectangular image without clipping, the trick is to select nothing at all. If no part of the image is selected and you choose the 90°cw or 90°ccw commands (or the ARBITRARY command for some other angle of rotation) from the Rotate sub-menu under the Image menu, PhotoShop will resize the image area automatically to handle the new dimensions (Figure 3-33).

FIGURE 3-33 *If you use one of PhotoShop's rotate commands on an unse-lected image, the whole image rotates and the image area is resized automatically to accommodate it. (Image from Wayzata Technology's Down to Earth by Josepha Haveman.)*

If you want to rotate only part of an image, however, and if that part is too long to fit within the current image area, you must enlarge the image area first to avoid clipping. To do so, choose the RESIZE command and enter the length of the image's long dimension—or a larger value—in both the Height and Width text boxes in the Resize dialog box. (The image's current dimensions appear in parentheses to the right of these text boxes.) Turn on the *Place at Center* option and click the OK button. The image area is now large enough to accommodate the image either vertically or horizontally. Select the part you want to rotate and use the ROTATE command to change its orientation as required. When the selection is oriented correctly, use the cropping tool to reduce the size of the image area if it turns out to be larger than necessary.

Transferring PC scans to the Mac

The best file format for transferring scanned images from a PC to the Macintosh is TIFF (Tagged Image File Format). Many Macintosh programs, including **PageMaker** and **Photoshop**, are able to read the transferred TIFF file without further modification or conversion.Thus, when you save a scanned image on your PC, select TIFF (or .TIF), not EPSF, as the file format.

If your Macintosh graphics or page layout program doesn't accept your PC-originated TIFF file, try a utility like **DiskTop** to change the file's Finder type to TIFF if it's something other than that (such as TEXT). If that doesn't work, you'll need to run the file through a conversion utility. If the scan is in black-and-white (not gray-scale or color), you can use the conversion utility called .Tif to TIFF that comes with **DeskPaint**. Alternatively, you can use the PC-to-Mac TIFF file translator found in **MacLink Plus/Translators** (used with Apple File Exchange) or **FlipTIFF**, a free conversion utility available from many user group software libraries and electronic bulletin boards.

Controlling alpha channels growth

In **PhotoShop**, alpha channels serve as reusable masks which can be dropped out of, or brought back into, an image file at any time; as a result, alpha channels are often vital to artwork creation and image retouching. The problem is that each new alpha channel in a Photoshop file (and one file can have up to 16 channels) increases the file's storage size by one-third, and the larger the file, the slower PhotoShop operates.

To keep your file from growing out of control, go to the Image menu, choose DUPLICATE from the Calculate submenu, and copy all the alpha channels, one by one, into a new file. For each channel that you copy, select New as the destination channel in the Duplicate dialog box (Figure 3-34). For safety's sake, it's wise to save your new file with a name that links it to the old file; for example, if your original image file is called "Bowl of Roses," call the new file "Masks for Bowl of Roses." Once all the alpha channels are copied, you can delete them from the original file to bring it down to a reasonable size.

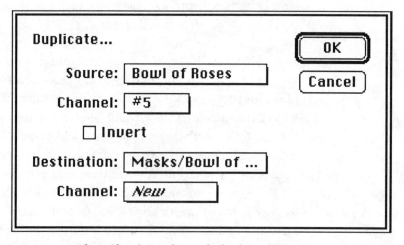

FIGURE 3-34 *PhotoShop's Duplicate dialog box allows you to move alpha channels from one file to another, one at a time. Use it to speed up PhotoShop's performance when you're working on a file with many alpha channels.*

Whenever you need one of the alpha channels stored in the new mask storage file, use the DUPLICATE command once again to copy it back to the original file, and then delete it when you're done.

Selecting complex shapes

Selecting a complex shape with the magic wand in **PhotoShop** is often quite difficult. If the shape is against a relatively uniform background (Figure 3-35), it often pays to use a little reverse psychology and work with the background rather than the shape itself.

There are two versions of this strategy. In one, you use the magic wand to select the background. Press the Shift Key and continue clicking with the magic wand tool to add background colors not included in the first click; choose the SIMILAR command in the Select menu to add isolated (discontiguous) areas of background to the selection. When all of the background is selected, choose the INVERSE command from the Select menu to deselect everything that was

FIGURE 3-35 *To select a complex shape against a uniform background, use PhotoShop's magic wand tool to select the background (as illustrated here) and then invert the selection. (Image from Down to Earth by Josepha Haveman.)*

selected (the background) and select everything that wasn't selected (the complex shape).

Alternatively, start by surrounding the object with a selection marquee using the rectangle or ellipse selection tool. Then deselect pieces of background within the marquee by clicking the magic wand on unwanted background areas while pressing the Command Key.

 ## Selecting everything but...

In **Photoshop**, it's sometimes useful to be able to paint or modify all of an image except for one small area. To do so, first select the area you don't want changed with any of Photoshop's standard selection methods. Then choose the INVERSE command from the Select menu, which will select everything except the small area you originally selected. Image modifications will now affect all parts of the image except the original selection.

Halftones

 ## Different line screens for different elements

The default line screen of all 300-dpi printers—60 lines per inch on most printers—is the best value for photos and graduated blends but not necessarily the best value for line art and type. To get the best of everything in **FreeHand**, specify different line screens for different elements on the same page with the HALFTONE SCREEN command in the Attributes menu. Use this command, for example, to specify a higher line screen for type and line work—giving you a tighter, darker image—and the default line screen for photos and blends.

Printing orientation and custom screen angles

Be careful when using special-effect screen angles other than the default 45 degrees in programs such as **FreeHand**. Because the screen angle is actually based on the output device, what is printed by your laser printer may not be what you get from your service bureau. For example, say you create and proof a graphic in portrait mode that will later be printed in landscape (transverse) mode on your service bureau's Linotronic. As shown in Figure 3-36, when the halftone screen is set to "line" and the screen angle to zero degrees, the logo's line pattern is horizontal in the portrait-mode LaserWriter proof; when printed in landscape orientation on a high-resolution photoimagesetter, however, the line pattern is vertical. To avoid problems such as this, be sure to let your service bureau know if you've set a screen at a nondefault angle and tell them which orientation is the correct one when printing.

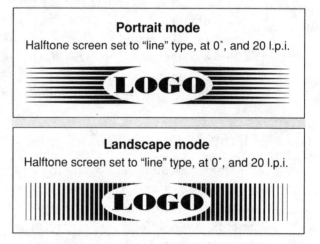

FIGURE 3-36 *Because the screen angle is calculated on the output device, different page orientations can produce different graphic images.*

Color

Visualizing CMYK colors

Do you spend a lot of time fiddling with CMYK values to get the color you're looking for? *Computer Color*, by Michael and Pat Rogondino, may help. It contains 10,000 color swatches arranged according to their CMYK (cyan, magenta, yellow, and black) values. You can flip through the book's 108 pages, find the color you want, and know immediately the corresponding percentages for cyan, magenta, yellow, and black.

Since the color swatches for the book were created in Illustrator 88, separated with Adobe Separator, output on a Linotronic 300 at 2540 dpi, and printed on coated stock, what you see are actual printed colors obtained from the Macintosh. Default screen angle settings were used throughout; moiré patterns in some of the color swatches indicate colors to avoid with these settings and printing conditions. Different applications, screen angles, resolutions, paper stock, and other variables will, of course, produce different results.

Drop-in Pantone color

Most image-editing and paint programs don't let you specify spot colors since images generally require process-color separations to reproduce a wide range of colors. Spot color separation features are more commonly found in page layout or ad makeup programs. Occasionally, though, you might want to approximate a Pantone (or other color matching system) color in an image you're editing or creating, even though it will be reproduced using process color, not Pantone inks.

To save time trying to duplicate a particular color, scan the Pantone (or other color matching system) color chips for the colors you want to use in your images and save the file. When you use your color paint or image editing program, open this file along with the file you're working on and use the eyedropper tool, common to most of these programs, to pick up the colors of the scanned color chips.

When PhotoShop tools don't work

In **PhotoShop**, certain painting and editing tools (including feather-edge selections, the paint brush, and the smudge tool) don't work on an indexed color image such as a color GIF file. To use these tools, convert the image with the RGB COLOR command. When finished, convert the image to the old format with the INDEXED COLOR command using the default settings for resolution, palette, and dither.

Naming colors

When you're naming colors in **Freehand**, it's sometimes a good idea to give each color a number and/or list its percentages at the end of the name. For example, you might give battleship gray the name 12-BlueGray-42c43m37y0k. The number can help you locate a color quickly and makes it easier to give graduated fills a name that means something. When you create a new graduated fill, for example, you could name it 4/12/216d, for the two colors used (4 and 12) and the gradation angle. The percentage shorthand at the end of each color name saves you from having to lookup the percentages in the Edit Color dialog box. To display the percentage shorthand in the Color Palette, drag the size box to increase the palette's width.

Creating a color library in your word processor

FreeHand color libraries are useful for storing related colors—such as those used in a particular publication—in one convenient place. If you know your CMYK percentages, you can use a word processor to create a FreeHand color library, and doing so is often much faster than using FreeHand's Colors dialog box. Here's how to do it:

1. Launch your word processor and open a new document.

2. Type:

```
ColorLibrary 1.0
LibryType MyColors
BeginColorDefs
name=(BlueGray)cmyk=(.40,.20,.10,.0)
EndColorDefs
EndColorLibrary
```

You can enter any name you wish after LibraryType instead of My-Colors. Type the first, third, and last two lines exactly as shown. Between them, define as many colors as you need, one per line, by naming colors and entering decimal values for cyan, magenta, yellow, and black (100 percent would be 1.00, for example) as shown in the fourth line.

3. Save the file as text only with a .clib extension at the end of the name, as in MyColors.clib. (The name can be the same as the one in the second line, or it can be a different name.)

Open the library with FreeHand's LIBRARY command (from the Color Palette's pop-up menu), specify whether you want process or spot colors, and add as many of the color definitions as you want to the Color Palette.

. . . .

 ## Cleaning a file before separation

When you prepare an **Illustrator** file for color separations, make sure that no extraneous, unwanted points or rules lie outside your illustration. Any unnecessary item like that will either give you an unwanted bounding box or cause a PostScript error.

. . . .

 ## A colored line on a colored background

If you're printing an **Illustrator** graphic containing a colored line that crosses a different colored background, you need to knock out the background color so it doesn't change the line's color. You also need to overlap the colors slightly to prevent gaps during printing. Here's what to do:

1. Draw the line, select it, and choose the STYLE command. In the Paint Style dialog box, select the desired stroke and color, and turn on the *Overprint* option.

2. With the line still selected, copy it (press Command + C) and choose the PASTE IN FRONT command (or press Command + F).

3. With the pasted line still selected, choose the STYLE command, reduce its overall stroke width by 0.6 point, and turn off the *Overprint* option.

When you print, the thinner line will knock out the background, and you'll have a .3-point trap on each side.

 ## Separating several graphics at once

In **FreeHand**, you can save on film charges by separating several small graphics at the same time. Just place them all on the same page and use the ¤ character (Shift + Option + 2) to make registration marks as follows: Define a process color called, for example, "Registration," made up of 100 percent of all four process colors (cyan, magenta, yellow, and black), and assign it to the first registration mark that you place on the page. Then copy that mark and paste one in all four corners of each separate graphic. The marks will appear on each piece of film in perfect registration.

File transfer and conversion

 ## Tracing a template in MacDraw

You can trace over an imported bitmap image in MacDraw II, just as you can in Illustrator or FreeHand; the major difference is that it takes a little more time and effort to set everything up. First, move the template graphic to MacDraw by copying it to the Clipboard in your paint program and then pasting it into a MacDraw document.

Next, since MacDraw doesn't automatically turn the template gray, you'll need to do so yourself to make it easier to trace. To do that, add yellow or blue to the pattern palette with the PATTERNS command in the Layout menu. Then select the bitmap image, press the Option Key (or click on the pen pattern box at the right end of the pattern palette), and click on the blue or yellow square in the pattern palette. This replaces the black of the original bitmap image with either blue or yellow, which you can easily trace over with black.

Finally, select the LAYERS command to create a second drawing layer on top of the bitmap template. Trace the image in the second drawing layer, and, when you're done, delete the template and its drawing layer.

 ## Transferring Ventura graphics

If you've used **Ventura Publisher**'s graphics tools to create a complex chart which you'd like to use in another Ventura document, you may have noticed that Ventura saves such charts as VGR (Ventura Graphics) files, but doesn't include that format among Ventura's graphic file import options.

To transfer a Ventura graphic from one document to another in the GEM or Windows editions, load the original document and copy the graphic to the Clipboard. Then load the new document and go to the appropriate page. In the GEM Edition, you'll also need to switch to graphics mode. Then paste the graphic.

If you need to transfer a Ventura graphic from the Ventura Publisher GEM Edition to the Windows Edition, use the OPEN command in the Windows Edition to load the GEM Edition chapter containing the Ventura graphic. Since the two versions use compatible file formats, the graphic loads without problem. You can then copy the graphic from the transferred document to other Windows Edition Ventura documents as we described above, but not to any other Windows applications, like PageMaker or CorelDRAW. For these and other Windows applications you can, short of recreating the chart, transfer it as an EPS file using the *Setup* options under the PRINT command:

1. In Ventura's Print dialog box, click the Setup button, and in the Setup dialog box click the Options button.

2. In the Options dialog box select the Encapsulated PostScript File option and enter a file name. Then click OK buttons until you're back at the main Print dialog box.

3. Print the page containing the Ventura graphic. Instead of sending it to your printer, the PostScript page information will be stored in the file you named above.

4. Place the resulting EPS file into PageMaker or other layout program in the usual way.

Note that Windows EPS files don't include image headers for on-screen display. Placed in PageMaker, for example, they appear as gray boxes, making them hard to crop since you can't see the actual image. They'll print fine, though. Also, don't bother trying to import the Windows EPS files into CorelDRAW since the Windows EPS format is incompatible with CorelDRAW's EPS import filter.

  ## AutoCAD to Mac EPS conversion

For converting **AutoCAD** drawings to EPS format, we recommend **PowerDraw Translator** for Macintosh by Engineered Software. The utility converts AutoCAD (DXF) and **Claris CAD** drawings into Encapsulated PostScript (EPS) files, fully editable in Adobe **Illustrator**. It's a single-step operation if your Macintosh is equipped with an Apple Super Drive, which can read DOS 3½-inch diskettes via the Apple File Exchange utility.

Using TIFF graphics in your word processor

Most Macintosh word processors can display only MacPaint and PICT graphics. But you can get around this limitation and insert black-and-white TIFF graphics (such as scanned images) in a word processor document with DeskPaint, a desk accessory which puts some stand-alone graphics programs to shame. DeskPaint can open TIFF files directly, and you can use the program's impressive collection of tools to edit them (Figure 3-37). Once an image is the way you want it, you can save it as a PICT or Macpaint format file. Or you can copy the image, or any part of it, to the Clipboard and paste it directly into your word processing document.

If you convert a TIFF image to PICT or use the Clipboard with Desk-Paint, it will retain its original size and resolution (pixels per inch). If you convert it to a MacPaint file, however, keep in mind that files in this format are always 72 pixels per inch and can be no larger than 576 by 720 pixels. Furthermore, in a TIFF to MacPaint conversion,

FIGURE 3-37 *With DeskPaint, you can open a TIFF file (such as this 300 pixel per inch paddlewheeler), edit it, and paste all or part of it into your word processing document. Note that all the desk accessory's tools and menus are inside the DeskPaint window.*

DeskPaint enlarges the TIFF image until its pixel density equals that of a standard MacPaint format. Thus, the overall size of a small 300-pixel-per-inch TIFF file is approximately quadrupled, while a large 300-ppi TIFF image is invariably cropped as a result of conversion.

Saving a PICT file in MacDraw II

To place a **MacDraw II** file in **PageMaker**, save it in PICT format by selecting the *PICT* option in the Save As dialog box. Be sure to give the file a new name (by appending PICT to the current name, for example) as well as a new format. If you don't, MacDraw will delete the original MacDraw format file; since the MacDraw file is more "sophisticated," deleting it may result in the loss of information that can't be recorded in the PICT file.

Convert your logo to PostScript outlines

Consider converting your company's logo to an all-outline Post-Script drawing if the logo contains text from one or more download-able fonts. This gives you maximum flexibility in sizing and scaling and frees up printer memory in projects that call for large numbers of downloadable fonts. Conversion to outlines often reduces print-ing time as well. If your logo is all type, convert the text to outlines with **Illustrator** or **Metamorphosis Professional** on the Mac, or use **CorelDRAW** or Micrografx **Designer** on the PC. If your logo contains bitmap graphics, **Streamline** can trace either the graphic alone or, if you prefer, both graphics and text. Use **FreeHand** or Illustrator to put the various parts together and/or touch up any rough spots.

Using PICT or TIFF graphics in Illustrator

To use a PICT, TIFF, or Paint (bitmap) image in an **Illustrator** for the Macintosh drawing (not as a template, but as part of the drawing itself), you must first convert the image to EPS format. There are a variety of ways you can accomplish this file format conversion:

- If the image is a scan, your scanning software may be able to save it in EPS format. Simply launch your scanning program, open the image file, select the Save As command, choose EPS as the file format, and save the file under a new name. This technique often has a major drawback, however. Most scanning programs are unable to create a preview image, so all you'll see in Illustrator is a box. This, of course, makes it difficult to visualize how the rest of the graphic interacts with the scanned image.

- Open a new document in FreeHand and import the image with that program's Place command. Choose Export from the File menu and save the file in Macintosh EPS format.

- Open the image file in **PhotoShop**. If necessary, use the Open As command so you can tell PhotoShop what kind of file it is. Select the Save As command, select the *EPS* option from the File Format pop-up menu, and save the file under a new name.

- If you don't have access to FreeHand or PhotoShop and your scanning software doesn't support EPS, you can use **PageMaker** to perform the conversion. Here's how:

1. Place the image in a new, one-page document in PageMaker with the Place command.

2. To eliminate excess page area in the PageMaker EPS file, create a custom page size that's only slightly larger than the image (Figure 3-38). To do so, first measure the size of the image with PageMaker's vertical and horizontal rulers. Then choose the Page Setup command, enter the appropriate figures in the Page Dimensions text boxes, and select *Tall* or *Wide* orientation as needed.

3. Select the Print command and click the PostScript button in the Print dialog box. Turn on the *Print PostScript to Disk* option and then the *EPS* option. Click the Filename button, give the new file a name (you'll probably want to end it with .EPS), select a destination for the file, and then click the OK and Print buttons.

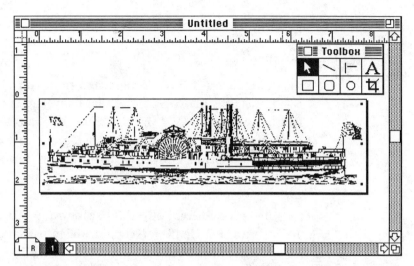

FIGURE 3-38 *To use a TIFF or PICT file in Illustrator, first place it in a PageMaker document and create a custom page size only slightly larger than the image.*

Keep in mind that there's an important caveat to this method: Both Aldus Prep and Apple's Laser Prep are automatically downloaded to your PostScript printer when you print an Illustrator drawing containing a PageMaker-generated EPS file. This could overload your printer's memory, so be careful to limit the number of downloadable fonts in your document if you use this technique. Also note that this technique does not work in Illustrator 3.0; to be able to place a PageMaker-generated EPS file, you must use Illustrator 3.01 or above.

Back in Illustrator, remember to use the PLACE ART command to insert the EPS file in your drawing. (Don't try to open the EPS file with the OPEN command; it won't work.) If you want to see the placed image while you're working on your Illustrator drawing, be sure to turn on the *Show Placed Images* option in the Preferences dialog box. To speed up screen redraw while you work, turn *Show Placed Images* off. With this option off, Illustrator won't display the placed image in Artwork mode—but will in Preview mode and when you print.

Lotus PIC on your Mac

You can use Lotus 1-2-3 PIC charts and graphs on a Macintosh with help from either of two Macintosh file conversion utilities: **PICTure This** by FGM or DataViz **MacLink Plus/Translators**. Both will convert Lotus graphs (.PIC format) into PICT graphics that you can open and edit in most Macintosh drawing programs (including **MacDraw** and **FreeHand**, though not **Illustrator**).

PICTure This comes as both an application and a DA and specializes in converting PC, UNIX workstation, Macintosh, and Amiga graphics to PICT (Macintosh PICT2 format). In addition to Lotus PIC, PICTure This can also convert to or from Lotus BIT, CGM (Computer Graphics Metafile), EPS (Encapsulated PostScript), PC Paintbrush PCX, Targa, Dr. Halo CUT, Amiga RIFF and IFF, PixelPaint, Letraset RIFF, MacPaint, TIFF, GEM IMG, Sun Raster, X11 bitmaps, CompuServe GIF and RLE graphics formats. FGM plans to include GEM line art (GEM) conversion in a future release. If you work primarily with graphics, including those created with computer systems other than Macintosh, then PICTure This is the program to use.

DataViz MacLink Plus/Translators work with the Apple File Exchange utility included with all Mac system software. The package focuses on word processing, spreadsheet, and database file format conversion. The package contains dozens of conversion options, though only a few concern graphics. These include PC Paintbrush (PCX)/PICT, and PC TIFF/Mac TIFF, in addition to Lotus PIC to PICT conversions.

Both programs do a good job converting Lotus PIC to editable PICT. PICTure This is more convenient to use, but the wealth of non-graphic format conversions offered by MacLink Plus/Translators certainly make it a great deal. One word of warning: because Lotus PIC is a vector graphic format, the circular portion of a pie chart, for example, is converted into numerous straight-line segments (a polyline) in the PICT file which makes for trickier editing, as when editing a pie chart, for example. In most cases, though, it's fairly easy to select and group the points that lie along a polyline and thereby create a more manageable graphic object.

Better EPS export

When exporting a drawing to an EPS format file in **CorelDRAW**, use the 512-x-512 setting for the on-screen representation of the graphic (at the Fixed Size prompt near the bottom of the Export window). While this uses a little more disk space than the 128-x-128 setting that Corel recommends, 512-x-512 provides a sharper preview image (Figure 3-39) when you place the graphic in Ventura Publisher or PageMaker.

FIGURE 3-39 *In CorelDRAW, the* 512 x 512 *Fixed Size option for an EPS file screen preview (bottom) provides a sharper image in your layout program than does the* 128 x 128 *Fixed Size (top).*

Creating clean, accurate traces

When using **Adobe Streamline**, set the noise level at zero (via the CONVERSION OPTIONS command) to improve accuracy and avoid losing any of the original artwork. To get rid of any stray, unwanted elements in the resulting image, open the tracing in **Illustrator** and select only the elements you want to save. Press Command + 1 to lock these elements together. Then press Command + A to select all the other elements, the unwanted ones, and delete them. This is a quick way to clean up all Streamline art, by the way, regardless of the noise level setting.

 ## Ventura graphics file alchemy

To make graphics available to GEM Artline, GEM Draw, and other PC programs, you can convert them from a variety of draw-type formats to GEM format with **Ventura Publisher** (GEM Edition). Simply load the graphic as Line Art with Ventura's LOAD TEXT/PICTURE command. Ventura will automatically convert CGM (Computer Graphics Meta-file), WMF (Windows Metafile), HPGL (Hewlett Packard Graphics Language), and even Macintosh PICT file format, into GEM format. You'll find the converted file, along with the original, in the original's directory. The new file will have the same file name but with a .GEM extension.

There are cases where this conversion technique doesn't work with GEM Draw and Artline. A highly complex Ventura-created GEM file may display a *Too many elements* message when you open it in GEM Draw or Artline, and will either fail to load or only partially load. PICT graphics converted to GEM via this technique tend to lose their text elements, and you may see a *Too many text elements* message when loading those files in GEM Draw or Artline. But aside from highly complex line art, the technique works fine.

 ## Using EPS graphics in your word processor

Most Macintosh word processors cannot display encapsulated Post-Script (EPS) graphics. But there are several programs that can convert an EPS graphic to a special PICT format which is acceptable to most word processors. The format includes a PICT image for on-screen viewing plus the original PostScript code; the PostScript part of the graphic is used only when you print and produces an image whose quality is equal to the original.

Although its primary function is special typographic effects, one program which can perform this conversion is **Smart Art**. To use Smart Art for this purpose, simply open the desired EPS file—the same way you would open a Smart Art special effects file—and select the COPY command. Switch to your word processor and paste the image into your document.

Alternatively, you can transfer an image directly from **Illustrator** or **FreeHand** using the Clipboard. To do so, open the PostScript file with one of these programs and select the image you want to transfer. Next, convert the image to the special PICT format and copy it to the Clipboard by pressing the Option Key as you select the COPY command. Finally, paste the image in the usual way into your word processor document.

 ## Windows screen capture

Are you writing documentation that requires screen shots of **Windows** software? Use Windows 3.0's built-in screen-capture function to copy part or all of the screen to the Windows clipboard. To copy the entire screen to the Windows clipboard, press the PrtScreen Key on your keyboard. To copy the active window only to the Windows clipboard, press Alt + PrtScreen. (If you have an older keyboard and you can't get the basic PrtScreen Key command to work, try Shift + PrtScreen or Alt + PrtScreen instead.) You can paste the screen shot directly into a Windows document. Or, you can save the contents of the clipboard as a clipboard file (.CLP) by using the SAVE AS command under the Clipboard utility's File menu. (To open the Windows Clipboard utility, double click the Clipboard icon in the Main program group.) Later, you can load the saved file back into the clipboard and paste it into a Windows application.

For deluxe screen captures, we like **Tiffany Plus**, a utility designed specifically for Microsoft Windows screen captures. Tiffany Plus lets you save either the entire screen or just the active window in color or gray-scale TIFF, color or black-and-white PCX, color or black-and-white BMP (Windows bitmap), or MSP (Microsoft Paint) formats. It can convert color to gray patterns. It also lets you capture directly to a disk file rather than through the Clipboard—although this can take longer than a minute depending on the speed of your computer.

 ## Making a fine image coarse

There are many ways to convert a smooth PICT or TIFF graphic to the angular, pixelated look of the MacPaint era: One technique that always works is to convert the image to a low-resolution (72-dots-per-inch) bitmapped graphic, and then enlarge it to exaggerate the jaggies. For example, if you are working with a PICT graphic, you might open it in **SuperPaint** and reduce the entire image to a half or a quarter of the desired final size; use the CUT TO PAINTING command to move the image to the bitmap layer; then enlarge the bitmapped image back to the desired size. The two globes in Figure 3-40 show just such a transformation.

If the image is in TIFF format and you are using it in a **PageMaker** document, you might try this method: Place the image in Page-Maker, enlarge it in the usual way, and then discard the original TIFF file so that the image in the PageMaker document is no longer linked to it. You will probably want to conduct a few trial runs with this technique since the results vary, depending on the resolution of the original TIFF file, the printer you're using, and the extent to which the image is enlarged.

FIGURE 3-40 *The globe on the right is a "pixelated" version of the one on the left, using the SuperPaint method described in the text.*

Shortcuts

Quick element information

A quick way to bring up the Element Info dialog box in **FreeHand** is to double-click on the element in question while holding down the Option Key.

Quick charts

You can use **Ventura Publisher**'s table function to quickly create bar charts like the one in Figure 3-41. For simple charts, this technique can be a real time-saver since you don't have to create a chart in a separate program and import it into Ventura, hence making changes

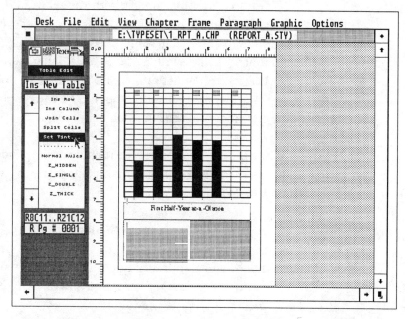

FIGURE 3-41 *You can create a bar chart using the table-making features in Ventura Publisher. Cells in the last column have been selected using the mouse cursor. A tint will be applied, like the completed bars to the left.*

to the chart is a one-step process. Here's how to do it using the GEM and Windows Editions:

1. Select the Text tool and place the insertion point where you want the table/chart. Then select the *Table* option with the INSERT SPECIAL ITEM command under the Text menu in the Windows Edition, or from the Edit menu in the GEM Edition.

2. At the Rows: and Columns: prompts in the Insert/Edit Table dialog box, specify the number of rows and columns you'll need. You'll need at least as many rows as the number of vertical increments you intend to show and an adequate number of columns for the bars and spaces between the bars. In percentage charts, for example, 20 rows are sufficient to graphically represent 0–100 percent in 5-percent increments.

3. To create each bar for the chart in the Windows Edition, select the required number of cells with the mouse (Figure 3-41 on page 179). Then use the Set Tint dialog box under the Table menu to fill in the column cells you selected. In the DOS/GEM Edition, the strategy is the same, but there's no Table menu. Instead click on TABLE EDIT beneath the Mode Selector icons on the upper left of the screen; *Set Tint* and other table editing options will appear in the window at the left sidebar.

When the chart is complete, you may want to hide the table's ruling lines, by changing the generated tags that apply to the table. Here's how to do that:

1. In order to view the generated tags so that you can select them, select the *Shown* option in the Preferences settings under the Edit menu in the Windows Edition, or select the SET PREFERENCES command under the Options menu and turn on the *Show Generated Tags* option in the GEM Edition.

2. Using the Paragraph tool, click on any cell in the table and tag it as Z_SINGLE. Then, using the Ruling Line Above options under the Paragraph menu, set the Height of Rule 1 to zero in the GEM

Edition. In the Windows Edition you'll have to first change the Width options to anything other than *None*, such as *Frame* or *Text*, before you can select rule heights under the *User-Defined* rule setting option.

You can generate an attractive chart with this technique. And, although it may lack the precision of charts from specialized software, you can easily edit it in Ventura.

Selecting objects *sans* control points

A common way to select a group of objects in **FreeHand** is to drag the pointer and surround the objects with the selection marquee. But if you select a collection of irregular shapes and lines this way, you also select all their control points, which has the undesirable side effect of decreasing the program's speed. One way around this is to Shift + click on each shape and/or line you want to select; this leaves the control points unselected. A more efficient method for large numbers of objects is to select all the objects and their control points by dragging the pointer and then deselecting all the control points by pressing the the Accent Grave Key.

Easy symbol access

Micrografx **Designer** is great for creating graphics elements that can be reused in building more complex drawings. But finding them again can be confusing if you or others in your group forget their names. For symbols you use frequently, create a new document and stockpile them at one edge of the page. When you start a new drawing that uses those symbols, open that document and save it with a different name; then as you draw you can move the symbols to the appropriate position on the page when you need them. Erase any extra, unneeded symbols before printing your final copy.

Selecting tools from the keyboard

In **FreeHand**, it's often easier to select a tool with a key command than to click on the desired tool in the toolbox. In most cases, pressing the appropriate key combination turns the tool on until you select some other tool:

Select tool	By pressing
Square corner	1
Round Corner	2
Ellipse	3
Line	4
Freehand	5
Combination	6
Knife	7
Curve	8
Corner	9
Connector	0 (zero)
Text	A

In some cases, the keyboard shortcut turns on the tool only while the key or keys remain pressed. Release the keys and the previous tool returns:

Tool appears	When pressing
Pointer	Command
Hand	Spacebar
Magnifying Glass (zoom in)	Command + Spacebar
Magnifying Glass (zoom out)	Command + Option + Spacebar

The right mouse button in CorelDRAW

In **CorelDRAW**, pressing the right mouse button normally gives you a fast, full-screen preview of the on-screen drawing. But many people overlook the fact that you can reprogram the right button to be a shortcut for zooming in at twice the magnification, editing text, or for editing nodes in objects you've drawn.

To program this alternative right-button function, use the PREFER-
ENCES command under the Special menu, and click on the *Mouse*
option button. The mouse option you select will take effect immediately, without restarting CorelDRAW.

 ## Multipurpose toolbox tools

Instead of adding more tools than you have room for to your
Micrografx **Designer** toolbox (using the Tools selections under the
View menu), you can double up on the functions of some tools. Instead of adding the Square tool to the toolbox, you can draw a square
simply by holding down the Ctrl Key as you draw with the Rectangle
tool. Holding down the Ctrl Key, you can draw a circle with the Ellipse
tool or a freehand line with the Polyline tool.

  ## Copy it first

When you're working on an element of a complicated graphic in
Micrografx **Designer**, **CorelDRAW**, **Illustrator**, **FreeHand**, or other
drawing program, copy the object before you alter it, and store the
copy off to the side of the page. Then, if you make a mistake that your
program's Undo feature won't correct, you can delete the altered object and drag the copy of the original back into place.

In Designer, you can duplicate an object quickly by holding down
the Shift Key as you drag the object away. In CorelDRAW you can
duplicate the object by typing Ctrl + D after it's selected. In Illustrator
for the Mac, select and start dragging the object, and then press the
Option Key; in FreeHand, select the CLONE or DUPLICATE commands.

Speedier saves in CorelDRAW

You can gain precious minutes every time you save a complex draw-ing in **CorelDRAW** by disabling the bitmapped thumbnail preview that CorelDRAW automatically saves with each drawing. This is the thumbnail that shows up in Corel's Open or Import windows (Figure 3-42), or in the Corel Mosaic file utility, so that you can see a file's contents before you open it. Here's how to change the CorelDRAW defaults in order to disable the thumbnails:

1. Use the Windows Notepad to open the CORELDRW.INI file in the CORELDRW subdirectory.

2. Go to the section labeled [CDrawConfig] and find the line that reads: CDRHeaderResolution=1.

3. Change the value 1 to 0 (0 means no header).

4. Save the CORELDRW.INI file.

To create and save previews again, repeat the above procedure and change the 0 back to 1.

Working in preview mode

Illustrator for the Mac doesn't allow you to work on a drawing in preview mode, as does FreeHand. If you have enough display area on your monitor, however, you can get around this restriction by opening two windows displaying the same document. Simply open the first window with the OPEN command and the second window with the NEW WINDOW command. Position the two windows side by side and place one in Preview mode (Figure 3-43). Any change you make in the other window is immediately displayed in the preview window. It's not quite the same as working on the preview image itself, but it's pretty close.

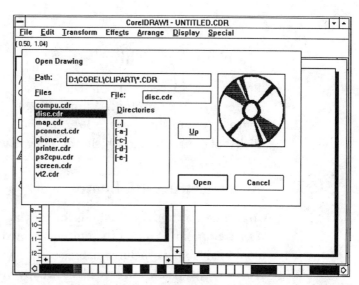

FIGURE 3-42 *CorelDRAW's thumbnail images in the Open Drawing window may aid file selection, but they increase the amount of time it takes to save a file.*

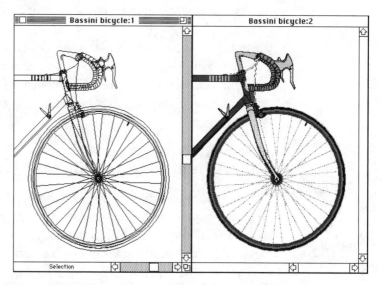

FIGURE 3-43 *In Illustrator, opening two windows for the same file and placing one in preview mode is as close to working in preview mode as you can get.*

Quick tool switching

Pressing the spacebar in **CorelDRAW**, except when editing text, activates the Pick (or pointer) tool with which you can select, size, move, or rotate your images. Pressing the spacebar while using the Pick tool returns you to whichever tool you were previously using.

Arts & Letters duplicates

Arts & Letters has two methods for copying objects. The Copy and Paste commands under the Edit menu are best used for placing a copy of an object in a different area of the page, far from the original. The Duplicate tool, however, places a copy wherever you drag it with the mouse; it's best for creating enhancements to the original object, such as 3-D and drop-shadow effects, or for replicating the same graphic a number of times to add density and depth to a composition. You can select the Duplicate tool either from the Toolbox or by selecting the Duplicate command under the Manipulate menu.

Remember: As long as the Duplicate tool cursor is displayed, you'll be making another copy every time you drag an object to a new position in the screen. Turn off the Duplicate function when you've made the necessary copies to avoid having to delete unnecessary extra copies.

Quickly replacing one object with another

Here's a trick you can use in any drawing or PostScript graphic program when you want to position one object precisely on top of another and then delete the object underneath. First draw a square or circle off to the side of the to-be-deleted object (such as the black text in the **FreeHand** example in Figure 3-44, top) and use the Group command to join the two together. Then move the other object (such as the gray text in the figure) into position on top of the grouped object. Deleting the original object is now easy: Click on the square or circle off to the side to select the group and press the Delete Key.

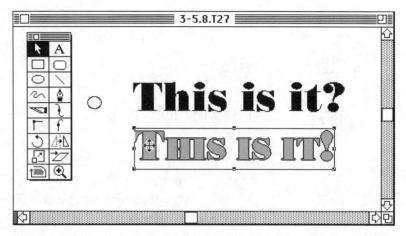

FIGURE 3-44 *First position the gray text directly over the black text by aligning the initial uppercase T's. Then, to delete the now unnecessary black text, select it—by clicking on the circle at the left with which it is grouped—and press the Delete Key.*

 ## Designer quick selections

The SELECT command in Micrografx **Designer** is an extremely powerful but frequently overlooked tool. It's found in the Edit menu and allows you to quickly choose objects on the screen by their properties (such as the color of backgrounds, lines, patterns, text, as well as line style and width, font style and size, and symbol ID). If you want to select every object on the screen that has a blue pattern color, for example, here's how:

1. Select just one of those blue objects.

2. Then choose the SELECT command, turn on the *Pattern Color* option, and then click on OK.

All the objects on the screen with a blue pattern color will be selected. As you might imagine, this technique enables you to get very specific with your selection; for instance, you could select every object on the screen that has a blue pattern color and a red line.

Text in graphics

CorelDRAW headlines

If you create your major headlines in **CorelDRAW**, you can apply special effects such as shadows, outlines, and 3-D effects, and kern the headline to perfection (Figures 3-45 and 3-46) using Corel's Shape tool—a task not easily accomplished in Word for Windows or the PC versions of Ventura Publisher, PageMaker, or WordPerfect. In addition, once the headline has been saved as a graphics file and placed in your page layout program, you can compress or expand it to fit perfectly into its allotted space.

If you have a PostScript printer, save your headline file in EPS format. If you use a LaserJet, DeskJet, or other non-PostScript printer, save the file as GEM format for Ventura Publisher, CGM for PageMaker, or WordPerfect Graphics format for WordPerfect.

Exporting CorelDRAW type as curves

If you're using one of the standard typefaces in **CorelDRAW**, you'll have no problems when transferring your CorelDRAW files from one computer to another. But if you have also installed additional typefaces from Linotype, Adobe, Bitstream, or other vendors (using CorelDRAW's WFN BOSS utility) and have used one of these non-CorelDRAW typefaces in your drawing, be sure the same typeface is installed in CorelDRAW on the computer to which you're sending the file. If the font's not installed, CorelDRAW won't be able to load the drawing properly.

One way to avoid such problems is to eliminate the need for installed fonts in drawings you transfer to another computer. To do so, click on all the text using installed typefaces, using the Pick (pointer) tool, and choose CONVERT TO CURVES from the Arrange menu before saving the CorelDRAW drawing. This changes the type from text to

Type Style

FIGURE 3-45 *Create headlines with tight kerning and special effects using CorelDRAW's shape tool.*

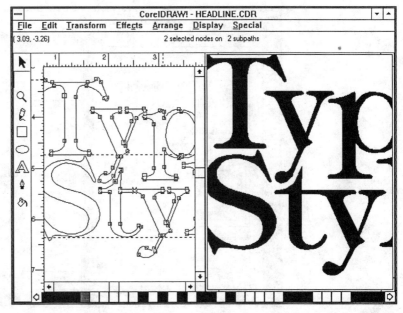

FIGURE 3-46 *Character outlines (y and t) have been edited in CorelDRAW for an interesting fit.*

graphics so that it can be loaded into CorelDRAW on any computer, regardless of the fonts installed.

This technique works well with headlines and other short sections of text. But if you want to export a longer section of text as EPS (Encapsulated PostScript), you may end up with a huge file. If your graphic contains a lot of text, don't convert the text to curves. Instead, select the *All Fonts Resident* option from the EXPORT command under CorelDRAW's File menu when exporting in EPS format. That way, the fonts are stored in the file and travel with the graphic.

Adding hidden notes to drawings

When working with complex illustrations in **CorelDRAW** or **Illustrator** that involve many objects or layers, you can easily add hidden, nonprinting notes about how the file is organized. Type your notes as text, directly on the artwork (see Figure 3-47). Give them a fill and a stroke of None so they do not print out or appear when Preview

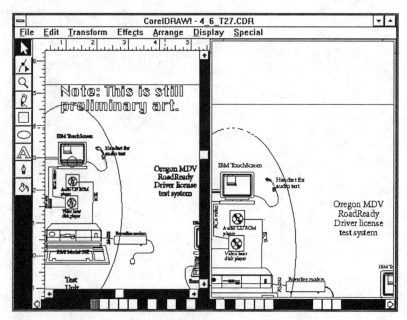

FIGURE 3-47 *You can add notes to your illustrations (top, left) that others can read on screen; give them a stroke and fill of None so they won't show up when printed or previewed (right).*

Illustration is selected. Or temporarily give them a fill of Black and stroke of None if you want them to appear on a draft copy.

Multiple text columns in FreeHand

An easy way to create precisely aligned columns of text in **FreeHand** is to clone the first text block and either drag it with the Shift Key depressed or use the MOVE command to move the clone horizontally. (Shear, rotate, reflect, and color the first block of text the way you want it before cloning.) Use the CLONE and TRANSFORM AGAIN commands to create additional text blocks, and move them the same distance as the first (Figure 3-48). All the clones will have the same attributes and will be aligned precisely with the first text box; the text in each remains fully editable. Double-click on each text block to edit the text within.

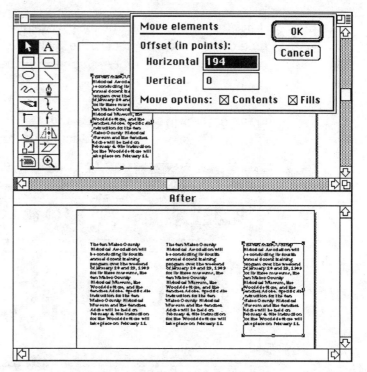

FIGURE 3-48 *Clone a text block in FreeHand and move it horizontally (top) to create two or more text blocks with the same attributes and baselines in exact alignment (bottom).*

· ·

 ## Converting text to a graphic

In **PageMaker** for the Mac, there's an easy way to convert text into a graphic which can then be scaled or distorted for special text effects. Here's how:

1. Use the pointer to select the text block containing the text you want to convert and copy it with the COPY command.

2. Open the Scrapbook, paste in the copied text block, and then close the Scrapbook.

3. Select the PLACE command, open the System folder, and double-click on the Scrapbook file.

4. Click the Place icon once on the page to place the converted text, and then click on any tool in the Toolbox to "unload" the place icon and delete any other scrapbook images that await placement.

You can now select the placed text and stretch, shrink, or distort it using any of PageMaker's standard graphic techniques (Figure 3-49).

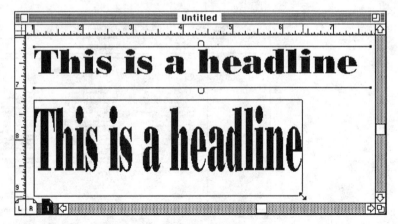

FIGURE 3-49 *Pasting a text block (top) into the Scrapbook and then placing it with PageMaker's Place command converts it to a graphic (bottom), which can be scaled or distorted in all the usual ways.*

You can also select and place an entire page as a graphic using this same technique. Before copying it, draw a 2-point rule around the page to define the page area; after it's been placed, reduce the image proportionally to the desired size.

 ## Text too tight in a curve

When applying text to a curve in **FreeHand**, the text can get over-crowded in tightly concave sections of the curve (Figure 3-50). Here are some things you can do to open up the crowded spots:

- With the SPACING command in the Type menu, add some space between the letters with the *Letter Space* option.

- With the HORIZONTAL SCALING command in the Type menu, decrease the width of the letters by specifying a scaling factor less than 100.

- With the BASELINE SHIFT command in the Type menu, move the baseline so it falls a short distance outside the curve. (This, however, subtly changes the shape of the curve.)

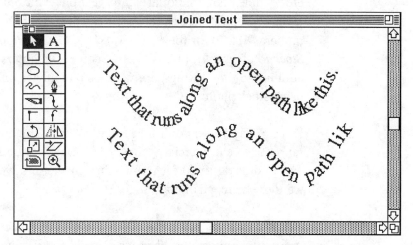

FIGURE 3-50 *Text in FreeHand as it originally appears after joining to a curve (top) and after applying a baseline shift of minus 2 points and 2-point character spacing (bottom).*

Most likely, you'll want to alleviate the congestion in the curve by some combination of these techniques. To adjust these three different options all at the same time, choose the TYPE SPECS command from the Type menu or press Command + T. Whichever method you choose, adjust text after it has been joined to a curve by simply clicking on the text/curve to select it and choosing the appropriate command from the Type menu.

Grab bag

  ## Photo mongering

If you have an image in mind but have limited photographic resources, try stock photos. The most common sources for stock photos, also known as "stock shots," are commercial agencies that sell the rights to use their photographs. They'll provide you with the necessary instructions and forms to ensure that you use their photos legally. To locate stock agencies in your area, ask your local photo shop for a list, or look in the yellow pages under "Photographs—Stock Shots." For a national listing, get hold of the *Stock Photography Handbook*, published by the American Society of Magazine Photographers (ASMP), or the *Stock Workbook/ The National Directory of Stock Photography*, published by Scott & Daughters Publishing. In addition to their listings, both books offer advice on obtaining and using stock photos.

You can pay anywhere from $100 to $700 for the one-time right to reproduce a commercial agency's photo. Large photos, color photos, and photos destined for publication covers or advertising run toward the high end of that range.

Other interesting sources of stock photos are collections owned by universities, museums, libraries, and historical societies. These collections tend to reflect the regional or topical orientation of the institutions that maintain them, but, typically, a university collection can provide prints for $5 to $20 each. The quality of the prints might be a concern since they're often prepared by student workers without a great deal of experience. In some cases, negatives may be checked out of such collections. Institutions with large collections include the New York Public Library, the University of Washington, and the University of California at Berkeley. The granddaddy of non-commercial collections is in the Library of Congress.

Digitized photos are also now available on CD ROM, for those of you with CD ROM drives attached to your computer systems. Comstock offers the **Comstock Desktop Photography** CD ROM volumes. Comstock's contract reguires that you order film transparencies for the final production of your publication and pay for licensing rights for each image you use. NEC's **PhotoGallery** includes over 1,500 gray-scale TIFF images covering a variety of categories. Like Comstock's CD ROM, you'll have to pay extra for final production rights and the film from the copyright holder. The **Professional Photography Collection** from DiscImagery, on the other hand, gives you unlimited reproduction rights, so you can print images without paying an additional licensing fee, though you can still order film transparencies for final production.

  ## Curing limitcheck blues

When using Autotrace in **Illustrator** or the tracing tool in **FreeHand**, it's possible to end up with a curve so complex (i.e., with so many points) that it won't print. You'll know that this is the problem when you get a "limitcheck" error message when attempting to print the image. Fortunately, the cure is an easy one: Simply cut the too-complex curve into two or more segments with the scissors tool. This not only solves the limitcheck problem, but it speeds up printing as well.

You can also use the above technique in **CorelDRAW**, but there's an easier and more convenient method that lets CorelDRAW do it for you:

1. Save your drawing.

2. Use the EXPORT command under the File menu to convert the drawing to GEM format.

3. Open a new, blank drawing, and import the GEM file you just created.

Corel automatically breaks up and bands graphics it converts to GEM format so that they don't become too complex. By importing them back into CorelDRAW, you can be assured the complex curves are already broken up into pieces PostScript printers and imagesetters can digest.

  ## What's a spline?

If you're getting confused hearing people talk about vectors, splines, or Bézier curves when they describe object-oriented computer graphics and outline fonts, that's understandable—especially given the way these terms get slung around.

A vector is a straight line segment extending in a given direction. Vector fonts, such as those used by Linotype in their older Linotronic 202N typesetters (many of which are still in use), are composed of numerous straight line segments. At type sizes larger than 18 or 24 points, you may start to see flat spots on the curves as individual vectors become apparent. Microsoft also includes a set of vector fonts with Windows.

Strictly speaking, a spline is a mathematically defined curve that smoothly links a series of points. The curve can form the outline of a text character or other graphical shape. In the broadest sense, a Bézier curve is a spline since it fits the above definition—although people often make a point of distinguishing between the two. In a Bézier curve, a single segment is defined by four points: a beginning and end point which are actually on the curve and two other points which affect its shape, even though they may be off the curve (Figure 3-51). If you've used Adobe Illustrator, Aldus FreeHand, Micrografx Designer, CorelDRAW, or any of a host of other drawing programs, you're no doubt familiar with manipulating a curve by dragging

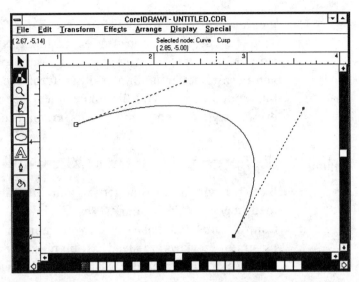

FIGURE 3-51 *This Bézier curve segment, created in CorelDRAW, can be reshaped by manipulating any of the four visible points—although only two of them are actually on the curve.*

"control points," which aren't necessarily on the actual curve. The points on the curve are often referred to as "anchor points."

Some font technologists draw a sharp distinction between splines and Bézier curves. In his 1987 book *Digital Formats for Typefaces*, Peter Karow distinguishes between splines and Bézier curves and provides a mathematical definition of what he calls a spline, with an accompanying illustration in which all points are actually on the curve.

Others use the terms somewhat interchangeably. Microsoft's literature on TrueType mentions that TrueType's quadratic B-splines are composed of "quadratic Bézier curve segments," described by 3 points with one point off the curve. These entail simpler math than the 4-point Béziers employed in Adobe-specified Type 1 fonts, which are referred to as incorporating "cubic Bézier" curves.

And if things are complicated enought, some people use the word *vector* to mean any kind of mathematically defined graphic (whether of straight lines, splines, or whatever) as opposed to bitmapped graphics, where an image is formed out of a fixed pattern of dots. That's the case in the often-used expression "raster to vector conversion." Many people use this phrase to describe what happens when you use Adobe Streamline or other autotrace utility to convert a bitmapped image (a TIFF file, for instance) into line art, for example, even though the line art that results is composed of Bézier curves.

Seeing graphics in QuarkXPress

If you're having a hard time getting your **Illustrator** graphic previews to display properly in **QuarkXPress** documents, open the Monitors Control Panel and make certain your monitor is set to 8-bit color. Illustrator previews are saved as 8-bit files; if your monitor is set for 24-bit color, Illustrator files will print but they won't show up on the screen.

Faster-on-the-screen CorelDRAW

When you're working in **CorelDRAW** with the preview window open, there are two ways to speed up the screen display:

- Use the PREVIEW SELECTED ONLY command (under the Display menu) to limit the preview to just the elements you're working on.

- Turn off AUTO UPDATE (also under the Display menu), so that the preview image only redraws when you click in the preview window. Keep in mind that AUTO UPDATE can only be turned back on if you've already selected SHOW PREVIEW.

Text-wrap around missing graphic

If you don't have a scanned version of an irregularly shaped image you'll be stripping in, you can use a photocopy instead to help you wrap text around it in **PageMaker**. Here's how:

1. Photocopy the graphic onto a clear sheet that's safe to use in your photocopier.

2. With your on-screen page view set to *Actual size* (not reduced or enlarged), put the transparency on your computer screen. (It should stick there by itself due to the screen's static electricity.) Slide it into position over the spot on the page where the stripped-in copy will appear.

3. Create a small stand-in graphic more or less the same size as the image on the transparency. The actual shape of the stand-in isn't all that important; a rule, circle, or square created with the approriate tool will do fine.

4. Use the text-wrap borders of the stand-in to adjust the text around the edges of the photocopied image.

On the final, printed copy, manually paste up or strip in the graphic, using traditional methods.

Page Layout

Design

Start with a sketch

Start with quick thumbnail sketches of any design job before turning to your computer. This is especially important for new users of a page design program who are stumped when faced with a blank screen. With sketches to work from, you can quickly create an on-screen design that looks like an actual page.

Save your layout as a template

Before you place text or graphics on a new page grid—whether it's for a newsletter, book, brochure, or ad—duplicate it and label it with the date and job name. This collection of in-house design "archives" can provide a starting point for future creative work and help you develop a corporate or company style.

Guideline guides

If you generate complicated **PageMaker** documents, you probably have a large number of ruler guides on the screen for positioning text and graphic elements. If you use the same layout templates repeatedly, you can keep track of what each guide is for by labeling them. Draw a short rule beginning and ending on the pasteboard that corresponds to a guide on your page (have it end close to, but outside, the edge of the page). Then use the text tool to type a label at the outside end of the new line (Figure 4-1), making sure the text block handles do not overlap the edge of the page. Repeat the process for each guideline. When you print your document, the labels and referencing rules will be invisible since they're on the pasteboard.

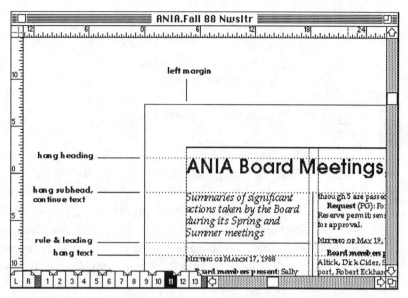

FIGURE 4-1 *Use text and hairline rules in PageMaker to label ruler guides and margins for easy identification.*

  ## Vertical grids

Good page layouts are based on an underlying grid on which you align graphics, headlines, pull quotes, and other items. Often times, though, a page design may use 3 columns of text, the design itself may bea 6-column grid. In **PageMaker**, you can use the program's column guides to help you position the vertical guides in a new page grid. Here's how:

1. With the COLUMN GUIDES command under the Options menu, enter the number of column guides you need. Set Space between columns to 0 inches, picas, or whatever; then click OK.

2. Drag ruler guides into position over the column guides to create the verticals for the grid.

3. Choose the COLUMN GUIDES command again. Enter the number of columns and the appropriate space between columns to create the actual column guides you'll use.

Aligning everything along the text column margins can make for an overly symmetrical, dull-looking page. Using a more complex page grid allows you to employ more spatial variety in your layout without sacrificing consistency.

Plan for length

When you design a publication, make sure your layout accommodates the lengthiest example of each element. In the text, find the wordiest titles and subheads. In tables, find the longest headings, categories, or longest numbers in columns. Use these in the prototype, along with average and short examples, to show how it all works together. Your sample may prompt your clients to rewrite or reorganize the material. And the earlier they do that, the better.

Right and left header conventions

In books and other lengthy, multisection documents, different information may or may not appear in right and left headers. Works of fiction often display the title in both right and left headers. Nonfiction publications usually place a major document division title (book, chapter, or part title, for example) in the left header and a minor division title in the right header. Although there's no one accepted scheme, the following is a list of the most commonly used header combinations:

Left-hand page	Right-hand page
Document title	Chapter title
Part title	Chapter title
Chapter title	Chapter title
Chapter title	Subhead
Subhead	Subhead
Appendix	Title of Appendix
Bibliography	Section title

Front and back matter conventions

If you're producing a full-length book or manual, you'll want to be sure that the acknowledgments, table of contents, index, bibliography, and the like—what is called front and back matter—are in the proper order. Authorities may differ over a few minor details, such as whether or not the glossary comes before or after the bibliography, but the sequence followed by most parts of a book is well established:

Front matter	
	Title page
	Copyright page
	Dedication
	Table of contents
	Lists of illustrations and tables
	Foreward
	Preface
	Acknowledgments
	Introduction
Main text	
Back matter	
	Appendixes
	Notes
	Glossary
	Bibliography
	Indexes

Front matter pages are often numbered with lowercase roman numerals while the main text starts a new sequence (beginning with the number one) in Arabic numerals. Back matter page numbers pick up, of course, where the main text leaves off. Don't forget, too, that all pages (including any blank pages) are counted, even if the page number is not printed. You'll find more detailed information about these and many related matters in *Graphic Design for the Electronic Age* by Jan V. White, one of our favorite reference books.

. . . .

Creating the layout

. . . .

  ### Centering graphics

A simple way to center a graphic or text block between the page margins in most page layout programs is to draw an X on the page and use it as a centering guide. Here, for example, is how to do that in **PageMaker:**

1. Draw two diagonal hairline rules from margin corner to margin corner on the Master Pages. The resulting X will appear on every page.

2. Drag the object to be centered until both top or both bottom corners sit on the upper or lower diagonals of the X (like the top sea

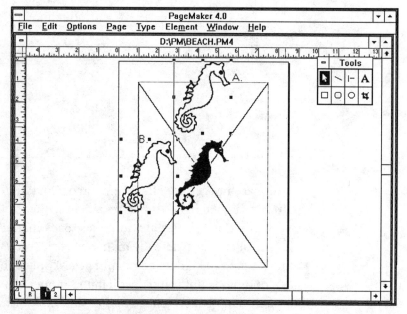

FIGURE 4-2 *Use diagonally intersecting lines to help center an object within the page margins.*

horse in Figure 4-2). The object is now centered horizontally. Drag a vertical ruler guide to the left edge of the object.

3. Now drag the object until both left or both right corners are aligned with the left- or right-hand diagonals of the X (like the sea horse on the left in the illustration).

4. Finally, while holding the Shift Key to prevent vertical movement, drag the object until its left edge aligns with the vertical ruler guide you placed in step 2.

The object is now precisely centered inside all four page margins.

Place rules after the text is finished

When laying out a page containing a number of rules in **Quark-XPress**, be sure to structure your text, placing it exactly where you want it, before you create any rules. Were you to move or adjust the text after the rules were in place, you would have to reposition all the rules as well since they're not connected to the text box. Another reason to leave the rules until last is that screen redraw is more sluggish with the added rules, and, as a result, most tasks take a little longer to accomplish.

A page within a page

Here's an easy way to use a page from one **PageMaker** document as an illustration in another PageMaker document:

1. Open the document containing the page you want to use as an illustration.

2. Choose the Print command or press Command + P. Enter the page number of the illustration page in both the From and To page range text boxes; then click the PostScript button.

3. Turn off all the currently selected options in the PostScript dialog box. Then turn on the *Print PostScript to Disk* option. Turn on the

EPS option, and, if there are graphics on the page, turn on the *Include Images* option.

4. Click the File Name button and give the file-to-be a name and a destination. Click the OK and Print buttons to create an EPS file of the PageMaker page.

5. Open the document in which you want to use the illustration page and turn to the page which is to display it. Choose the PLACE command or press Command + D. Locate and select the EPS file you just created, click the OK button, and place the graphic in the usual way.

You now have a full-size graphic of a full-size PageMaker page sitting on another PageMaker page. Reduce the graphic to the required size and draw a rectangle around it to define the page's boundaries (Figure 4-3).

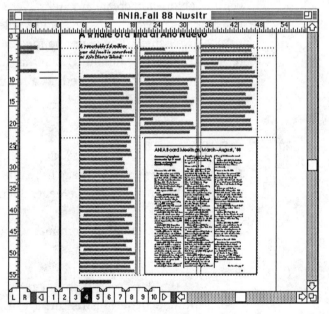

FIGURE 4-3 *Use the* Print PostScript to Disk *option to use one PageMaker page as an illustration in another PageMaker page.*

Saddle-stitch layout

Single fold, saddle-stitched booklets are relatively easy to produce on laser printers. You simply print two pages per side on both sides of the paper, stack the sheets, fold them down the middle, and staple the spine. The hard part is getting the page order right since most publishing programs, including PageMaker and Ventura Publisher, lack built-in tools to automate such a layout. As you've no doubt noticed if you've tried it, you can't simply print pages sequentially on each side of the paper because, in a saddle-fold, right and left halves of each sheet end up at opposite ends of the booklet. It's a tough layout to visualize; we sometimes resort to folding a couple of pieces of paper in order to see the page-order relationships in a saddle-stitched booklet.

As an alternative to paper folding, you can use the following pencil-and-paper trick to figure out your saddle-stitch page order. Suppose, for example, that you're working on a 12-page, two-up layout:

1. List the even-numbered pages in descending order, from 12 to 2 in a column on the left side of the page.

2. To the right of the first column of numbers list the odd-numbered pages in ascending order from one to eleven (as in Figure 4-4). You should now have two columns of numbers side by side.

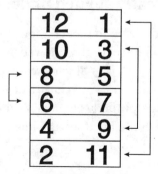

FIGURE 4-4 *Creating a simple table like this makes it easy to plan the layout of a saddle-stitched booklet.*

3. Draw a connecting line between the top and bottom pairs of numbers, then between the second to the top and second to bottom pairs, and so on (see the illustration).

Here's what your pencil pushing reveals: Each number pair in your table indicates which two pages lie next to one another on and unfolded sheet. (Notice that pages six and seven are the only consecutive pages positioned on the same piece of paper. That's because they're on the center spread, the page lying on the inside of the fold.) The lines connecting different pairs indicate which two pairs of pages will be printed on opposite sides of a single piece of paper. When they're stacked in order (the top three pairs stacked facedown with 12-1 at the bottom) folded together and stapled on the fold, they'll read in the correct order from cover to cover.

If you use a PC and frequently print saddle-stitched booklets on PostScript printers or photoimagesetters, you may want to invest in the **Double Up** utility from Legend Communications. With Double Up you print your document to disk as a PostScript language file, and then load that file into the utility. Double Up will automatically reorder the pages, create the proper margins, and print trim and registration marks, among other features. It even lets you enter paper thickness adjustments to compensate for "creep," the difference in side margins after trimming, especially noticeable when you're folding a lengthy publication.

Neatly aligned underscores in forms

Problem: To create a form in a page layout program containing a column of terms followed by underlined spaces (for example, Name: _____). If you create the underlines with strings of underline characters, you'll have a devil of a time keeping the right ends of the lines properly aligned. If you create the underlines by drawing rules with the line tool, the lines won't move with the text if you change the layout.

Solution: Set a flush-right tab at the right margin, and specify the underline character as the tab leader (Figure 4-5). If your page layout program allows it, set the leader spacing to 0. Then, for each entry in the form, type the text, press the Tab Key, and press Enter or Return.

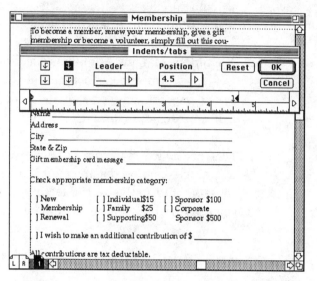

FIGURE 4-5 *If you use underline tab leaders to create the underscores in a form, as in this PageMaker document, the right ends of all the underscores will be neatly aligned.*

One column in a two-column document

If you sometimes need a one-column first page in an otherwise two-column-per-page **Ventura Publisher** document, you can create one by placing a frame over the entire first page and setting it in a single column. But you can also create the one-column page using the underlying frame so that text flows from the first page without interruption. Here's what to do:

1. After setting the underlying frame for two columns, go to the first page of your document and select the *Insert New Page Before Current Page* option, using the INSERT/REMOVE PAGE command from the Chapter menu. Ventura will create a new, blank, first page for your document.

2. With the new first page created, select Frame mode in the GEM version, or use the pointer tool in the Windows version, and click on the underlying page to select the base frame.

3. From the Files list windows, select the name of your text file. It will load onto the page (and following pages) in two columns.

4. From the Margins & Columns dialog box under the Frame Menu, change the number of columns to one. This will apply only to the new page you have created; the rest of the document will still be in a two-column format.

This tip also works to create a single two-column page in an otherwise single-column document; it is a less intuitive but equally acceptable alternative to the technique described below in "Two columns in a one-column document."

- -

 ## Two columns in a one-column document

One way to create a two-column format in an otherwise single-column **Ventura Publisher** document is to create a new two-column frame over the underlying frame. The only drawback is that text won't automatically flow onto that frame, as it does with the underlying frame. There's an easier way (which won't inhibit automatic text flow) to create a temporary two-column (or more) format. It involves adding a thin frame down the center of the underlying frame. The added frame splits the page into two columns and becomes the gutter between the two. Here's how to do it:

1. Create a new, thin frame running from the top to bottom margin, splitting the page into the columns you want (Figure 4-6).

2. While the new frame is still selected, make sure that the *Flow Text Around* option in the Sizing & Scaling dialog box under the Frame menu is set to *On*, and that *Horiz. Padding and Vert. Padding* (also under Sizing & Scaling) are set to zero.

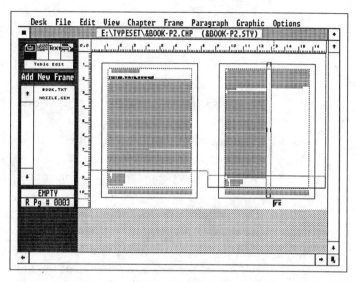

FIGURE 4-6 *A narrow frame placed down the middle of an underlying page (as in the right-hand page of the Ventura spread above) forces text to flow around it, forming two columns.*

3. Also in the Sizing & Scaling dialog box, you can make fine adjustments to the frame width (which is, in fact, your between-column gutter width) by entering the desired dimension in the Frame Width text box.

Your text will automatically flow down each side of the narrow frame (forming two columns) and onto the following pages.

Grouping objects in PageMaker

Unlike **QuarkXPress** and most drawing programs, **PageMaker** for the Mac lacks a GROUP command for fusing two or more objects together. The Scrapbook, however, turns out to be an adequate, if inelegant, substitute. Here's how it works:

1. Select all the items you want to group together and cut them with the CUT command.

2. Open the Scrapbook (by selecting it under the Apple menu) and PASTE in the cut items.

3. Choose the PLACE command and place the cut objects back on the page; if they were the last item pasted into the Scrapbook, they should be the first graphic placed with the Place Scrapbook pointer. Select any tool in the Toolbox to "unload" the pointer and cancel any other graphics from the Scrapbook.

The placed items are now grouped together as a single object. If you later want to restore the grouped items to their original, ungrouped status, simply paste the Scrapbook copy instead of placing it.

One word of caution about this technique: Our favorite PageMaker newsletter, *ThePage*, reports that grouping objects this way can convert hairlines and half-point lines to one-point lines. Copying to Solutions' **SmartScrap** (instead of the Scrapbook) and pasting (instead of placing) the objects back into PageMaker not only solves this problem but is also simpler and faster.

Equal horizontal spacing

You can divide an area or object on a page into equal horizontal slices simply by using vertical ruler guides and a diagonal rule. For example, here's how to divide a box into five equal parts:

1. Place six vertical ruler guides at regular intervals within the box— it doesn't matter where they fall or how far apart they are, as long as they're equally spaced and are placed inside the box.

2. Draw a diagonal rule from where the left-most guide meets the top of the box down to where the right-most guide meets the bottom of the box.

3. Place horizontal ruler guides at the points where the diagonal rule and the vertical ruler guides intersect (Figure 4-7). These will mark your five equal horizontal divisions.

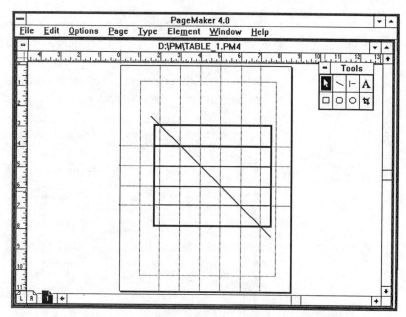

FIGURE 4-7 *Drawing a diagonal line through evenly spaced vertical ruler guides makes it easy to divide an area into equal horizontal segments.*

  Equal vertical divisions

You can use **PageMaker's** *Force justify* text alignment option to create equally spaced vertical guidelines across your page, column, or other measure. You might, for example, want to equally space a series of graphic elements across a page or column. Here's how to do it:

1. First type a series of vertical bars, obtained by pressing Shift + \, and highlight the line of bars.

2. Select *Force justify* from the Alignment submenu under the Type menu. Forced justification will spread the bars evenly across the text block you've created—no arithmetic needed.

3. Drag vertical ruler guides over the evenly spaced bars (Figure 4-8), and delete the bars.

Rotate the bars 90 degrees using PageMaker's text rotation function to position evenly-spaced horizontal ruler guides.

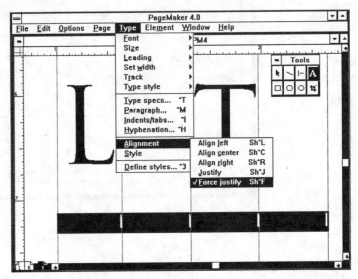

FIGURE 4-8 *PageMaker's* Force justify *alignment option will equally space a series of bar characters across a text block. Use them to align vertical ruler guides.*

Creating camera-ready signatures

QuarkXPress's multiple-select and rotation features make it easy to generate camera-ready, four-page signatures. To create an eight-page newsletter to imageset as two four-page signatures, for example, first design the entire newsletter as a standard 8½-x-11-inch document. Then create a new 17-x-22-inch document with two blank pages. Go to page 1 of your completed newsletter, select the Item tool, and choose SELECT ALL; open both documents and place them side-by-side in any view except Thumbnail. Now drag the entire page into the 17-x-22-inch document. Repeat for pages 8, 5, and 4, arranging the pages in signatures and rotating them 180 degrees

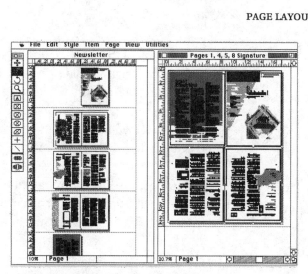

FIGURE 4-9 *You can create camera-ready, four-page signatures using QuarkXPress's multiple-select and rotation features.*

when required (Figure 4-9). Repeat the process for the remaining pages to make page 2 of the signature document.

 Orderly text flow

Because **Ventura Publisher** flows text into frames in the order in which the frames were created, you may find that your text doesn't flow in the order you want—especially when you add a new frame to a page. This can also create problems with automatic numbering since the numbers (section or figure numbers, for instance) won't appear in the proper sequence.

One simple way to overcome this is to delete the frames containing the out-of-sequence text and then reinsert each frame in the order in which you want the text to flow. If your layout is complex and precise, and the idea of recreating a number of frames makes you feel ill, try the following technique.

If most of the layout is affected, first make sure you've saved the chapter. Then, starting from the end of the layout and working back to the beginning, click on each out-of-sequence frame in turn and choose the REMOVE TEXT/FILE command (under Edit menu in the DOS/GEM Edition, under the Frame menu in the Windows Edition), selecting *Frame* as the *Remove from* option in the ensuing Remove File dialog box. That will clear the text from each out-of-sequence frame. Now, having clicked on the frame, select *List of files* as your *Remove from* option. That will clear all the frames of text, though you'll have to reload the text file (with the LOAD TEXT/PICTURE command under File) when it's time to reflow the text.

Then, starting from the beginning of the out-of-order portion of your layout, select each frame, in the correct order, and choose CUT FRAME and then PASTE FRAME for each one in turn.

The cut-and-pasted frames will remain their original positions, but text will now flow in the order in which the frames were cut and pasted. To flow the text, simply select each frame in order and click on the text file name in the Files window (Windows), or in the file assignment box on the left-hand sidebar (DOS/GEM).

Signature line via an inline rule

In contracts, memos, and other documents, you often need to create signature lines with the expected signatory's title printed beneath the rule. In **PageMaker**, you can use the program's inline graphics capability to create a signature line. Here's how:

1. With the straight-line drawing tool, create a rule of the desired length, select it, and CUT it to the Clipboard.

2. Then with the text tool, type the official's title or other designation.

3. Place the cursor at the beginning of the text and press either Return or Enter.

4. Move the cursor to the beginning of the new blank line you've just created, and PASTE in your rule from the Clipboard.

5. To center-align the text with the rule, make the text block the same width as the rule (Figure 4-10), and choose the *Center* option via the ALIGNMENT command under the Type menu for the text.

To bring the signature line and the line of text closer together, select both lines and decrease their leading.

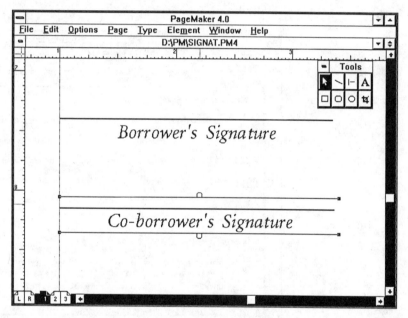

FIGURE 4-10 *The signature line in this PageMaker layout is an inline graphic in the paragraph above the single line of text.*

Handy Ventura breaking tags

You can quickly force a new column or new page in the PC editions **Ventura Publisher** without typing in a lot of carriage returns or adjusting the frame. Add two tags that have the same attributes as body text but that are set for *Column Break After* (Figure 4-11) and *Page Break After*. Name the styles NEWCOL and NEWPAGE or something else equally descriptive. Apply the tags to force a page break after a paragraph.

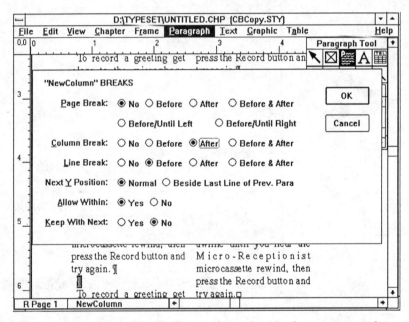

FIGURE 4-11 *A tag which specifies a column break after a paragraph is a quick way to force a new column.*

Copying tab settings

There are several ways you can copy tab settings from one paragraph to another in **PageMaker**:

- To copy tab settings from one paragraph to any number of immediately following paragraphs, do the following:

1. Select the paragraph whose tab settings you want to copy by triple-clicking the Text tool within the paragraph. Don't release the mouse button at the end of the triple-click.

2. Drag down the text column to select all the paragraphs.

3. Select the INDENTS/TABS command from the Type menu. Without making any changes in the Indents/Tabs dialog box, close it by clicking the OK button or pressing Return.

All selected paragraphs now have the same tab settings as the first selected paragraph.

- To copy tab settings to paragraphs which aren't immediately below the model paragraph, create a style based on the model paragraph's tab settings. Then apply that style to the paragraphs which should have the new tab settings.

- To change the tab settings for all paragraphs formatted in a particular style, edit the tab settings for that style in the Edit Style dialog box. Your new settings are automatically copied to all paragraphs already formatted in that style. These new settings are also copied, of course, to any paragraphs you format in that style in the future.

- To copy tab settings to all text blocks created in the future, select any tool except the Text tool and specify the desired tab settings in the Indents/Tabs dialog box. These settings become the default settings for all future text blocks created in that publication.

  Power paste in PageMaker

If you cut or copy and then immediately paste an object in **Page-Maker**, the pasted object is normally offset from the original by about an eighth of an inch (diagonally, down and to the right). But if you press the Option Key as you choose the PASTE command (or press Option + Command + V on the Mac or Shift + Control + P on the PC), the object is pasted back in the exact spot from which it was cut or copied. This can be useful if you want to clone an object, but it has other ramifications as well.

You can use Option + PASTE, for example, to copy or move an object from the current page to exactly the same position on another page. You can also use it to copy or move an object to exactly the same position on another page in another document, as long as the other document has the same page size as the original one.

Another way to use Option + PASTE is to "step and repeat" an object across the page. (Two step and repeat sequences—the two trajectories of a bouncing ball—appear at the bottom of the document page in the window in Figure 4-12). Here's how:

1. Select and copy the object you wish to step and repeat with the COPY command (or press Command + C on the Mac or Control + C on the PC).

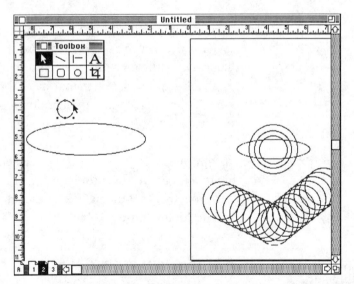

FIGURE 4-12 *In the document page on the right side of this PageMaker window, two different paste techniques have created a step-and-repeat bouncing ball and a precisely centered stack of circles.*

2. Paste the copy directly on top of the original with Option + PASTE (Option + Command + V on the Mac; Shift + Control + P on the PC).

3. Drag the copy to a new position.

4. Use Option + PASTE again to create a second copy. The second copy will automatically place itself the same distance and direction from the first copy as that first copy is from the original.

5. Continue to use Option + PASTE to step and repeat as many copies as you need.

Beware of one caveat: The position you have copied from and the location you intend to paste to must both be visible in the document window. If the position you've copied from is somewhere off screen, the object will be pasted in the center of the window. Thus, for a successful step and repeat, make sure the current view displays all of the area in which you'll be working.

To create a stack of objects centered around some imaginary point, you can take advantage of the fact that objects are pasted in the center of the screen when their origin is off screen. For example, let's say you want to stack a group of circles and ellipses so that they all have the same center point. These are the steps you would take on the Mac:

1. Create the objects you want to stack on the far edge of the pasteboard.

2. Select an object and either cut it or copy it.

3. Choose the FIT IN WINDOW command (or press Command + W) to center the document page in the window and move the object's original position off-screen.

4. Choose the PASTE command (or press Command + V); this pastes the cut or copied object in the center of the page.

5. Scroll back to the edge of the pasteboard and repeat steps 2 through 4 for each object in the stack.

In Figure 4-12 on page 222, for example, we have already stacked three circles and an ellipse in the center of the document page on the right and have selected a fourth circle in preparation for adding it to the stack. Note that using the FIT IN WINDOW command—rather than scrolling the document page into position—is very important; because the command always places the document page in exactly the same position in the window, it ensures that the stacked objects are all centered on precisely the same point.

Zoom in to align

In graphics and page layout programs, the accuracy with which you can visually position an object or baseline varies with the view. Generally speaking, the higher the view's magnification, the greater the accuracy. A 100-percent or actual size view, for example, gives you approximately 1-point accuracy. In contrast, a 200-percent view provides about ½-point accuracy, and a 400-percent view about ¼-point accuracy.

Precise pasting

In **PageMaker**, you can move a text block or graphic from one page to the same spot relative to the margin on another page—even if the pages are different sizes—using a box as a guide. (If exact, not relative, page placement is called for, the technique described earlier in "Power paste in PageMaker" will be faster.) These are the steps:

1. Draw a box against a corner margin of your page to serve as a placement guide. Change its Fill (under the Element menu) to Paper so that it will be easier to select.

2. With the guide box snug against the margin corner, select both the box and the item you want to move, and then COPY them to the Clipboard.

3. Select the new page and PASTE the items onto it.

4. With both the box and object still selected, drag the box (with the other object tagging along) to its original margin corner (Figure 4-13). Ungroup the item and box and delete the box.

This tip also works with **QuarkXPress** and **Ventura Publisher**.

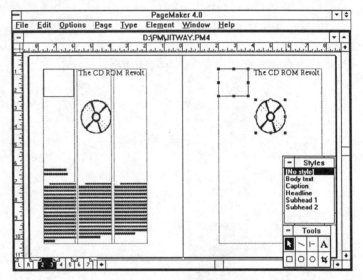

FIGURE 4-13 *The box and the graphic have been copied and pasted to a new page, where the box serves as a positioning guide for the graphic.*

Creating your own pasteboard

If you'd like to use a pasteboard in any PC version of **Ventura Publisher**, don't let the fact that it doesn't have one stop you:

1. Make your page one size larger than necessary using the *Paper Type & Dimension* options of the PAGE SIZE AND LAYOUT command under the Chapter menu).

2. Highlight the base frame with the pointer tool and use the SIZING & SCALING command under the Frame menu to specify your actual page size (Frame Width, Frame Height). Also set the Upper Left X

and Upper Left Y in the GEM Edition (Left Side and Top Side in the Windows Edition) so they position the page toward the center of the paper dimensions you specified above.

With the base frame the size you want, you can use the dead space for your pasteboard (Figure 4-14). To make a pasteboard element available on every page, drag it into the pasteboard space and select the REPEATING FRAMES command. Before printing the chapter, reset the page size to match the base frame size.

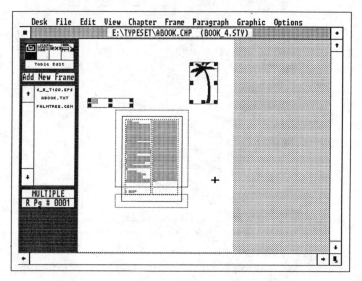

FIGURE 4-14 *Placing a smaller base frame on a larger paper size yields an effective pasteboard in Ventura, which lacks one otherwise.*

  ## Custom page sizes

Ventura Publisher's PAGE SIZE & LAYOUT command under the Chapter menu allows you to pick half-size, letter, legal, tabloid, and other preset sizes for your page. You can, though, customize the dimensions of your page by adjusting the Frame Width and Frame Height of the underlying frame with the SIZING AND SCALING command under the Frame menu (Figure 4-15) on the PC, or via the SIZE & POSITION command in the Frame menu on the Mac. While you're cruising the Sizing and Scaling window, set Upper Left X and Upper

Left Y in the GEM Edition to .5 inches or greater to allow room on the paper for crop marks. In the Windows Edition set Left Side and Top Side, and in the Mac Edition enter values for Left and Top. Ventura will use the Frame Width and Frame Height dimensions as your true page size and will place crop marks accordingly.

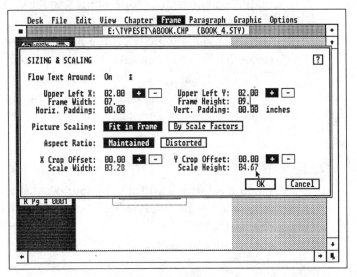

FIGURE 4-15 *However you set your Ventura paper size—letter, A5, legal—the Sizing and Scaling command settings under the Frame menu reflect your document's true page size, and crop marks will print accordingly.*

Get organized for Ventura

When beginning a **Ventura Publisher** publishing project on the PC, your first priority is organization. Create a subdirectory from your root directory and copy the needed text and graphic files into that subdirectory. To help identify them, use an acronym or other abbreviation for the name of the subdirectory; use the same acronym in the names of the text, graphics, and working files.

For example, in a disk subdirectory titled HTPB for a How to Publish Books project, you should see files named in an organized way, like this: text files named HTPB-1.txt, HTPB-2.txt, HTPB-3.txt, and so on; graphics files named HTPB-1.eps, HTPB-1a.eps, HTPB-2.eps,

HTPB-2a.eps; and Ventura working files named HTPB-1.chp, HTPB-2.chp, or HTPB-1.cap, HTPB-2.cap.

File names aren't all that need careful organization. Tags can get confusing and confused quickly. Establish the basic parameters for the Body Text tag such as font, point size for body copy, line spacing, alignment, etc., and document them. Then base as many of the other tags as possible directly on the Body Text tag. This will speed the creation of new styles and tags for your project. Also, consider printing out some sample text indicating the formating hierarchy of your design (such as major head, minor head, subhead1, subhead 2, etc.). This will serve as a template for your design associates.

Header and footer efficiency

When creating a **Ventura Publisher** design, define the headers and footers last. Otherwise you'll end up with more work if you make any changes to your top, bottom, left, or right margins since Ventura doesn't automatically adjust the headers and footers when you alter the margins.

Quick stepped rules

You can create stepped rules in **Ventura Publisher** on the PC by layering rules of different widths and lengths one above the other. To produce the rule shown in Figure 4-16, for example, set up three blank paragraphs with different Ruling Line Above settings—the first with a thick short rule, the second with a thinner, longer rule, and so on.

Then, using the BREAKS command under the Paragraph menu, set the *Line Break* option for the second and third paragraphs to *No* and the Next Y Position option to *Normal*. The text should be part of the last paragraph and widest rule.

Chapter Two: The Norman Kings

FIGURE 4-16 *Three paragraphs are used to create this Ventura stepped rule: two with just rules, the last paragraph with a thin rule and text.*

One-column, two-sided text wrap

Ventura Publisher on the PC will automatically flow text around both sides of a frame added in the center of a column. For example, if you place a graphic in the frame, Ventura automatically wraps the text down the left side of the graphic first, then down the right side. This in essence forms two columns, one on either side of the graphic: You read down one side first, then down the other.

For a slender graphic, though, you might want Ventura to break a line at the left edge of the graphic and continue it from the right edge. That allows you to read the text across the column, from margin to margin, skipping over the graphic as you do. One way to do this is to create a stack of one-line-high frames over your graphic frame (Figure 4-17 on page 230). Since each of these little frames is only one-line high, Ventura can flow only one line of text on the left side of the frame before it moves over to the right side, which is exactly what you want. Since this happens to each frame in the stack, the text appears to skip over the graphic. Here's how to set it up:

1. In the Frame Typography dialog box (under the Frame menu), set the Move Down To 1st Baseline By option to *Inter-Line*.

2. Draw the frame for the graphic, making sure that *Line Snap* is turned on. (You'll find *Line Snap* under the Options menu in the

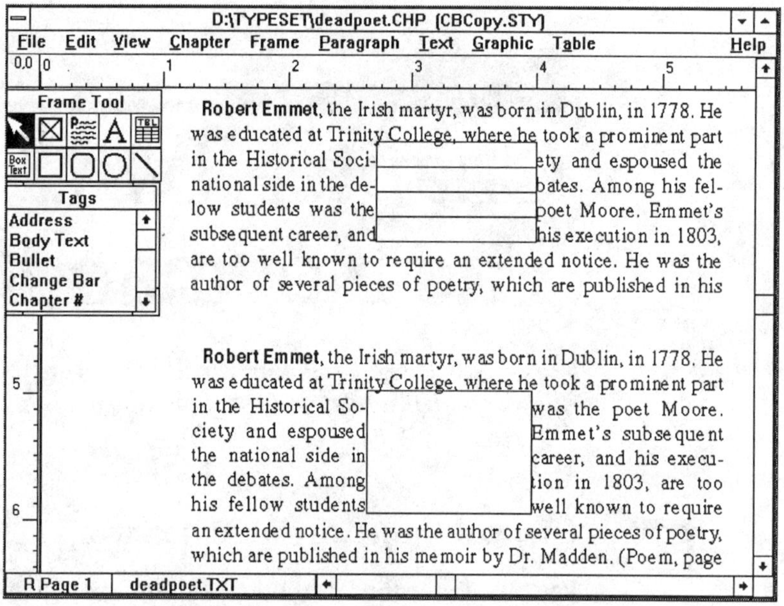

FIGURE 4-17 *A stack of single line-high frames in Ventura causes text to break on either side of a graphic (upper paragraph of illustration)—instead of first flowing down the left side and then down the right side (bottom paragraph).*

GEM Edition or under the View menu in the Windows Edition). Then load the graphic into the frame.

3. Use the Sizing & Scaling dialog box under the Frame menu to turn *Flow Text Around* off. Your text should now run directly over the image: so far so good.

4. Now draw a new one-line-tall frame across the width of the frame that contains your image, relying on *Line Snap* to give it the height of a single line.

5. Create a stack of identical one-line-tall frames to fill up the frame containing the image. You may want to move the graphic frame out of the way temporarily as you position the one-line frames. Make sure you give the frames a hollow fill and no ruling lines around, and turn on *Flow Text Around*.

6. Here's the tricky part. You'll notice at this point that text on either side of the frame doesn't line up properly. To fix that, first turn off *Line Snap*.

7. Now select all the one-line frames by clicking on one of them, then holding down the Shift Key as you click on each of the others. Drag the group of frames so the upper edge of the top frame aligns with the baseline of the line above (not with the cap height of the next line, which is how Ventura's line snap orients them).

Now each line of text will skip from one side of the graphic to the other.

Printing closer to the bottom edge

In the GEM and Windows editons of **Ventura Publisher** it's normally not possible to laser-print text within the ½-inch "dead zone" at the bottom of letter-size pages. You can, however print to within ¼ inch of the page bottom by setting Paper Type to Legal under the Page Layout menu and by specifying a large bottom margin. A bottom margin of 3¼ inches will give you the equivalent of a ¼-inch margin on letter-size paper.

Let the ruler do the calculations

Let your page layout or drawing program's ruler do the arithmetic for you when you're trying to align elements equidistant from the right and left margins. Many programs, including **QuarkXPress**, **Page-Maker**, **FreeHand**, and **MacDraw II**, let you move the zero point of the ruler to any place on the page. If you move the ruler's zero point to the middle of the page, ruler markings march away from the zero point in both directions. This makes it easy to center text blocks or graphic elements; all you need to do is position the right and left or top and bottom object boundaries so they fall on the same ruler value on both sides of the zero point. For example, the fact that the right boundary of the ship being moved in Figure 4-18 falls on the right 1½-inch mark and the left boundary falls on the left 1½-inch mark (as indicated by the dotted lines on the horizontal ruler), confirms that the graphic is centered on the page.

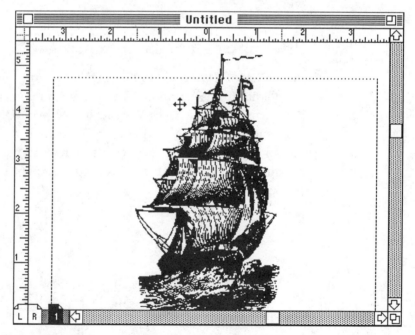

FIGURE 4-18 *Moving the ruler's zero point to the middle of the page makes it easy to center a graphic.*

Similarly, if you want to position an object a certain distance from the right margin, move the zero point to that margin. Then use the markings on the left side of the zero point to measure the desired distance. When you're done, you can leave the zero point where it is, move it back to its original position, or move it to yet another useful location, ready to position another object.

LaserJet overlay problem

If you want to position clip art on top of a ruled border in **Ventura Publisher** for the PC without having the border show through the graphic, you'll run into problems when the page is printed on a Hewlett-Packard LaserJet Series II. That's because the LaserJet Series II—and other printers using Hewlett-Packard's older PCL (Printer Control Language) Level 4—can't print a lighter object over a darker object without the darker object showing through.

As a workaround, you need to create a ruled border that doesn't pass beneath the clip art. Instead of creating the ruled border using Ventura's RULING BOX AROUND command from the Frame menu, you'll have to draw line segments that stop at the edges of the graphic. Here are the steps:

1. Select the frame with the border running under the graphic.

2. Make note of the frame's height and width in the Sizing & Scaling dialog box under the Frame menu.

3. In the Grid Settings dialog box reached via the Graphics menu, turn on *Grid Snap* and enter a Horizontal Spacing value equal to the frame's width and a Vertical Spacing value equal to its height.

   With the grid set up this way, you'll be able to draw lines the length of the sides of the frame only. This will ensure their precise intersection at the corners of the frame. (Later you'll switch to a finer grid setting in order to draw short lines along the side of the frame that passes beneath the graphic.)

4. From the Line Attributes dialog box under the Graphic menu, set the line thickness, and choose rounded line endings to ensure smooth joins at the corners.

5. Draw lines from corner to corner along the three unbroken sides of the frame. The grid snap will make it easy to draw straight lines from corner to corner along each edge of the frame. Hold the Alt Key down while you draw in order to keep the lines to a vertical or horizontal orientation.

6. For the fourth side, change your grid setting to a smaller interval so you can draw a separate line from each corner to the edge of the graphic. You may have to turn off Line Snap to make fine adjustments to the locations of the rules' inner end-points

When you print, the graphic will appear to overlay the rule al though the rule, in fact, doesn't extend under the graphic at all.

Autoflow for short columns

PageMaker's Autoflow feature automatically flows text from column to column on a multi-column page and from page to page. Normally, autoflowed text blocks automatically start at the top margin. But you may want to reserve space at the top of the page for text or graphic elements yet to come. If so, you can use PageMaker's text-wrap feature to force autoflowed text blocks to start lower down on the page, with the tops of all columns properly aligned. Here's how:

1. First, create a horizontal line across your page. Then choose *None* in the Lines dialog box to make the line invisible.

2. With the line still selected, choose TEXT WRAP under the Options menu, and adjust the line's text-wrap boundaries over the areas where you don't want text to flow (Figure 4-19).

3. When you place your text with Autoflow, it flows from column to column, each column starting at the graphic's boundary.

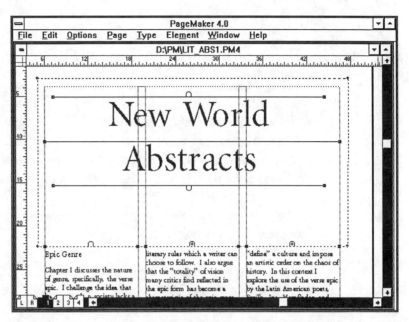

FIGURE 4-19 *Setting a boundary (the dotted line) with the Text Wrap feature in PageMaker is a quick and easy way to create shorter than normal autoflowed text columns, all properly aligned.*

To make sure lines are aligned from column to column, place text starting at the top of the column, regardless of where you've located the text-wrap boundaries. To further ensure text alignment across columns, select *Custom* as your Vertical ruler in the Preferences dialog box under the Edit menu. Then enter a value in points equal to the leading of your body text. Make sure you've selected *Snap to rulers*, also under the Options menu.

Moving the graphic's boundary up or down will shift the top margin of all the columns of text while keeping the tops of all columns in alignment.

Using only some master page items

In **PageMaker**, it's possible to use some master-page items on a given page, but not on others—for instance, on a chapter title page where you would want to eliminate the header. To eliminate just one item, such as the page number, cover the item with a box. Format the box with *None* selected under the Line submenu and *Paper* (opaque white) selected under the Fill submenu of the Element menu.

To eliminate a number of master-page items, it's best not to use lots of opaque boxes. Instead:

1. Go to the appropriate master page, select all, and COPY everything to the Clipboard.

2. Return to the document page, paste the copied master items, and, if necessary, adjust them (while they are all selected) so that they cover the automatic master-page items exactly.

3. Turn off *Display Master Items* in the Page menu so the automatic master-page items no longer appear on that page.

4. Delete the copied and pasted master-page items which are not needed.

Temporary Ventura ruler guides

Ventura Publisher doesn't offer nonprinting horizontal and vertical guides for aligning elements, but you can mimic them, at least temporarily. Click on the intersection of the ruler lines in the upper left hand corner, and then drag the pointer to another place on the page. As you do this, horizontal and vertical lines track the movement of the pointer (Figure 4-20). You can use these temporary lines to easily check the alignment of objects.

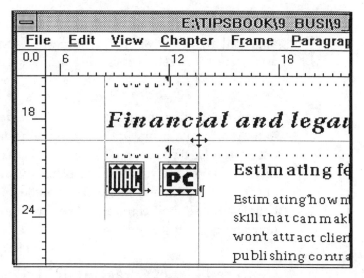

FIGURE 4-20 *Dragging the pointer from the ruler's 0,0 point out onto a Ventura page displays dotted lines that you can use to align and position elements precisely.*

Working with text

Turning off hyphenation for specific words

If you're using **PageMaker** or **QuarkXPress** with hyphenation turned on, insert a soft hyphen (Command + Hyphen on the Mac, Ctrl + Hyphen in PageMaker for Windows) in front of any word you want to keep intact. The halves of currently hyphenated words immediately reunite and drop to the next line when you do this. If the word isn't currently hyphenated, the soft hyphen "prefix" will prevent it from breaking in the future, even if it falls at the end of a line.

"Unloading" the text icon

No doubt it's happened to you in **PageMaker:** You accidentally click on a windowshade handle and the pointer turns into the text icon, ready to flow text. The question is, how do you get rid of ("unload") the text icon and get back to work? It's easy. Whether the text icon appeared accidentally or on purpose, you can cancel the text icon and any further text flow by clicking on any tool in PageMaker's Toolbox.

If, before unloading the text icon, you accidentally press the mouse button and create an unwanted text box, don't select the text box and cut or delete it. If you do, you'll delete the text as well as the text box. Instead, to preserve your text and delete only the text box, simply drag the box's bottom windowshade handle up until it hits the top handle. Choose another tool or click elsewhere on the page and the now-empty text box will disappear.

Centered text over ragged right

If you want to center type—such as a headline—above a column of ragged right text, gauge the placement by the eye. If you center it using the appropriate fomatting command in your page layout program, the type usually looks as if it's too far to the right (Figure 4-21).

FIGURE 4-21 *The headline on the left was centered by PageMaker; the headline on the right was centered visually.*

Highlighting text with rules instead of boxes

To highlight subheads and other short paragraphs with a colored or shaded gray box, you can use **PageMaker** for the Mac's or **Quark-XPress**'s paragraph rules instead of the box drawing tool. In Page-Maker, you can create highlights up to 24 points high. To create the 24-point highlight at the top of Figure 4-22, for example, you would follow these steps:

1. Place the insertion point anywhere within the text you want to highlight.

2. Choose the PARAGRAPH command from the Type menu (or press Command + M), and, in the Paragraph dialog box, click the Rules button.

3. In the Rules dialog box (Figure 4-22, bottom), specify 12-point (the maximum weight) rules for both above and below the paragraph. Select the appropriate line width (Width of Text or Width

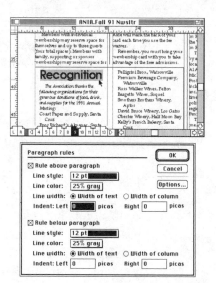

FIGURE 4-22 *The headline in the PageMaker window (top) is highlighted with a pair of paragraph rules. The Rules dialog box (bottom) displays the settings for these rules.*

of Column) and line color. (You may need to define a new tint or gray shade with the DEfine COLORs command if the desired shade is not already listed in the Line Color pop-up menu.)

4. Click the Options button in the Rules dialog box. In the Paragraph Rules Options dialog box, specify 2 picas above the baseline for the top rule and zero picas below the baseline for the bottom rule. (These settings are what cause the rules to overlap the text.)

5. Click OK in each dialog box until you return to the main window.

Back in the main document, check to see how well the highlight is centered over the text; if the highlight is too high or too low, adjust the values in the Paragraph Rules Options dialog box by a few points, positioning the highlight precisely. The text will overprint the rules, so you can reverse the text or knock it out in spot separations.

In XPress, the principles are more or less the same; the differences are in the details. These are the steps for the example in Figure 4-23:

1. Select the text you want to highlight.

2. Choose the RULES command from the Style menu (or press Command + Shift + N), and, in the ensuing dialog box, turn on the *Rule Above* option.

3. In the Paragraph Rules dialog box, specify the desired color, shade, length, and width (up to 504 points, or 7 inches) for the rule. You'll probably want to keep the default style, which is a solid (as opposed to dotted or dashed) rule.

4. In the Offset text box, enter a negative offset value to center the rule over the text. Since this text box expects a percentage value, enter the appropriate unit of measurement after the offset value (as in the dialog box in Figure 4-23). In most instances, a small offset value will do.

5. Click the Apply button to see the results of your work. You will probably need to adjust the offset value by a point or two to position the highlight exactly where you want; then click the Apply button again to see the results of your adjustment.

6. Click on OK when the highlight is the way you want it.

Keep in mind that the text to which you apply the rule can also be any color or shade; so you can, for example, create reverse type on a black rule. Another convenient aspect of the technique is this: A paragraph rule can be part of a style definition; thus, highlighting type is as easy as applying a style.

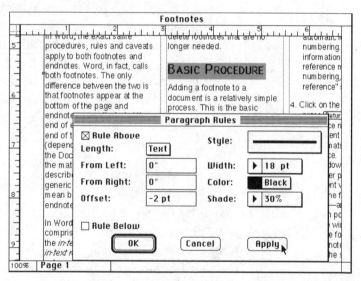

FIGURE 4-23 *You can also use paragraph rules in XPress to highlight text.*

  Creating a style based on existing formatting

Here's how to quickly create a style based on an existing paragraph's format in **PageMaker**:

1. Place the insertion point anywhere within the appropriately formatted paragraph.

2. Press the Command Key on the Mac or the Control Key on a PC and click on *No Style* in the Styles Palette.

3. In the Edit Style dialog box which then opens, specify the desired Based On style and Next style.

4. Enter a name for the style and save it by clicking the OK button.

Your new style should now be listed in the Styles Palette.

 ## Global changes

Because the PC editions of **Ventura Publisher** use text-based text formatting codes, you can view them and edit them in your word processor. This gives you the opportunity to make certain kinds of global formatting changes that you can't make directly in Ventura. Suppose, for example, that you want to change the type style for each instance of a certain phrase in your document to bold italics; here's how you can do it using your word processor's search and replace features:

1. Open the relevant text file in your word processing program.

2. Search for the phrase you wish to reformat. Replace it with the same phrase plus the <BI> code (including the angle brackets) in front and the <D> code at the end. For example, you'd search for the words *Peachpit Press* and replace each occurrence with <BI>*Peachpit Press*<D>.

3. Save the file using the same file name.

When you open the chapter containing the file in Ventura, you should see the new formatting.

  ## Standard weight tab leader dots

Tab leader dots in **PageMaker** take on the style of the preceding character (Figure 4-24). Thus, the leader dots following a character in boldface (such as a major heading in a table of contents) will be in boldface, those following a character in outline style will be outlined, and those following a a standard weight character (such as a regular table of contents entry) will be of standard weight.

You can convert leader dots in bold, outline, or any unwanted style back to standard weight by first inserting a fixed space (Option + Spacebar on the Mac, Ctrl + Spacebar on the PC) between the last character of styled text and the first leader dot. Then select the fixed space and apply the Normal style (from the Type Style submenu). The leader dots will acquire the style of the fixed space and will change to standard weight (Figure 4-24). You can use this technique to change the size and the font of the leader dots as well.

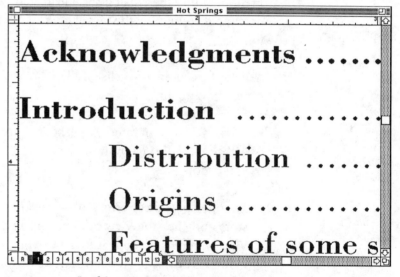

FIGURE 4-24 *In this 400-percent PageMaker view, you can see that the leader dots following the first contents entry are bold, like the entry text, and the leader dots following the third and fourth entries are standard weight, also like the corresponding contents entry. The second entry is in boldface; its leader dots are of standard weight because the entry is followed by a fixed space in the Normal type.*

Moving text between documents in PageMaker

To read or copy the text in another **PageMaker** document, you used to have to close the current document, open the other document, find the desired text, read or copy the text, close that document, and reopen the original document. But PageMaker's story editor now provides access to the text of a second PageMaker document without having to leave the current document. Here's how:

1. Choose the PLACE command from the File menu or press Command + D.

2. In the ensuing Open dialog box, locate and select the PageMaker document containing the text of interest. Then click the OK button.

3. A dialog box containing a list of all the stories in the selected document now opens:

   • To read the text of interest, select the appropriate story in the list and click the View button. Cancel the PLACE operation when you're done.

   • To copy a portion of a story to the current document, select the story and click the View button. Select what you want in the View window and copy it to the Clipboard by pressing Command + C in the Mac version or CTRL + INSERT in the Windows version. Cancel the PLACE operation, and, back in the current document, insert the copied text with the PASTE command.

   • To copy an entire story to the current document, place it in the usual way by selecting the story and clicking the OK button.

Effective and efficient style names

Since style names in **Ventura Publisher**, **PageMaker**, and other page layout and word processing programs are listed alphabetically, it's often helpful to choose names that keep related styles together. For instance, if you have a style for numbered lists called "num list," call the style for list headings "num list head," rather than "head num list."

Alternatively, you may find it useful to prefix some of your style names with a number. By numbering the most commonly used styles, they'll move to the top of the style list, where they are most conveniently selected. By numbering styles in the order in which they appear on the page—such as 1Head for a heading, 2Subhead for a subheading, 3ParFirst for the first paragraph after a subheading, 4ParStndrd for subsequent body paragraphs, and so on—the style names are easily found and can be applied in the order in which they appear in the style list (Figure 4-25). In addition, if the program you're using allows you to specify styles from the keyboard (as in **Microsoft Word** 4.0 for example), styles prefixed with a number can be applied by typing a single number rather than a long name.

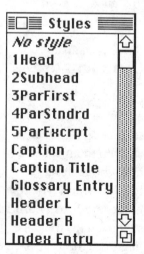

FIGURE 4-25 *Numbering the most commonly used styles, as in this Ventura style list, will cause them to move to the top of the styles list, where they're easily located and selected.*

Back-to-front copy editing is best

When you make final copy editing or proofing changes to a long document in your page makeup program—especially if you're checking it against hard copy, start at the last page and work back to the first. Because the text doesn't shift position before you get to it, the lines on screen will correspond to the lines of your hard copy and changes will be easier to locate.

Plain print-out for the editor

To print an unformatted version of an already-formatted **Ventura Publisher** document—for marking copy revisions, for example—simply load your document, and then load the Default style sheet. To do that, use the Load Different Style command under the File menu in the GEM or Windows editions, or the Switch Style command in the Mac's File menu. The chapter will reformat according to the Default style sheet, which contains only a Body Text tag, and will ignore other tags you've added. Change body text interline spacing to double spacing; then print. Obviously, you can adapt this tip to any page layout or word processing program that lets you easily switch style sheets.

Comment text

PageMaker documents that travel around your office network for approval can include everyone's comments right in the document (Figure 4-26). Create a style called "Comments" and a text block to contain them, located on the pasteboard, so they won't print. Everyone who reviews the document can make a copy of the comment's text block and type remarks in it, or in the Story Editor. If the comments apply to a particular page, you'll need to place the text block so it overlaps the page. If some comment text blocks do overlap the page, use the Type Specs command under the Type menu to set the text color of the Comments style to white (Paper) so the comments won't print.

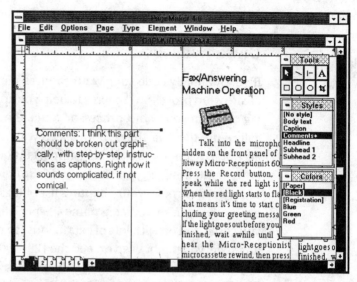

FIGURE 4-26 *A style for text with the color set to Paper lets you add textblocks containing comments and notes that appear on screen but not when printed.*

  Greek text in color

In page layout programs that let you specify colored text as part of a style or tag, you can assign a color to text of a particular style in order to identify it when it's greeked. That way you can quickly page through a document in reduced view to see if and where the style or tag is applied. Don't forget to change the text attributes of each style back to black before the final printing.

This tip works fine with **Ventura Publisher** (Mac, GEM, and Windows) and **QuarkXPress** since greeked text appears in the assigned color. **PageMaker** on the Mac and PC, though, always displays greeked text as gray. You can still use colors to check your styles in a reduced view in PageMaker for the Mac: Just set the *Greek text below* option in the Preferences dialog box to zero to avoid greeking altogether; expect slower page redraw as a result, however.

Unwanted tags

If you manually code your **Ventura Publisher** text, take the time to create word processing macros to help you apply Ventura paragraph tag codes in your word processor. Since the macros will automatically enter the tags, they'll both speed your text entry and maintain accuracy. Accuracy is especially important because every tag name entry containing a typo, such as *@Frist Paragraph =* , becomes a unique tag name in your chapter's list of tags. If you and other staff are applying numerous tag names, especially to a long document, you could end up with lots of extraneous tag names unconnected to any style; you might even exceed the 128-tag limit per style sheet. In any event, you'll have to remove them one by one via Ventura's Update Tag List dialog box (under the Paragraph menu).

  ## Easy style sheet label

Try using a **Ventura Publisher** tag name to display useful information about your chapter's style sheet. Simply add a tag that starts with 0, !, or some other low-sorting alphanumeric character, followed by a short description, like the date the style sheet was created, the document for which it was created, or whatever (Figure 4-27). The tag is used only as a heading for the list of tags, not for formatting text. Ventura lists tags alphabetically, so a low-sorting prefix will put the new tag at the top of the list. To keep its information up-to-date, you can edit this tag name each time you revise the style sheet.

  ## Breaking a line of text manually

To break a line manually, without starting a new paragraph, most page layout and word processing programs have what is called a soft return or an end-of-line mark. In many Macintosh and PC programs, including **Microsoft Word**, **PageMaker**, **Ventura Publisher** Macintosh Edition, and **MacWrite II**, soft returns are entered by pressing Shift + Return. In the PC Editions of Ventura Publisher, enter a soft return by pressing Ctrl + Enter.

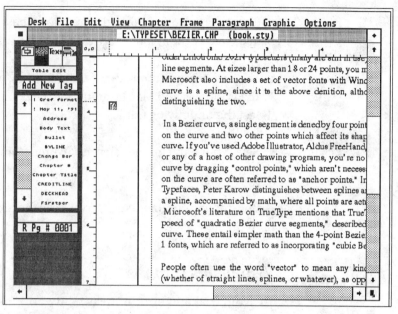

FIGURE 4-27 *Use a dummy tag, such as the one at the top of the tag list, to display useful info about your style sheet.*

Loading multiple text files

In **Ventura Publisher**, you can load a series of text files onto the underlying frame of a single chapter by inserting a new page at the end of the chapter after you've loaded the first text file. Use INSERT/RE-MOVE PAGE under the Chapter menu on the PC editions to add the page; use the INSERT PAGE AFTER command under the Chapter menu in the Mac Edition. Then go to the new, blank page and select the underlying frame. You'll then be able to load another text file from the assignment list in the GEM Edition, from the File List Window in the Windows Edition, or from the File List Window or ADD TEXT command on the Mac.

Proper text flow on a new page

If you've inserted a new page in the middle of a document in **Ventura Publisher's** using the INSERT NEW PAGE command on the PC, or the INSERT PAGE BEFORE or INSERT PAGE AFTER command on the Mac, you may have noticed that the text flows past the page, leaving it blank. Here's how to make the text flow onto this new page:

1. Select the Frame mode in the GEM Edition, or the pointer tool in the Windows and Mac Editions, and click on the new page to select the underlying frame.

2. Select the name of the relevant text file from the file assignment list.

As soon as you complete step 2, you'll see the text automatically flow onto the new page.

Visual aids for tabs

To avoid trial and error or heavy-duty arithmetic, try using **Page-Maker**'s vertical ruler guides as a visual aid for setting tabs and indents for tabbed text. Here's how:

1. Drag the vertical ruler guides onto your page to visually mark where you want the tabs or indents positioned.

2. In *Actual Size* page view, align the zero mark on the Indents/Tabs ruler (under the Type menu) with the left margin guide (Figure 4-28).

3. Use the vertical guides to help determine the placement of tabs along the Indents/Tabs ruler.

Ventura function key tags

In **Ventura Publisher**, you can assign tag names to function keys to save time while tagging text. But you should always leave the F10 Key assigned to Body Text (the default setting). That's because it's often impossible to use the paragraph tool to tag paragraphs that have unusual line break settings—they may overlap other paragraphs, or another paragraph may overlap them. You can, however, place your cursor in the problem paragraph, using the text tool, and press the

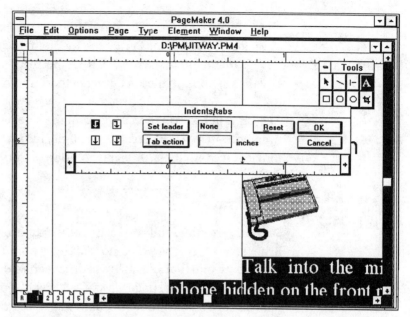

FIGURE 4-28 *Use vertical guides to help set tabs and indents on the In-dents/Tabs ruler.*

F10 Key to temporarily change its tag to Body Text, with normal line breaks. After editing, use the paragraph tool to tag them with their original tags.

  ## Vertical captions

If you want a vertical caption to run up the side of a frame in **Ventura Publisher**, try the following:

1. Use the Anchors & Captions dialog box under the Frame menu to select *Left* or *Right* instead of the usual *Below* or *Above* as the *Caption* option.

2. Type in the caption at the Label text box, and click OK.

3. Tag the resulting element with a new tag called "Rotated," or something equally descriptive.

4. Set the Vert. Alignment option for this tag to *Top* in the Alignment dialog box under the Paragraph menu (in the PC versions) or the Tags menu (on the Mac). Then set the Text Rotation option to *90* if the caption's on the left border of the frame, or *270* if on the right.

The caption text will then appear on the side of the frame, reading from bottom to top if you chose a 90-degree rotation, or top to bottom if you chose the 270-degree rotation option.

Sight-saver

Save time, trouble, and your eyes by including in your **Ventura Publisher** style sheet a "view" tag for editing use only. For this paragraph tag, select a font that's easy to read on screen whether you're working in reduced or normal page views—such as 14-point Helvetica. On a Mac, 12- or 14-point New York or Monaco would also be fine. If you assign the tags to function keys, you can switch a paragraph to your view tag, edit it, and then switch it back to its original tag, all without leaving text-editing mode.

This tip is by no means confined to Ventura Publisher, by the way; it works with any program with style-sheet functions. It's especially useful in programs such as **QuarkXPress**, which let you assign styles to function keys for quick paragraph tagging. You won't need this tip with **PageMaker** since you can set the default font for the Story Editor to any size and typeface you want.

New styles from old

To create a new style based on an existing style in **PageMaker**, first select the DEFINE STYLES command from the Type menu. In the Define Styles dialog box, select the existing style on which you want to base the new one. Then click on the New button. The Edit Style dialog box will now open with all of the selected style's attributes already entered. Make the necessary changes, give the new style a different name, then click on OK to save it.

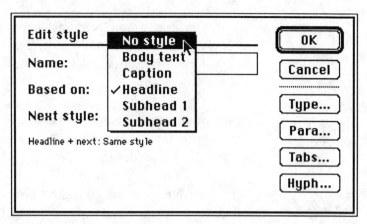

FIGURE 4-29 *Select* No Style *in the Based On pop-up menu to cut the link between a new style and the style from which it was derived.*

Keep in mind that styles created in this way are "linked" to the style on which they are based. If you subsequently alter the original style, that change will also affect any linked styles. To sever the link to the original style (so that a change to the original has no effect on the new style), select the *No Style* option in the Based On pop-up menu in the Edit Style dialog box (Figure 4-29).

If the style you want to base your work on is in another document, you must first copy that style to your current document. To do so, click on the Copy button in the Define Styles dialog box, and select the document containing the desired style. All styles from the other document will be copied; if both documents contain styles with the same name, the copied styles automatically replace the existing style in the current document. Be careful.

Generating multiple indexes

When you need to generate more than one index in **Ventura Publisher**—say, indexes of both names and subjects—use Ventura's Hidden Text feature and your word processor's search-and-replace function to prepare your text for indexing. Here's how:

1. Insert the Ventura index entry codes (<$IIndex entry>) in your text file using a word processing program; but, instead of the $I prefix,

use the Hidden Text prefix $!, followed by an identifying code of your choice, such as I1. Your entry might read <$!I1Name index entry> for name index entries; or <$!I2Subject index entry> for subject index entries.

2. When it's time to generate the indexes, first use your word processing program to search for all instances of $!I1 and change them to $I to "unhide" them.

3. After generating the first index in Ventura, return to your word processing program, and convert $I back to $!I1 in order to hide those entries again.

For the second index, "unhide" the entries coded as !I2 (in our example) as described above, and again generate the index in Ventura.

Graphics as bullets

Ventura Publisher's SPECIAL EFFECTS command under the Paragraph menu has an option that will automatically place a bullet character at the beginning of a paragraph, making it easy to create bulleted lists, for example. Trouble is, that feature only uses text characters or dingbats as bullets. You can, however, use a custom graphic as a repeating bullet using Ventura's anchored frame feature. Here's how:

1. Create a frame, load the graphic you want to use for the bullet in the frame, and select the ANCHORS & CAPTIONS command from the Frame menu.

2. Give the frame an anchor name in the Anchor text box.

3. Put your cursor at the start of the paragraph where you want the bullet to appear and, in the PC editions, select the INS SPECIAL ITEM command from the Edit menu; then select the *Insert Anchor* option. On the Mac, select the FRAME ANCHOR command from the Insert Special Item submenu of the Text menu.

4. Enter the name you previously entered as the frame anchor and select the *Relative, Automatically At Anchor* option. You can repeat the process, using INS SPECIAL ITEM, or FRAME ANCHOR as many times as you want; Ventura will automatically copy the frame and graphic wherever you specify.

Uniformly spaced bullets

In bulleted lists of fully justified text in **PageMaker,** the width of the space after the bullet often varies from item to item. There are two ways you can eliminate this variation and establish a uniform amount of space after each bullet. One is to enter a tab (rather than a space) after each bullet and set a tab marker at the appropriate distance on the ruler in the Indents/Tabs dialog box (Figure 4-30).

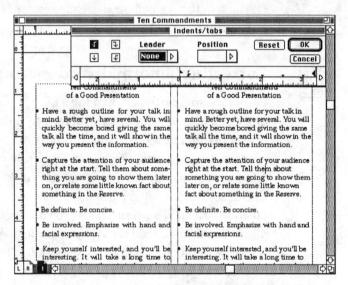

FIGURE 4-30 *In the column on the left, the size of the single space between bullet and text varies. On the right, there's a tab between bullet and text, and a tab marker on the ruler creates a uniform bullet-to-text distance.*

The other method is to enter one or more nonbreaking spaces—rather than standard spaces—after each bullet. Nonbreaking spaces don't vary in width, regardless of how the line justifies. There are four kinds of nonbreaking spaces in PageMaker:

- The em space, equal in width to the current font size (Shift + Command + M on the Mac, Ctrl + Shift + M on the PC).

- The en space, equal to half the current font size (Shift + Command + N on the Mac, Ctrl + Shift + N on the PC).

- The thin space, equal to one fourth the current font size (Shift + Command + T on the Mac, Ctrl + Shift + T on the PC).

- The fixed space, where size is dependent on the font (Option + Spacebar on the Mac, Ctrl + Spacebar on the PC).

Correcting abnormal word spacing

From time to time (when opening a file originally created on someone else's Mac, for example), you may find that the text in a Page-Maker document is displayed with unusual and/or unsightly word spacing. You can sometimes straighten out such abnormalities by raising and lowering the windowshade handles for the text blocks that need fixing. A better alternative, however, forces a global recomposition of all text and corrects word spacing throughout the document. To do this, hold down the Option Key while selecting the HYPHENATION command. Don't select a text block beforehand, and be prepared to wait while PageMaker puts all its ducks in a row. When the Hyphenation dialog box finally appears, simply click either the OK or Cancel button to return to a document which looks the way it should.

Working with graphics

  ## Tracking picture placement

If your publications contain a great many stripped in graphics, you may have trouble keeping them all organized. To keep order among them as they travel from your office to the printshop, label the photo layout boxes on the pages with letters of the alphabet, using a text block created for that purpose. Then label the photos with the page and box letter: 1/A, 4/C, and so forth. With these precautions, verifying photo placement is easy.

 ## Creating "combs" for fill-in forms

No doubt you've had to deal with those irritating "combs" on forms and registration cards, those horizontal rules marked with evenly spaced vertical divisions in which you have to enter your name or address or credit card number, one letter or number per division. They look like they might require some rather precise graphics work. But, should you want to inflict a "comb" on others, you can make one easily in **QuarkXPress** or **PageMaker** without resorting to a single graphics tool.

Here's how to create a comb in XPress:

1. Draw a text box and type a sequence of vertical lines using a sans serif (Helvetica, for example) uppercase I or the vertical line character (Shift + \), each one separated by a space character. If n is the number of entry spaces you want in the comb, enter $n + 1$ uppercase I's. End the line with a Return.

2. Select the line of I's.

3. If necessary, adjust the height of the I's by selecting a larger or smaller point-size.

4. Choose the RULES command from the Style menu. Specify Rule Below in the Rules dialog box; select the solid rule and the *Text* option from the Length pop-up menu.

5. If necessary, specify a negative baseline shift of two or three points so that the bottoms of the I's touch the rule beneath.

6. Select the *Justified* option from the Alignment submenu (under the Style menu).

7. Choose the H&Js command from the Edit menu. In the H&Js dialog box, create a new H&J (hyphenation and justification) specification containing a large Flush Zone (2 to 6 inches, depending on the length of the comb). Save it under an appropriate name, such as "Comb." (The large Flush Zone force-justifies the line across the length of the text box.)

8. Apply the new H&J specification to the still-selected line by choosing the FORMATS command from the Style menu and selecting the *Comb* option you created from the H&J pop-up menu.

Once the comb is completed, move it into position following the text label in the form. You can now enlarge or reduce the text box to fit the space available; the spaces between the I's in your comb will adjust automatically and evenly (Figure 4-31).

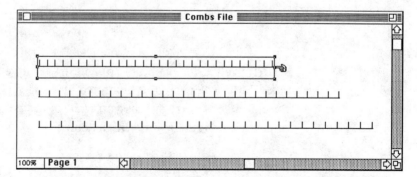

FIGURE 4-31 *These form fill-in guides or "combs," created in XPress, are just a series of Helvetica upper-case I's with a Paragraph Rule below.*

To create a comb in **PageMaker**, follow these steps:

1. With the text tool, type a sequence of vertical lines using either a sans serif uppercase I or the vertical line character (Shift + \), each one separated by a space character. If *n* is the number of entry spaces you want in the comb, enter *n + 1* uppercase I's.

2. Select the sequence you just entered.

3. If necessary, adjust the height of the verticals by selecting a larger or smaller point size.

4. Choose the PARAGRAPH command from the Type menu. In the Paragraph Specifications dialog box, click the Rules button. In the Paragraph Rules dialog box, turn on the *Rule below Paragraph* and *Width of Text* options.

5. If the bottoms of the verticals don't touch the rule beneath, choose the TYPE SPECS command and select the *Subscript* option from the Position pop-up menu in the Type Specifications dialog box. If the vertical bottoms still don't touch, lower the subscript position in the Type Options dialog box (which is opened via the Options button in the Type Specifications dialog box). Or, if you're using the vertical line character, select a different font with a longer vertical line.

6. Select the *Force Justify* option from the Alignment submenu (under the Type menu).

Move the comb into position after the text label in the form; enlarge or reduce the text block to fit the space available.

Using color correctly

If we had to name the one thing that most frequently trips up desktop publishers, we'd have to say it's color. And if pressed to name the best single guide to using color correctly (or at least intelligently), we'd have to say *Color for the Electronic Age* by Jan V. White. This book won't tell you how to make a complex color separation in Illustrator, but it does explain when and why you should use color (not, it should be noted, simply as decoration) and how to use it effectively—in charts and graphs, in type, in graphics, in page designs, and in presentations. *Color for the Electronic Age* is written in a witty and highly readable style, and it's chock-full of colorful illustrations. If you're one of those desktop publishers who occasionally uses color without really understanding why, this book is essential reading.

Ventura spot-color graphics

Ventura Publisher won't let you directly assign spot colors to graphics. For that reason, graphics always print out on the spot color separation overlay that's labeled as black, along with any black text. But with a little deft jockying of Ventura's spot color feature, you can cause the graphics to print out as a spot color overlay for any color you choose.

Suppose, for example, you are creating a newsletter using three spot colors: red for subheads, blue for icons (small, imported clip-art symbols), and black for body text. Your goal is to print the newsletter as three separate overlays. To do that, set the color for your subheads to red and the color for all your other text tags to an arbitrary color, say green. Assuming that there are no other graphics in your newsletter, this means that the clip-art icons will be the only element left in black.

Now print—with the *Spot Color Overlays* and *Crop Marks* options turned on in the Print dialog box under the File menu. The result will be three separate overlays for each page, one for the subheads, one for the icons, and one for regular text. The subhead overlay pages will be labeled correctly as red. The colored icon and regular (black) text overlays will be labeled incorrectly as black and green, respectively. Now all you have to do is cross out the incorrect labels and write in the correct ones before taking your pages to the printer.

Centering graphics quickly

Here's a quick and easy way to automatically center a graphic horizontally within a column in **PageMaker**:

1. Place your graphic at the left edge of the column in which you want the graphic centered (top, Figure 4-32).

2. Drag the graphic's lower right corner handle to stretch it across to the right-hand column guide (center, Figure 4-32).

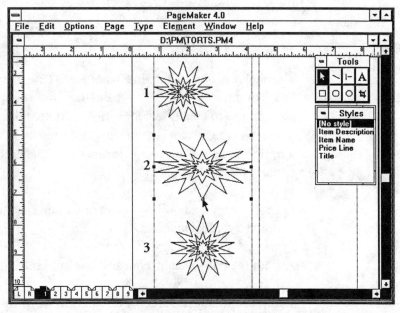

FIGURE 4-32 *You can center a graphic by stretching it to fill the column (top) and then clicking its bottom center handle while holding down the Shift Key (bottom).*

3. Place the pointer on the bottom center handle of the graphic, hold down the Shift Key, press the mouse button for a second or two, and then release it.

When you release the mouse button, the graphic will bounce back to its original height-to-width ratio (bottom, in Figure 4-32) and will be centered horizontally in the column (and vertically between where you clicked with the pointer and the point to which you dragged the lower right handle). To readjust the vertical position without messing up the horizontal placement, press Shift as you drag the image up or down.

Picking up lines under guidelines

If you point to and click on a rule that sits on a guideline in **Page-Maker**, you invariably pick up the guideline instead of the rule. To select the rule instead of the guideline, press the Command Key on the Mac or the Control Key in Windows when you click on the rule.

Finer dotted line

The choice of dotted lines in **PageMaker**'s Line dialog box under the Element menu is pretty limited. But there are a couple of techniques you can use to create a wider variety of dotted lines. The first technique uses the box tool to draw finely dotted lines. It's only effective for printing on 300 or 400 dpi printers, not imagesetters. Here's what to do:

1. Draw a very shallow box, about one point high (or wide, if you're doing a vertical line).

2. With the box selected, choose *None* from the Line dialog box.

3. Choose different screen percentages from the Fill dialog box under the Element menu, thus varying the density of the dotted line that results.

On low-resolution printers, the thin box will appear as a dotted line.

Another technique involves overlaying reversed text on a horizontal rule to make the rule look dashed:

1. Draw a horizontal rule of the weight and length you need.

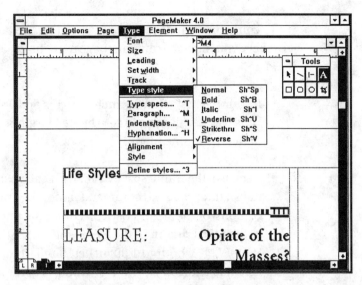

FIGURE 4-33 *Place a series of reversed bar characters over a rule in Page-Maker to create custom dashed rules.*

2. Create a text block the length of your rule.

3. Choose a suitable Zapf Dingbats character, such as ▮ (lowercase y) or ▮ (lowercase z), and type it into your text block, spacing the characters as needed for the effect you want.

4. Once the text block is set, position it over the rule, select the text, and set to Reverse (from the Style selections under the Type menu).

When the type turns white, the underlying rule appears dashed (Figure 4-33).

  ## Labeling spot-color overlays

When printing spot-color overlays in **Ventura Publisher**, you need to leave space outside the underlying frame where Ventura can print crop marks and the name of each overlay's color. That means that on 8½ by 11-inch paper, the underlying frame can't extend to the edge of the page, otherwise there won't be room for the crop marks and overlay name.

To compensate for the space required for the crop marks and color labels, you must narrow your page margins accordingly. Here's what to do:

1. If your page is to have 1-inch margins on all sides, set the underlying frame's margins to zero in the Margin & Columns dialog box under the Frame menu.

2. Decrease the frame size by 1 inch on each side. To do that, select the SIZING & SCALING command under the Frame menu in the PC editions, or the SIZE & POSITION command under the Frame menu in the Mac Edition. In the GEM edition, set the Upper Left X and Upper Left Y both to 1.00 inches. Similarly, enter 1.00 inches for Left Side and Top Side in the Windows Edition, or Top and Left in the Mac Edition.

3. Set the Frame Width to 6.50 inches and the Frame Height to 9.00 inches.

The smaller frame compensates for the lack of margins, and Ventura now has room to print the spot color name at the edge of each page, plus automatic registration and crop marks if you request them.

· ·

Tinting a table column

You can easily tint an entire column in a **Ventura Publisher** table, even one that extends across several pages. You need only select a starting point. When you select a tint, Ventura will automatically extend the tint to the bottom of the column. Here's what to do:

1. Select the table tool.

2. Click on the top horizontal line of whichever cell will be the upper limit of the column area you want to tint.

3. Choose the *Set Tint* option from the Table menu in the Windows Edition, the Table Edit assignment box in the GEM Edition, or via

the CELL BACKGROUND command from the Tables menu in the Macintosh Edition.

4. Make your choice of tint or shade of gray, and press Enter.

The tint will then flow from the cell border you selected to the bottom of the table, regardless of the length of the column.

Sharper on-screen TIFF images in XPress

In **QuarkXPress**, the resolution of the on-screen version of a TIFF or RIFF file is normally 36 dpi. You can increase that to a crisper, more detailed 72 dpi (as illustrated in Figure 4-34) by pressing the Option Key when you click the Open button in the Get Picture dialog box. Note, however, that increasing the on-screen resolution increases both the file size and the RAM needed to display it.

FIGURE 4-34 *The display resolution of a TIFF file in XPress is 36 dpi (left), but you can increase it to 72 dpi (right) for a more detailed image.*

Hiding Ventura table rules

If you select one of the outside edges of a **Ventura Publisher** table and try to hide the line, you won't succeed. To get rid of the line, you'll have to remove all four edges of the table and then restore only three of them. Here's what to do:

1. Using the table tool, click on any of the border rules at the edge of the table. A thick gray line will appear along the outer edge of the table cell you clicked to indicate that it's selected.

2. In the GEM Edition, select Edit Table Settings from the Edit menu; then turn of the *Box Around* option . In the Windows Edition, select Change Settings from the Table menu; then, under the Rules section of the Insert/Edit Table dialog box, change the B*ox Around* option to *NONE* or *Z_HIDDEN*. In the Mac Edition, select the EDIT TABLE command under the Tables menu and turn off the *Box Around* option. This will delete all four outer edges of the table.

3. Now select one of the table edges that you want to reappear. To select a table edge, simply drag the table tool along the length of that edge.

4. In the GEM Edition, with the table edge selected as above, click on Z_SINGLE or Z_DOUBLE in the Assignment List on the left side of the screen. In the Windows Edition, select the CUSTOM RULES command under the Table menu, and then select the *Z_SINGLE*, *Z_THICK*, or *Z_DOUBLE* option from the pop-up menu. On the Mac, select either the *Z_SINGLE* or *Z_DOUBLE* option from the Custom Rules submenu under the Tables menu.

Repeat steps 3 and 4 for each edge of the table which you want to reappear. The edge you don't recall with steps 3 and 4 will remain hidden.

· ·

 ## Rotated graphics in PageMaker

Since you can't rotate a graphic once it's been placed in **PageMaker**, you must rotate it before placing it in PageMaker. But what if the image is a scan, for example, and no image-editing software is available? If you have a copy of **FreeHand**, you're in luck:

1. Place your graphic in the middle of a blank PageMaker page. To make things easier later on, you may want to reduce the page size so that the graphic fits just inside.

2. Set the image-control options for the lightness and contrast you want, plus the screen angle and screen frequency if you're using a gray-scale image.

3. Print the page to disk as an EPS file using the *PostScript* option in the Print dialog box.

4. Launch FreeHand and place the newly created EPS file in a new document with FreeHand's PLACE command. Your graphic will appear with object handles where the corners of the PageMaker page had once been.

5. Select the image and use Freehand's Rotate tool to tilt it. (You can also use other tools to flop or skew the image.)

6. Use FreeHand's EXPORT command to create a new EPS file containing the altered image.

7. Back in PageMaker, complete the job by placing the new EPS file.

The graphic will now appear on the page at the angle of rotation specified in FreeHand.

Bisecting boxes

In **PageMaker** for Windows or Macintosh, you can use the handles in the middle of the sides of a selected box as a guide for placing a horizontal or vertical line precisely through the middle of the box.

1. Select the box and drag a vertical or horizontal guide so that it is aligned with the center handles.

2. Making sure you've turned on SNAP TO GUIDES under the Option menu, draw the line on top of the guide (Figure 4-35).

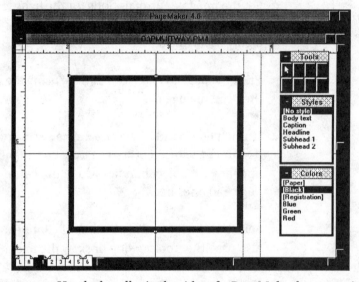

FIGURE 4-35 *Use the handles in the sides of a PageMaker box to position ruler guides that bisect the box.*

Scanning technical illustrations

When you want to scan small technical illustrations or other complex, fine-line art for use in **QuarkXPress**, scan the images at 800 dpi as black-and-white line art. Save the document as a TIFF file. When you import it into XPress, hold down the Shift and Command keys to bring the file in as true black and white with no halftone screen.

The screen preview will look a little choppy, but the printed image will look great.

Accurately positioning graphics in Ventura

In **Ventura Publisher**, accurately positioning a graphic is much easier if you attach it to a small frame (about 2 inches square). Using the SIZING & SCALING command (PC versions) or the SIZE & POSITION command (Mac version) under the Frame menu, you can move the frame (and the graphic with it) in increments as small as one one-hundredth of a point. The graphic doesn't need to be inside the frame as long as the frame is selected when you draw it. In Figure 4-36, for example, the "Wonder Box" rectangle is automatically repositioned when the selected frame to which it is linked is repositioned.

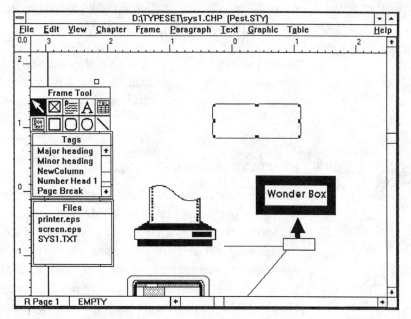

FIGURE 4-36 *You can precisely position the "Wonder Box" (above) in Ventura by moving its attached frame in tiny increments with the Sizing & Scaling dialog box.*

Deleting unnecessary graphic duplicates

With **Ventura Publisher** for the PC, you can save disk space by re-moving large TIFF or PCX image files from your disk once you've finished your page layout. Ventura converts image files to GEM image format (with an .IMG extension), so you can live without the original image file once the conversion has taken place.

Once you've loaded, cropped, and scaled the original image in Ventura, simply select its frame and load its IMG counterpart to replace the original file. For example, load PICTURE.IMG into the frame for PICTURE.TIF. The IMG file replaces the TIFF or PCX file on the page while retaining the correct sizing and scaling. You can then archive the original TIFF or PCX files. (You'll need them to make any further changes, though.)

When you reopen the chapter file after archiving the PCX or TIFF files, ignore messages indicating that those image files can't be located. After you save the chapter again, these messages won't reappear.

Preserve your text wrap

Graphics, especially color scans, slow down the screen redraw as you work on other layout tasks unrelated to the image. Fortunately, if you plan to paste or strip images into your page layout document, you don't need to keep position-only scans in the document once you've determined their placement and text wrap. The trick is to preserve the image's text-wrap borders even though the image itself is deleted. Here's a technique for **PageMaker** that lets you do just that:

1. Keep a small, low-resolution TIFF file on hand (preferably one that doesn't contain a visible image) for use as a space-filling "blank."

2. Once you've finished setting TEXT WRAP borders around a for-position-only scan (Figure 4-37), select the image and substitute the

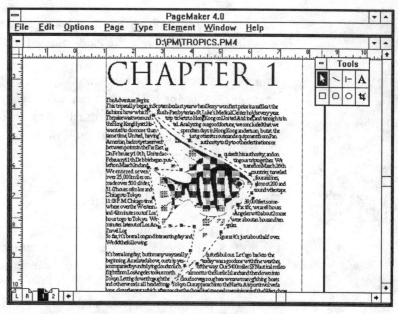

FIGURE 4-37 *Use a scanned image to create a text-wrap with PageMaker's Text Wrap command.*

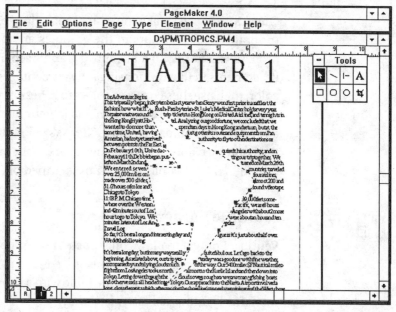

FIGURE 4-38 *Remove the for-position-only scanned images—but still preserve your PageMaker text-wrap—by substituing a small blank TIFF file using the* Replace entire graphic *option.*

blank, low-resolution TIFF file, making sure to click the *Replace entire graphic* option in the Place dialog box.

Your original scan will be replaced with the blank one (Figure 4-38 on page 271), saving both memory and screen redraw time, but the irregular wrap border you laboriously worked out will remain unaltered. Had you simply deleted the image, your text wrap-border would have disappeared along with it.

Permanent drawing tools

When using **Ventura Publisher**'s graphics drawing tools, hold down the Shift Key in the PC editions, or the Command Key in the Mac Edition, to prevent Ventura from automatically selecting the pointer after an object is drawn. This way, you can create any number of objects without having to reselect the same tool for each new object.

Using color Illustrator graphics in XPress

QuarkXPress can't make spot color separations of imported **Illustrator** graphics if the colors in the graphics are made up of different process-color tints. To make sure a graphic separates properly, draw its elements in Illustrator using only percentages of a single process color; then use those process colors in XPress as your spot colors. Or use Pantone colors for the elements in your Illustrator graphic, and add the same Pantone colors to XPress's color palette. When adding the Pantone colors in XPress, make sure that the *Process Separation* option in the Edit Color dialog box is turned off.

Multiple paragraphs in a cell

Ventura Publisher allows only one paragraph per table cell, which is often not enough for a sophisticated layout. To get around this limitation, you can augment the table with a superimposed frame of more freely formatted text. Here's how:

1. Create the table in one frame and overlay it with another frame containing text (Figure 4-39).

Underlying table

Rates for Long-Distance Service		

Call	Voicequick	Talknet
S.F.-N.Y. Weekday, 2 p.m. 8 minutes	$6.80	$7.26
Chicago-Dallas Weekday, 7 p.m. 8 minutes	$12.76	$14.14
Atlanta-Denver Weekday, 9 a.m. 5 minutes	$18.45	$21.84

Final appearance

Rates for Long-Distance Service		
Call	Voicequick	Talknet
S.F.-N.Y. Weekday, 2 p.m. 8 minutes	$6.80	$7.26
Chicago-Dallas Weekday, 7 p.m. 8 minutes	$12.76	$14.14
Atlanta-Denver Weekday, 9 a.m. 5 minutes	$18.45	$21.84

Overlaid text

FIGURE 4-39 *The cities and the calling times in this figure are in separate paragraphs in a text frame overlaying the table, but it all appears as a single table.*

2. In the text frame, set up the columns to match the cell widths in the table. Use blank lines and tabbed column tags to control the spacing in the text frame.

3. In the table frame, Ventura Publisher won't let you set the length or depth of each row in a table directly, but here are a couple of workarounds:

- Use Ctrl + Enter on the PC, or Command + Return on the Mac, instead of Enter at the ends of lines in the table. That way, you can control the cell lengths by breaking lines without creating new paragraphs.

- You can vertically expand a row by creating a new paragraph tag for the row's cells and specifying a larger Below setting in the Spacing dialog box under the Paragraph menu.

This technique also lets you mix text in the table with text and graphics in the overlaying frames.

Window view shortcuts

Changing the view for all pages

To change the page view (*Actual Size, Fit in Window*, etc.) for all pages at once in a **PageMaker** for the Mac document, press the Option Key while selecting the desired view from the Page menu. Be sure to select the desired view command from the menu; adding Option to a keyboard command doesn't work.

Selecting both page and view

When changing from one page to another in **PageMaker**, you don't have to wait for PageMaker to complete drawing the new page before selecting the view you want. In fact, you can save a lot of time by typing the keyboard shortcut for the desired page view immediately after clicking on the icon for the page you wish to view. PageMaker will then switch to the new page and turn on the appropriate page view in one relatively quick maneuver.

Super close-ups in XPress

Although the View menu in **QuarkXPress** offers a maximum magnification of only 200 percent, you can actually display XPress documents at up to 400-percent magnification. One way to display a super close-up is to select the Zoom tool and keep clicking on the document until you reach the desired magnification. The amount of magnification increases in 25-percent increments with each click. (It decreases in 25-percent increments if you press the Option Key when you click.) The current magnification is displayed in the View Percent field in the lower left corner of the window (Figure 4-40).

If you have a specific magnification in mind, there's a quicker way to zoom (in or out). Simply double-click in the View Percent field and enter the desired magnification from the keyboard (type a number

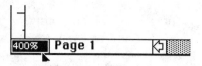

FIGURE 4-40 *XPress's View Percent field is in the lower left corner of the document window.*

between 25 and 400; you don't need to type the percent sign). Press Return and the view changes instantly to the desired magnification.

Easy two-sider

When you're working on a double-sided, single-page document—such as a flier or brochure—you can save time by inserting a blank first page in your page layout document and working on pages 2 and 3 in a facing-pages view. This way, you can see both sides of your page on a single screen and not waste time switching between pages. Remember to print only pages 2 and 3 or to delete the blank first page when the document's finished.

Alternatively, instead of inserting a blank first page, specify the starting page as page two if your page layout program allows. That way you won't have to remember to omit the blank page when printing.

Fast fit-in-window views

To turn directly to the *Fit in Window* view of any page in **PageMaker**, hold down the Shift Key when you click on the page icon for the desired page. This also works as a shortcut for the page you're currently working on: Press Shift and click on the current page's highlighted icon to change from any view to the *Fit in Window* view.

Quick scrolling in Ventura

In **Ventura Publisher,** it's possible to see the part of your page that extends beyond your monitor without using the scroll bars. To shift the screen view, position the pointer at the edge of the visible portion of the page as close as possible to the area you're trying to see. Then press Ctrl + N (assuming you're in the *Normal View*) or Ctrl + E (if you're in the *Enlarged View*). Ventura quickly redraws the screen with the screen center shifted slightly toward the pointer location. Press Ctrl + N repeatedly to scroll further.

To move the view a long way in one jump, press Ctrl + R to switch momentarily to Reduced View; then move the pointer to another part of the page, and press Ctrl + N. The screen will be redrawn in *Normal View* and centered over the new cursor location.

Zooming in on a specific location

PageMaker has several handy shortcuts for zooming in on a specific part of the page. In any reduced-size view on the Mac, for example, hold down both the Command and Option keys and click on the part of the page you want to see; in Windows, simply click with the right-hand mouse button. PageMaker changes the view to *Actual Size* and centers the screen around the clicked-on area. If you hold down the Command, Option, and Shift keys and click, on the Mac, or Shift + click with the right-hand mouse button in Windows, Pagemaker zooms in to a 200-percent view.

In *Actual Size* view, however, something quite different happens if you Command + Option + click on the Mac or click with the right-hand mouse button in Windows. Instead of centering on the clicked on location in *Actual Size* view, PageMaker zooms out to *Fit in Window* view. Thus, Command + Option + click on the Mac and clicking with the right-hand mouse button in Windows provide a convenient way to move around in a two-page spread on a small screen:

• To change to *Fit in Window* view and to see where you want to move to, press Command + Option + click on the Mac or click with the right-hand mouse button in Windows anywhere in *Actual Size* view.

• To change to *Actual Size* view and move to the clicked-on location, press Command + Option + click on the Mac or click with the right-hand mouse button in Windows on a specific location in *Fit in Window* view.

- To change to *Fit in Window* view and to see where you want to move to, press Command + Option + click on the Mac or click with the right-hand mouse button on a specific location in *Actual Size* view.

Other shortcuts

Text selection shortcuts

Here are some quick shortcuts for selecting text in **QuarkXPress**:

- Double-click to select the word the insertion point is in.

- Click quickly three times to select the line the insertion point is in.

- Click quickly four times to select the paragraph the insertion point is in.

- Click quickly five times to select the entire story.

Easy Ventura indexing

Although you can create index entries in **Ventura Publisher** itself, it's often easier to do so in your word processor beforehand. To do so, use your word processor's search and replace function to create index entries in your text. For instance, if you're indexing the word computers, search for the word *computers* and replace it with *<$Icomputers>*. If your word processor lets you confirm each change, use this option to apply the index entry only to meaningful references.

Easy flush-left-flush-right text

To easily combine flush-left and flush-right text on the same line in **PageMaker**, place a tab between the two bits of text. Highlight the whole line (or lines) and change its ALIGNMENT (under the Type menu) to *Align right* (Figure 4-41). The type on either side of the tab will rest flush against opposite margins.

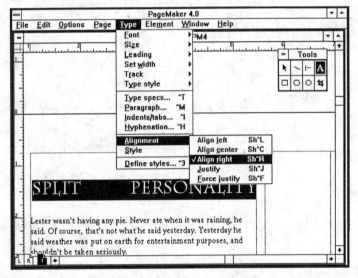

FIGURE 4-41 *For a flush left and right line in PageMaker, place a tab midway in the line; then format the line as* Align right.

  More shades of gray

In **PageMaker**, you can get a wider variety of gray screens than offered in the Element Fill submenu by using the DEFINE COLORS command (you'll find it in the Element menu). In the Define Colors dialog box, click on the New button. In the Edit Color dialog box that appears, select CMYK as the color model, set the cyan, yellow, and magenta values to zero, and set the black value to the percentage gray screen you want (Figure 4-42). Give the new color a descriptive name, like "25% Gray," which is how it will be listed. On the Mac, use the Color Palette to apply your new screen. To select the screen in PC PageMaker, choose it from the Define Colors menu.

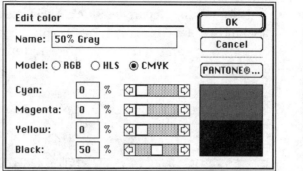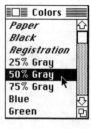

FIGURE 4-42 *Use the CMYK color model in PageMaker's Edit Color dialog box (left) to define a custom-gray screen. Apply the screen by selecting it in the Color Palette (right).*

Clearing a cluttered page

To get a clutter of **PageMaker** ruler guides off the page quickly once they've served their purpose, simply select COPY MASTER GUIDES from the Page menu. The unneeded guides will disappear and be replaced by the ones on your master pages. If there are no ruler guides on your master pages, the page will be cleared of ruler guides entirely.

Closing chained dialog boxes

To close the current dialog box and all the dialog boxes leading to it in **PageMaker**, press the Option Key on the Mac or the Alt Key on the PC as you click an OK or Cancel button.

Hot-linked tables

PageMaker for Windows comes with an import filter that lets you place a table created with Aldus's Table Editor directly on the page using the PLACE command. If the table was saved in the Table Editor's native .TBL format, PageMaker will automatically create a hot link between the original table and the copy in your publication. From this point on, hold down the Ctrl Key and double-click on the table in your layout to launch the Table Editor with the table loaded and ready for editing (Figure 4-43). After you make changes, save the table and exit the Table Editor; PageMaker automatically updates the table in your layout to reflect the changes you've made.

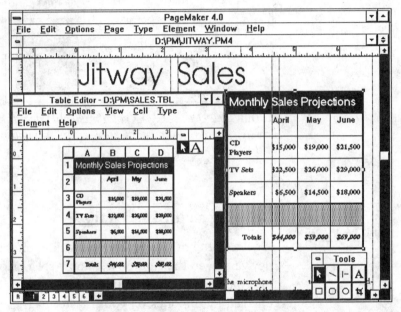

FIGURE 4-43 *Double-click an Aldus Table Editor table in a PageMaker document, and Table Editor will pop up with the original table loaded and ready to edit.*

  ## Multiple tagging

To select multiple paragraphs for tagging in **Ventura Publisher**, hold down the Shift Key and click on paragraphs one at a time with the paragraph tool in the PC version or with the tag tool on the Mac.

 ## PageMaker shortcuts in a desk accessory

You'll find a wide diversity of **PageMaker** for the Mac shortcuts, tips, and techniques summarized in **PM4 Shortcuts**, a well designed and helpful desk accessory by Mark Teranishi and Paul Sorrick. It's divided into ten panels, each covering a separate topic, including editing shortcuts, key combinations for special characters used in text or the Find and Change dialog boxes (Figure 4-44), page view and window shortcuts, and power user tips. PM4 Shortcuts is shareware and is available from many Macintosh shareware libraries.

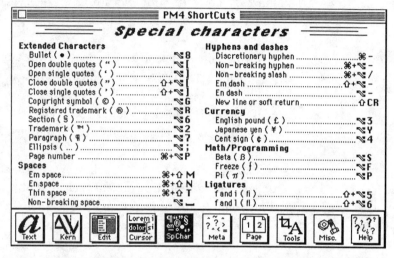

FIGURE 4-44 *Each of PM4 Shortcuts' 10 panels of information, like the one shown here for special characters, is displayed by clicking on the appropriate icon at the bottom of the window.*

  ## Ready-made Ventura headers

Ventura Publisher style sheets don't save headers and footers. But here's a way you can avoid having to format headers and footers for each chapter when you're creating multichapter documents in Ventura Publisher. Simply create a blank chapter containing the headers and footers you'll use throughout the publication. Use the blank document as a template to begin new chapters, and remember to save each new chapter under a new name.

Shift + click to select multiple objects

Normally, when you click on an object in a Macintosh graphics or page layout program, that object is selected and all previously selected objects are deselected. Pressing the Shift Key as you click, however, converts your click into a toggle switch that's useful when you want to select a group of objects:

- If you Shift + click on an unselected object, that object is selected and all previously selected objects remain selected.

- If you Shift + click on an already selected object, that object is deselected and all previously selected objects remain selected.

Note that you can use Shift + click by itself to select any number of objects and deselect mistakenly selected objects. You can also use Shift + click to add objects to or subtract them from a group of objects selected by any other selection technique.

Version restoration in PageMaker

In **PageMaker** (for both the PC and the Mac), the REVERT command, found under the File menu, normally restores the last version of the file saved using the SAVE or SAVE As commands. A modified form of the REVERT command, however, allows you to backtrack to the last mini-saved version of your document, rather than to the last saved version. Unlike a regular save, a mini-save occurs each time you go to another page or use the PRINT command. To go back to the last mini-save, hold down the Shift Key when selecting the REVERT command, and you'll be greeted with a "Revert to last mini-save?" message (Figure 4-45) instead of the usual "Revert to last saved version?" message. Reply in the affirmative to restore the last mini-saved version of the document.

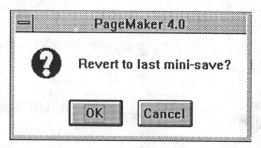

FIGURE 4-45 *PageMaker's mini-save can restore a previous version of your document, even if you forgot to save it.*

  ## Ventura tools from the keyboard

If you have a small display and want to devote all of it to your current document, or if you simply want to eliminate unnecessary clutter in **Ventura Publisher**, you can close the Tool box and select many of its tools with keyboard shortcuts. In fact, whether the Tool box is open or closed, and no matter which tool is currently selected, these key commands allow you to select tools from the keyboard:

Select tool	By pressing (Macintosh Edition)	By pressing (GEM and Windows Editions)
Pointer	Option + Command+ U	Ctrl + U
Tag	Option + Command + I	Ctrl + I
Text	Option + Command + O	Ctrl + O
Table	Option + Command + P	Ctrl + P

If the pointer is currently selected, there's one other shortcut you can use to select a tool from the Tool Box:

Select tool	By pressing (Macintosh Edition)	By pressing (GEM and Windows Editions)
Frame tool	Ctrl + 2	Ctrl + 2

 ## A Revert command for dialog boxes

In **QuarkXPress**, pressing Command + Z will return a dialog box to the settings it had when you first opened it. If you botch a complex dialog box setting, this keyboard shortcut is a lot quicker and easier than reentering everything or canceling and reopening the dialog box.

Scrolling on a standard Apple keyboard

The **QuarkXPress** manuals describe keyboard scrolling for the extended keyboard only (using the Home, End, Page Up, and Page Down keys). What the manual doesn't tell you is that six additional scrolling shortcuts are available in QuarkXPress on both the standard and extended keyboards:

Key combination	Scrolls
Ctrl + K	One screen straight up
Ctrl + L	One screen straight down
Ctrl + A	To the top of the document
Ctrl + D	To the end of the document
Ctrl + Option + K	To the top of the previous page
Ctrl + Option + L	To the top of the next page

Changing a graphic wrap

When changing the text-wrap boundary around an irregularly shaped graphic in **PageMaker**, press and hold the Spacebar while you make your adjustments. This prevents the text from rewrapping each time you change the boundary (Figure 4-46) and saves you from having to wait for each rewrap. When you're finished with your adjustments, release the Spacebar and the text rewraps around the new graphic boundary in one fell swoop.

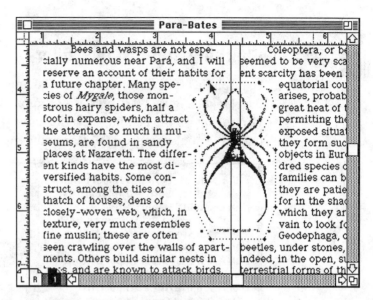

FIGURE 4-46 *The Spacebar is depressed while the text-wrap boundary of this PageMaker graphic is adjusted.*

PageMaker tools from the keyboard

If you have an extended keyboard, you can use the following keyboard shortcuts to select tools in **PageMaker** for the Mac:

Key combination	Selects tool
Command + Spacebar	Pointer
Shift + F1	Pointer
Shift + F2	Diagonal line
Shift + F3	Perpendicular line
Shift + F4	Text
Shift + F5	Square-corner rectangle
Shift + F6	Round-corner rectangle
Shift + F7	Circle/ellipse
Shift + F8	Cropping

If you don't have an extended keyboard, you can use a macro utility such as **Quickeys 2** or **Tempo II Plus** to assign easy-to-remember key combinations to clicks on each of the tools in the toolbox window.

Checking your installed filters

To display a list of all currently installed import and export filters in **PageMaker** (Figure 4-47), press the Command Key on the Mac or the Control Key on the PC and select the ABOUT PAGEMAKER command under the Apple menu on the Mac or the Help menu on the PC.

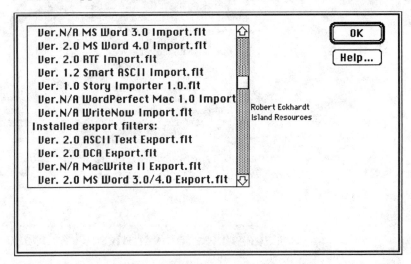

FIGURE 4-47 *Press Command and select About PageMaker on a Macintosh to see a list of installed filters.*

 ## Self-loading Ventura chapter

If you often work with the same **Ventura Publisher** GEM Edition chapter file, you can create a batch file that simultaneously loads both Ventura and your chapter. To do so, copy and rename your VP.BAT or VPPROF.BAT file. You can give the file any name you want so long as it ends with .BAT. Preferably, the name should indicate which document the batch file automatically opens in Ventura.

Open the copy in a text editor and enter immediately after the term *VP* or *VPPROF* the complete path and filename of the chapter you want to load automatically. Be careful to avoid changing anything else in your file, or Ventura may not work. The batch file should look something like the following when you're done (The /S= tells Ventura what screen driver to use; the /M= tells it which mouse to use.):

```
ECHO OFF
D:
CD \VENTURA
DRVRMRGR VPPROF yourfile.chp/S=SD_GENS5.VGA/M=01
```

Back at the DOS prompt, when you want to load Ventura enter the name of the custom Ventura batch file and press Return. Ventura will load and then automatically load your chapter.

  ## Pasteboard shortcuts

To move two or more elements from page to page in **PageMaker**, don't cut and paste one item at a time; use the pasteboard that surrounds the document instead. Simply drag one or more items onto the pasteboard, click on the page to which you want to move the elements, and drag the items onto that page. If you can't remember where something is stored on the pasteboard, display the entire pasteboard (Figure 4-48) by pressing the Shift Key while you select the FIT IN WINDOW command.

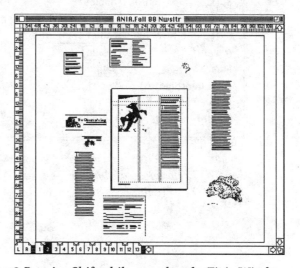

FIGURE 4-48 *Pressing Shift while you select the Fit in Window command will show you PageMaker's entire pasteboard.*

· ·

Grab bag

· ·

 ## Approximate points versus real points

In most Mac applications, an inch is equal to 72 points. This is technically incorrect since the actual measurement is closer to 72.27 points per inch. As a result, most Macintosh type sizes, leadings, and measurements will appear slightly larger than, and not match up to, properly calibrated type rulers or to type that has been set at a traditional type house. This discrepancy has been attributed to paper stretch that occurs during printing, but in fact that's not the case.

QuarkXPress provides a solution to this problem by allowing you to specify the points-per-inch ratio in the General Preferences dialog box (Figure 4-49). You can enter any value between 72 and 73 points per inch, in .01-point increments. Changing the ratio affects only future actions, not previously placed text or graphics.

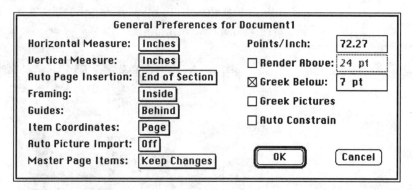

FIGURE 4-49 *Specify the customary 72 points-per-inch in QuarkXPress's General Preferences dialog box—or something closer to the actual amount, 72.27 points-per-inch.*

Disappearing pasteboard items

Normally, objects on **PageMaker**'s pasteboard remain there, regardless of which page is currently in view. But sometimes items on the pasteboard mysteriously disappear: You drag an item onto the pasteboard, for example, change pages, and discover that the item you've just moved to the pasteboard has vanished. You return to the page on which the item originally appeared and, *voilá*, it reappears on the pasteboard. So what's going on here?

If an object appears on the pasteboard only when a certain page is displayed, then that item is still attached to a particular page. In PageMaker's view, a graphic or block of text is attached to a page when any part of it, even a very small part, overlaps the page (Figure 4-50). Even if the overlapping part is currently invisible—and text or graphic handles are often invisible—the object is still attached to the page. Dragging an object so that the object and all its handles are entirely off the page solves the problem and places it firmly on the pasteboard.

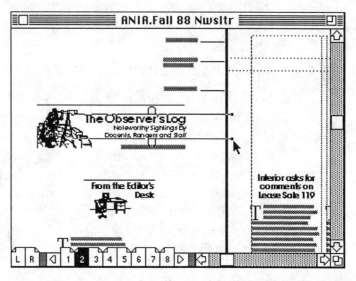

FIGURE 4-50 *Because its text handles overlap the page, the Observer's Log text block is still attached to the page.*

When files are saved in the "wrong" place

Our readers occasionally complain that **PageMaker** sometimes saves documents in the "wrong" folder. To understand how this happens, you need to know that if no document or an untitled document is open, PageMaker knows about only one folder (or subdirectory in the PC version): the one that was most recently opened. (If you haven't opened any folders since launching PageMaker, it knows about the PageMaker folder.) When you save a document for the first time, unless you specify some other folder, PageMaker automatically stores it in the only location it knows—the most recently opened folder. If the most recently opened folder is the one containing the graphic you just placed, for example, the document is saved in that folder unless you instruct PageMaker differently.

To ensure that your documents are saved in the proper place, it is essential that you check the drive and folder (or subdirectory) designations in the Save dialog box. Documents saved in the "wrong" location are almost always caused by a failure to check the file destination when saving. If the wrong drive or folder is indicated, select the correct one in the usual way before clicking the Save button.

Tamper-proof style sheets

In order to prevent others in your workgroup from altering a style sheet in **Ventura Publisher**, you can "write-protect" the style sheet file. On the Mac, you can do this by opening the style sheet file's Get Info box (by pressing Command + I) in the Finder and turning on the *Locked* option. On the PC it's also easy to write-protect the style sheet. The Norton Utilities, Xtree, and several other DOS utilities let you set the DOS file attributes, including the "read only" attribute. In Windows, open the File Manager and use the CHANGE ATTRIBUTES command under the File Manager's File menu.

On the PC you can also write-protect a style sheet by using the DOS ATTRIB command. Here's how:

1. At the DOS prompt, change to the directory where your style sheets are located.

2. Type in the DOS command `ATTRIB +R filename.STY`, using the actual name of your style sheet. The `+R` argument in the ATTRIB command line turns on the read-only attribute for the named file. (You can later turn the read-only attribute off using the same command, except this time you enter `-R` instead of `+R` in the command line. With read-only turned off, you'll be able to make changes to the style sheet again.)

Whichever method you use, the style sheet will become a "read-only" file, and Ventura won't save any changes made to it. A style sheet file specified as read-only will appear listed at the top of the screen in PC versions with the characters -RO appended. If you try to save the chapter after making style changes, you'll be prompted to save the style sheet under a new name (Figure 4-51.)

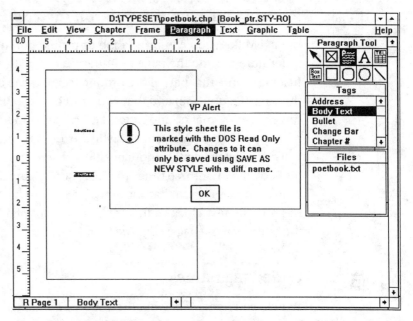

FIGURE 4-51 *On the PC, a write-protected Ventura style sheet is indicated by the suffix –RO after the style sheet name in the window's title bar.*

Restoring Ventura after a crash

Sometimes when **Ventura Publisher** for the PC freezes up and forces you to restart your computer, you may find that the program no longer works correctly. Instead of reinstalling the entire program, search in the Ventura directory for files that end in .INF and delete them (especially VPPROF.INF in the DOS/GEM Edition, and VPWIN.INF in the Windows Edition). These files contain information such as your previous option settings; if they're ever corrupted, Ventura will become hopelessly confused.

Deleting these troublesome files will return the program to its factory defaults, and Ventura will recreate the files as it needs them. You may have to reset some of your favorite options, but you'd have to do that anyway if you reinstalled the program.

Printing off-page production instructions

In **PageMaker**, you can print a job or production number, date, or other note outside the page boundary, along with the crop marks. Just make sure that part of the production note's text block overlaps the page (Figure 4-52) and that you print on paper large enough for the page, crop marks, and notes. Ordinarily, something positioned off the page on the pasteboard won't print, but with this overlap it will print. If you want the note positioned at the bottom of the page, hit Return two or three times to create some blank lines before entering the message so that the actual text doesn't overlap the page. Position the text block so the upper section of blank lines overlaps the bottom of the page, with the typed part hanging off the page.

Coded tag names

To help you remember what the **Ventura Publisher** tags you've created actually do, give each a coded name. Indicate the amount of left and right indent and how the paragraph line breaks are set.

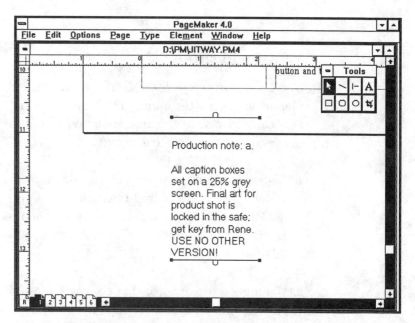

FIGURE 4-52 *Create a printed production note in PageMaker by hanging one end of an off-page text block just over the edge of the actual page.*

For example, your coded tag name might read vb_0_2306_l. In this case, the letter *v* indicates a vertically tabbed column, so the tag name will appear with the other vertically tabbed column tags (which you'd use to arrange separate paragraphs in a tabular format) in the paragraph tag list. The *b* indicates that the tag is for the first column (line break before, not after); an *n* would indicate a middle column (no line breaks), while an *a* would be for a right column (break after, not before).

The next number in the sample tag name indicates the left indent—in this case 0, since it's for a left margin column. Following that is the right indent of 23 picas, 6 points. The last letter indicates left text alignment: R would mean right alignment, C centered, and so on. You can, of course, devise your own tag naming system based on this strategy.

Ventura file finder

If you ever forget which directories a **Ventura Publisher** chapter's files are in, several techniques can help you re locate them on your PC's hard drive. One technique relies on Ventura's MULTI-CHAPTER or MANAGE PUBLICATION commands:

1. Choose the MULTI-CHAPTER command under the Options menu in the GEM Edition, or the MANAGE PUBLICATION command under the Files menu in the Windows Edition. Then select the chapter and click on *Open*, as though you were going to add the chapter in question.

2. You'll get a list of all of that chapter's files (Figure 4-53): text, graphic, and style sheet files. The list will include the complete path and drive specification for each file, enabling you to find any file easily.

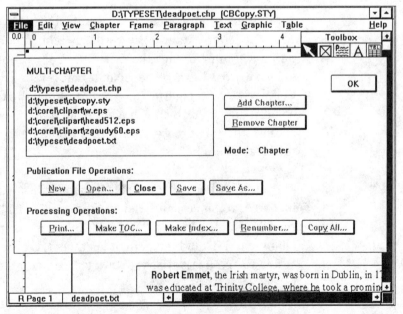

FIGURE 4-53 *Use Ventura's Manage Publication command in the Windows Edition to find all of a chapter's files.*

Another technique locates the style sheet, and text and graphic files for a single chapter, or for all the chapters in a publication file. And you don't need the Ventura Publisher program for this one. Simply view the chapter's .CHP file (or publication's .PUB file) on screen, using the DOS TYPE command. If you're not adept at DOS, use a DOS utility, like XTREE, which lets you view the contents of files (among many other functions). Or use a text editor that can load and display plain, unformatted text. The first few lines of .CHP or .PUB files contain what you're looking for: the names and disk directories of the text, graphics, or chapter files included in the documents, as well as the style sheet that was used (Figure 4-54).

```
← ↑ ↓ → Scroll  0..9)speed  G)oto  H)ex  S)et  PgUp  PgDn  Home  End  Return
#D 100Z 0ZZA 0005 0001 0Z 0Z 80 0000 0000 D:\TYPESET\REPORT_A.STY
_  80 × 80 × 80 × 80 × × × ×
#T 01 C:\SHOWPAGE.TXT × × ×
#I 01 C:\TIPSHOTS\3_CHAPT\5_5_T5.PCX × 0Z80 01E0
#G 07 C:\TIPSHOTS\1_CHAPT\5_5_T3.EPS 0040 0140 007D
#T 01 E:\TYPESET\BEZIER.TXT × × ×
#T 01 E:\TYPESET\1_RPT_A.TXT × × ×
#FN × × × × ×
#FT '''' '''' '''' '''' '''' '''' '''' '''' ''''
#BT FF × . . . × × × × . × × × × × × ""
_  × × × × × × × × ×
_  × × × × × × × × ×
_  × . . × × ×
#BT FF × . . . × × × × . × × × × × × ""
_  × × × × × × × × ×
_  × × × × × × × × ×
_  × . . × × ×
#BT FF × . . . × × × × . × × × × × × ""
_  × × × × × × × ×
_  × × × × × × × ×
_  × . . × × ×
#RT
#RT
#RT
```

FIGURE 4-54 *Peek into a Ventura Publisher chapter file (.CHP), as we did above, by using the XTREE utility. You'll see the names and locations of the text and graphic files it includes, plus the style sheet used.*

CHAPTER 5

Presentations

Charts and graphs

  ## Better charts and graphs

We have four favorite guides to better graphmaking. Two of these are by Edward Tufte. His *Visual Display of Quantitative Information*, a modern classic in the theory and practice of statistical graphics, includes a remarkable diversity of illustrations, both in era and subject matter, from Napoleon's march to Moscow to the chromosomes of humans and monkeys. His more recent *Envisioning Information* examines the design of data representations of all kinds: timetables, maps, meteorological charts, the Vietnam Veterans Memorial, musical scores, electrocardiograms, postage stamps, time series, dance notation, and much more (see Figure 5-1). These are thoughtful and thought-provoking books, and great sources of inspiration.

For more how-to advice, however, refer to our other two favorites. *Using Charts and Graphs* by Jan V. White is a treasure-trove of contemporary examples, design ideas, inventive variations on standard themes, and chartmaking techniques, most of which lend themselves to graphics creation on a Mac or PC. *Designer's Guide to Charts and Diagrams* by Nigel Holmes, art director of *Time* magazine, is also an excellent source of ideas and advice on the graphic display of data. More than the other books mentioned here, however, Holmes' suggestions require an artistic flair for successful execution, and they can make your publication look like a *Time*-clone if you're not careful.

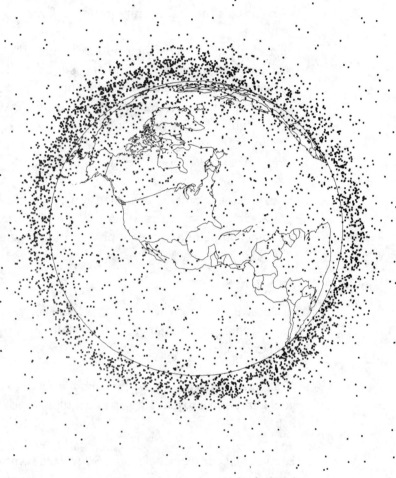

FIGURE 5-1 *The distribution of orbiting space junk, one of hundreds of enlightening illustrations in* Envisioning Information.

   ## Quick accurate bar charts

You can create accurate bar charts quickly in drawing programs like **CorelDRAW**, Micrografx **Designer**, **MacDraw II**, and others that display the dimensions of objects as you draw them. For example, here's how you might create a vertical bar chart:

1. Draw a narrow vertical rectangle. Then duplicate it to create as many bars as your bar chart requires.

2. Align the duplicates by their bottoms, and adjust the height of each bar by selecting the bar and dragging its top handle. The vertical dimension shown on screen can be interpreted as the value for the bar. A value of $1.25 million, for example, corresponds to a bar height of 1.25 inches, assuming your rulers are set in inches.

3. After the bars are properly sized, group them.

You can enlarge or reduce the dimensions of the chart without distorting the relative bar values. When you're all done, export the chart in a format compatible with your presentation program.

Quick pie slices

With a drawing program like **MacDraw II** or **Canvas**, you can create simple pie charts in a matter of minutes. Here's how, using MacDraw II as an example:

1. Calculate the degrees of arc for each pie slice. To do so, convert your chart values to percentages and multiply each percentage by 360.

2. Launch MacDraw and select the SHOW SIZE command from the Layout menu.

3. Select the Arc tool and, with the Shift Key depressed (to create an arc of a perfect circle), drag out an arc. The radius of the arc should be the same as the radius of the pie you want in your chart; the figures at the bottom of the window show the radius of the arc as you draw it out. Turn Autogrid off (in the Layout menu) if you want a radius length other than the ones the grid allows.

4. Choose the RESHAPE command from the Edit menu and drag an end of the arc to create a slice of the proper size for your pie. The

degree values displayed at the bottom of the window will tell you when you have an arc of the correct radius (Figure 5-2).

5. Repeat steps 3 and 4 for each slice of the pie chart.

Select your pie slices and fill them with different colors or patterns. Then move them into position to create a proper pie.

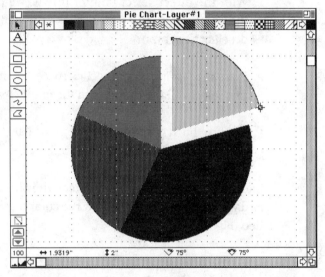

FIGURE 5-2 *MacDraw's Reshape tool allows you to convert an arc into a wedge of the correct size for a pie chart.*

Don't ungroup Illustrator graphs

Be careful not to ungroup the objects in an **Illustrator** for the Mac graph. Doing so converts the graph to a conventional collection of graphic objects and deletes all the links to the values in the Graph Data window. Since the UNDO command cannot regroup an ungrouped graph, there's no way to recover the links once they're deleted. And, once the links are gone, changes in the data are no longer automatically reflected in the graph.

Subtler shadows for your graphs

Illustrator's shadowed graph style creates solid black shadows which may be too bold for your publication (Figure 5-3, top). Here's how to change the default black shadows to something a little lighter:

1. With the direct select pointer (the white pointer—chosen from the pointer tool subpalette), click on an empty part of the page to deselect the graph.

2. Press the Option Key and click twice on any part of any shadow; this selects all the shadows in the graph.

3. Choose the STYLE command from the Paint menu, select None for the stroke, and specify the desired color or gray shade for the fill.

Back in the main document, check the shadows in Preview mode and you'll see that they are now the color or shade of gray you specified (Figure 5-3, bottom).

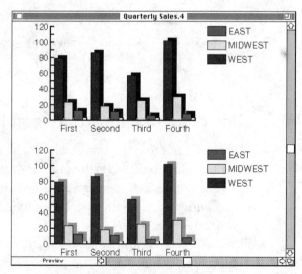

FIGURE 5-3 *A shadowed graph with Illustrator's default black shadow (top) and with a custom shadow (bottom).*

Changing the fill in a complex graph

Graphs created with **Illustrator**'s graph tool often contain several filled areas representing a single data group, for example, the four bars and corresponding legend for the western sales group in Figure 5-4. You can change the pattern or color of each area individually, but it's easier to change them all at once. Here's how:

1. Choose the direct selection tool (the white pointer, available from the tools subpalette). Click on an empty part of the page to deselect the graph.

2. Press the Option Key and click twice on the legend (not the text, but the box next to it) of the desired data group. This selects all the areas associated with that group—both legend and data areas—as illustrated in Figure 5-4.

3. Choose the STYLE command from the Paint menu and select the desired color, gray shade, or pattern.

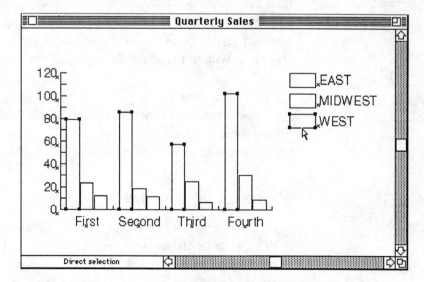

FIGURE 5-4 *To make a universal change to all chart elements corresponding to a single data group, select all the areas representing that group with the direct selection tool.*

Back in the main document, turn on Preview mode and you'll see that all the areas representing the specified data group are now in the selected color, shade of gray, or pattern.

Color

  ### Color clip art for presentations

Color clip art appropriate for presentations is hard to come by. High quality, color clip art in EPS format is not that difficult to find, but **MacroMind Director** (if you're creating animated presentations) and many slide recorders cannot handle EPS artwork. Also, on-screen drawing of EPS images in presentation programs is relatively slow. On a Mac, PICT is the best file format for color presentation clip art, and the best PICT collection we've seen for this purpose is **ClickArt Color Graphics for Presentations** by T/Maker. This collection of over 250 PICT2 color images (see Figure 5-5) includes an appropriately business-like variety of arrows, borders, backgrounds, financial symbols, detailed drawings of computers, printers, telephones and other office equipment, flags and maps, people at work, and more. A complete printed catalog of images with a comprehensive index is included with this multi-disk set.

ClickArt Color Graphics for Presentations is also available in .WMF (Windows Metafile) format for presentations on the PC and in EPS format (both Mac and PC) for high-resolution output, such as color separations and print publications.

  ### Sharper colors for video

If you record your computer presentations on videotape, you may notice that some of the colors—especially vivid reds and bright blues and violets—look fuzzier and less defined than they do on your computer screen. This is because videotape can't accommodate highly saturated colors. To prevent such blurring, use no more than an 80-percent level of any given color, and add a few percentage points of

FIGURE 5-5 *Gray-scale renditions of color clip art from ClickArt Color Graphics for Presentations.*

other colors. The less-saturated colors will look very similar to saturated colors on your computer screen and will record much more accurately on video.

Color: 24-bit quality at an 8-bit cost

Although **MacroMind Director** supports 24-bit color, the amount of RAM and hard disk space used by 24-bit images can significantly limit the complexity of your animations. It isn't always necessary, however, to use 24-bit art to achieve high-quality results; 8-bit color artwork can look surprisingly good when it's generated from a 24-bit original.

To generate "low cost, high quality" color, first create the original art in 24 bits using **PixelPaint Professional**, **Studio/32**, **Adobe Photoshop**, or **ColorStudio**, taking advantage of these applications' superior blending, filling, and transparency features. Then, within the paint program, convert the file to an 8-bit image that uses the System Palette (the Mac's 256 default colors), or better yet, an Adaptive or Custom Palette (256 colors custom picked to best suit your image). You'll end up with a rich-looking, 8-bit image that can be less than one-fourth the size of its 24-bit equivalent.

 ## One bit for two colors

Use 1-bit (black-and-white) castmembers in **MacroMind Director** whenever you need only two colors to adequately render an object in your presentation. By converting one or more castmembers to 1-bit graphics, you can realize considerable memory savings. You can also significantly increase playback speed for many sequences.

Convert any bitmap castmember to 1-bit by selecting it and choosing the COLOR DEPTH command in the Cast menu. After the castmember has been dragged onto the stage, you can replace its black and white pixels with any two colors in the color palette. To do so, select the castmember (on the stage), open the Tool Window, select a foreground color from the Tool Window to replace the black pixels, and select a background color to replace the white pixels.

 ## Animated cards in color

Although **HyperCard** allows you to open external color windows, it still doesn't support color on the cards themselves. **MacroMind Player** lets you launch **MacroMind Director** animations from within HyperCard, however, and MacroMind Player also has a useful feature that plays an animation as an overlay on top of the card, a feature which can be used to colorize (and animate) your HyperCard presentations.

First, use a screen capture utility (such as Mainstay's **Capture**) to grab an image of the card you want to colorize. Insert this image into the bottom (first) channel of a new MacroMind Director animation. You'll use the card image to keep the dimensions of your animation within the area of your HyperCard card.

With Director's paint tools, create color artwork to place over the card image in your animation. Keep the first frame of your animation blank except for the card image. This will allow you to insert transitions (dissolves, wipes, and so on) for your color artwork when it first appears, and to preview exactly how the animation will look once it's in HyperCard. When the animation sequence is finished, delete the card image from the cast and score before saving your work.

Back in HyperCard, compose your card script as follows:

```
on openCard
playmovie "Art for a Color Card",movienoclear,movienoupdate
end openCard
```

When the card is opened, there will be a slight delay as the animation is loaded. Your color artwork will appear on the card, complete with wipes, dissolves, and other visual effects if you have included them. Then HyperCard will resume control.

No fades or color cycling in 24-bit

If you're working in 8-bit color in **MacroMind Director** and intend to change at some point to 24-bit color for a video transfer, keep in mind that color cycling and palette-related transitions such as fade to black or fade to white don't work in 24-bit color. The solution to this problem is either to avoid using these effects in your animation or, if you do use them, avoid switching to 24-bit color for the video transfer.

Quick color selection

AutoDesk Animator's Home panel offers a choice of only eight colors at a time; to use any of the other 248 available colors, you normally have to interrupt your work, display the Palette panel, select a color, and then return to the Home panel. If you've already used the color you want, though, you can avoid this rigamarole: Just move your pointer over the desired color and press the F1 Key to select it. The next tool you use—the fill tool, for example—will automatically employ the color selected via the F1 Key.

. . . .

Start an animation with a new palette

In **MacroMind Director**, modifying an existing color palette as you develop an animation can lead to complications such as unwanted color shifts and color conflicts between palettes. Instead of altering existing palettes, it's often better to start a new animation by creating a new palette. Then add new colors to that palette as needed.

The first color in a palette is always white and the last is always black. It's best not to change the rest of a palette to all black or all white, so we recommend that you start a new palette in a new animation by changing all but the first and last colors to a dark gray. Here's how:

1. Open the Palette Window by choosing the PALETTE command from the Window menu. Drag the window's size box to make the window large enough to work in.

2. Select the next-to-last color in the palette, the dark gray in the lower right corner, by clicking on it once. Copy it with the COPY command.

3. Select the second color in the palette, the near white in the upper left corner. Paste the dark gray in this position with the PASTE command.

4. In the dialog box that now appears, give your new palette a name and click the OK button.

5. Drag the pointer from the second color (the pasted gray) to the next to last color (the original gray) in order to select all but the first and last colors in the palette.

6. Choose the BLEND command from the Palette menu to change all the selected colors to dark gray.

Now use your new palette for the cast members you add to your animation, replacing the grays with new colors as needed. As you fill your palette, fill the color squares sequentially and row by row; this will leave blank rows in which you can create color blends for color cycling.

Type and text

  ## Make presentation type visible

Because they're projected, presentation slides and overheads require some special type treatment. For slides, use graphics with a dark background and light type; deep shades of blue with light yellow are particularly easy to read. For printed presentations or overhead transparencies, dark type on a light background works best. By using strong color contrasts, you can keep the house lights high enough for your audience to see you as well as your presentation.

 ## Use anti-aliased text in your presentations

The Mac's 72-dpi screen resolution can impair the readability of small type in an animation. Also, if you're animating for video, sharp-edged text creates video "artifacts" that severely decrease readability. Solve both problems by using anti-aliased text in your animations. To do this, create the text in **PhotoShop** or Letraset's **ColorStudio** with Shapes, remembering to turn on the *Anti-aliased* option in the Type Style dialog box. Save the text in PICT format and import it as a color cast member. If the text has a color background, generate the background along with the text so the two can be properly blended along the edges.

A disadvantage to this method is that the text can't be edited after it's imported into **MacroMind Director**. As a result, you might want to use regular "jaggy" text in your animation until size, color, and positioning are finalized, and then create anti-aliased text as a finishing touch. See Figure 5-6 for an example of the difference between anti-aliased and standard text.

Anti-aliased text
Standard text

FIGURE 5-6 *Examples of 48-point Goudy demonstrating the difference between standard Macintosh text and anti-aliased text on screen.*

Easy presentation notes

Here's a good way to stay on course while delivering a presentation using slide or overhead transparencies. Print them as reduced thumbnail views, several to a page, on plain paper, and use these as your notes. You can then jot comments in the margins about the points you want to emphasize—for easy reference during your presentation. In **PageMaker**, for example, select the *Thumbnails* option in the Print dialog box to print up to 16 reduced-size pages on a single piece of paper. This may be too many for effective speaker notes, but you can print fewer if you need larger thumbnails that are easier to read.

Shimmering metallic type

Metallic type that appears as if it glints in a bright light is easy to create in **MacroMind Director**. These are the steps you follow:

1. Open the Cast Window and select the next available castmember.

2. Open the Palette Window and select the Metallic color palette from the pop-up menu.

3. Open the Paint Window, select the Text tool, and choose Gradient from the Ink Effects pop-up menu on the left side of the window (below the paint tools).

4. Type the desired text in the Paint Window, selecting the appropriate font, size, and style from the Text menu.

5. Select the GRADIENT command from the Paint menu, select the *Castmember* option from the Range pop-up menu, and select the *Dither Adjacent Colors* option from the Method pop-up menu. Select the desired gradient direction from the Direction pop-up menu. Select the color gradient you want your type to display by clicking on the left end of the gradient bar and selecting a dark color from the left side of the pop-up color palette. Click on the right side of the gradient bar and select the light color at the opposite end of the same row in the color palette. Click the Set button, note that the text is now filled with the selected gradient, and close the Paint Window.

6. Open the Score Window, select the first cell of the first channel, and drag the newly created text castmember onto the stage. Its castmember number should now appear in the selected cell.

7. With the first cell of the first channel (the beginning cell) still selected, choose the COPY command. Select an ending cell later in the channel (depending on how long you want to display the text) and choose the PASTE command. (Drag the text to a new position on the stage at this point if you want the text to move as well as glint in the animation.)

8. Drag through the first channel in the Score Window in order to select the beginning and ending cells and all the cells in between. Select the IN-BETWEEN command from the Score menu to fill in all the empty cells in the selected part of the channel.

9. Drag through the Palette channel in the Score Window in order to select the cells directly above those with the text castmember.

(Scroll up in the Score Window if you can't see the Palette channel.) Select the SET PALETTE command from the Score menu.

10. In the Set Palette dialog box, turn on the *Set Color Cycling* option. There are several styles of color cycling you can create, but for now let's just turn on the *Over Time* option.

11. Still in the Set Palette dialog box, select the two rows of colors that correspond to the color gradient you picked in step 5. Select the one row that cycles from dark to light and one that cycles from light to dark; the first color in the first row and the last color in the second row should be the same. (This ensures a smooth, seamless cycling of colors.) Click the Set button.

Now click the Play button in the Panel Window and watch what happens to the gradient-filled text on the stage; it should cycle through the selected colors as if reflecting a bright light. The trick to this effect is to cycle over a range of colors that starts and ends with the same color, with a lighter or darker shade of that color in the middle. Although the Metallic Palette makes it easy to select such an auto-reversing gradient, you don't have to use the Metallic Palette to achieve the effect. You can create your own palette, fill a sequence of cells with a gradient of colors, select the colors, reverse them, and fill the cells that follow with the reversed gradient. You can then use this handmade, auto-reversing gradient to create a custom glimmer effect.

Creating balloon-style caption boxes

A good way to make your point in a presentation graphic is to literally point it out. A pointed caption box (Figure 5-7) comes in handy for that purpose: It's simply a rectangular (hence, easily drawn) version of a cartoon text balloon. Here's how to create and use this type of caption box in most presentation and drawing programs:

1. Use a polygon drawing tool to create a rectangle with three extra handles on each side. Give the box a white fill, so the text is easily read against the white background. This will serve as your caption

box template—save a copy for future use. Polygon tools vary somewhat from program to program, but you generally create the handles by clicking at three separate intervals as you draw each side of the box.

2. Enter the text you want, and then scale the completed rectangle as required to enclose the text.

3. Select the rectangle and then choose whichever command lets you reshape the polygon. Drag the middle handle on the side from which you want the pointer to extend, as we did in Figure 5-7.

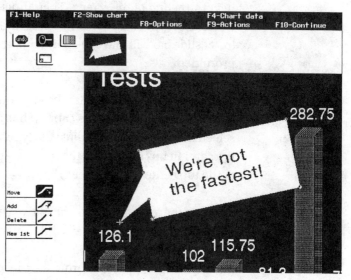

FIGURE 5-7 *Text pointer boxes, like this one created in Harvard Graphics, emphasize the important points in your presentation.*

Harvard Graphics has a special caption box feature that converts any box you draw into a caption box. You can quickly create a caption box, rotate it or skew it for special effect, then convert it into a polygon to further customize it. Here's how:

1. Draw a box with the Box tool from the tool palette.

2. While the box is selected, click the color icon at the upper left of the screen, and, from the pop-up color menu, select a white fill for the box.

3. With the box still selected, click on the caption box icon from the assortment of box style icons at the upper right of the screen. Four box style icons will appear which allow you to choose the side from which the pointer will extend.

4. The box may not appear to change after you've applied the desired caption box style. If that's the case, find the two slide bars located near the center of the screen. Their functions vary depending on which tools you're using. In this case, dragging the arrows on the lower slide bar will make the pointer part of the caption box more prominent.

5. Select the Text tool and enter the caption text in a text box. Then drag the text block into the caption box. With the text block still selected, you can quickly adjust the type size for a better fit within the caption box by clicking the right or left arrows on the slide bar at the top center of the screen.

6. To rotate the text and caption box as we've done in the illustration, first hold down the Shift Key while you click on the box and the text block to select them both, and then select Group from the tool pallete. Use the Rotate tool from the tool palette to rotate the caption box and text. If you want to further modify the shape of the caption box after rotating it, select the text caption box, then select Ungroup from the tool palette.

7. If you want to change the direction of the caption box pointer, as we did in Figure 5-7 on page 313, you'll first need to convert the box to a polygon. To do that, select the box and then click the *To poly* icon from the tool palette. Then, to adjust the pointer, click the *Edit pts* icon and editing handles will appear at points along the polygon. You'll notice that the pointer side of the caption box is composed of three additional handles, just as we described in

the first technique above. To slant the pointer downward as we've done, simply drag the handle at the tip of the pointer.

In Harvard Graphics, you can store your customized pointer boxes in a special library file, so they're easy to retrieve.

Presentation and production

  ### Readable overhead projections

When creating presentation transparencies for overhead projection, use landscape orientation for your pages. All too often projectors are set up in a way that causes the projected image to narrow toward the bottom. Transparencies created in portrait orientation tend to lose brightness and focus near the bottom, with only the upper portion of the image remaining legible. Landscape orientation keeps your image in the upper area of the projection, where it's most readable.

  ### Perfect overlays

Need to make a presentation using a series of overlaid transparencies? Try this in **Illustrator:**

1. Create the elements of your presentation.

2. Use the PAINT command to give each separate overlay element a different color.

3. Use ADOBE SEPARATOR with the *Spot color* option turned on to print the image on a PostScript printer; on a monochrome printer, each overlay will print in black and white; on a color printer, each overlay will print in a different color.

When you give the presentation, the objects in each overlay will line up perfectly as you lay transparency on transparency.

Know your slide recorder

When producing a slide presentation, it's important to know from the very beginning what kind of slide recorder will be imaging your slides. Not all recorders have the same image area on a 35-mm slide; in fact, the image area can vary from model to model. If the recorder's slide area does not match the default slide size of your presentation software, and if the default size is larger than the recorder's image area, parts of your presentation will appear clipped. Knowing which slide recorder you're going to use means that all the slides you create will be neither too large nor too small.

Sound that requires less memory

To avoid eating up a lot of RAM and disk space when creating an animation with music in **MacroMind Director**, don't use digitized sounds. Instead, send basic MIDI commands to an external sequencer (mixing board) attached by a MIDI interface to your Mac's serial port. Since MIDI sounds are generated outside the computer from simple instructions, you don't have to store digitized versions of the sounds on your hard disk. Director doesn't have to find room for the sounds in RAM, and the Mac doesn't have to spend precious computation time creating the sounds. The result is more economical use of hard disk space and RAM and significantly better sound.

Creating in-between shapes

With the BLEND command in **FreeHand** or the Blend tool in **Illustrator**, you can easily transform one shape into another, creating a sequence of intermediate shapes. With sequences of in-between shapes, you can create a smoothly flowing animation in **MacroMind Director** where a letter mutates into a number (as in Figure 5-8), for example, or a frog metamorphoses into a prince. And it's a lot easier than trying to generate such shapes in Director itself.

To import a sequence of in-between shapes into Director, first create the blend in FreeHand or Illustrator and ungroup the objects. Next use the Scrapbook FKey supplied with Director (and easily installed with Suitcase II or MasterJuggler) to copy each shape in the ungrouped blend, one at a time, and paste it into the *Anim Scrapbook* which the FKey creates. Then open Director, choose the IMPORT command, and select the *Anim Scrapbook* (you should find it in the System Folder). Director automatically pastes the sequence of in-between shapes into the next available positions in the Cast Window.

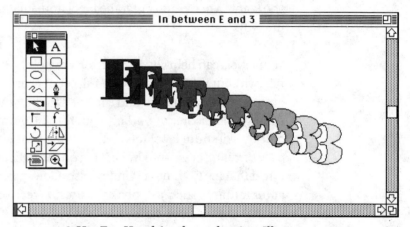

FIGURE 5-8 *Use FreeHand (as shown here) or Illustrator to generate in-between shapes for use in a transformation animation in Director.*

  ## Maintain a consistent image

Make your presentation layouts consistent with your corporate identity: typefaces and type styles, colors for backgrounds, rules and borders, and spatial relationships between elements should match the corporate logo and design concepts. One way to ensure consistency is to create presentation templates and require everyone in your organization to use them.

 ## Quick scrolling in a score

You can quickly scroll the Score Window in **MacroMind Director** to the first or last frame of your animation sequence by pressing the Return and Tab keys. Return takes you to the first frame and Tab scrolls the score to the last frame of your animation.

. . . .

Labels help find frames fast

Add short, memorable labels to important frames of your **MacroM-ind Director** animation in the Comments channel in the Score Window. The Comments channel is marked with a black triangle and is the top channel in the Score Window. Drag a triangle onto the frame you want to mark, and enter the label immediately to the right (Figure 5-9).

Your labels can help you find significant points within the presentation without having to scan the full set of channels for the defining event or castmember. To find a labeled frame, you can scroll rapidly through the score, or you can open the Comment Window and quickly skip from label to label (with the Score Window automatically scrolling in unison) by clicking on the right or left arrows. Don't forget that the Comment Window also allows you to attach extended commentary (such as speaker notes, directions, or storyboard scripts) to your necessarily brief labels.

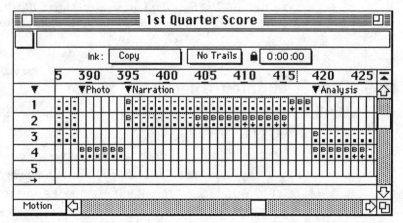

FIGURE 5-9 *Adding short labels to frames in MacroMind Director's Score Window helps you to return to those frames quickly.*

Short field names facilitate global style changes

In **SuperCard**, you can change the style of a field throughout an entire presentation to experiment with different fonts, font sizes, and font styles. To change the style of one or more fields in a presentation, create a SuperTalk script that searches through the cards and sets the textFont, textSize, and textStyle properties of the named fields to the desired characteristics. You'll find it easier to refer to fields in a script if you remember to give short, simple names to the fields in a Super-Card presentation.

Changing the master for only a few slides

If you make changes to a **Persuasion** master slide that affect placement, size, and/or color, the changes will affect all the slides in the presentation that are based on that master. To make a change affecting only one or a few slides, create a new master slide by selecting NEW from the Go To Master submenu of the View menu. Base the new master on the original master (which remains unchanged), give the new master a different name, and edit it as desired. Finally, for all the slides you want based on the new master, go to each slide and select the new master slide from the Master pop-up menu at the bottom of the window.

Grab bag

Cloning objects and their scripts

In **SuperCard**, if you want to create a new object with the same script as that used in an existing object, clone the existing object and its script with the DUPLICATE command (in the SuperEdit environment) or the COPY and PASTE commands. This is usually a lot faster than creating a brand-new object and using the script editor to copy the script from one object to another.

Managing memory in Director

Here are a number of ways you can reduce file size, save disk space, and speed up your **MacroMind Director** animations:

- As you work on a file, occasionally select the SAVE AS command to replace the working file with a freshly updated copy.

- At convenient points in the creation of a file, periodically choose the DELETE UNUSED CAST command and then the CLEAN UP CAST command. (You may want to use the SELECT CAST command first to make sure that you aren't discarding cast members that will be needed later on.)

- Before importing them into Director, shave unwanted or unnecessary areas off PICT images.

- Whenever possible, reuse existing castmembers instead of creating new ones.

Keep in mind that file size on disk is not the same as the amount of RAM required to run a file. Director files are compressed when you save them to disk. As a result, the amount of RAM required can be much greater than the file size. Use the above four techniques to keep both RAM requirements and file size to a minimum. The following can help reduce the appetite for RAM as well:

- One by one, select castmembers and press Command + T to open the Cast Info dialog box and see how much memory each castmember requires. Such a survey shows how a presentation's memory needs are distributed and may reveal that one or more castmembers use especially large amounts of memory. Consider replacing particularly memory-hungry castmembers with smaller ones.

- Select ABOUT MM DIRECTOR from the Apple menu to see how RAM is allocated for the current animation (Figure 5-10). You can reduce the amount of RAM devoted to the screen buffer by reducing the color depth of the monitor being used for the stage (in the Monitors Control Panel); at most, color depth should be set to the highest depth required by the castmembers. You can reduce the RAM used by cast and score with the techniques already described. In any event, always make sure that there's at least about 250K of free memory available while you're working on a movie; you'll need this free RAM for cutting, pasting, and undoing work in the Paint Window.

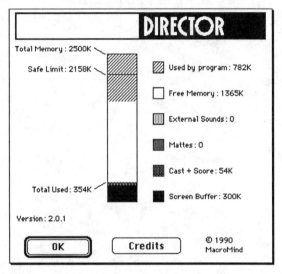

FIGURE 5-10 *The About MM Director Window reveals how RAM is used by the current animation.*

 ## Setting the Director memory partition

By increasing the memory partition devoted to **MacroMind Director** in System 7 or in MultiFinder under System 6, you'll be able to open larger files and you'll experience fewer slow-downs or dislocations due to memory shortages. Here's how to increase the program's memory allocation:

1. Make sure that Director is not currently running. If it is, quit it.

2. Back on the desktop, select the MacroMind application icon (click on it once), and choose Get Info from the File menu (or press Command + I).

3. Enter an amount larger than the 2,048K minimum in the Application Memory Size (System 6) or Current Size (System 7) text box. Close the Get Info dialog box.

In general, give Director as much memory as you can spare, 3,000K to 4,000K or more if possible.

CHAPTER 6

Hardware

Printers

Dusting a laser printer

Since stray toner particles and paper dust can cause printing problems, blow them away while you have your laser printer open. Don't use your lungs to do the job, however; use a canister of compressed air, available at most camera shops.

Save paper, stop the startup page

The test page that prints each time you turn on your PostScript or PostScript language compatible laser printer is for most people a waste of both time and paper. Some printers have a front control panel that allows you to turn off the startup page with the press of a button. Other printers, like the QMS 410, ship with printer utilities that let you select numerous printer options, including the option to stop printing the startup page.

If you own a Mac and you're using System 7, you can turn off a PostScript LaserWriter's startup page by launching the LaserWriter Font Utility (you should find it on your System 7 More Tidbits disk) and choosing the SET STARTUP PAGE command from the Utilities menu. If you're still using System 6 and own the utility **Widgets** (part of CE Software's MockPackage Plus Utilities), you can cancel the startup page by selecting that program's DISABLE STARTUP PAGE command.

If neither Mac utility is available or if you work on a PC, you can turn off the test page by sending a few lines of PostScript code to the printer. Here's how:

1. Type the following in any word processor and save it as an ASCII or text-only file:

```
serverdict begin 0 exitserver
statusdict begin
false setdostartpage
end
```

You can name the file anything you like; we'll assume for the moment that you've saved it as STOPTEST.PS.

2. Download the file to the printer. From a PC, you can download the file using the DOS COPY command. Assuming that the printer is connected to the PC's parallel port, enter the command COPY STOPTEST.PS LPT1: (or LPT2:, COM1:, or COM2:, depending on your PC set-up), and hit the Return Key.

   To download the file from a Mac, use the DOWNLOAD POSTSCRIPT FILE command in the File menu of Adobe's **Font Downloader** (included on every Adobe font disk) or a PostScript download utility, such as Adobe's **SendPS** or CE Software's **LaserStatus** (part of MockPackage Plus Utilities). SendPS is available from users groups or from the Adobe forum on CompuServe (type GO ADOBE at the CompuServe prompt).

   Note that during the download you'll get the message, "exitserver: permanent state may be changed," which, though ominous, is exactly what you want to see. The next time you turn the printer on, the test page should not print.

   The test page, of course, has some useful information printed on it, such as the printer's lifetime page count, installed memory, and PostScript interpreter version number. Thus there may be times when you do want the printer to print a test page. To turn the test page back on, simply change the word "false" to "true" in the Post-Script code described above and download the code again. Or launch Widgets again and select its ENABLE STARTUP PAGE command.

Easy access with a lazy susan

If you find yourself crawling around your laser printer to perform tasks that can't be accomplished easily from the front, place it on a rotating television stand of the appropriate size. Make sure that the printer and power cables have sufficient slack so that you can rotate the printer a half revolution in each direction; this should be enough to give you easy access to all parts of the printer.

 ### LaserJet age in pages

PostScript printers produce a test page showing the lifetime total of pages printed unless that function has been de-activated. Here's how to get the same lifetime page count from a LaserJet:

1. Press the On Line button to take the printer off line.

2. Hold down the Print Fonts / Test Key for about five seconds until "05 SELF TEST" is displayed.

3. Release the button and wait for the printer to produce its test sheet.

At the top of the test sheet is the total page count.

 ### Fighting faded images

White horizontal streaks on laser printer output can be the result of having exposed the printer's EP (electrophotographic) cartridge or drum unit to light. To avoid streaks, don't expose a cartridge to normal room light for more than 5 minutes and never expose it to direct sunlight. White vertical stripes or faint areas on the printed page are caused by a lack of toner or by a dirty corona wire. To clean the corona wire on a Canon CX or SX cartridge, locate the long slot that's covered with a thin plastic strip. Insert the felt-tip plastic cleaner which comes with the cartridge and move the cleaner back and forth several times.

True printer speed

PostScript printers, like other laser printers, have a speed rating defined in pages per minute. But whether you own a 4, 6, or 8 page-per-minute printer, you've probably wondered why few if any of your documents have ever printed out that fast. PostScript and PostScript compatible printers almost invariably print slower than their rated speed, and the first page of a document usually takes longer than the rest.

The pages-per-minute speed rating on a laser printer is like the miles-per-gallon economy rating of a car—there's highway driving and there's city driving. Adobe Systems, the company whose PostScript page description language is built in to most PostScript language processing printers, uses a document of 3,500 characters in its speed test. But the test is performed after the characters are rendered for printing and "cached," that is, stored in the printer's memory and ready to go—definitely highway driving. Adobe's test yields fast results for another reason as well: the test page, unlike many real pages, has no graphics.

In a real document, some city driving is required before the printer can begin cruising at highway speed. Before a character can be printed, its outline must be converted to a bitmap—an array of electronic 0s and 1s that describes the printed character. The conversion takes about 0.01 seconds or less for a standard character in ordinary text and substantially longer for large or complex characters. PostScript saves each character's bitmap in a cache to avoid repeating the conversion each time it prints a character. The time-consuming conversion process is why the first page or two takes longer to print. A similar process takes place for graphics: they generally aren't cached and so must be re-rendered each time the graphic is used. Hence, graphics slow down the entire print job.

Using LaserWriters with PCs and Macs

There are times when Macs and PCs don't get along well in a work-group setting. Apple LaserWriters in particular aren't very obliging to PC users since they lack a Centronix parallel port, the relatively fast and convenient printer interface found on virtually every PC and PC-specific printer. But LaserWriters do include a RS-232C serial connector for connecting PCs although, sad to say, it's a slower interface and it's less convenient than Centronix parallel—since serial cables vary in the way they're wired and numerous communication options inevitably confuse most computer users.

As a further inconvenience to everyone in the workgroup, when it comes time to switch the printer interface from LocalTalk (for Mac printing) to serial (for PC printing), you often can't just simply change a switch setting at the rear of the printer. With the original LaserWriter, LaserWriter Plus, IINT, and IINTX, if you blithely make the setting change without first unplugging the printer's LocalTalk connector to remove the printer from the LocalTalk network, you'll soon discover that the Macintosh network has gone dead. Electronic mail, file servers, printers, everything on the same network cable as the PC-connected LaserWriter is suddenly unavailable.

To avoid network problems on the original LaserWriter, LaserWriter Plus, IINT, and IINTX, you must disconnect the printer from the AppleTalk network before you switch it to serial configuration. To do this safely, turn off the printer and unplug the LocalTalk connector, but leave the LocalTalk cabling attached to the connector. Then switch the printer's communication mode to serial and turn the printer back on. Reverse the process when you reactivate the Local-Talk port. Since the LocalTalk and serial ports operate more independently in this printer, network crashes are not nearly as common with the Personal LaserWriter NT, but the above precaution is also advised for that printer since the Personal LaserWriter NT may transmit noise through its LocalTalk port while the serial port is activated. This can jam the network, slow it down, or cause random transmission errors.

This is not, by the way, a problem that's endemic to all desktop laser printers offering LocalTalk plus serial and parallel connections. Most PostScript printers now on the market let you switch communication options electronically via the option menu on their front panel displays, and they do so without disrupting LocalTalk networks. Some, like the QMS PS 410, the Abaton LaserScriptLX, and the Laser-Writer IIf and IIg can automatically switch between their LocalTalk, parallel, or serial interfaces depending on which one is receiving a print job. The QMS and Abaton printers can also automatically detect whether you're sending a PostScript language print job or one in Hewlett-Packard PCL-4 (LaserJet Series II) format, and then switch to the appropriate interpreter or emulation.

If you have only a few PCs among your largely Mac network, a better way to solve the LW's serial/LocalTalk switching problem is to invest in an AppleTalk adapter for each PC. That way they can have equal access to printers and Mac file servers. We've used such a set-up for years at *Publish*.

Faster LaserWriter serial port connections

If you've purchased or inherited a LaserWriter to use with your PC, there are some inexpensive ways to speed up the connection between your computer and the printer's serial port. Although the default data transfer rate of the LaserWriters' serial port is 9,600 baud (which in this case amounts to 9,600 bits per second), you can increase that rate considerably. The maximum serial communication rate of the LaserWriter and LaserWriter Plus is actually 19,200 baud; for the LaserWriter IINT, IINTX, and Personal LaserWriter NT, it's 57,600 baud. Achieving the higher rates is a two-part process. First you configure the printer to the higher rate, and then you set your PC to communicate at the higher rate. Here's how to set up the Laser-Writer:

1. Switch the LaserWriter's interface from LocalTalk to serial Post-Script Batch mode using the rear switch setting as described in the printer manual. The switch setting and how you change it depends on which model LaserWriter you have.

2. Connect the appropriate serial cable between the computer and printer serial ports. If your dealer doesn't sell a cable specifically labeled for serial connection with laser printers, ask for a "null modem" cable, which should work fine. Remember, LaserWriters use the 25 pin (DB25) serial connector while most PCs now use the 9 pin (DB9) connector, so you'll want to ask for a DB25 to DB9 null modem cable for serial connection to a laser printer. If your dealer can't help you, your local computer cable specialty shop will know how to make one for you.

3. With the proper cable connected, send the printer the commands that raise the serial communication speed to the highest setting. There are two ways to do that:

- The technique we prefer, and it's certainly the easiest method, is to use a PostScript printer utility that lets you choose the desired setting change from a menu. The utility program then sends the required commands and reconfigures the printer for you. There are several programs we like to use for this purpose. One is **PrintCache** by LaserTools, which can also serve as a print spooler for DOS and Windows programs. Another is **PS-Plot** by Legend Communications, which also offers a variety of other options: downloading Macintosh PostScript fonts from your PC, printing Hewlett-Packard Graphics Language files, and converting Adobe Type fonts so that they can be downloaded using the DOS COPY command.

- If a suitable PostScript printer utility is not available, you can write your own PostScript code that specifies the required change, and then send it to the printer using the DOS COPY command. Obviously this requires some modest PostScript programming skills, but most LaserWriter manuals provide the necessary details. Use a text editor to write the PostScript code; a typical listing to switch the printer's serial port baud to 19,200 baud would read like this:

```
serverdict begin 0 exitserver
statusdict begin 25 19200 68 setsccbatch
```

For those who can't read PostScript code, the number *68* is one of several available sets of serial communications protocol options which you can choose to match the communications protocols of the software you're using. It stands for "8 data bits, one stop bit, no parity, using hardware handshaking (DSR/DTR)." You don't need to know what that means; just make sure to use a similar set-up at the PC end.

At this point, you'll need to change your software settings to match the faster serial communication rate you set for your LaserWriter. Here again you have a couple of options, depending on the software you use. If you only use Windows software to print to the LaserWriter, you can increase the speed of your computer's serial port to a maximum of 19,200 baud via the Windows control panel. Here's how:

1. Double-click the Control Panel icon in the Main program group in Window's Program Manager.

2. In the Control Panel menu, double-click the Ports icon.

3. Select the *Com1*, *Com2*, or other port option as appropriate, and then click the Settings button.

4. From the Ports-Settings dialog box that appears, select *19200* in the Baud Rate text box, making sure that the rest of the settings (Data bits, parity, etc.) match those previously set for the printer.

5. Back in the Control Panel menu double-click the Printers icon. In the Control Panel Printers dialog box, click the Configure button, and then select the serial port (the one you set up in step three) from the *Ports:* selections.

Unfortunately for Windows users, font downloaders like Linotype's or Adobe's PSDOWN run under DOS, and are limited to the DOS default of 9,600 baud. Unless you use another utility to enhance the port speed when Windows isn't running, you'll need to rely on the printer's built-in fonts, or on automatically downloading fonts. One alternative is to use the **Micrografx PostScript Driver for Windows** instead of the standard PostScript driver supplied with Windows. The Micrografx driver has a handy option for manually downloading fonts to your PostScript printer, which automaticall transmits at the rate set by the Windows communication port options. (See "A better Windows PostScript driver" in Chapter 7 for a full discussion of the Micrografx PostScript driver.)

Most DOS software, like WordPerfect and Ventura Publisher GEM Edition, and DOS font downloaders, use your PC's default serial baud rate of 9,600 baud (19,200 baud for PS/2s). If you want non-Windows applications to take advantage of an accelerated serial printer connection, we recommend several alternatives:

- PrinTools' **PrintCache** will spool your print job, say from WordPerfect, and send it through a serial port at up to 115,000 baud. In addition, PrintCache can be used to configure your LaserWriter's serial port for higher speed. With it you can set up both your software and LaserWriter IINT, for example, to to communicate at the printer's maximum 57,600 baud rate.

- LaserTools' **Printer Control Panel**, like PrintCache, will also speed up your PC's serial port, but it won't automatically reconfigure your printer or spool your print jobs. It does, however, automatically send print jobs to the correct printer if you have more than one attached to your computer. For most PostScript printers that switch between PostScript language interpretation and Hewlett-Packard Printer Control Language via software commands, Printer Control Panel will automatically switch the printer to match the jobs you print.

Using Printer Control Panel, for example, you can juice up your PC's serial port to 57,600 baud. Then all you have to do is print to the parallel port (LPT1:, LPT2:, etc.), and Printer Control Panel automatically redirects the print job out the supercharged serial port. We've been using this set-up with an Apple Personal LaserWriter NT and Ventura Publisher GEM Edition, printing at 57.6K baud. Interestingly, the Adobe PCSEND utility for downloading Type 1 fonts via your computer's parallel port works just fine using Printer Control

Panel's accelerated serial port. Also, both PrintCache and Printer Control Panel can be configured to work with Windows 3.0.

Fitting fonts in your LaserJet

You'd think 400K of soft fonts would fit easily into a Hewlett-Packard LaserJet Series II printer with 512K of memory, but it won't. You may be able to download that many fonts, but you'll get memory errors when you attempt to print even one simple text-only page. This is because, of its 512K, the Laserjet Series II has only about 395K available for storing fonts *and* printing. For all practical purposes, you need to limit yourself to about 290K of fonts. That's not much when you consider that a 12-point font typically takes up 15 to 25K of printer memory, and a 24-point font requires 100K or more. Regardless of size, the absolute limit is 32 downloadable fonts. Ten downloaded softfonts is, in general, a practical upper limit for the LaserJet Series II.

Monitors

Avoiding screen burn-in

Screen burn-in occurs when a bright, static image is displayed for long periods (such as a lunch break) and etched right onto the screen; this burned-in image creates a ghost that haunts your screen forever after. While everyone agrees that you should avoid screen burn-in, opinions differ about the best way to go about it.

Not so long ago we printed a tip, sent in by a respected display manufacturer, which suggested that it's better to use a screen saver utility than to simply darken the screen manually using the contrast control. If the screen is completely black for long periods while the monitor is on, so this frequently heard argument goes, the electron gun can become contaminated with unfired electrons that can in turn permanently reduce the brightness of the screen. A screen saver that draws some sort of everchanging image supposedly doesn't effect the electron gun in this way, and the best screen saver is one that creates a bright, mobile display that is equally distributed over the screen.

According to other video engineers that we've talked to, however, it's simply not true that displaying a completely blank, black screen for long periods can damage the monitor. The only thing that's "better" about a screen saver program, say the engineers, is that it never forgets to kick in when you go to lunch or take a break; people who manually turn down the contrast are rarely as reliable. Furthermore, they add, a plain, black screen may be better, though less entertaining, than a fancy screen saver display since it doesn't exercise the tube's electron gun unnecessarily.

So who are you going to believe? We tend to believe the engineers we've talked to, but until someone delivers the official party line, we use a screen saver at its most modest, mostly black display module. (Well, we sometimes entertain ourselves by turning on the more colorful display modules.) And what are our favorite screen savers? For the Macintosh, we like **Pyro! 4** and **After Dark 2**. Both offer a variety of animated, screen saver displays, and both allow you to select preferred operational details (such as always using the same display or rotating a number of different displays). The aesthetics of individual display modules are, in most cases, customizable as well.

After Dark, however, tops Pyro! in two ways. It provides optional sound effects for many of its displays, which means that clocks tick, lightning bolts thunder, and aquarium bubbles go glug-glug. In addition, After Dark offers a greater number of display modules which are, on the whole, more entertaining and more colorful—to our taste anyway (Figure 6-1). For its squadrons of flying toasters (toast darkness is adjustable) and its ability to convert your current screen into a sliding-square puzzle, After Dark is irresistible.

FIGURE 6-1 *In After Dark's aquarium-like screensaver module, you can select the number of creatures and the speed with which they swim. Aquatic flying toasters have been spotted on occasion among the many types of fish, jellyfish, seahorses, and crabs.*

  ## Brightness or contrast: which comes first?

Regardless of whether you use a color or monochrome monitor, the correct procedure for setting the contrast and brightness is as follows:

1. Set the brightness control. Turn the brightness control all the way up, and then turn it down just until the unused areas at the edge of the screen (the background raster) turn black. If these areas are black even at the highest brightness level, leave the brightness control at full throttle.

2. Adjust the contrast control to whatever level appeals to you.

Once brightness is set, leave it. To accommodate changes in ambient light and/or viewing comfort and to dim the screen when you're not working at the computer, adjust only the contrast control.

Degauss is *de rigueur*

Like us, you probably find those diagrams of the Earth's magnetic field a little hard to relate to. But even if you can't see it or touch it, the Earth's magnetic field really does exist, and it can have a noticeable effect on your color monitor. It can, for example, generate residual magnetic fields within a monitor, fields which increase in strength the longer the monitor is turned on. Rotating or tilting the monitor while it's on can also add to the build-up of residual magnetic fields. The problem is, these residual fields can cause purity problems—subtle and not-so-subtle tints which muddy other colors and add color to areas that are supposed to be white.

To minimize residual magnetic fields and their concomitant purity problems, you should be sure to degauss (demagnetize) your color monitor regularly. All color monitors automatically degauss when you turn them on, so turning a color monitor off at night and on again in the morning is a good way to ensure a daily degauss. (Turning it off at night also slows a monitor's gradual but inevitable decline in brightness.)

If you need to reposition the monitor (if it's on a swivel stand, for example), try to move the monitor only when it's turned off. If you can't avoid moving your monitor while it's turned on, or if you detect purity problems developing at any time, degauss the monitor. Some color monitors, such as the Apple 13-inch High Resolution Color Monitor, have a degauss button on the back—just give it a push. If your monitor does not have a degauss button, turn it off and then on again instead.

Cleaning the screen

Probably the most effective way to clean a monitor screen is simply to wipe it with a soft, dry tissue. Water and many cleaners can leave a residue on the monitor that is just as distracting as fingerprints. In the long run, a little elbow grease will keep your monitor looking cleaner than a commercial preparation will. It also costs less.

Cleaning an anti-glare screen

When cleaning a noRad anti-glare/anti-radiation screen—or any similar screen made with finely woven mesh—don't use a dry cloth and elbow grease. Instead, rinse off dust and dirt with distilled water, not tap water. Tap water, whether from a well or a public water supply, will leave mineral deposits on the mesh and cloud the screen.

  ## Radiation and what to do about it

Lately there's been a lot of discussion about video monitors, the radiation they emit, and the danger this poses to human health. Monitors produce several types of radiation, including ultraviolet rays and X rays, in addition to creating electromagnetic fields. Recent concern has been focused on extremely low-frequency (ELF) fields that previously were thought to be too weak to have any biological effects. One reason for the new concern is that research has shown that the body itself uses weak ELF fields within its tissues to regulate cellular functions; by mimicking or interfering with those internal fields, the ELF fields produced by monitors have the potential for deleterious effects.

Unfortunately, the jury is still out on just how hazardous monitors are—if, indeed, they are a hazard at all. We know that ELF intensities vary widely from one type of monitor to another and that color monitors generally produce stronger ELF fields than monochrome monitors. But the facts aren't in on whether large-screen monitors produce more radiation than smaller monitors, for example, or if one make or size of monitor is more of a threat to one's health than another make or size.

Until the biological and health issues are resolved, it makes sense to do what you can to minimize your exposure. Several tests have shown that ELF fields are stronger at the rear than at the front, and strongest of all at the sides of a monitor: Avoid sitting beside or behind someone else's monitor. Don't sit too close to the screen, either. A good rule of thumb is that you should not be able to touch the screen with arm and fingers extended. (If you can't read the screen when it's that far away, maybe it's time to visit the eye care professionals.)

Those interested in learning more about the health effects of monitors will find plenty of food for thought in *Currents of Death* (Simon & Schuster, 1989) and "The magnetic-field menace" (*Macworld*, July 1990), both by Paul Brodeur. Another excellent source of in-depth information on the subject is *VDT News*.

Disks and hard drives

  ## Leave it on or turn it off?

We're often asked which is better for a hard drive (and the computer it is connected to), leaving it on all the time or turning it on and off as usage requires? The hardware vendors we've talked to generally agree that leaving a hard drive turned on, even when you're not using it, has a deleterious effect on the drive since drive bearings and other mechanical parts have finite life spans and slowly but surely wear out while the drive is on. The electronic parts of the computer can "wear out" as well—although for different reasons. The best advice seems to be to leave the computer and drive turned on if you'll be away from it for only a short time. Turn everything off, however, if you don't intend to use it for the next three or four hours or more.

 ## Two sides for the price of one?

It sure is tempting to recycle old single-sided disks as double-sided ones. But read our lips: Don't do it. Both types of disks are basically the same, and single-sided disks can almost always be initialized as double-sided, but there's a potential for problems later on. Manufacturers test double-sided disks on both sides for faulty media—flaws in the magnetic coating of the disk—but test single-sided disks only on one side. As a result, single-sided disks may have a marginal or inadequate magnetic coating on the second side.

A marginal disk often initializes properly and may work perfectly for a while, but it's a time bomb waiting to go off. And when it does go off, your data is lost along with the disk. Since there's no way for you to distinguish a good second side from a marginal one, we recommend that you never format single-sided disks for double-sided use. The money you'd save is nothing compared with the cost of reconstructing lost data later on.

Double-duty for your backup device

In a publishing network, use a removable hard disk drive like Iomega's Bernoulli Box as your file server's backup storage instead of using floppies or streaming tape. If your main hard disk goes down, you can often work directly off the removable backup pack without having to restore the backup onto another hard disk, as you would with diskette or tape backups. In addition, you can move the drive to other workstations or file servers on the network to temporarily replace some other hard disk that's out of commission.

Jukebox clip art

If find you spend too much time switching CDs while you search for a particular clip art image, you should consider buying a multi-disk CD ROM drive. At the time this went to press, the only moderately priced multi-disk CD ROM drive currently on the market was Pioneer's $1,295 Model DRM-600, which handles six CDs in jukebox fashion. An extension of Pioneer's consumer audio technology, the DRM-600 also plays audio CDs through your stereo. Six CDs load into a removable holder; although it's really a single drive, each CD appears as a separate drive volume on your PC or Mac.

There are faster single-disk CD drives on the market, but the DRM-600 can change disks in 4–7 seconds, making it very convenient if you're planning to work with multiple clip art volumes. Apple's CD ROM drive, for example, has 500 ms average access time, compared to 600 ms for the Pioneer drive. Other single disc drives rate up to 300 ms but cost almost as much as Pioneer's 6-disk DRM-600.

Defragmenting hard disks

When you use a hard drive, the files it contains tend to become fragmented—stored in sectors scattered throughout the disk, instead of in groups of neighboring sectors. As fragmentation increases, disk performance declines because the disk mechanism has to search farther to find all the parts of a fragmented file. Top performance is easily restored, however, by defragmenting the disk—moving the parts of each fragmented file to a sequence of contiguous disk sectors. You can defragment a disk yourself by backing it up (twice, just in case one backup goes bad), erasing it, and copying all the files back on again. But only a masochist with lots of free time would defragment a hard disk this way.

On a Macintosh, we use **DiskExpress II** because we're not masochists and, more importantly, because the program is fast and easy to use. DiskExpress II can defragment disks while you work, and it can prevent fragmentation from recurring once a disk is defragmented. It can also decrease the time it takes the drive to find a file by storing frequently used files in one area and less frequently used files in another (thus minimizing the distance the read/write head must travel to find frequently used files). **Speed Disk**, part of The Norton Utilities, offers some unusual enhancements, including a remarkable, though perhaps not very useful, map of your hard disk (Figure 6-2). But because it cannot defragment a disk while you work or prevent future defragmentation, Speed Disk is not our first choice.

Here is one note of caution about disk optimizers like DiskExpress II and Speed Disk: If you install a background "undelete" utility, such as the ones in SUM II or 911 Utilities, defragmentation will very likely destroy its ability to recover previously deleted files.

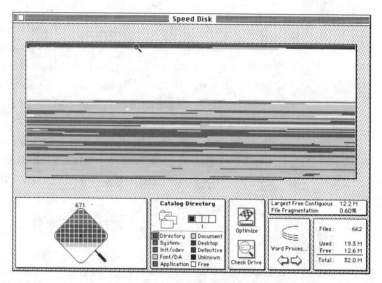

FIGURE 6-2 *Speed Disk's hard disk map uses different colors or shades of gray to indicate different types of files (free space is white); with the magnifying glass you can enlarge small areas to pinpoint the location of specific files.*

The benefit of a faster disk drive

Want a faster computer but can't afford it? Consider buying a faster hard disk. Many paint, draw, and page layout programs are disk intensive; that is, they spend a lot of time shuffling data back and forth between the hard disk and RAM. To spend less time waiting for your program and more time using the program's features, invest in a drive that has an access time of about 19 milliseconds or faster. You'll notice a big difference in performance.

Mice and keyboards

    ## Mouse maintenance

Is your Mac or Windows cursor lurching in fits and starts instead of sliding smoothly across the screen? Then it's time for a little internal mouse cleanup. Turn the mouse over and rotate the retaining ring counterclockwise so it pops loose and releases the mouse ball. Remove the ball and give it a good wipe with a clean, lint-free cloth. In the pocket where the ball sits are three rollers that get gummed up over time. You can gently remove most of the gunk with a small screwdriver, hairpin, or, our favorite, the clip end of the plastic top to a Bic pen. The rest should come off with a clean pencil eraser, but don't rub so hard that eraser crumbs fall into the mouse housing. Reinstall the ball, twist on the retaining ring, and you're back in business.

Bus versus serial mice

Bus mice attach to your PC via an interface card that mounts in one of the computer's expansion slots. People often assume that a mouse connected via such a direct bus interface is "faster" (by which most people seem to mean more responsive) than one connected via one of the computer's built-in serial ports. They make this assumption because serial connections to laser printers, and serial communication via modems is relatively slow.

The truth is, bus mice and serial mice are about equally fast and responsive. Some bus mice use a parallel data interface, many others use serial data interchange; in both cases, the data transfer rate is about the same—and not appreciably faster than a serial mouse. The IBM PS/2 mouse, though it plugs into a special connector on the PS/2, is in fact a serial mouse.

The real issue boils down to your PC's configuration. If all of your serial ports are tied up connecting modems or printers, then a bus mouse is the clear choice, provided you have a spare expansion slot in your PC. If, on the other hand, your PC is stuffed with expansion cards like a digital Thanksgiving turkey, a serial mouse is in order, provided you also have a spare serial port.

Learning to mouse

If you're new to using a mouse, you can speed yourself through the awkward developmental stages by using it awhile with your non-dominant hand (your left hand if you're right-handed, for example). When you switch back to your usual hand, you'll feel more adept with the mouse—positively professional. You might even discover your nondominant hand mouses better.

  ## Sticky key remedy

Faced with a sticky key on a Macintosh ADB keyboard, you could take the keyboard to your dealer for repairs (or replacement). Sticky keys can often be remedied easily at home or in the office, however; doing it yourself is quicker and cheaper, too. Here's what to do:

1. Buy a can of compressed air and some WD-40 lubricant.

2. Flip the keyboard over onto a clean, dry surface and carefully un-screw the back cover. Remove the back cover, lift the circuit and key assembly up, and flip it upright.

3. Use the compressed air to remove any gunk that has accumulated around the circuitry and key assembly. You'll probably be sur-prised at how much stuff has insinuated itself into the innards of your keyboard.

4. Use a wooden tongue depressor to carefully pry the sticky key's cap and stem out of its socket.

5. With the plastic applicator straw attached to the nozzle of your WD-40 can, squirt the smallest possible amount of lubricant down the hole where the stem of the key fits. Replace the key cap and give it a little exercise; it should now travel freely up and down.

6. Reassemble the keyboard.

For more about keyboard repairs and the like, you might want to invest in a copy of *Macintosh Repair and Upgrade Secrets* by Larry Pina. Pina's well-illustrated chapter on keyboard repairs covers only Macintosh 512 and Plus keyboards, but the concepts are the same for ADB keyboards and the details (such as the number of screws you must remove to open the back) differ only slightly. The book also explains how to replace a broken key, how to properly clean a mouse, how to adjust a Plus or SE monitor, and quite a bit more.

Central processing units

Buying a new 386

If a new 386 PC is in your future, you should ask the following questions about your prospective system's memory set-up:

- Does it have a motherboard RAM cache for the 386 processor?

A RAM cache improves a computer's performance, so you definitely want a computer that has one. A RAM cache keeps frequently used instructions in special high-speed memory where the 386 processor can get to it very quickly, much more quickly than it can in the low-speed RAM that forms the bulk of the system memory. RAM caches typically use fast (25 nanosecond) chips known as static RAM chips since those chips don't need the extra computer clock cycles to maintain the information they store. Too bad they're so expensive; otherwise our computers would simply use static RAM chips for all of the system memory. Instead, to keep the machines affordable, slower but cheaper dynamic RAM chips are used for the 2 to 16 megabytes of system memory that people typically install on 386 machines.

RAM caches are generally 64K to 256K in size. Although you might think that the bigger the cache the better, perhaps more important than the size of the RAM cache is the design of the cache controller. A good cache controller has logic that figures out which information the processor is most likely to need and keeps that information in the high-speed RAM cache. A good cache controller is one that yields a high number of cache "hits," and so cuts down the number of trips the 386 processor has to make to the slower RAM. There's no way you can judge the efficiency of a cache in a casual inspection, but some form of RAM cache is better than none at all.

By the way, don't confuse the term *RAM cache* with the term *disk cache*. A RAM cache enhances the performance of RAM memory; a disk cache enhances hard disk performance. A disk cache hangs onto frequently accessed information stored on your disk and keeps it in RAM. Since RAM access is faster than disk access, you notice better system performance in applications like desktop publishing, where the software frequently accesses your hard disk. An effective disk cache is usually about a megabyte in size, and PCs don't normally come with built-in disk caches. Some large capacity disk drives, especially those designed for use as file servers, have built in disk caches, some as large as 4MB.

- Does it have a zero wait state memory architecture?

If you can afford it, always pick a machine designed with zero wait states. In computers with slower, less expensive memory architecture, brief pauses must be introduced into the memory access cycle so that a fast processor (like the 386) doesn't outpace the slower memory. These scheduled pauses are called *wait states*; the processor waits out one or more computer cycles while the slower memory circuitry catches up. A machine designed with zero wait states is faster since it spends more time computing and less time waiting. Even a single wait state slows down the computer significantly, although the overall slowdown depends on other things, such as the effectiveness of the RAM cache, if there is one.

- How much RAM fits on the motherboard?

The 386 processor generally has faster access to the dynamic RAM mounted directly on the 386 motherboard than it does to the RAM added via expansion cards inserted into the computer's expansion slots. That's because expansion cards share a special "expansion bus," and the expansion bus often operates at a slower speed than the processor's bus. Also, further processing delays occur because extra computing cycles are required to manage the bus. Thus, the more RAM that fits on the motherboard, the better. A machine that can hold only 4 MB of motherboard RAM (often called "CPU-speed" RAM) doesn't leave you much room in the faster CPU-mounted RAM for next year's version of Windows or OS/2, or future applications that will inevitably require more RAM.

New life for an old Mac

Is there a 512KE Mac in your office with nothing to do? Install a fax/modem and use your old Mac to download electronic mail from services such as MCI Mail or CompuServe when rates are lowest in the middle of the night. Use a telecommunications program like **MicroPhone II**, whose script feature allows you to automate the entire download procedure, initiating the transfer at any time you set. Or, you can write a macro to do the job with a macro utility such as **Tempo II Plus**. If you like, attach a timer to the modem so it is turned on only when it's in use.

CP/M based computers

There are a surprising number of writers who stick by their sturdy KayPros or other CP/M-based machines. Over a decade ago, these machines were selling like hot-cakes while the far more expensive IBM PC and compatible computers were gradually taking over the personal computer marketplace.

Typically these older systems run early versions of WordStar on the CP/M (Control Program/Microcomputer) operating system. Sooner or later your publication will have a contributor who still uses one of these warhorses and submits a file on a 5¼-inch floppy disk from his or her machine. You'll pop the diskette into the A: drive of your

DOS-based computer, type DIR A: for a directory, and after a few seconds you'll read on your screen:

```
General failure reading drive A:
Abort, Retry, Fail?
```

This is clearly not welcome news, especially around deadline time. The problem is that each CP/M machine, whether a KayPro 2x, Morrow MD3, or venerable Osborne, used its own disk format, which of course isn't IBM compatible.

Fortunately there are several disk media conversion utilities for both the KayPro (and other CP/M machines) and IBM PC compatible computers. These utilities steal control of the computer's diskette drive hardware and make it act like a disk drive from another computer system, so either your author can convert the file to PC format before submission, or you can convert it after you receive it. Two such programs are Microsolutions' **UniForm** utility and Intersecting Concepts' **Media Master**. Both are available for both MS-DOS and CP/M machines. If you're a Kaypro 2x user, for example, these utilities will allow you to format a disk in IBM format and copy or save your files to that disk so any PC can read the disk and its files.

If you own a PC and are the receiver of CP/M files, an alternative and less expensive solution is Sydex's **22DISK** DOS shareware program which reads, writes, and formats about 300 different diskette media formats, including the once common KayPro 2X and Morrow MD3. If you don't find it on your local bulletin boards you can download it from Sydex's own BBS (503/683-1385) or order it direct. We've used it at *Publish* with great success. **XenoCopy-PC** for the PC also handles a huge range of disk formats and is easier to use, though more expensive than 22DISK.

If you only occasionally need CP/M to DOS disk conversion, you might find it more convenient to use a disk conversion service in your area. While walk-in service ranges between $35 to $70 per disk, mail order conversion is cheaper. Fog International Computer User's Group in Daly City, California, for example, charges nonmembers only $10 per disk, with a $10 set-up fee. Fog International is, in fact, the group to which WordStar often refers their CP/M software customers.

Keep in mind one caveat concerning CP/M to DOS conversions, however: Some CP/M-based computers, like the NorthStar models, used what are called hard-sector diskettes. These diskettes had evenly spaced holes punched through the media near the hub of the disk; the disk drive relied on the holes to determine the placement of data sectors and the location of the data. As a result, since current drives use electronic signals rather than holes, there's no way your IBM PC drive can read the data on hard-sector diskettes, no matter what conversion utility you use. You'll need to find a professional conversion service that has the machinery to read hard-sectored diskettes. To tell if you're dealing with a hard-sectored diskette, find the small hole in the diskette covering. Watch that hole as you rotate the disk within the cover, and count the holes that appear on the actual disk media as it turns. If you count more than one hole per revolution, you're holding a hard-sectored disk.

The difference between 386 and 386SX PCs

PC publishers shopping for new computers often ask us about the difference between 80386SX-based PCs and ordinary 80386-based PCs. Here's our standard non-technical answer, which includes a little microchip history as well:

The 80386SX was introduced in June, 1988, about three years after the 80386DX. The 80386SX design is nearly identical to its more powerful sibling. The chief difference is that the SX has only a 16-bit data channel (bus) to your computer's main memory, which is half the channel width of the 32-bit memory bus used by the 80386DX. In terms of actual processing, the 80386SX, like the 80386DX, works with 32 bit data; but it's a two-step process to get the 32 bit information into the chip via a 16 bit path. Picture a 32 lane freeway chopped down to 16 lanes, and you can see the speed trade-off. Still, the SX chip is about $100 cheaper for computer vendors, and, equally important, it uses cheaper 16 bit memory chips and other cheaper circuitry, resulting in computers priced $300 to $500 less than similar models with 80386DX processors. That's not necessarily a significant difference if you're buying just one computer, but it is if you're ordering 5 to 5,000.

Oldtimers will remember a similar state of affairs regarding the Intel 8086 chip (with 16 bit memory access) and the 8088 used by the original IBM PC. The 8088, though 16 bit on the inside (like the 8086), had a half-size (8-bit) memory channel. For IBM, the choice was a price performance trade-off since 8-bit memory and other support circuitry were cheaper than similar 16-bit parts at the time, and IBM wanted a relatively inexpensive machine.

So while PCs using Intel 80386SX microprocessors are usually less expensive than those using 80386DX chips (currently referred to as simply 80386), they also tend to run slower, with some exceptions. If we sound like we're fence-sitting a bit on the performance issue, it's because we've found some 80386SX machines that work faster overall than bargain basement 80386DX machines. This is due, in part, to the fact that there is now a 20 megahertz version of the SX chip (the original was 16 megahertz), and this higher speed SX chip reduces overall performance differences between 80386SX and 80386DX—especially in instances where an SX machine packs a better disk drive and RAM cache than a DX machine. In addition, most programs running under DOS and Windows on a 80386DX machine don't take full advantage of 32-bit data access anyway.

As always, keep in mind that raw processor speed is tempered by memory speed, memory cache designs, coprocessor speeds, video performance, and disk access rates. You have to evaluate the performance of the whole system. SX-based systems take advantage of the same Windows virtual memory, extended memory access, and multi-tasking features, as do 80386DX-based systems. However, if you're working primarily with full-color graphics (especially with scanned images), CAD, or complex graphics illustrations (in Corel-DRAW or Designer, for example)—or wherever seconds count—spend the extra money for a full 80386-based computer (the DX is also available in even faster 25MHz and 33MHz versions). Otherwise, the 80386SX should do fine.

80286 vs. 80386SX-based PCs for publishing

There are some really great buys in 80286-based computers, and many people ask us whether they're obsolete with the latest offering of 80386SX-based computers. Our answer is no, they're not obsolete, and the faster 15 or 20 mHz 286-based models aren't slower than comparable 386SX-based computers. Intel is pushing the 386SX over the 80286 as the new chip for entry level computers, partly because they've been the sole supplier of the chip until recently. With the 286 they face greater competition since two other companies, AMD (Advanced Micro Devices) and Harris Corp., are licensed to produce and market various versions of the 286. Still, 80286-based computers, especially if they're of the 12 to 20 megahertz variety, work fine with Windows if you install the 4 MB of memory and the faster hard drives that often come with 386SX systems. Under Windows, unlike the 80386SX, the 286 will only run a single DOS program, not several; it can't use hard disk space as overflow memory for Windows applications, and it doesn't perform multi-tasking as effectively. But many PC publishers don't rely on those features. It's fashionable these days to dump on the 286, but don't be a slave to fashion and dump the 286-based computers you've already paid for, or relegate them to mundane, non-Windows tasks. They can still perform for you if configured comparably to 386SX-based machines.

Grab bag

AppleTalk subnets for speed

Printing traffic can seriously slow down AppleTalk networks. If there are some heavy printer users on your network, you can isolate them on a subnet using a network bridge device such as **Hayes' Inter-Bridge**. Putting the printer and its most frequent users on the subnet localizes their network traffic but keeps the printer available to everyone on the net.

One switch for all

The more often you flip a power switch, the more likely it is to fail. Power switches for computer hardware can be expensive to replace, and when they break they put your equipment out of commission for a while. It is thus a good strategy to attach all your equipment to a multi-plug surge suppressor, and use the surge suppressor switch to turn them all on and off together. Since the switches on your computer and its peripherals remain in the on position at all times, wear and tear on your hardware power switches is eliminated. If the switch on the surge suppressor goes bad, your hardware is still in working condition, and the surge suppressor can be replaced quickly and cheaply.

Saving documents after a crash

If your Macintosh bombs or freezes and no amount of effort on your part brings it back to life, there's one more tactic you can try before heading for the Reset button (if there's a bomb dialog box on the screen) or the Reset switch (the frontmost of the two switches on the little, user-installed, plastic doodad stuck to the side of your Mac). This tactic works only some of the time, but it's always worth a try since unsaved work is invariably lost when you reset the computer.

The technique is simple. First, press the Interrupt switch (the second switch on the plastic doodad, behind the Reset switch). A box with a ">" in the upper left corner may appear on screen. If it does, type G Finder and press Return. With luck, and if you've been working under System 7 or System 6 with MultiFinder turned on, you'll return to the Finder and your unsaved documents. Immediately save your documents, quit all applications, and select RESTART from the Special menu. Restarting after recovery is vitally important. Do not simply continue working after an Interrupt switch recovery; your Mac may be in a fragile state and may crash again.

System software

Managing files and documents

Long file names in the Open dialog box

In the standard Macintosh Open dialog box, the endings of long file names are replaced by an ellipsis, making some files difficult or impossible to tell apart. If you can't resist using long file names, there are several ways to see more of them in the Open dialog box. One way is to use **Super Boomerang** (part of Now Software's Now Utilities). Super Boomerang squeezes together the letters of long file names in the Open dialog box; all but the longest file names are displayed in their entirety. **NameViewer** (AaStar Technologies), another solution to the problem, takes a different approach. It displays the full file name of the selected file plus your choice of additional file information (such as date or time created, file type or creator, and file size), either automatically at the bottom of the Open dialog box (Figure 7-1) or in a pop-up box at the press of a key. NameViewer is shareware and is available from many electronic bulletin boards and user group software libraries.

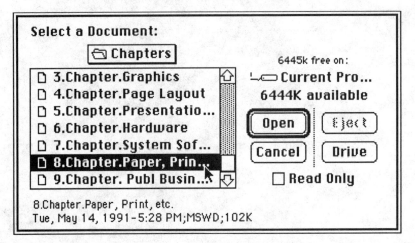

FIGURE 7-1 *NameViewer displays the full file name of the selected file and other information at the bottom of the Open dialog box.*

Keeping track of publication files

Help yourself recognize which publication you've saved on a 5¼-inch diskette by printing a scaled-down version of the first couple of pages using a PostScript printer. The miniature pages can then be placed inside the disk jacket along with the disk. If you draw a blank with the file names printed on the disk label, the scaled-down print version of the publication should help jog your memory.

Lost chapters

If you've mistakenly deleted the original chapters (CHP files) from a **Ventura Publisher** (PC editions) publication, don't bother trying to recover them by means of the document's multichapter (PUB) files. You can't use the PUB file to reconstruct CHP files because the PUB file only contains pointers to CHP files; it does not actually replicate the information contained in those files.

Your only hope for recovering CHP files is to either use a file recovery utility, such as the Norton or Mace utilities, or else look on your hard disk for files with an $HP extension. These are backups to the corresponding CHP files. They're automatically generated by Ventura if you've turned on the *Back Up Copy* option under the Preferences selection of the Options menu in the GEM Edition, or if you've selected *Yes* as the *Keep Backup Files* option in the Set Preferences dialog box under the Edit menu of the Windows Edition. To recover the text in these $HP files, use the DOS RENAME command to give them CHP extensions, keeping the remainder of each file name unchanged. First, for safety sake, copy the .$HP extension files to diskette(s). Then use the DOS command `REN *.$HP *.CHP` to automatically rename all files with a $HP extension in the specified subdirectory so that all have a .CHP extension instead. Then load the chapters as usual.

Managing your INITs

If your Macintosh System folder looks anything like ours, it's stuffed with startup documents (INITs) which the Macintosh automatically loads at startup. Many handy utilities come in INIT format, and INITs are also supplied with many types of hardware (such as CD ROM players and large-screen monitors). Frankly, INITs tend to proliferate like coat hangers in a dark closet. Unfortunately, when a lot of INITs congregate in a System Folder, they can misbehave. A conflict between two or more inimical INITs can prevent one or more of them from functioning properly or, worse, cause your Mac to crash.

To help determine the cause of and to resolve INIT conflicts, an INIT manager is extremely handy. We've always preferred Microseeds Publishings' **INITPicker**, but a recent newcomer, **INIT Manager** from Baseline Publishing, has made the choice much more difficult. Both programs allow you to turn INITs on and off, create and select startup sets containing different combinations of INITs, and rearrange the order in which INITs load (a common technique for eliminating conflicts). Both are able to identify and disable some, if not all, troublemakers. INIT Manager can generate a detailed startup report, which the technically inclined can use to pinpoint otherwise intractable problems. INITPicker, however, has a more elegant interface (Figure 7-2), a better manual, and in some instances is faster than INIT Manager. Ultimately, we still have a slight preference for INITPicker, but either one of these programs will serve you well.

 Finding the "Application Not Found"

Generally speaking, if you double-click on a document, the Macintosh will launch the appropriate application and automatically open the document as well. But sometimes—if you double-click on a text-only document, for example, expecting to open your word processor—you'll get an "Application Not Found" message.

The problem is that many text-only files, such as text files downloaded from an E-mail system, are not properly linked to the

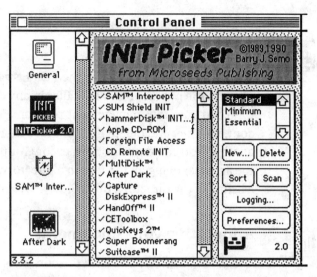

FIGURE 7-2 *In INITPicker, only checked INITs are run at startup, and you can select (from the list on the right) from any number of user-defined INIT sets.*

application that created them, or if they are, they're linked to a word processing program that you don't have. You can usually open such files by launching your word processing program first and selecting the file with the program's OPEN command. The same problem occurs with generic PICT files, and much the same solution applies as well.

If you get the "Application Not Found" message frequently, you should consider using **HandOff II**. Once installed in your System folder, this utility allows you to link specific types of files to specific applications, such as plain text files to your word processing program. You can also use it to link one application's files to another application (such as old MacPaint files to SuperPaint) or to link all files with names ending in a certain suffix to a particular application (for example, to link all converted PC text files whose names end with .*wrd* to Microsoft Word). Once specific file types have been linked to specific programs, you can double-click on any file to open both it and the appropriate application.

Built-in file manager

You can use **WordPerfect** for the PC's LIST FILES command, which displays the names and sizes of files in any directory, as a substitute for a separate file management program. With List Files, you can copy, rename, and delete files, or move them from one directory to another. You can tag multiple files for group operations by pressing the asterisk; to tag all the files in a directory, press Alt + F5. To print a listing of the directory, press Shift + F7.

Annotating your documents

Use the comments text box at the bottom of a file's Get Info window to keep notes on that document as it moves through your edit cycle (Figure 7-3). Editors and designers can add pithy comments, their initials, and the date, for example, every time they make changes to the document.

To open a file's Get Info window, click once (don't double-click) on the document icon in the Finder to highlight it, and then select GET

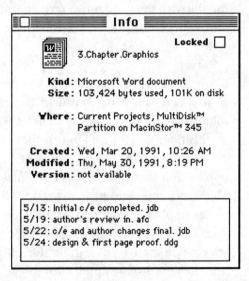

FIGURE 7-3 *Use a file's Get Info window to keep notes on a document as it passes through the edit cycle.*

INFO from the File menu or press Command + I. If you turn on the *Locked* option in the upper right corner of Get Info window, you'll prevent anyone from making changes to the document. Locking a file in this fashion is a fairly effective if somewhat devious way to force others to review the collected comments. An editor who wants to work on the locked document will have to open the Get Info window and turn the *Locked* option off and will see the comments which appear just below.

Keep in mind that Get Info comments are stored in the disk's Desktop file. (Although, or perhaps because, it is vital to the proper functioning of your Mac, the Desktop file is normally invisible to humans.) If you find it necessary to rebuild the Desktop file, all the notes for all the files on that disk or drive will be erased. (Rebuild the Desktop file by pressing Command + Option while inserting a floppy disk or mounting a hard drive.)

Fast file and application launching

In the average Macintosh hard disk, applications, documents, and more are stored in a complex (but, one hopes, orderly) hierarchy of folders within folders. To find a file or application, you frequently must climb laboriously out of one nested sequence of folders and dive into another. Too often, the shortest route to a needed file is anything but a straight line, and wrong turns are frustratingly easy. Listing all your commonly used applications and files in a menu is a good way to avoid such folder floundering. Instead of searching through folders, you simply select the desired file or application from the menu. System 7 allows you to do just that, in fact, by creating aliases and adding them to the Apple menu. But two utilities, **Hand-Off II** from The Handoff Corporation and Icom Simulations' **On Cue**, go a step or two farther.

Although both utilities improve upon several System 7 inovations, HandOff II is the more versatile of the two (and as of press time, the only one of the two that's System 7 compatible). Both On Cue and HandOff II create a menu (standard menu bar variety or pop-up, your choice) containing a user-defined list of commonly-used applications and documents; in both, documents are organized according to application and listed in submenus appended to the appropriate applications. But in HandOff II, you can group applications together in submenus (Figure 7-4). Select the category name, and the default application (the one marked with a check) opens; select any other application within the submenu to open that application.

You can also specify a collection—what HandOff calls a briefcase—of documents belonging to several applications and add it to the menu; select the briefcase, and its applications and documents are opened all at once. And you can specify a color depth (black and white, 16 colors, 256 colors, etc.) for each application, so that when you switch from one to the other, the color depth changes accordingly. As good as the program is, however, HandOff II's manual leaves a lot to be desired; plan to spend some time figuring out just what HandOff II can do and how it works.

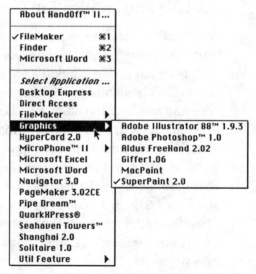

FIGURE 7-4 *To minimize menu clutter, HandOff II's pop-up menu can group applications into category submenus.*

Cryptic names protect files

You can prevent other people from accessing your DOS files by placing a hidden character in the file name. When you name the file,
make one of the characters a blank by holding down the Alt Key and
typing 255 on the numeric keypad. It's best to begin or end the name
this way, so the missing character isn't apparent; otherwise a space
will appear in the file name. Someone snooping among your files
won't know about the hidden character, so they won't be able to enter
the correct file name in order to open the file. This technique won't
stop a determined computer hacker. Neither will it stop anyone
from wiping them out with wildcard DOS commands like DEL * . *,
which erases all files except those with read-only or hidden system
file attributes. But it will stop anyone from casually or accidentally
altering your files.

This technique also works with directory names, so you can tuck
your files away in their own disguised subdirectory. Give the subdirectory name an extension using the Alt-255 combination—people don't usually expect subdirectories to have file extensions
anyway. Anyone entering the subdirectory name for a file path in a
DOS command will get an *Invalid Directory* error since they omitted
the hidden character. DOS file utilities, such as XTREE Professional,
that let you choose subdirectories via on-screen menus will circum-
vent the protection provided by this technique. Windows File Manager won't let you access a directory disguised this way, however,
since it will report that a disguised directory contains no files, even
if it does.

Tools for Open and Save dialog boxes

We often discover that we need to perform some minor task, such as
creating a new folder, after we've opened the Mac's Save dialog box.
Normally, this means cancelling the dialog box, doing the deed, and
then opening the dialog box again. But if you have a utility like Aladdin Systems' **Shortcut** o r **SuperBoomerang** (p a r t of Now
Software's Now Utilities), you can easily perform simple tasks such

as creating a new folder from within the Open or Save dialog box. Both these programs allow you to move quickly to commonly-used files and folders, delete files, rename files, create new folders, and find lost files—all within Open and Save dialog boxes (Figure 7-5). The file and folder menus in both utilities list the most recently opened files and folders; you can also instruct them to list certain files and folders at all times.

In SuperBoomerang, you can create permanent file and folder lists specific to individual applications. SuperBoomerang also appends a submenu of user-defined and recently opened files to an application's OPEN command. Shortcut, on the other hand, is distinguished by its ability to work with files archived by Aladdin Systems' StuffIt Classic and StuffIt Deluxe. Shortcut can list the files in a StuffIt Classic archive, unstuff a stuffed file, and, if you own StuffIt Deluxe, compress a file—all from within Open and Save dialog boxes. We tend to like the clean and simple interface of Shortcut; neither program, however, will disappoint.

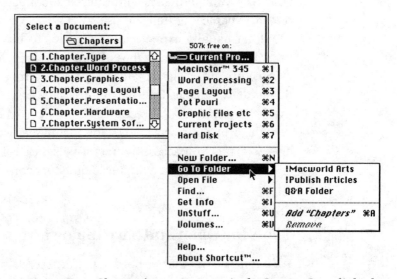

FIGURE 7-5 *From Shortcut's pop-up menu in the Open or Save dialog box, you can create a new folder, find a lost file, or move quickly to a different volume or a commonly-used folder.*

Quick start for multiple documents

Here's a quick way to resume working on a project that involves a number of different documents on the Macintosh. In the Finder, select the files you want to open by pressing the Shift Key as you click on each one. Then, with the Shift Key released, double-click on any one of the selected files. If all the documents belong to the same application, and if that application lets you open multiple documents (PageMaker for the Mac is a notable exception here), the application will launch and all the selected documents will open automatically.

If you're using either System 6 with MultiFinder turned on or System 7, you can select documents from several different applications. When you double-click on any one of the selected documents, all of the corresponding applications will launch and open their documents automatically. In System 6, the selected documents must all be in the same folder (the applications, of course, can be stored anywhere). System 7's hierarchical view, on the other hand, allows you to select multiple documents no matter where they're stored.

Managing memory

Memory use in Windows

Since 386SX computers have come down in price, lots of folks are begging their bosses to buy them one instead of a 80286-based computer. Many 386SX-based machines come with only 2MB of memory, and we're often asked how to set these machines up to get the maximum performance under **Windows** with this less-than-ample amount of memory. Here's our advice:

- Whether on not you intend to run DOS applications and Windows applications under Windows, configure your system with 640K of conventional memory and the remainder as extended memory. If any of the DOS programs you intend to use require LIM EMS (Lotus, Intel, Microsoft Expanded Memory Specification) memory, configure your system with the maximum amount of LIM EMS memory those DOS applications use and leave the remaining memory as extended memory (preserving 640K of conventional memory, of course). Windows will emulate EMS memory for any Windows application that requires it.

Expanded memory is a special type of added memory, designed to give specially written programs (including earlier versions of Windows) access to more RAM than the 640K that DOS can use. It employs a complex scheme to temporarily swap portions of memory from areas DOS *can't* use into memory areas that DOS *can* use. Extended memory is more straightforward. It extends in one large block above the one megabyte of memory space used by DOS and can be accessed directly by operating systems or programs (like OS/2 or Windows 3.0) that use the extended memory accessing features of the 80286 or 80386 microprocessors. Since extended memory entails less rigamarole, it operates faster than expanded memory. Maximizing the amount extended memory available results in better Windows performance.

- You can reserve more memory for your programs by minimizing the amount reserved exclusively for the Windows SmartDrive disk cache. (The disk cache keeps disk information on call in system memory for faster file access.) To do that you'll need to edit your system's CONFIG.SYS file. Use the Windows Notepad accessory, or even more conveniently, type SYSEDIT at the RUN prompt command line from the File menu of the Windows Program Manager. This will launch the Windows System Configuration Editor and automatically load the CONFIG.SYS, AUTOEXEC.BAT, WIN.INI, and SYSTEM.INI files for editing.

  In the CONFIG.SYS file, you'll see an entry like this:

```
DEVICE=C:\WINDOWS\SMARTDRV.SYS 768 512
```

The first of the two numbers at the right end of the entry is the maximum size of the disk cache (in bytes), much of which Windows will release to programs that need more memory. The second number is the amount of memory reserved exclusively for the disk cache, the amount that SmartDrive won't release. Change that second number to something lower, say 64, and then reboot your computer.

But before you get too worried about available memory, remember that Windows running in 386 Enhanced mode, as it does on your 80386SX-based computer, uses its virtual memory capability to temporarily swap portions of application program code and data from memory to your hard disk should you run out of extended memory. If you're curious, double click the About Program Manager button under the Program Managers' Help menu. Unless your disk drive is full, you'll probably see a listing of free memory which is much greater than the RAM you have available. Much of that free memory is actually free hard disk space.

Since disks (being mechanical) are slower than RAM, Windows will run noticeably slower when it has to rely on virtual memory. You can, however, minimize the problem and speed up virtual memory (and file access in general) by optimizing your hard disk with products like Norton Utilities Speed Disk, which defragments disk files so the computer doesn't have to jump around the disk to read a whole file. Also, setting up a permanent swap file for Windows will further speed up virtual memory by giving Windows more direct access to the disk space. Here's how to set up a permanent swap file:

1. Exit Windows. Then restart Windows in Real mode by typing WIN/R and pressing Return at the DOS prompt. Window's Real mode runs in your computer's conventional memory only, just as did versions of Windows prior to 3.0.

2. Run Windows SWAPFILE.EXE utility by typing SWAPFILE at the RUN command under the Program Manager file menu. SWAPFILE can only run in Windows Real mode because the utility makes

direct function calls to DOS, which aren't permitted in Windows' Standard and Enhanced modes.

3. The Swapfile dialog box will appear and report the amount of free space on your disk plus the maximum amount of space that can be used for a swapfile. The Swapfile dialog box prompts you with a recommended swap file size that's usually some rather large proportion of your free disk space, so enter the amount you think you'll really need. If you work with large scanned images, or like to keep lots of applications loaded and ready to run, then create a large file (10 MB and beyond). Otherwise, keep it around 3 to 6 MB.

The maximum swapfile size refers to the largest clump of available disk sectors that are unbroken by random sectors of stored information—often referred to as "unfragmented disk space." You may find that the maximum swapfile size is smaller than the total free space on your disk. This means that your disk is fragmented, to some extent, with free space interspersed between blocks of recorded data. If the maximum swapfile space is less than what you'd like to specify, defragment your disk by using a disk optimizing utility, or by backing up your entire hard disk, reformatting it, and restoring your files. Keep in mind that swapfile disk space is only used for virtual memory swapping and nothing else. Unless you have hard disk space to waste, don't blow more disk space on it than you need.

Windows can only create swapfiles on disks formatted using 512K disk segments. We've occasionally run into hard disks that used larger segments and special partitioning drivers in the CONFIG.SYS file; these hard disks will not allow you to install a permanent swap file. No need to panic; just rely on Window's temporary swapfile unless the disk vendor can find a workaround for you. Be forewarned that their workaround may entail repartitioning and reformatting your drive, which most likely won't be worth the effort.

Jump start Windows applications

To save start-up time on your PC, it's possible to automatically open **PageMaker** for Windows and also load Table Editor (PageMaker's companion table editor, included in version 4.0) each time you launch Windows. You can do so by editing your WIN.INI file (in the Windows subdirectory) as follows:

1. Using Windows Notepad, open WIN.INI and find the "run=" line at the beginning of the file under the Windows heading. Change this line to read: `run=PM4.EXE`.

2. To automatically load Table Editor, change the "load=" line in the same file to read: `load=TE.EXE`.

3. Save your WIN.INI file, and then exit and restart Windows (type `WIN`) for the changes to take effect.

Now PageMaker will open in an active window and Table Editor will load as an icon at the bottom of the screen each time you start Windows. This tip should work with most Windows programs if you include the program directory as part of the PATH statement in your MS-DOS AUTOEXEC.BAT file, or if you include the application's full path name in Window's WIN.INI *run=* line. (The computer has to know where your application resides in order to launch it.)

Windows and GEM memory management

On the PC, many **Ventura Publisher** fanatics prefer the look, feel, and speed of the GEM Edition—but prefer Windows-based graphics and spreadsheets programs like **CorelDRAW** and **Microsoft Excel**. Trouble is, GEM and Windows use different memory configurations. Ventura Publisher GEM Edition, with its professional features and the EDCO hyphenation dictionary enabled, requires about 1.5 megabytes of LIM EMS (Lotus, Intel, Microsoft Expanded Memory Specification) memory. Windows and Windows applications, on the other hand, don't require EMS memory and actually run better in extended memory. Here are several ways you can accommodate both:

- If possible, configure your memory added above 640K as part-expanded and part-extended. (See "Memory use for Windows" earlier in this chapter for an explanation of expanded and extended memory and how they work with Windows.) Some memory expansion boards (like Intel's Above Board Plus) let you partition the memory on the board in just this way. Alternatively, 386 memory management software, like Quarterdeck's QEMM-386 or Qualitas' 386MAX, let you create a mix of expanded and extended memory out of the memory installed above 640K on your 386 computer. In either case, reserve enough expanded memory (LIM EMS) for Ventura GEM Edition and leave the rest as extended memory. Both Windows and Ventura will then have extra memory they can use.

- If your memory set-up doesn't allow for a mix of expanded and extended memory, another solution is to create two CONFIG.SYS files (which set up your expanded memory and other options at startup) and then use batch files to activate one or the other:

  1. Name the CONFIG.SYS file that configures your extra memory for Ventura as CONFIG.XVP and name the CONFIG.SYS file that configures suitable memory for Windows as CONFIG.WIN.

  2. Create one batch file, named USEWIN.BAT, containing the following command lines:

     ```
     cd c:\
     erase CONFIG.SYS
     copy config.win CONFIG.SYS
     ```

  3. Create another batch file, NOWIN.BAT, with these command lines:

```
cd c:\
erase CONFIG.SYS
copy config.xvp CONFIG.SYS
```

4. If you don't already have a BAT directory on your hard disk for batch files, create such a subdirectory and add it to your AU-TOEXEC.BAT file's PATH command. Save both of the above batch files in the BAT directory.

Now, with all your batch and config files in place, let's say you've been working with Ventura GEM Edition and now want to use CorelDRAW in Windows. To do so, quit Ventura and type USEWIN at the DOS prompt, reboot the computer, and start Windows. On the other hand, if you've been using Windows and want to switch to Ventura GEM Edition, you'd quit Windows, type NOWIN at the DOS prompt, and reboot the computer before starting Ventura GEM Edition.

Keep in mind that Ventura needs all the base 640K memory it can get, so unload any RAM resident utilities you don't need. If you use a 386-based computer, use 386MAX or any of several other utilities which let DOS run RAM resident utilities, plus mouse and network drivers, into the DOS-addressable conventional memory space above the 640K. This area is normally reserved for video RAM, system ROM, and other functions, but there's usually unused memory space available. The new DOS 5.0 can also move RAM resident utilities and drivers to these reserved memory areas.

With clever memory management you can actually get Ventura Publisher GEM Edition and Windows to run simultaneously on a 386, a set-up that allows you to conveniently switch between GEM Ventura, Windows applications, and other DOS programs. Using Qualitas' 386MAX, for example, at *Publish* we've been able to run Ventura Publisher GEM Edition under Windows, including the professional features and the EDCO dictionary, and several other programs. To do so, we allocated the mix of extended and expanded memory. But, most important of all, we made sure that the 386MAX utility, the mouse driver, Window's SmartDrive driver, and the DOS memory resident SHARE utility were all moved out of the 640K memory area into reserved RAM space. Fortunately, the Maximize utility that comes with 386MAX automatically sets up our computer's AU-TOEXEC.BAT and CONFIG.SYS files to take care of all this.

Here's why it's important to maximize the amount of base 640K memory available for your DOS programs: Windows creates a special DOS window for each DOS application (like Ventura Publisher GEM Edition or WordPerfect) that you run under Windows. Each of these DOS windows acts like a separate DOS environment with its own copy of DOS in which to run. (These DOS windows are also called "virtual machines" since each window acts like a separate DOS computer and relies on a special "virtual machine" feature of the 386 chip.) Trouble is, if your 640K of base memory space has been whittled down to 490K because you've loaded memory-hogging pop-up utilities, network and mouse drivers, disk cache utilities and the like, then the memory associated with each separate DOS window (virtual machine) you open will be reduced to the same degree. For example, on a standard Windows set-up on our LaserMaster 386 WinEngine, with mouse driver, SHARE, HIMEM.SYS, and SMARTDRV.SYS loaded, only about 530K of the original 640K remains free. Likewise, any DOS windows we open have only about 520K left to run a DOS application—rather tight for Ventura GEM Edition. On the other hand, after using 386MAX Maximize utility and rebooting our 386, we have 580K remaining of the original 640K. Each DOS window gets about 570K—and Ventura runs nicely, though you may run out of memory if your document uses large, complex graphics.

Good medicine, preventive and otherwise

Healing the sick file or disk

Individual files can become corrupted and refuse to open for a variety of (mostly arcane) reasons. And even the most cautious Mac owner has been known to erase a file or reformat a whole disk accidentally. Although there's no foolproof way to prevent such traumas, complete recovery is often possible with the right tools. If the damage is minor, Apple's **Disk First Aid**—a utility program included in the Macintosh System disks—may be able to repair a floppy disk for you. But if Disk First Aid doesn't help, you'll need an industrial strength recovery utility.

For file recovery, the tools we've found most helpful are those in **911 Utilities**. Only recently patched together from several different programs, 911's seams still show. As a result, making sense of it all requires a little extra effort on your part. And, unlike some other file recovery programs that run more or less on automatic, 911 expects you to be an active participant in the recovery process. But the program's Troubleshooting Guide is invaluable, and, with its help, 911 Utilities can salvage all but the most hopelessly wrecked file. In addition, 911 Utilities is unique in its ability to pull unformatted text from word processor and page layout documents which are hopelessly wrecked.

For repairing flaky or crashed disks, on the other hand, we prefer the **Norton Utilities for the Macintosh**. In addition to performing all the standard recovery procedures, Norton Utilities can shake down a troublesome disk better than anything we've seen. The program checks to make sure that the number of files in the directory and the number on the disk are the same, that areas recorded as "in use" actually do contain files, and that two files are not assigned the same location on the disk—and fixes these problems when they are discovered. It fixes folders that won't open and files that won't delete. It searches out duplicate copies of the System and Finder. And it checks every file on the disk for missing Finder icons, incorrect Finder information (bundle bits), and more. If your disk isn't clean and sober when Norton gets through with it, then it's likely that nothing will straighten it out.

SUM II (Symantec Utilities for the Macintosh) is also a popular choice for file and disk recovery, one that we've used frequently with success. It's not our favorite, but it's cheaper than buying both Norton and 911; anyone who purchases a copy will definitely get his or her money's worth.

Relieving backup pain

Sadly, even the best recovery program cannot resuscitate a disk whose time is up. When your hard disk is laid to rest atop Boot No More Hill, you better hope that there's a recent backup of your critical files somewhere back at the ranch. Unfortunately, most backup programs succumb to the proverbial featuritis double-bind: The more flexible the program is (by offering all kinds of options and customizable features), the more difficult it is to use. As a result, many Mac owners fail to back up as often as they should, and some don't back up at all. These folks, of course, are just asking for trouble.

For those who feel that backing up is an especially onerous task, there are two Macintosh backup programs, SuperMac's **DiskFit** and Microseeds' **Redux,** which we feel relieve backing up pain better than most. Both programs are easy to use, yet relatively powerful, and impose no size limit on the file to be backed up. Both also reclaim and reuse disk space on existing backup disks during incremental backups (many programs simply tack new and changed programs onto the end of the current backup sequence).

Some backup programs store backup files in standard Finder file format while others, in a quest for greater speed, store files in a proprietary format comprehensible only to the backup program. Many people are uncomfortable if they can't view and retrieve their backup files in the Finder, and they worry that the translation to and from a proprietary format increases the possibility of backup errors. If this describes you, use DiskFit; it always creates Finder-readable backup files. DiskFit can also perform an unattended backup (after you leave for the night, for example) and then turn off your Mac II when it's finished.

Redux (Figure 7-6) is also an excellent choice for backup, so long as you're not concerned about backup file format. It only stores backup files in Finder-readable format if all the files you want to backup fit on a single backup volume (such as a removable hard drive). Otherwise, the program stores backup files in a format only Redux can understand. Backing up with Redux is, however, about as easy as it gets. Power users also like Redux since they can automate backups with Redux's scripting language BackTalk.

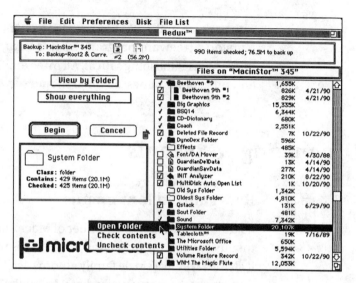

FIGURE 7-6 *Pop-up menus make it easy to view and select files for Redux to back up; information about the selected folder (left) and all currently selected files (top) is always available.*

Keeping viruses at bay

Our readers hardly need to be reminded (we hope) that a computer virus can put a Mac out of commission just as effectively as a flu virus can lay you low. Even worse, a really nasty virus can destroy data stored on a hard or floppy disk. Since the only Mac immune to virus attack is one that's switched off, an anti-virus program is an essential part of every software library.

Of the anti-virus programs for the Mac, we especially like **SAM** (Symantec AntiVirus for Macintosh). It has all three elements essential to effective virus protection: It can locate and in many instances eradicate existing infections. It lurks in the background and prevents new infections from occurring. And last but not least, Symantec operates a virus hotline which informs callers of the latest viral strains and alerts registered users of new viruses by postcard. You can enter new virus definitions manually, or dowload a new virus definition file; either way, you don't have to wait (or pay) for a software upgrade.

Although we prefer SAM, other Mac owners we know swear by John Norstad's freeware program **Disinfectant**, Microcom's **Virex**, or Microseeds Publishing's **Rival**. All three eradicate existing infections and prevent new ones; all three should serve you well.

....

Organizing your fonts

....

 ### Reorganized font menus

As time goes on and the number of Macintosh fonts increases, Font menus are getting longer and longer. This might not be so onerous if all the faces in a single family automatically grouped together, but, unfortunately, they usually don't. In Adobe's standard font naming scheme, for example, the names of all bold faces begin with an uppercase B and thus all cluster together; italic faces all begin with an I and make their own cluster; and bold-italic faces begin with BI and make yet another cluster. Since they don't begin with a special prefix, the roman (plain) faces are scattered all up and down the menu. All told, it's hard to imagine a less convenient system.

Fortunately, there are several ways you can better organize your Font menu. One is to use the utility programs that come with **Suitcase II** and **MasterJuggler** to group related fonts into families (combining Times with Times Italic, Times Bold, and Times Bold Italic, for example). The result of such groupings is that only the main family name is listed in the Font menu; to specify a face other than the roman face, you apply the appropriate style (*Bold, Italic,* or both). The drawback to this method is that only four style variants—usually roman, italic, bold, and bold-italic—are grouped together. In complex families with additional faces, such as light, semibold, and condensed, the extra ungrouped faces still clutter the Font menu.

An alternative solution, one that deals better with the complex font family problem, is **Adobe Type Reunion**. A Font menu modified with Type Reunion lists only font families. Each family name leads to a submenu, from which all the faces in that family, no matter how numerous, can be selected (Figure 7-7). Type Reunion is in most respects an elegant way to clean up a font menu, but it, too, has its drawbacks. For one thing, every face, even the Roman face, must be selected from a submenu; if you're not fond of submenus, Type Reunion is not for you. Equally irritating is the fact that scrolling font lists remain as disorganized as before.

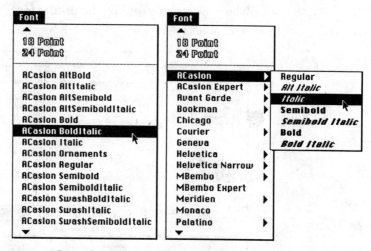

FIGURE 7-7 *This is the same Font menu, with (right) and without (left) the help of Adobe Type Reunion.*

 Maintaining space with rarely used fonts

Do you have a lot of fonts installed in **Windows**, fonts that you hardly ever use but which take up a lot of valuable hard disk space? To free up some of that hard disk space for more productive uses, you can remove seldom-used fonts and replace them only when you need them. Here's how: Copy the WIN.INI file from your Windows directory and the .PFA (or .PFB) files from your PSFONTS subdirectory onto floppy disks. Then use the Windows Control Panel to remove from your hard disk the fonts you don't need. When you need them again, just copy the appropriate WIN.INI file to the Windows sub-directory and font files to the fonts subdirectory.

. . . .

Store your font files somewhere else

You can clean up a System Folder cluttered with an overabundance of font files (in System 7 as well as in System 6) by installing a font utility such as **MasterJuggler** or **Suitcase II** and storing screen and printer fonts in one or more folders either inside or outside the System Folder (Figure 7-8). As long as you keep screen font files and the corresponding printer font files in the same folder, your applications will have no trouble finding the printer fonts when it comes time to download them.

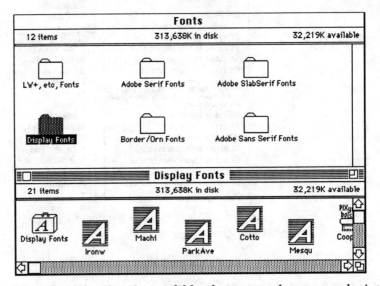

FIGURE 7-8 *To eliminate System folder clutter, store the screen and printer files for your PostScript fonts in a special Fonts folder, organize them in any convenient way, and install them with Suitcase II or MasterJuggler.*

Grab bag

A better Windows PostScript driver

The PostScript driver for Windows 3.0 that's included with Micrografx Designer 3.1 offers a wider range of printer choices and printing options than the one Microsoft supplies with Windows. It's also available directly from Micrografx for $199. The Micrografx driver makes font handling much easier since it has menus for installing and downloading PostScript fonts. Windows only offers that convenience with Hewlett-Packard LaserJet fonts. With the Micrografx driver you can download PostScript fonts to printer memory or to an attached SCSI drive, but you can also change your mind and specify that the fonts automatically download when you print.

The Micrografx driver can also help you avoid "limitcheck" PostScript errors on high-resolution imagesetters. This type of error often occurs when printing a document too complex for the imagesetter to process. For files that are having trouble printing, you can adjust the driver's Curve Quality setting from the default of 100 (highest quality) to a slightly lower setting, which in most cases will simplify the print job enough to squeak by without visibly affecting print quality. If you have trouble with hairline rules printing too thinly, you can use the Default Line Width setting to force all rules to a minimum width—4 pixels, for example.

You should be aware that the Micrografx driver ignores any PostScript fonts you've already installed for use with the Microsoft driver. You'll need to use the Micrografx driver to reinstall the font information, a simple process with the most recently released version (2.6) of the driver. You won't find much mention of the Micrografx PostScript driver in the Designer 3.1 documentation, but it's fairly well covered in Designer's on-line Help function.

· ·

Saving keystrokes with macros

Most Mac owners would prefer to issue a single command, rather than a sequence of ten or twenty keystrokes, to achieve the same result. Such commands are called macros, and a utility that creates macros is a great way to eliminate repetitive typing and boost your productivity. We particularly like three Macintosh macro programs. Apple's **MacroMaker** is a real low-brainer; using it requires little brainpower on your part, and MacroMaker offers relatively little braininess in return. Since it is part of the Macintosh System software, however, the price (free) is right.

QuicKeys 2 from CE Software is a powerful macro utility for people who have a hard time understanding what macros are all about. Dozens of useful mini-macros (such as QuickQuotes, which enters the correct open or closed quotation mark when you press the Apostrophe Key) are listed in separate menus, organized by category, and virtually ready to run (Figure 7-9); all you have to do is assign them a key combination. Many complex macros can be constructed simply by stringing together two or more of these easy-to-understand

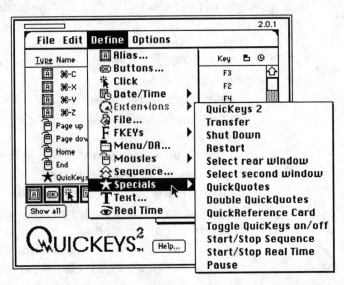

FIGURE 7-9 *Many simple macros can be defined in QuicKeys 2 simply by selecting them from a submenu and assigning them a key combination.*

mini-macros. But Affinity Microsystems' **Tempo II Plus** is the one for true macronauts. It beats the pants off all other macro utilities and can do almost anything you ask of it (if you're prepared to expend the effort to tell it how). Compared to the other two programs, however, it's not especially easy to use and thus isn't recommended for beginners.

Start-up batch files

If you use Windows 3.0, you may be surprised to know that you can bypass the Applications Manager and launch a Windows application and one of its documents directly from DOS. To do so, make yourself a special DOS batch file name GO.BAT as described below. Then, every time you want work on a Windows document, simply type GO then batch filename in the DOS command line, then a space and the filename of the document.

Within the GO.BAT batch file, you'll need to specify the correct directory and path for the application, and document file directory. For example, let's assume that Windows 3.0 is in the directory WINDOWS on drive C, that CorelDRAW is in directory \CORELDRW on drive C, and that you keep all your drawings in directory CORELDRW\PIX on drive C. To create the batch file for this set-up, type the following lines at the DOS prompt, ending each line with a Return:

```
COPY CON C:\GO.BAT
CD C:\WINDOWS
C:WIN C:\CORELDRW\CORELDRW C:\CORELDRW\PIX\%1.CDR
```

To save the file, press Ctrl + Z, or the F6 Key, and then press Return. You can also create the batch file using the Windows Notepad accessory, or any text editor that save files in ASCII format (plain text, without formatting codes). Simply omit the first and last lines of the command list above and save the text under the name GO.BAT. The %1 in the batch file is a placeholder, or variable, which is replaced by the first term after the batch file name when the batch file is run. Of course, you can create similar batch files for any Windows programs, such as Designer or PageMaker.

Quick system file editor

Need a fast way to modify your **Windows** configuration files? Here's one: Select the File menu's RUN command from Program Manager, type SYSEDIT in the Command text box, and click on OK. This opens the Windows System Configuration Editor (SysEdit), which immediately opens your AUTOEXEC.BAT, CONFIG.SYS, WIN.INI, and SYSTEM.INI files in four cascading windows. SysEdit's File, Edit, and Search menus enable you to easily modify these vital files, use the SAVE command to save your changes, and make printouts of each file. That's a whole lot faster than using Windows Notepad to edit each file individually.

Paper and Printing

Laser printing

  ### Precision positioning on the page

The cassette paper-feed mechanism on many laser printers cannot place the printed image in exactly the same position on every page every time; instead, the image tends to wander slightly from page to page. If you need precise image placement—to print on sheets of small, self-adhesive labels, for example—you may find that inserting sheets one by one in the manual sheet feeder produces more satisfactory results.

  ### Two paper stocks in a single tray

Make your laser printer's paper tray do double duty by loading the tray with the two paper stocks you intend to use. Place one sheaf faceup and the other facedown with a piece of stiff cardboard between them. You'll be able to flip the sandwich over and quickly re-insert it into the tray whenever you need to switch from one stock to the other. Placing an extra piece of cardboard on the bottom of the tray makes it easier to remove the paper stack when you need to flip it.

 ### Don't rely on the low toner-level light

If you use different toner cartridges for different print jobs (black toner for some, blue toner for others, for example), don't expect the Low Toner Level light on a LaserWriter II to warn you when one of the cartridges is low. (Of the four LaserWriter II status lights, the Low Toner Level light is the orange one second from the left .) All models of the LaserWriter and LaserWriter II use page counts as a rough indicator of toner level. In the LaserWriter, the page counter is inside the toner cartridge, so swapping cartridges is not a problem. In the LaserWriter II, however, the counter is in the printer, and replacing the toner cartridge resets the counter back to zero. Thus, if you swap toner cartridges with any frequency, you'll run out of toner long

before the orange toner light turns on. In this situation, the only reliable indicator of toner level is print quality—so keep your eye on
the printed page, not on the warning light.

Conserving toner

Save yourself some money on toner cartridges by setting your laser
printer to print as lightly as possible or as lightly as you're willing to
go until you're ready to print final copies. If you can tolerate lightly
printed proofs, you can double the life of your cartridge.

Touching up black areas

Water-based, washable marking pens are good for touching up or
filling in solid black areas on laser-printed originals. The water-
based markers don't dissolve toner, as do the solvent-based permanent markers.

Cheap raised lettering

You can create raised lettering when printing business cards on a
laser printer by spraying the printed cards with five to ten thin coats
of clear lacquer. The lacquer sinks into the card stock but builds up
on the toner. After it's dry, the lettering looks and feels like professionally printed raised lettering.

Higher resolution via photo-reduction

Sharpen camera-ready copy from desktop laser printers by printing
type and graphics at 200 percent of final size and then making a pho-
tostat at 50 percent. This is particularly handy for smaller pages or
page elements that just fit an 8½-by-11 inch page at double-size. This
trick bypasses the vagaries of downloading fonts to an imagesetter,
but you should restrict its use to larger type and bolder graphics.
Small type can turn muddy and hairlines can disappear in the reduction process.

Even less sizeable photo-reductions can reduce the jaggies of 300-dpi type and graphics destined for the printing press. A 17-percent reduction reduces 12-point type to 10 points, enough to largely cure the jaggies that shows up on diagonal strokes (the result of the laser printer's square printing dots).

With 17-percent reduction, you can expect the remaining jaggies to be further reduced during the printing process. That's because the jaggies don't reproduce very sharply on an offset printer and tend to smooth out. This is an old and proven technique of which many publishing beginners aren't aware.

Don't overdo Ventura's collator

Ventura Publisher for the PC's automatic collating option (in the Print dialog box accessed via the File menu) is handy, but make sure to turn it off when you don't need it or when haste is essential. When the collating feature is turned on, even one-page documents take nearly three times longer to print than when it's turned off.

Properly scaled bitmapped images

Bitmapped graphics, such as black and white TIFF or paint-format files, have fixed resolutions that often conflict with the resolution of your printer when scaled. To get the bitmap to print smoothly, you must resize it by the proper percentage. Otherwise you get very noticeable banding when printing the image.

PageMaker on both the Mac and PC takes care of the proper scaling automatically: If you hold down the Mac's Command Key or the PC's Control Key while dragging the corner handle of a bitmap, the image will jump between the sizes which are compatible with the resolution of the printer you've selected.

In other applications, you need to figure out the proper resizing percentage with the following technique. Begin by dividing your bitmapped image resolution (in dots per inch) by that of your printer. In the case of the Mac Paint file and a typical laser printer, this value is 72/300, or 0.24. Therefore, when printing to a standard laser printer, 24 percent is the base percentage; scaling a bitmap by any whole-number multiple of 24 percent—48, 72, 96, and so on—will ensure that it prints with the best quality.

If you're printing to an imagesetter with a resolution of 1270 or 2540 dots per inch, the numbers don't work out quite as smoothly. The base percentage is not an even number (it's about 5.67 percent), but the best scaling values turn out to be multiples of 17 percent, such as 34, 51, 68, 85, and 102 percent.

  ## Cover-weight paper jams

Paper jams can be a problem when printing on rough-textured, cover-weight stock on a laser printer. One way to eliminate this inconvenience is to switch to paper with a smoother surface. Another solution is to flatten the leading edge of each sheet with a burnishing tool or the curved plastic top of a cheap ballpoint pen.

  ## Reducing fountain-fill banding

Troublesome banding can appear on printed copy when you use the fountain-fill function in **CorelDRAW**. To lessen the banding when printing to a laser printer, select Print Options under the File menu and increase the number of Fountain Stripes. Start with 80 fountain stripes and experiment—a larger area fill will require more stripes. Beware: The higher the stripe number, the more slowly the screen will redraw, and the longer your file will take to print. To save time when drawing and printing early proofs, select a small number of Fountain Stripes, such as 5.

 ## Manually download PostScript header

PostScript printing is faster if you prevent PostScript header files from loading automatically with each job. Ventura's header file (also called a preamble file) contains PostScript program routines that an application uses while printing. Instead, manually download the header so that it's always available and doesn't have to be downloaded for each separate job. This is easy to do, but the steps are different, depending on whether you're using GEM or Windows editions. These are the steps for Ventura Publisher GEM Edition:

1. Delete the file PS2.PRE from the Ventura subdirectory.

2. In its place, copy the file PERMVP.PS from the POSTSCPT subdirectory of the Ventura Utilities disk to your Ventura subdirectory.

3. Prior to starting Ventura, download the file PERMVP.PS to the printer using the DOS COPY command.

For Ventura Publisher Windows Edition (and other Windows applications) you can use features in the Windows PostScript printer driver to prevent the automatic loading of the Windows PostScript header. Here's how:

1. Open the printer dialog box either from your application's PRINTER SETUP command or by double-clicking the Printers icon in the Windows Control Panel.

2. In the PostScript Printer dialog box, select the Options button. In the Options dialog box which appears, click the Header button.

3. In the Header dialog box select the *File* option. A text entry window appears, prompting you to enter a file name. You're about to create a header file (which you'll download shortly), so give it descriptive name, such as PS-HEADER.PS. Then click OK.

4. You should be back in the Options dialog box. In the Header selection area, select the *Already downloaded* option. Then click OK to close the Option dialog box and again to close the PostScript Printer dialog box.

5. Before you print the document, open a DOS window by double-clicking the DOS Prompt icon in the Main program group under Program Manager. Then use the DOS COPY command to

download the header file you just created. For example, the command `COPY PS-HEADER.PS LPT1:` will download the header to a printer attached to your parallel port.

6. After downloading the header, type `EXIT` at the DOS prompt to close the DOS Prompt window and return to the Windows Program Manager.

The header file is now stored on disk, so each time you turn on the printer and start printing with Ventura, you should download the header as in steps 5 and 6. Downloaded this way, the PostScript header remains from job to job until the printer is turned off.

Optimum printer climate

Does your laser printer show a light fog of toner on the edge of type and graphics but only on winter weekends? Do you find that turning down the toner density makes it worse? Do you wonder what's going on?

Most likely, if your laser printer is acting up in this way, it suffers from winter-time weekend chills when the thermostat is lowered in many offices to conserve energy. If this is the correct diagnosis, you should turn the heat up instead of turning the toner density down. Specifically, you should heat up the room for at least half an hour before you use a chilled printer. A laser printer should be kept in a room above freezing and below sizzling (32 to 95 degrees Fahrenheit) when not in use. While printing, it should be kept at a temperate 50 to 91 degrees.

Humidity is also a factor in laser printer print quality. Again, avoid extremes and keep the printer's environment—and that of the paper you use—between 20 and 80 percent relative humidity. If you can't afford a room dehumidifier, avoid the loss of laser print quality in humid environments by zapping your paper in a microwave oven for a few seconds before printing. Baking the stationary this way drives out absorbed moisture, helping the toner achieve a better bond during printing.

Legal paper without a legal tray

Even if you don't own a legal-sized paper tray, you can still print on legal-sized paper with a LaserWriter II. To do so, first turn on the *US Legal* option in the document's Page Setup dialog box. When you're ready to print, choose the *Manual Feed* paper source option in the Print dialog box. Then feed legal paper through the manual paper feed on top of your regular paper tray. Feed the sheets one by one, always waiting to feed a new sheet until the previous sheet begins to exit the printer.

Printing invitations

Since a 4½-inch-square card is rather awkward for laser printing, printing formal invitations on a laser printer such as an HP Laserjet Series II or Apple Laserwriter IINT requires a few accommodations. To overcome the size problem, print several cards on one sheet, and then cut each sheet with a paper cutter into individual invitations.

The published paper-weight specification for Canon LBP-SX engine printers—including Laserjet Series II and Laserwriter II models—is 16- to 20-pound bond paper when you use the paper output tray on top of the printer. You can use up to 36-pound bond paper if you use the fold-down output tray on the back of the printer. In practice, your printer can handle up to 70-pound stock without jamming, provided you open the back tray. Be careful, however; a steady diet of 70-pound paper (or even just a fairly sizable print run of it) may not be good for your printer.

A finer shade of gray

When using a 300-dot-per-inch printer, you can obtain finer-looking light gray fills in **PageMaker** for the Mac by importing them from **FreeHand**. Here's how:

1. On an empty FreeHand page, draw a square. Once it's drawn, it should remain selected.

2. Select the FILL AND LINE command from the Attributes menu. From the Line pop-up menu on the right, select the *None* option. From the Fill pop-up menu on the left select the *Basic* option, and from the Color pop-up menu select the *Tint* option.

3. In the Colors dialog box that now opens, select black as the Based On color, enter a tint of 5 percent, and name the new tint *5% gray*. Click the OK button.

4. Back in the main document, make sure the square is still selected. Select the HALFTONE SCREEN command from the Attributes menu and enter a screen-ruling value of 80 lines per inch.

5. Choose the EXPORT command from the File menu and save the file in Macintosh EPS file format. Give the file an appropriate name, such as *5% Gray.EPS*.

6. Place the FreeHand file in Pagemaker; size and position it as needed.

The imported gray screen will either be very faint or invisible on your monitor but will look like a smoother version of PageMaker's standard 10 percent fill when printed. A 10 percent screen from FreeHand will approximate a 20 percent PageMaker fill. This technique also works with QuarkXPress, though you'll need to experiment to discover which tints in FreeHand produce the desired printed screen.

Printing problems and prep file changes

If you have trouble printing a **PageMaker** for the Mac document, try changing the printer driver from PageMaker's Aldus Prep to Apple's Laser Prep. Unless you specify otherwise, PageMaker uses the Aldus Prep file. To specify Apple's Laser Prep instead, press the Option Key as you choose the PRINT command. Click the OK buttons in the ensuing LaserWriter Print Options and Page Setup dialog boxes to reach the standard LaserWriter Print dialog box. Check to see that the correct print options are turned on and, once again, click the OK button. This simple printer driver switch won't cure all your ills, but it often resolves otherwise puzzling printing problems and is always worth a trying when all else fails.

. . . .

Toner cartridges

. . . .

Pre-owned toner cartridges

Given the price of new toner cartridges and the environmental cost of simply throwing them away, it's not surprising that we often are asked for our opinion on refilled toner cartridges. They certainly are cheaper than new ones, and in many cases they may last longer (many cartridges are refilled with more toner than the original had). But are they safe and of equal quality?

On the issue of safety, we can report that problems are possible. We know of several cases in which a laser printer was damaged by a refilled toner cartridge. In one case, the cartridge spilled toner inside the printer. In the second case, the toner was of poor quality; it spread into the printer and gummed up the printer gears. In both cases, an incredibly extensive cleanup job was required before the printer could be used again.

On the issue of quality, we can tell you our own experience is mixed. Not all refilled cartridges are alike, and quality certainly varies from vendor to vendor. It can also vary quite a bit from cartridge to cartridge from the same vendor (more so, we believe, than the variation we've seen in new cartridges). Thus, you may need to experiment a bit to find a vendor in your area whose cartridges are of consistently high quality.

When looking for a quality source, keep in mind that a reputable refilling outfit will open a cartridge, clean it completely, add toner, and then reseal it. Avoid toner cartridge vendors that simply drill a hole in a used cartridge and fill it with more toner: (1) the cartridge hasn't been cleaned, (2) drilling a hole in the side may contaminate the cartridge with plastic particles that can scratch the printer drum, and (3) you'll be in a mess of trouble if the hole's plug comes unglued.

Generally, though, people seem satisfied with refilled toner cartridges and printer manufacturers have, by and large, learned to like them. As for us, do we send our cartridges to a refiller for recycling? Absolutely. Do we use recycled cartridges in our own laser printers? Not on a regular basis, not yet anyway....

  ## Washing out toner

If you get laser printer toner on your clothes, always wash it out with cold water. Heat bonds toner in your printer (by melting it onto your pages), and in like fashion hot water will seal the toner to clothing.

  ## Breaking-in toner cartridges

It sometimes happens that documents printed immediately after installing a new toner cartridge appear faded instead of crisp black. This is most often a problem with Canon-based printers (such as a LaserWriter or LaserJet). If this happens to you, turn the density dial on the printer to full black. Then print about 10 or more pages of solid black until the toner darkly and evenly covers the page. If one half of a page is faded, or if a page has light and dark streaks, remove the toner cartridge and gently rock it from side to side several times (don't turn it upside down). Then place it back in the printer. This should distribute the toner more evenly and eliminate the faded or streaked areas.

  ## Disposable toner cartridges—what a waste

Even if you prefer not to exchange an empty toner cartridge for a refilled one, you don't have to add your spent cartridges to the crush at the local landfill. If you use Hewlett-Packard laser printer toner cartridges, you can send the cartridges back to Hewlett-Packard. They'll disassemble and reuse or recycle the component parts of the cartridge and its packaging. By early 1992, prepaid UPS labels will be included with all H-P toner cartridges; until then, you can obtain a recycling kit (including instructions and a prepaid UPS label) from an H-P dealer or by calling 800/752-0900, extension 1872. (In Canada, call 800/387-3867, department 129; in Toronto, call 678-9430, extension 4981.) In addition to reducing waste, H-P's recycle program donates fifty cents to both the Nature Conservancy and the National Wildlife Federation for each returned cartridge. Apple is expected to have a similar program, by the way, but at the time this went to press, no formal announcement had been made.

If you want to make a little extra return on your investment, some cartridge recyclers will pay cash for your trash. For example, in addition to accepting empty cartridges for refilling, Alpha Laser Cartridge will purchase empty laser cartridges (new empties only, not previously recycled empties) for most common laser printers for $5 per cartridge plus your shipping cost. You must repack the cartridge in its original box and include the cleaning rod; the company sends you a check (or credits your account) after receiving the cartridge.

Color printing

Thin lines and small type in color

Thin lines (.25 point or less) and delicate type at small point-sizes should be composed of no more than two process colors. Most high-speed presses are not precise enough to register with exactness all four plates on such thin elements.

Color printing on a laser printer

A perfectly reasonable, low-tech way to print in two or more colors is to use different color toner cartridges and put your pages through a laser printer several times. This technique won't hurt your printer, but it can be a bit of a chore. The main drawbacks are the inconveniences of switching toner cartridges and the laser printer's lack of precise control over registration. The latter, of course, means that the placement of the different colored elements will vary from page to page. This technique works fine, however, when precise registration is not crucial. For the most consistent registration possible in a laser printer, use the manual paper feed instead of the paper tray.

Easy-trapping spreads and chokes

When working with color graphics in **Illustrator**, **FreeHand**, **Corel-DRAW** and other drawing programs, you'll often want graphic elements that border each other to actually overlap slightly. That way, no gaps appear between the elements after color separation and printing (a problem that occurs when the registration of the printing plates is slightly off). *Trapping* is the term the pros use for this color printing technique, and there are numerous ways to achieve it.

An easy way to specify the amount of overlap with accuracy and control is to increase slightly the width of the overlapping graphic's stroke—the line that defines the shape. If you give a graphic object a thicker stroke, its outline will expand slightly in all directions. That slight spreading is exactly what you need to achieve the trap. Remember, though, a stroke builds from the center of its path, half of its width extending into the object and the other half extending outward. So if you want a 1-point trap for a blue dot, for example, enter a 2-point blue stroke. Set the stroke to overprint and the interior fill not to overprint (so that it will cutout the portion of the underlying graphic which it covers). That way you don't print the underlying color under the whole object, but only where you've created a spread with the stroke to trap the two colors.

In some cases there's a simpler way to avoid trapping problems: Make sure that any overlapping objects have at least one process color in common—this is especially useful when you're printing colored type on a colored background. Any gaps that do occur will appear in the common color and will not be as noticeable.

Jumbo color PostScript printouts

Want to turn your document or drawing into a billboard? ReproCAD of Lafayette, CA, has a national network of service bureaus that can print color PostScript graphics up to 42 inches wide by 12 feet long. ReproCAD licenses their Megachrome system; call ReproCAD (415-/284-0400) and they'll help you find a Megachrome service bureau near you.

Once you've located a convenient Megachrome service bureau, you can bring in a printable color PostScript file (preferably EPS) on a Mac or PC floppy, or you can arrange to transmit the file by modem. Blue Print Service Company of San Francisco (415/495-8700), for example, will send you a kit with order forms and pricing, including a detailed and easily understood set of instructions and comments on preparing the proper PostScript files from GEM Ventura Publisher, Corel Draw (and other Windows 3.0 applications), Harvard Graphics, Aldus FreeHand, PageMaker 4.0 for Macintosh, and Adobe Illustrator. They also include a sample process color chart to help you with color matching on the Versatec plotter used in the process. According to our contacts at ReproCAD, you'll get the best color matching with your software by specifying colors in CMYK.

Prices for Megachrome printing average around $10 a square foot (printed on presentation bond). For example, a 36- x 48-inch Megachrome poster printed at Blair Graphics, 213/829-4621, in Los Angeles costs $120 for the first print and $78 for reprints (65 percent of the first print). You can also specify transparency film or velum material. Blair, for example, can print your image on Megatrams plastic laminate, suitable for exterior signs; the price of the plastic laminate is 80 percent more than the price of presentation bond.

Avoid excess spot-color overlays

Ventura Publisher can print eight spot colors, each as a separate overlay. To avoid printing all eight separation pages when you're only using two or three spot colors in your document, select DEFINE COLORS under the Paragraph menu. Then, under Color Settings, disable the colors you're not using; Ventura then prints only the spot-color overlays you need.

Registration for spot color overlays

For spot color overlays, many strippers will not use registration marks which fall outside the page area. This is especially true when the pages need to be stripped close together. To keep the strippers happy, try placing a registration mark in the footer or the header or (preferably) both.

Staying within the color limit

When a **FreeHand** or **Illustrator** file is sent through a prepress link, it's converted into a linework format that has a color limit of about 255 colors, a number easy to exceed if the artwork contains color blends. If you do exceed the limit, the file won't go through the link properly.

One way to avoid this problem is to strip out color gradations, leaving those areas blank and indicating the area to be filled with a keyline. With your instructions, the prepress operator can recreate the gradations on the high-end console. Not only does this eliminate the color-limit problem, but your gradations will appear smoother as well. As with all special instructions, however, always consult the prepress house first to make sure that what you want to give them is, in fact, what they want to receive.

Glossy thermal printer black

To obtain a nice, glossy black from a color thermal printer using a four-color ribbon, use a mix: 100 percent of all the process colors, including 100 percent of black. This also ensures that any gaps left during the black pass are filled in, giving your document a very professional appearance. You can play this effect against a straight 100 percent black, which may look matte in comparison. You could try a glossy black background with matte black lettering, for example, or vice versa.

Prepress links and trapping

When working with Crossfield's **StudioLink**, Scitex's **V.I.P.**, Hell's **ScriptMaster**, or other desktop-to-prepress links, remember that the automatic overprinting and trapping you specify in page layout or PostScript-illustration software doesn't translate through the PostScript link. Although you should consult with your prepress house first, here's a possible workaround: Use a separation utility and print the four separation files to disk. By sending these files through the link individually, the prepress console operator can re-assemble the plates and hold all your trapping and overprinting specifications.

Richer process-black

In process printing, a simple 100-percent black often yields muddy results on the press. Many printers create richer blacks by combining one or more of the process colors (cyan, yellow, and magenta) with black. For example, try 50-percent cyan plus 100-percent black, and use this new color instead of the default black available in your application. Check with your print house for its recommendations, too.

Add a color test icon to your documents

Before proofing or printing a color job, insert in your document a simple color icon that can act as a test for proper color and registration. Your test icon should be a simple graphic composed of adjoining swatches of 100-percent values of the four process colors (cyan, magenta, yellow, and black). Create your icon in **Illustrator**, for example, and place it in the trim margin of FreeHand, PageMaker, QuarkXPress, or Illustrator pages as a guide for your printshop. On the proof, check the colors in the icon for accuracy and check their alignment for proper registration.

Document preparation for better printing

Scanning at the right resolution

To save disk space and printing time, don't scan images at resolutions that are higher than necessary. For line art to be used at the same size and printed on a laser printer, a scan at 300 dpi should be sufficient; for line art which is to be enlarged or printed on an imagesetter, you'll probably want to scan at a higher resolution (or, in any event, at the highest resolution the scanner allows).

For gray-scale images used at the same size, the optimum scanning resolution is about twice the line-screen rating that you use to print the image. On a LaserWriter with a default screen of 60 lpi, for example, the optimum scanning resolution is 120 to 150 lpi. If a gray-scale image is to be scaled up or down, use the following formula to determine the optimum gray-scale scanning resolution:

$$\text{line screen} \times 2 \times \text{percent scaling} = \text{scanning resolution}$$

According to the above formula, if the image needs a 50-percent reduction, the line screen (lpi) and scanning resolution (dpi) values will be the same. On the other hand, if the image needs a 150-percent enlargement, the scanning resolution value will be three times the line screen value. If you don't know the size change as a percentage and the image is scaled proportionally (the same amount both horizontally and vertically), this formula will give it to you:

$$\text{final image width} \div \text{original image width} = \text{percent scaling.}$$

Keep in mind that the calculated optimum scanning resolution is probably not optimal in every conceivable circumstance. Always judge the output quality of your images for yourself, and adjust the scanning resolution if you're not satisfied.

Scrap those pasteboard scraps

Like a real table surface, the pasteboard area (outside the page boundaries) in **PageMaker** is a great place for sticking scraps and miscellaneous pieces while working on a page. But when you go to print the page, PageMaker processes those extra items internally even though they don't print. To speed printing, remove scraps from the pasteboard, either by deleting them or by moving them to a blank page (be sure not to print that page). This becomes particularly important when you send the files to a service bureau. The extra items outside the page make the file much larger and drastically slow down a high-resolution imagesetter.

Finding and fixing incorrect fonts

In **QuarkXPress**, it's easy to check your documents for fonts that you don't intend to use and that you believe you've replaced or deleted. Because a stray period or space in the wrong font could overload the printer and prevent your document from printing, this is a useful exercise. To find errant fonts in an XPress document, choose the Font Usage command from the Utilities menu. In the Font Usage dialog box (Figure 8-1), open the Find What Font pop-up menu to display the fonts required by the current document. If you see a font

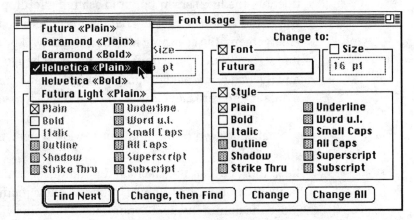

FIGURE 8-1 *In XPress's Font Usage dialog box, you can search for and change fonts, font styles, and font sizes.*

that shouldn't be there, use the Find Next and Change buttons to locate and replace text that's incorrectly formatted.

Enter ligatures with search and replace

Use the search and replace function in your word processing or page layout program to replace fi and fl letter pairs with the corresponding ligatures. Convert fi combinations to *fi* with Option + Shift + 5; replace fl with *fl* by pressing Option + Shift + 6. (You'll probably see only a hollow square in your Change dialog box when you specify these special characters.) These two ligatures are available in all fonts that follow the standard Macintosh character set. Many fonts have other ligatures as well that you can search for and replace in the same way.

Eliminating unexpected font changes in Word

It wasn't so long ago that you skated on pretty thin ice whenever you tried to print a document on someone else's Macintosh. Far too often in those days, when a document was printed from a Macintosh other than the one it was created on, text that was supposed to be in one font unexpectedly changed to another font. Fortunately, these unexpected font substitutions are largely a thing of the past. Unfortunately, one program in which they still occur much too frequently is **Microsoft Word** for the Mac.

Unexpected font changes used to be a big problem because, for much of the Mac's existence, it was standard procedure to specify fonts by their Font ID numbers. But this method had a serious flaw: Font ID numbers sometimes changed during installation with the Font/DA Mover. As a result, unexpected font substitutions occurred whenever someone moved a document from one system (with one set of font ID numbers) to another system (with the same fonts but a different set of font ID numbers).

To resolve these problems, Apple requested that applications specify fonts in a document by their names instead of their ID numbers. Most applications—including PageMaker, QuarkXPress, and Adobe

Illustrator—now follow this guideline. As a result, unexpected font changes are rare in these programs. A few applications have yet to mend their ways, however, and Word has the distinction of being perhaps the most prominent violator of the font name guideline. That's why unexpected font changes remain a common problem in Word documents.

But don't despair: There's a workaround that you can use until Microsoft takes the hint and deigns to follow Apple's guideline. To ensure that the fonts in a Word document print correctly, save your Word documents in RTF (Interchange) format, not in Word's native format. RTF format specifies fonts by name (the name on the Font menu, not the PostScript name) and preserves all of your other formatting as well. The receiver's copy of Word will faithfully convert the RTF file back to Word format and interpret all of the fonts correctly, thereby eliminating any font mix-ups.

Calculating an unbanded blend

Illustrator and **FreeHand** generate custom gradient fills by creating a sequence of objects which gradually change, step by step, from one tint to another. For a smooth, unbanded blend of shades, you need to specify the right number of steps for the blend. And the proper number of steps is a function of the number of available gray shades and the total span of the blend (black to white, for example, or black to 50 percent gray).

Here's the formula for calculating the number of gray levels available:

$$G = (dpi/lpi)^2 + 1.$$

In this equation, *dpi* is the resolution of your printer, *lpi* is the halftone line screen frequency, and G is the number of gray levels. Here's the formula for calculating the correct number of steps in the blend:

$$S = (G \times \%T) - 2.$$

As before, G is the number of gray levels, and %T is the percentage of the tint change (1.0 for black to white, for example, or 0.5 for black to 50-percent gray).

Here is an example of how these two equations are used: Take a typical imagesetter whose default screen frequency is 90 lpi; at 1270-dpi resolution, the number of grays available from that imagesetter is $(1270 / 90)^2 + 1$, or about 200. For a blend from white to black (a 100 percent change in tint) on this printer, you'd use $(200 \times 1.0) - 2 = 198$ steps to take advantage of all the gray values. To create a gradation over a smaller range, say from 30 percent red to 70 percent red (a 40 percent change), you'd use $(200 \times 0.4) - 2 = 78$ steps to create a smooth blend.

For a 300-dpi laser printer, try a few calculations yourself. At the default line screen of 60 lpi, you'll find that the printer can create a maximum of 26 different gray levels (including black and white). Thus, at a full blend (from black to white, for example), you should specify 24 steps.

Shades of gray aren't all the same

When you're using a PostScript laser printer to produce proof documents and a PostScript photoimagesetter to print final masters, be aware that shades of gray may differ between the two versions. Although many printer drivers can compensate for the differences between laser printers and imagesetters, dark shades on the laser printer may still appear darker on the imagesetter, while light shades on the laser printer may appear lighter on the imagesetter. Shades of gray that appear very light on laser-printer proofs may fade away completely when typeset. Thus, if you proof screens on a laser printer, respecify your light screens for about 10 percent darker before sending them to a high-resolution imagesetter. Likewise, dark screens proofed on a laser printer should be lightened 5 to 10 percent before printing on an imagesetter.

Better scans in PageMaker

Generally speaking, gray-scale scans in TIFF format that look fine on screen often lack contrast when printed. If you use **PageMaker** for the Macintosh and **PrePrint**, here's a quick way to spruce up your scans that's a lot easier than adjusting PageMaker's image controls:

1. Launch Preprint and open the gray-scale TIFF file you intend to use in PageMaker.

2. Choose AUTO ENHANCE from the Image menu.

3. Save your changes. Repeat with the other scans you'll be using and quit PrePrint when you're done.

Place your auto-enhanced images in PageMaker in the usual way. When you print your document, you should find that your altered scans are sharper with better contrast.

Tab-less text indentation

Most graphics programs—such as **FreeHand, CorelDRAW,** or **Micrografx Designer**—don't offer tab stops for numbers or text. Simply hitting the spacebar to position your columns of numbers isn't a good idea since the width of a space character is not the same as the width of a numeral. But since numerals, in most cases, have the same width, you can use hidden numerals to accurately align columns of numbers. Simply type in extra numbers as invisible space holders, reversing them (white against a white page, for example) so they don't show.

Previewing an entire PageMaker document

Want to preview an entire **PageMaker** document quickly before printing from the Mac or PC? First put all document pages in the same view: On the Mac, press the Option Key while selecting the FIT IN WINDOW command (or any other page size command appropriate for previewing); on the PC press Alt + Shift or Alt + Control while choosing the desired page view. Next, on both the Mac and the PC, press the Shift Key while selecting the Go To PAGE command and continue to press the Shift Key until the first page of the document is fully drawn. PageMaker will automatically display each page or spread in the document, from first page to last, and will repeat the cycle when it reaches the last page. Click the mouse button to halt the cycle at any time.

Imagesetter (service bureau) printing

  ## Use film for sharp type and halftones

For sharp type in small sizes, ask your service bureau to produce negative film instead of paper copy on its imagesetter. Your print shop can then work with the negative directly, rather than photographing camera-ready copy. Because it's a first generation copy, a negative from an imagesetter produces text which is sharper and clearer—this is especially true at small text sizes—than that produced by a second-generation negative derived from camera-ready mechanicals.

When you're printing gray-scale halftone images on paper with a high-resolution photoimagesetter, don't use a line screen higher than 110 lines per inch. The dots in line screens higher than 110 tend to close up when the paper halftones are photographed to generate a plate-making negative, producing a dark, high-contrast image at the press. To get good quality line screens at frequencies higher than 110 lines per inch, you'll need to print the halftones on film, not paper. Your print shop can then strip in the film when preparing the master negatives.

Special effects mean special expense

Don't overdo special graphic effects such as gradient fills. Aside from risking a display of poor taste, you may run out of patience (and money) printing or typesetting them.

Specify lines per inch

If you are printing on high-quality paper, you may desire a finer line screen than the program's defaults call for. If so, be sure to specify the lines per inch you wish graphics and screens to have—in addition to specifying the resolution—when sending files to a service bureau for imagesetter output.

Provide copies of graphics

It's a good idea to provide copies of all of your document's graphic files along with your layout file when you send your job to a service bureau. If one of the graphics in the layout file causes a problem during imagesetting, you can ask the service bureau to suppress or delete the problematic graphic from the page. The service bureau may then be able to print the image separately using the copy. You can give the page and the graphic to your printer who can then strip the graphic into the final negative. This adds a step to the process, but at least it won't delay your job.

Telecommunication costs

Telecommunications should be cost-effective, so consider how much time it'll take before you transmit your files over the phone lines. Several factors affect transmission time: the transmission rate you intend to use, your service bureau's capability to receive the files at that rate, and the number of graphics your files contain. Figure that at best a 2400 bps modem transmits about 240 bytes of your file per second. Hence, a 24K file will transmit in roughly 100 seconds, or about 1¾ minutes under ideal conditions. (And conditions are rarely ideal.)

If your service bureau is across town, it's probably cheaper to transmit the file for the price of a local call than to have it delivered. If your service bureau is farther away, the price of the required long-distance call may be rather steep. Some service bureaus have electronic bulletin boards that permit you to send files in the wee hours, when the rates are lower. You can trim some of the cost that way, but remember that an overnight service can deliver an awful lot of files on disk for just $12 to$15.

For page layout documents that include scanned images, remember to telecommunicate the image files along with the actual document file. Otherwise, unless the additional files are present, some pages will print with low-res bitmapped images. **Ventura Publisher**, for example, maintains links to a chapters text and graphics files but doesn't incorporate them into the actual chapter file. In **PageMaker**, you can opt to link external files to your documents and thus not incorporate them into the document file. Scanned image files larger than 64K are automatically placed via an external link. In either case, as with Ventura, you must send along the externally linked files that compose the document.

Service bureau tele-compatibility

If you're purchasing or upgrading your telecommunications software, you should plan to buy the same program that your typesetting service bureau uses. If it means buying a new program, it will be worth the convenience. Telecommunications programs are notoriously difficult to decipher, and, if you and your bureau use different programs, the bureau staff may not be able to help you adjust your program to communicate with theirs. The result can be hours of frustration and wasted time.

The truth about hairlines

If you use one printer to proof and another to print, refrain from using an application's hairline rule choice: It may not reproduce consistently when printed. Traditionally, hairline rules are the thinnest rule a printer or imagesetter can produce; they're not of any standard dimension. Because these rules are not given a standard point-size, their thicknesses will vary depending on the resolution of the printer. Specify a ¼-point rule if that's what you want.

Submit the PostScript file instead

To avoid problems for your service bureau, create and submit a Post-Script version of your word processing or page layout file. This eliminates the need for the service bureau to load all the screen fonts, which is helpful if you've forgotten to note which fonts are in your file and/or haven't supplied the service bureau with a set of the required screen fonts. With this method the service bureau only needs the printer fonts that are located on its output device's hard disk. (Make sure, though, that the service bureau uses the same version of Apple's Laser Prep file that you do.)

You can write a PostScript file to disk from virtually any Macintosh application. In a few programs, the Print dialog box includes an option for printing a PostScript file to disk. There's one in **PageMaker** for the Mac, for example, which leads to a dialog box with a variety of print options (Figure 8-2). Most programs, however, don't have a

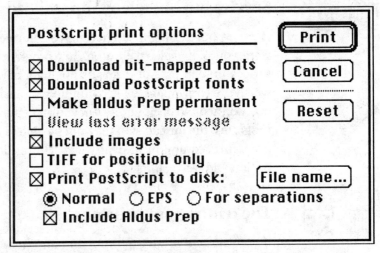

FIGURE 8-2 *PageMaker's PostScript Print Options dialog box allows you to create a PostScript version of your document.*

PostScript print-to-disk function. Here's how to create a PostScript file in programs such as these:

1. Select the PRINT command.

2. *Immediately* after clicking the OK button in the Print dialog box, press Command + Shift + F in most Macintosh programs. In **Free-Hand**, you need only press the F Key; in **QuarkXPress**, press Command + F. (In both programs, press Command + K if you want the information in Apple's Laser Prep incorporated in the PostScript file.) If you have successfully intercepted the print instructions, "Creating PostScript File" will appear briefly on screen instead of the standard printer status box.

Files are printed to disk under the file names *PostScript0*, *PostScript1*, and so on. Note that some print spoolers, including Apple's Print-Monitor, do not permit printing to disk. If you use an unsympathetic print spooler, turn it off before attempting to create a PostScript file.

Sending Ventura files to a service bureau

Here's our advice on sending a lengthy **Ventura Publisher** (GEM or Windows edition) document to your service bureau:

*   Carefully proofread your documents, using page proofs from your own laser printer. Cutting corners here will only increase your costs and waste considerable time if you have to rerun your job in order to correct errors.

*   To streamline printing at your service bureau, send them a Post-Script language print file of your document instead of the Ventura document files. The numerous files that make up a Ventura document increase the likelihood of confusion, even at a well organized service bureau. To create a PostScript file in the GEM Edition, choose *Filename* as your *Output To* option in the Set Printer Info dialog box under the Options menu. Then print as usual. In the Windows Edition, use the *Encapsulated PostScript file* option in the Options dialog box accessed via the PRINTER SETUP command

under the File menu. Then print the document. Since PostScript print files are quite large, you'll want to use high-capacity 1.4- or 1.2-megabyte floppy disks. If your file fills two or more disks, be sure to use a file backup utility that can split the file over several disks. Also make sure the backup utility is compatible with what your bureau uses; otherwise they won't be able to restore the file at their end.

- Unless your document is uniform in design, send a set of page proofs from your laser printer. This will help the bureau spot unwanted font substitutions and other printing problems.

- Find out what your service bureau prefers concerning the number of pages per print file. Some shops like a 20-page limit, in which case you can use the page range options of either the GEM or Window's edition's print menu to break your chapters down into smaller print files.

- Clearly label each floppy with the names of the files it contains, and attach a note to each floppy disk jacket explaining which page numbers in your document correspond to the file names. This helps your service bureau check the job for completeness.

  ## Copying Ventura files

To copy **Ventura Publisher** files to floppy disks, use the COPY ALL command from the Options menu of the GEM Edition. Or, for the Mac and Windows Editions, use the Multi-Chapter dialog accessed via the MANAGE PUBLICATION command under the File menu. If you just use the DOS COPY command on the PC, or copy from the Finder on the Mac, you won't be able to open the document on the floppy disk because the file path names stored in the chapter file are no longer correct and do not lead to the files stored on the floppy.

 ## Make print files smaller

If you're printing a **Ventura Publisher** document to disk as a PostScript file for your service bureau to print, the file size will increase dramatically if any fonts in the document are set to automatically download. That's because the printer driver, while autodownloading fonts for a job, may download the same font several times, though for different parts of the job. As a result, the PostScript file may contain duplicate copies of the same font, which would greatly increase its size. For a short document, this size increase may not be significant, but it certainly matters for a long document. Aside from increasing the file size, the document will also take longer to print since the extra font information in the file takes extra time to process.

In most cases, you'll need to specify all the fonts in the document as *Resident* so they don't automatically download. Ventura Publisher GEM Edition won't download a font specified as *Resident*, even if you're printing to a file. The assumption is that it's already been manually downloaded to the printer. How you accomplish this depends on the edition of Ventura you're using. Here's how to prevent automatic font downloading in the GEM Edition:

1. Open the file you intend to convert to PostScript language.

2. Select the ADD/REMOVE FONTS command from the Options menu.

3. In the Face selection box in the Add/Remove Fonts dialog box which now appears, click on the font you wish to specify as *Resident*.

4. With the font selected, consult the last option in the Style selection box. If it says *Download*, click on the word *Download*. It should then change to *Resident*, which is what you want. If the entry already says *Resident*, leave it as it is.

5. Repeat the last two steps for every font used in your document.

For the Ventura Publisher Windows Edition, and Windows applications in general, it's not an easy matter to control whether a font automatically downloads or not. You'll need to edit Window's WIN.INI file to make changes in the softfont initialization entries, and then reset the entries to resume normal printing. Here's how:

1. Make a backup copy of the WIN.INI file. Then open it using the Windows Notepad accessory or any word processor or text editor that let's you save text in ASCII format (plain text, free of special formatting codes).

2. Scroll down to the key word *[PostScript,LPT1]* (or *[PostScript, COM1]*, *[PostScript,LPT2]*, etc., depending on the printer port you're using). Directly below this header, you'll see some font entries that look like this:

```
softfonts=26
softfont1=c:\psfonts\pfm\morg____.pfm
softfont2=c:\psfonts\pfm\moi_____.pfm
softfont3=c:\psfonts\pfm\mosb____.pfm,c:\psfonts\mosb____.pfb
softfont4=c:\psfonts\pfm\mosbi___.pfm,c:\psfonts\mosbi___.pfb
```

3. To prevent a font from auto-downloading, delete the part of each *softfont#* entry after the comma, as we've done for the first two entries above. This removes the reference to the actual font file (.pfb), leaving only a reference to the Printer Font Metrics file (.pfm). Make the deletion for each font used in your document.

4. Save the WIN.INI file, exit Windows, and then restart Windows.

5. Print your document using the *Encapsulated PostScript file* option in the Options dialog box accessed from your application's PRINTER SETUP command or from the Printers icon in the Windows Control Panel.

In order to restore auto-downloading of the fonts whose WIN.INI entries you altered above, copy the backup WIN.INI file back into your Windows subdirectory.

A welcome alternative to this rather convoluted procedure is to invest in Micrografx' PostScript driver for Windows, which lets you control PostScript font status from a simple menu. See "A better PostScript driver" in Chapter 7 for more information about the Micrografx driver.

Fortifying your page finals

To make plain-paper laser printer finals that can be used and reused for several pasteups (such as box ads for newspapers), cover your laser pages with clear, adhesive-backed acetate film. They'll be durable enough for weeks of use.

Spot-cleaning imagesetter paper

To remove felt tip or ballpoint pen marks from photoimagesetter paper, use a commercial glass cleaner with ammonia, such as Windex, on a soft cloth or tissue. If it doesn't work at first, don't be afraid to rub harder. The paper holds up well to rubbing, and the mark will soon disappear or at least fade considerably.

Comments in PostScript files

When sending a PostScript language text file—such as a Ventura or Pagemaker document printed to disk—to a remote printer or to a service bureau, you can add identifying comments or instructions at the beginning of the file. Open the PostScript language file with your word processor and add your comments, prefacing each comment line with two percent signs (%%). Make sure you save the file again as an ASCII or a text-only file.

The two percent signs (%%) at the start of each comment tell the PostScript interpreter to skip over what you've written; your comments won't print; they won't even be read by the PostScript interpreter. You should notify your bureau that comments are in the files (they won't know otherwise).

Proper diskette labeling

To help your service bureau keep track of your disks (and to assist your own archiving efforts), create a label form so that all your disks are labeled consistently. The label should contain clearly marked entry spaces for the job number, job description, file name, program and fonts used, and the date. Also, send labeled laser proofs of your job. If you're telecommunicating your files, fax your proofs as well. The service bureau will need the printed proofs in order to reliably troubleshoot problems, especially unexpected font substitutions.

  ### List the fonts in your illustrations, too

When filling out your service bureau's job request form for a page layout document, be sure to list all the fonts used in any EPS or PICT graphics. These fonts will be called upon when the document is printed. For instance, if you have manipulated some Caslon 3 text in Aldus FreeHand, saved the FreeHand file as an EPS file, and placed it in a PageMaker document, you must include Caslon 3 in your PageMaker document font list. If you don't list the font and your service bureau fails to install it as a result, the text in the placed graphic will print as an unsightly bitmap.

 ### BYO suitcase to the service bureau

For every service bureau print job, Mac owners should create a suitcase containing all the screen fonts used in that particular job. Send the suitcase to the service bureau along with the files you want printed. This will eliminate any font ID problems and prevent the unexpected and unwanted substitution of one font for another.

Offset and other printing

  ### Let the offset printer add the screens

Using laser-printed gray screens as background for text and graphics can be handy if you're producing overhead transparencies or a document that will be photocopied. But grays can cause problems when shooting negatives to make plates for offset printing. The camera setting required to pick up a light gray may cause the text to darken and "fill in," whereas the setting that makes the text crisp may cause the light gray screen to "drop out."

Thus, if you intend to use gray screens in an offset job, show your print shop an example before you deliver the camera-ready copy. You may find that the camera operator prefers to produce the screen in the shop, using conventional halftone techniques.

Short runs at the press

Picture yourself in this press run situation: You order a run of 8,000 booklets, and the printer delivers only 7,500. When you complain, the printer cites "trade customs" and says that it's OK for the shop to deliver up to 10 percent less or 10 percent more than the quantity you ordered. It may surprise you, but the printer's right; this is a valid trade practice.

As long as you're not charged for those missing 500 booklets, the underrun is permissible according to the *Trade Customs and Printing Contract* adopted in 1985 by the Printing Industries of America (PIA) and other graphic arts organizations. The section on the custom regarding overruns and underruns reads as follows: "Overruns and underruns not to exceed 10 percent on quantities ordered, or the percentage agreed upon, shall constitute an acceptable delivery. The printer will bill for actual quantity delivered within this tolerance."

The practices outlined in *Trade Customs and Printing Contract* aren't legally binding, but they do provide a basis for resolving disputes over such issues as price quotations, charges for preparatory artwork, ownership of printing plates, overruns and underruns, charges for alterations and proofs, production schedules, and shipping charges.

Avoid unnecessary do-it-yourself expenses

In general, if your spot-color scheme is fairly simple, it's cheaper to let the print shop do it than to use your software's spot-color separations function. The cost of printing the extra separation pages at your service bureau may be more than your print shop would charge to do the same separations from a black-and-white mechanical in which the spot colors are marked with tissue overlays. To find out if that's the case, run a test page and have your print shop estimate how much the color work would cost.

Dot-gain compensation

You've probably noticed that finished documents tend to come back from your commercial print shop looking slightly darker than the original typeset pages. This phenomenon is known as dot gain: When the ink from a printing press spreads into a sheet of paper, type looks slightly bolder, and individual halftone dots tend to grow in size, diminishing detail and color clarity. Scanned photographs or halftone artwork show the most degradation and can come out looking muddy.

Aldus **PrePrint** allows you to compensate for dot gain by choosing options in the Press Controls dialog box that correspond to specific paper stocks. Choosing the *Uncoated* option automatically prints halftone dots 8 percent smaller than normal; choosing Newsprint shrinks your dots as much as 20 percent. You'll loose some contrast and definition this way, but you'll avoid most over-inking problems.

Better results from laser-printed masters

Material printed from laser-printed masters can vary widely in quality. Here are two pointers for getting the best printed results from laser-printed originals.

Most printers have an intensity control that should be turned to a fairly light setting. (Contrary to what you might expect, for Canon engines, like those in LaserJets and LaserWriters, 0 is the darkest and 9 the lightest setting.) You should use a light setting because the offset process—both the creation of a film negative and the printing itself—will tend to smooth the slightly jagged edges on laser type, making characters somewhat darker in the process. Make sure, though, that the setting isn't so light that the thinnest parts of letters break up.

It's also important that you choose your laser paper carefully. Some specialty papers are actually too glossy for toner to adhere to reliably, and tiny gaps may show up. Instead of using a specialty stock, you might try a 70-pound stock with an enamel coating on both sides. This coating provides a good surface for holding both toner and pasteup wax. Ask the printer to overexpose the film slightly. This, like a lighter intensity setting in the laser printer, will help keep your type from fattening up during production.

Paper

Printing on recycled paper

One of the fifty things a publisher can do to help save the earth is print on recycled paper. In the lingo of the paper industry, the term *recycled* actually means that a paper is at least 50 percent recycled paper. Such papers are either comparable to or slightly lower in quality than nonrecycled paper, and the color is usually not quite as white. As the following table of estimates shows, printing a book on recycled paper can add to the unit price of the book, depending on the printer and the length of the book. As the move toward recycled paper gains momentum, however, we expect the price of recycled paper to drop even as the quality improves.

Estimator	10,000 copies of	Unit print, recycled	Unit price nonrecycled
Consolidated Printers	208-page book	$1.36*	$1.22
Berkeley, CA	416-page book	$2.32*	$2.06
Viking Press, Eden	208-page book	$1.31**	$1.25
Prairie, MN	416-page book	$2.15**	$2.08
	*60# Simpson recycled.	**60# Viking offset recycled.	

Save money using stock paper sizes

Trim size is the first decision, not the last one, in a design. Consult your print shop to find out which trim sizes are the most economical.

For example, a 7-by-9-inch book may cost as much as 40 percent more than a 6-by-9-inch book with the same number of pages. Therefore, go with the more economical size unless your book requires a less common size to accomodate large-size graphic or special text formatting.

Papers of equal look and feel

While paper weights are based on the actual weight (in pounds) of a ream of paper, different types of paper have different basic sizes (the paper size used in the weight computation). For bond, the basic size is 17 inches by 22 inches; for cover stock it is 20 inches by 26 inches; for text, offset, and coated papers it is 25 inches by 38 inches. As a result, bond paper of a given weight doesn't look or feel like offset paper of the same weight, and 50 lb. offset paper is quite a bit lighter than 55 lb. cover stock. The following table, adapted with permission from our favorite PageMaker newsletter, *ThePage*, indicates roughly equivalent weights for three types of paper stock:

Bond	Offset	Cover
16		
20	50	
24	60	
28	70	
32	80	
	100	55
		65

Paper for inkjet printers

Unlike laser printer toner, which is fused onto the page at high temperatures, inkjet printer ink is more like the ink in a fountain pen. Rather than sticking to the surface of the paper (which is what toner does), it is absorbed into the paper. Thus, a paper with good absorbency is required; if you use a smooth, relatively non-absorbent paper, the ink spreads (rather than sinking in) and the results are usually less than satisfactory.

Output quality varies with paper choice more in some inkjet printers than in others—the Apple StyleWriter is an example of a printer in which paper choice is critical—but all seem to work best with just a few kinds of paper. Unfortunately, no two inkjet printers prefer the same paper; you'll need to experiment some to find just the right one. For inkjet printers with cut-sheet feeders, try these relatively inexpensive papers for proofing and day-to-day printing tasks: Weyerhauser's First Choice (a standard laser paper); Masterpiece's Recycled LaserSharp DTP (a smooth and bright recycled paper); Masterpiece's WoodStocks DTP (earth-toned and speckled recycled papers); and Masterpiece's Firebrites DTP (for colored papers).

In general, for the best quality output (such as for master copies you intend to send to the printer), use a bond paper with a high cotton content. We've had good luck on a StyleWriter, for example, with Crane Crest NIP; it is 100 percent cotton and, as a result, on the expensive side. We've also tested and been much impressed by pre-production samples of InkJet Ultra. This paper is designed for final copies from inkjet printers, and, contrary to our generalization, it contains no cotton at all. It can be used for pasteup and is even more expensive than Crane Crest NIP. All the papers mentioned above are available from PaperDirect; InkJet Ultra is sold exclusively by Paper-Direct.

  ## Picking the right paper

Selecting the right paper is an often neglected part of the publishing process. An excellent guide to all things paper is *Papers For Printing* by Mark Beach and Ken Russon (Coast to Coast Books). Essentially two books in one, the first half explains everything a publisher needs to know about paper types (grades, ratings) and features (basis weight, grain direction, size, opacity, ink holdout), as well as how to write paper specifications, decide on a quantity, and compute costs. There are many excellent illustrations, a glossary of terms specific to printing papers, and a state-by-state listing of paper suppliers. The second half of the book is a collection of 40 sample sheets, each sheet identified by paper type and printed with an identical set of nine color and nine black-and-white images and a sample of text. The binding allows you to remove the samples so you can test and compare the advantages and deficiencies of different paper types for different print jobs.

For testing the way a particular job will appear on a particular paper, it's hard to beat the PaperKit from PaperDirect, a mail order house that specializes in papers for laser printers, copiers, and offset printing. The PaperKit is a big box full of sample sheets of just about every paper that PaperDirect carries: recycled papers, card stock, dual-purpose laser/copier papers, classic, coated, and cotton rag single-purpose laser papers, pastel and neon colored papers, marbled and parchment papers, and papers with pre-printed borders, blends, and background designs and graphics. Find the paper that you're interested in, pull it out of the box, and print a test run on the printer you'll be using.

Included with the PaperKit is the PaperSelector, a handy, pocket-size swatch book of available papers; it makes an excellent reference/reminder after the sample sheets in the PaperKit have been tested and discarded. In most instances, matching envelopes are available for the papers that PaperDirect carries. PaperDirect also carries laser-safe clear and opaque labels, perforated and scored sheets, three-fold and four-fold brochure sheets, translucent vellum, overnight stiff-paper mailers, and a variety of other innovative desktop publishing paper products.

Special printing tasks

Iron-on documents

To print on materials that are too large or thick to feed through your laser printer—posterboard for a sign, for instance—you can iron on your document instead. With any program that allows mirror-image printing, simply print on the glossy side of a sheet of label-backing paper from label sheets. The image adheres to the slick paper, but transfers cleanly when ironed face down onto barn doors, posterboard, or other material that won't feed through your printer.

Printing two pages on one

Printing facing pages side-by-side on one sheet of paper or film can cut your service bureau charges in half. Here's one way to double up your pages in PageMaker for the Mac and for Windows:

1. With your document loaded, drag the ruler's zero point just outside the upper-left corner of the left page of a two-page spread.

2. Choose the PRINT command. Then click the Options button in the Print dialog box.

3. In the Print Options dialog box, turn on *Tiling*, and then select the *Manual* option.

Now, when you print out an even-numbered (left-hand) page, the right page will tag along with it, printing on the same sheet if the sheet is large enough. If you choose to print all the pages (by selecting the *All* Page Range option in the Print dialog box), all but the first page (the right-hand opener) will print two-to-a-page. Crop and registration marks will not print for the right page, so if you need those you'll have to create your own in a draw or paint program. Also, keep in mind that you'll need room on the sheet for both pages plus crop marks (if you use them). On a Linotronic 300 or a LaserWriter, the practical page size limit (with *Letter* selected for the Paper and *Wide* for the Orientation) is slightly more than 5 by 8 inches.

Alternatively, if you use a Mac, you can print two sheets to a page from virtually any program with Portfolio Systems' **DynoPage**. Once installed, DynoPage adds two extra dialog boxes to all your applications, one to the PAGE SETUP command (Figure 8-3) and one to the PRINT command. The options in these dialog boxes allow you to print two, three, four, or more application pages (reduced, actual size, or enlarged) per actual printed page. All you have to do is specify the way the pages should be laid out on each sheet of paper, and DynoPage handles the rest.

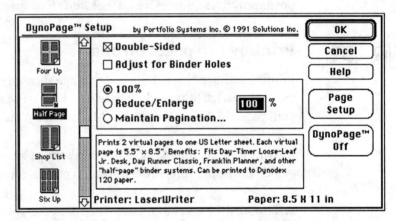

FIGURE 8-3 *The DynoPage Setup dialog box appears after you click on OK in your application's Page Setup dialog box. With it, you can choose a layout that prints two or more pages on a single sheet of paper.*

  Easy duplex printing

You don't need a duplex printer (which prints on both sides at the same time) to print double-sided documents; any laser printer will do the job. The easiest way to print both sides is to first print all the odd-numbered pages in reverse order from the end of document to the beginning, and then turn the paper over and print all the even numbered pages. But if your software won't let you print from back to front and/or print only odd or even-numbered pages, here's an easy technique that prints two double-sided copies of a single document:

1. Print your document as you normally would.

2. Re-sort the pages by putting each even-numbered page in front of the odd-numbered page that precedes it. For example, if you printed a 10-page document, you should sort your printed pages in the following order: 2, 1, 4, 3, 6, 5, 8, 7, 10, 9.

3. Re-stack the pages to reverse the order. For example, the pages in the stack in step 2 would now be 9, 10, 7, 8, 5, 6, 3, 4, 1, 2.

4. Place your pages in the paper feed tray facedown, so that the printer will print on the blank side of each page.

5. Print the document again.

6. You'll find that the pages are stacked in pairs; separate the two documents by placing every other page into one of two stacks, as you would deal cards to two players.

You now have two double-sided copies of the printed document.

If you own a Mac and prefer not to deal with even- and odd-numbered pages or printing back-to-front and front-to-back, you can let **DynoPage** handle all of this for you instead. In addition to printing two or more application pages on each printed page, as described in "Printing two pages on one," DynoPage also automates double-sided printing from within any application. If you turn on its *Double-sided* option, DynoPage prints half the pages on one pass, alerts you to turn the pages over and reinsert them in the paper tray, and then prints the remaining pages on the second pass. To print a standard duplex document (printing each application page full size, one to a printed page), you simply select DynoPage's *Full Page* option. Or you can elect to print two or more application pages on each side of a printed page. Either way, DynoPage automatically organizes the application pages so that they are in correct numerical order when the sheets of paper are cut (to separate the individual mini-pages, if two or more are printed per sheet) and stacked.

Duplex printing cautions

OK. You've read tips in *Publish* and elsewhere on using Hewlett-Packard LaserJets and other Canon-engine-based printers for duplex printing (printing on both sides of the page). Ah...but the LaserJet (and many LaserWriter) manuals warn against it. So, who are you supposed to believe?

On the one hand, it's true that many manuals warn against sending a laser-printed page back through the printer. They state that doing so may lead to curled paper, degraded print quality, and paper-handling problems. On the other hand, according to Hewlett-Packard's technical support staff, it won't void your warranty to try duplex printing this way. However, if you call them and complain about the above side effects after attempting duplex printing, they'll simply recite the warning in the manual. Don't expect any encouragement from them, in other words. And for good reason: The warning is legitimate.

The problem with print quality can occur when the toner on the already-printed side of the page gets reheated as the page passes over the hot fuser roller for the second time; some toner transfers back onto the fuser unit and ends up on the cleaning pad. Two things may result: lighter copy on the first printed side and a dirtier cleaning pad. You can't do anything about the print quality, but you can order extra cleaning pads from Hewlett-Packard's Corporate Parts department, 800/227-8164, part #RG1-0966-000CN. Normally you only change cleaning pads when you replace the toner cartridge; you may need to do it more often if you print duplex, however.

Paper curl occurs because paper from the paper bin takes a curved path through the printer. If you're determined to use these printers for duplex printing, you can reduce the paper curl and resulting paper-feed problems by lowering the rear paper tray. Paper will then travel a straight path through the printer, suffering less curl. Your pages will come out in reverse order, though. Another trick you can try if you're printing multiple pages is to first print all the odd-numbered pages, and then set them in a stack to cool and flatten out before printing the even-numbered pages on the reverse sides. We've had good results this way.

Printing T-shirt transfers

Designer T-shirts are the rage. Now there's a way to get your Free-Hand, Illustrator, CorelDRAW, or other draw program illustration onto a T-shirt without having to create silk screens. If you own a Canon-engine laser printer, you can use BlackLightning's **Iron-On Heat Transfer Toner** and print your own color iron-on transfers. Simply pop a BlackLightning toner cartridge into your LaserJet, LaserWriter, LaserJet IIP, or other Canon-based printer, and print your design onto plain paper with the image reversed. The toner contains sublimation dye granules that can withstand the heat of the printer's hot fuser roller but that releases the dye under the heat and pressure of a clothes iron or heat press. Since evenly applied heat and pressure are required for smooth-looking color application, images larger than the surface of a hand-held clothes iron should be applied with a larger-area heat press.

You can order Blacklightning cartridges for Canon CX, SX, and LX printers in a variety of colors including cyan, yellow, magenta, black, red, green, and blue. Cartridges come in 300-copy economy size and 2,200-copy professional size. BlackLightning is also willing to custom-mix toner for Pantone and other colors for an extra charge. You can print multi-colored images by printing on the transfer paper more than once, changing color toner cartridges between passes. BlackLightning's documentation includes tips for handling paper during the multi-pass process. A prep spray for all-cotton cloth and a toner solvent are included in each package.

Sending PostScript files to the printer

PC owners can use the DOS COPY command to send a PostScript file to the printer. If you use a Macintosh and need to print a PostScript file, however, you'll need a special utility since the Macintosh Finder only moves files to different disks or folders—not to printers, as does the DOS COPY command. By far the most economical of such utilities are Adobe's **SendPS**, which is available from user groups or from the Adobe forum on CompuServe (type GO ADOBE at the CompuServe prompt), and Apple's LaserWriter Utility, part of the Macintosh System 7 Software. Another is **LaserTalk**, a more comprehensive, PostScript utility from Adobe, on intended primarily for PostScript programmers. A fourth is **LaserStatus** from CE Software (part of MockPackage Plus Utilities). LaserStatus is a desk accessory which can send PostScript files to the printer, download previously defined sets of fonts, determine how much memory is available for downloadable fonts, and other neat stuff.

 ## White type on black

Unlike PostScript printers, the old **LaserJet Series II** isn't capable of printing reversed type (white type on a black background) unless you download a special reversed font into the printer. To reverse an existing font, you'll need to obtain a special utility like **Font Special Effects** by Softcraft. Font Special Effects is capable of altering existing Laserjet fonts in a variety of ways, including reversing black and white. (Each character in the reversed font will print as a black box surrounding a white letter.) Other options include obliquing, scaling, and applying patterns, shades, and shadows.

 ## Choosing the proper prep file

When printing to a PostScript printer or imagesetter, **PageMaker** for the Mac gives you the option of using the Aldus Prep printer driver or Apple's Laser Prep printer driver. (Aldus Prep is the default choice; press the Option Key when you choose the PRINT command and click the OK buttons in the ensuing dialog boxes to select Laser Prep.) What difference does it make which one you choose?

Pagemaker documents print faster with Aldus Prep, especially when you're using downloadable fonts. Also, scaled bitmapped graphics print better with Aldus Prep, and bitmapped graphics in Pagemaker can be smoothed only when using Aldus Prep. APD (Aldus Printer Description) files, which work only with Aldus Prep, give you access to printer options that are unknown to Apple's Laser Prep, such as multiple paper trays and different paper sizes; they also provide for more accurate rule thickness and screen density. APD files provide Aldus Prep with important information about the type of printer you're using, so more options remain available when using most print spoolers. Also, Aldus Prep provides better support for printing files to disk, and it requires a little less printer memory than does Laser Prep.

There are a few occasions, however, when Laser Prep is a better choice for Pagemaker printing. When Laser Prep is already stored in your printer's memory from a previous print job, using Laser Prep with Pagemaker saves the printer memory that would otherwise be used for Aldus Prep. Pages containing Adobe Illustrator graphics will automatically download Laser Prep during printing, so choosing Laser Prep at print time will, again, let you avoid loading both drivers. Finally, Laser Prep works with Apple's PrintMonitor print spooler, while Aldus Prep does not.

  ## Printing right to the edge

If you're still printing with a LaserWriter Plus, you may find that the usable page area for a legal-size sheet—6.7 by 12.8 inches—is just too small. Although there's no simple way to enlarge a PostScript printer's printable area, there are a couple of workarounds you can try. If your laser-printed page isn't going to be your final, distributed product, you can get around this limitation by tiling your publication. First, in your page layout program, create a custom page size about an inch longer and wider than a legal-size sheet. Then lay out your publication, print it using your page layout program's *Tile*

option, and paste the tiles together to produce an 8.5-by-14.0-inch master for printing at your local printshop.

An alternative to tiling is to create your document with legal-size dimensions and then print it on a different printer at your service bureau. For example, printers such as the Dataproducts LZR 2665, the PS Jet Plus, the QMS PS 800II, and the TI Omnilaser 2115 have a usable page area of 8.0 by 13.5 inches on a legal-size sheet; the Laserwriter IINT and IINTX offer a usable page of 8.0 by 13.8 inches on a legal-size sheet. And the Linotronic 100 and 300 both utilize the entire 8.5-by-14.0-inch page area.

Increased efficiency with Lettersmall page size

If you have at least a 2-inch margin on all four sides of your page in **PageMaker**, you can print faster on a PostScript printer and make more printer memory available for downloaded fonts by selecting Lettersmall as the paper size in the Print dialog box. The speed and downloadable font improvements result from the fact that the printer uses less memory to process the smaller page. On the Mac, select the *Lettersmall* option from the Paper pop-up menu in the Print dialog box (Figure 8-4). On the PC, make your selection from the printer Setup dialog box.

```
┌──────────────────────────────────────────────────────────┐
│  Print to:  Gutenberg                          ╭─────────╮ │
│                                                │  Print  │ │
│  Copies: ▐█▌   □ Collate □ Reverse order       ╰─────────╯ │
│                                                ╭─────────╮ │
│  Page range: ◉ All  ○ From │1│    to │1│       │ Cancel  │ │
│                                                ╰─────────╯ │
│  Paper source: ◉ Paper tray  ○ Manual feed     ╭─────────╮ │
│                                                │Options..│ │
│  Scaling: │100│ %  □ Thumbnails, │16│ per page ╰─────────╯ │
│                                                │PostScript..││
│  Book: ○ Print this pub only  ○ Print entire book          │
│                                          ┌──────────────┐  │
│  ──────────────────────────────────     │  Letter      │  │
│                                          │ ✓Lettersmall │  │
│  Printer: │LaserWriter II NTX│  Paper:   │  A4      ▖   │  │
│                                          │  A4small     │  │
│  Size:      8.5 H 11.0   inches  Tray:   │  B5          │  │
│  Print area: 7.7 H 10.2  inches          │  Legal       │  │
│                                          └──────────────┘  │
└──────────────────────────────────────────────────────────┘
```

FIGURE 8-4 *Note that the Print Area (lower left) is smaller than usual when the Lettersmall option is selected in the Paper pop-up menu in PageMaker's Print dialog box.*

Printing Illustrator images that contain screens

Use **QuarkXPress** to print **Illustrator** files that include screens. This gives you control over the number of lines per inch, which is useful when printing comps on a laser or thermal printer.

CHAPTER 9

Publishing as a Business

Financial and legal matters

Estimating fees for layout jobs

Estimating how much to charge your desktop publishing clients is a skill that can make or break your business; charge too much and you won't attract clients, charge too little and you'll starve. Most desktop publishing contractors use a time-based method for preparing their estimates. To prepare an estimate this way, break each job down into as many separate components as possible, and then estimate the time you'd normally take for each one. Add up the total and multiply by an hourly rate. For a project prepared with **Ventura Publisher** or **PageMaker**, for example here are some of the components you might include in your estimate:

- creating the layout design

- setting up style sheets

- installing any special fonts

- preparing graphics

- cleaning up text files to remove unnecessary elements like superfluous tabs and double spaces between sentences

- laying out pages

- printing the drafts

- proofing

- producing final imagesetter output

Make sure you always get a representative sample of the final document from your client before you make the estimate, and take a careful look at the client's text files to see how much cleaning up they'll need. After coming up with a preliminary estimate, add a fudge factor to compensate for misjudgments in your estimate and for unforeseen delays. Finally, compare the estimate to your actual experience with similar jobs.

Alternatively, or as a way of double-checking a time-based estimate, you can use a standard setup charge and a standard per-page charge, based on the nature and complexity of the document. For example, the estimate for a newsletter layout might be based on a setup charge of $250 and a per-page charge of $75. Prior experience and a good record of past projects and their costs are especially helpful in determining what your standard charges should be.

It is important to consider prevailing norms in your area as well. Clients and service bureaus in a given area usually have some idea of what constitutes a reasonable price for a particular type of job, and you should be able to determine the local average rates by asking around. For example, one contractor noted that, in our area, software companies expect to pay $25–$30 per page for illustrated manuals. Trade books with no graphics and single-column layouts go for $10 per page, including typesetting.

Be careful not to set your bids too low. Desktop publishers tend to undercharge when they're starting their business. That way, unfortunately, you'll end up with clients who think that good work comes cheap. Later, when you realize your mistake, you'll either have to convince them to accept higher prices or get new clients.

  ## Games and patents

Drawing programs like Illustrator, FreeHand, CorelDRAW, or Designer are great tools for designing board games. But if you've designed and printed samples of a unique board game, one which you think will be the next "Trivial Pursuit" or "Clue," you face a problem. How can you distribute samples or show potential publishers the game and at the same time ensure that someone doesn't copy your idea?

First thing: hire a lawyer to formulate a confidentiality or nondisclosure agreement. Then have anyone who might have a commercial interest in your game sign it before showing them your game. That doesn't protect the "idea" of the game, but you can sue for damages should anyone violate the agreement.

The legal protection of your game falls into three areas of law: copyrights, trademarks, and patents. Copyright law protects your game board's art and layout, printed game rules and instructions; the expression of your game idea; but not the concept or idea itself. Protecting the "idea" of the game goes beyond copyright protection. Look at most board games, and you'll see a copyright notice, a trademark registration, and occasionally a patent notice. Trademark registration makes it illegal for someone to use the name or logo design: in short, the identity of your game. Patent law actually protects the idea behind your game, and you can get a patent if you can demonstrate novelty or uniqueness behind its design or mechanics.

Unfortunately, getting a patent takes time and money. You could spend thousands of dollars obtaining a patent and not receive it until after your game has been published, hit its peak, and been forgotten. Still, patents and trademarks can serve a useful function (just having a patent pending may be enough to keep the wolves at bay); for more details about patents call the United States Patent Office (703/557-3158) and ask for patent and trademark information. For more specific information, we like a book called *Inside Santa's Workshop* by Ron Weingartner and Richard Levy.

Whether you're contemplating a patent or not, it's always a good idea to put a copyright notice on your game board and its container in this form: "© John Doe 1991." To register your copyright, request a form from the Copyright Office hotline at (202/707-9100). There's a $20 filing fee, and you'll need to include one copy of the game if it's not yet published and two copies if it's been published already. For more information about copyrights, call 202/479-0700 or write to the

Information and Publications Section, LM-455, Copyright Office, Library of Congress, Washington, D.C., 20559.

Mail-order businesses and banks

If you're trying to establish a mail-order book or catalog publishing business, you may have difficulty opening a bank account capable of receiving credit card payments. That's because many banks are reluctant to extend this service to businesses that operate without a store front. However, you can usually overcome the bank's reluctance if they know you personally or professionally, or if you're recommended by a personal acquaintance of the banker. Since most accountants maintain a close relationship with at least one banker, your accountant may be able to open the necessary doors.

Marketing and promotion

Credits increase your visibility

Increase your visibility by suggesting that grateful clients give credit to your design or layout in the masthead of their publication, or propose adding your byline and phone number to posters and flyers.

Focus on the design

The first time you show a client a layout or design you've done on the computer, don't show your fresh, sharp, laser-printed pages. Instead, trace the printed pages by hand, quickly greek in the copy, and show the traced version. That way, your client will concentrate on the design concept rather than on the technology, your choice of typeface, and other less important details.

Following Postal Service guidelines

If you are preparing and printing mailings in-house, follow Postal Service addressing guidelines. This will ensure that your letters make it through the new high-speed automated processing system with all due dispatch. The U.S. Postal Service publishes a number of envelope and return-mail addressing guides: Two small pamphlets, "Addressing for Success" (Notice 221) and "Addressing with Bar Codes" (Notice 53), nicely summarize the basics. A larger booklet, "A Guide to Business Mail Preparation" (Publication 25), offers a more comprehensive set of guidelines, and a second booklet, "Postal Addressing Standards" (Publication 28), explains the proper format of the address itself in almost excruciating detail. All the publications are free, and available through your local postmaster.

Here are a few guidelines to get you started:

- Print the address entirely in uppercase letters and avoid using punctuation marks. Insert two spaces between the state abbreviation and the ZIP code. The name of a foreign country must appear alone on the last line.

- If there is an "Attention" line, it should be placed immediately above the name of the recipient.

- Typefaces that work well include Friz Quadrata, Futura Medium, Helios, Helios Light, Helvetica, Helvetica Light, Optima, Univers, and Univers Medium. Avoid using boldface type.

- Use 10- or 12-point type with an extra 4 points of leading for the address. To print six lines per inch on mailing labels, use 8-point type on 12 points of leading, but make sure the typeface you're using meets the 80-mil minimum character height (a mil is 1/1000 of an inch).

- If you're using mailing labels, make sure that they're horizontal (plus or minus five degrees) when applied to the envelope.

You can't automate good design

Don't arbitrarily hand a design task over to someone on your staff who knows how to use page-layout and graphics programs but lacks design experience—even if doing so appears to be a cost-effective strategy. Consider the consequences of presenting a less-than-polished image to your clients and potential customers. You'll then realize the importance of getting professional design help if you don't have the expertise to maintain a good image. Although remarkable advances have been made in computer technology, no hardware or software developer has yet come up with the equivalent of a graphic designer in a box or on disk.

Book distribution and marketing

With desktop publishing tools it's possible to produce and publish an entire book, and many people, ourselves included, have done just that. Unfortunately, there's been no comparable revolution in book marketing and distribution, which remains a complex and convoluted business. Here are some good sources of information for those of you embarking on the marketing/distribution phase of your book publishing careers:

- Other small publishers. To find other small publishers in your area, you should contact the Publishers Marketing Association at 213/372-2732, or COSMEP (The International Association of Independent Publishers) at 415/922-9490.

- Books. Dan Poynter's classic *The Self-Publishing Manual* is good for a quick orientation. John Kremer's *1001 Ways to Market Your Books* is an incredibly rich assortment of practical book-marketing tips.

- Back issues of book marketing newsletters. Three newsletters covering book marketing are the *COSMEP Newsletter* (published by the International Association of Independent Publishers), the *PMA Newsletter* (published by Publishers Marketing Association), and *Book Marketing Update* (published by Ad-Lib Publications). In each case, you can contact the publisher for an index of back issues and then order those newsletter issues that address your particular interests.

- Free newsletters published by book printers. Some book printers publish newsletters with tips on production and marketing as a service to current and prospective customers. Two good ones are Griffin Printing's Signature, at 213/245-3671, and Thomson-Shore's Printer's Ink at 313/426-3939.

 ## Mail merge for page layout

To capture your prospective client's attention and keep their interest, your promotional material should look a lot better than average. Most high-end word processing programs have mail merge facilities that make promotional mailings relatively easy, but they don't have the typographical and layout finesse that the best promotional broadsides require. Most page layout programs, on the other hand, have primitive mail merge functions or none at all. Fortunately, you can merge a mailing list into a single-page **Ventura Publisher** document and thereby print a personalized promotional using a list of names from your database. To do this, generate a name list from your database as a text file to load into Ventura Publisher. The last line of each address of the generated file should include a paragraph tag that specifies a page break. Here's what a segment of your database-generated ASCII file might look like:

```
John Smith
275 York Terrace
San Francisco, CA 94117
@PAGEBREAK = Dear John,
Jane Bamburg
55 Saturn Staircase
San Francisco, CA 94118
@PAGEBREAK = Dear Jane,
```

Load the file onto the underlying frame, not any frames you've added. That way, Ventura will create a new page for each address when it encounters the tag for a style containing a page break. (Of course, you must create the style in your document, one which specifies the required page break.) Place the body of the document—the parts that don't change—in one or more added frames. You'll need to make those frames appear on each newly created page. To do so, select each frame and choose the REPEATING FRAME command from the Frame menu.

Production

New procedures: trust but verify

When preparing production schedules, allow ample time to compensate for bugs, bombs, and other computer-related anomalies. It ain't over 'til it's over, and the job isn't done until it's invoiced and delivered. If you haven't tested a procedure, don't assume it's the answer to all your problems just because you read it in a magazine or software manual.

When the production of a publication involves several steps using different application programs (for example, preparing tables in Excel, formatting them in Microsoft Word, and then placing them in PageMaker), do a dry run with a small sample of the material. With this experience under your belt, you can fine-tune your checklist of steps and avoid unpleasant surprises later on.

A ready-made publishing tool kit

A quick and convenient way to equip yourself with all the standard tools for publication design, preparation, and production is to buy a copy of *Graphics Master 4* by Dean Phillip Lem. In addition to its many reference pages covering halftone screens and color illustrations, typography, printing, proofing, and production, the book contains, among other things: a circular proportional scale, a 10-inch line gauge and ruler, process-color guides for both coated and uncoated paper, charts of paper weights and sizes and envelope sizes, a typeface catalog that includes character-per-pica information and specimen paragraphs, and a special copy-fit calculator.

Bullets make better place holders

For place holders that stand out against body text, replace the "TK" used by veteran writers with bullets. We think you'll have to admit that this phone number to come, •••/•••–••••, is pretty hard to overlook.

The fine art of bookmaking

Interested in applying your desktop publishing skills to that nearly lost art of limited-edition books? A good introduction to the fine art of bookmaking is Adrian Wilson's *The Design of Books*. (It's currently out of print, so try your local library.) Although written in the days before microcomputers, its explanations of design, paper, binding, and the like are no less valuable and insightful. Wilson was one of America's premier book designers, and reading his book is like apprenticing with a master of the craft.

For more up-to-date information, try the quarterly journal *Fine Print*. Each issue has a variety of articles of interest—essays on typography, type design, and the design of literature, illustrated reviews of current books, and so on—and advertisements from firms specializing in printing and binding supplies. Included with each issue is an eight-page newsletter containing a comprehensive calendar of events, a list of upcoming classes and workshops, and a classified ad section.

Write your own computer manual

Don't wait till the next disaster-before-a-deadline strikes to dig out the technical support number for your favorite application. Write down technical support phone numbers, current software versions, and software serial numbers in a small notebook and keep it next to your computer. Even better, expand the notebook into a personal reference manual containing all sorts of other notables, including the macros you've created, shortcuts that are difficult to remember, favorite tips from this book, and so on.

Scanning by hand

With hand-held OCR scanners such as **The Typist** from Caere Corporation coming onto the market, you may be tempted to cancel your typing lessons and take up the tango instead. But wait—put down the phone! These devices, while they *do* work, have some limitations that the vendors don't advertise. From our experience, in fact, there are many tasks for which a hand-held OCR scanner is not an effective tool, many tasks which could be accomplished faster and more accurately by entering text from the keyboard the old-fashioned way, or by using a full-size OCR system.

For example, if you need to enter text from the pages of a book, you should not use a hand-held OCR system. Here's why: Even if the book is narrow enough to allow for a single pass with the handheld scanner, it's darn near impossible to keep the scanner on track toward the bottom of the page. That's because some of the roller guides (on which the hand-held scanner glides) roll off the end of the page as you move the scanner nearer the bottom. When that happens, the scanner lurches momentarily, resulting in an error in the scan, and consequently a serious error in the OCR translation, which may converting the lower part of the page into gobbledygook. It's often a time consuming, eye-straining process to locate the errors, locate the correct text on the book page, and coordinate hand-entry of the appropriate corrections in the appropriate locations. Add that time to the 30 to 60 seconds it's already taken the OCR software to translate the scan and insert the text (with errors) into your word processor, and you may be wasting far too much time.

Of course, if the book page can't be scanned in a single pass, your problems are only compounded. Though some hand-held scanners claim the ability to automatically stitch together text from separate overlapping scans, we inevitably find repeated text and skipped segments of text in multi-pass scans, and it takes careful, time-consuming, and eye-straining proofreading to uncover and correct the errors. The same holds true for magazine articles that cover several columns which you need to merge into one body of text.

Difficulties similar to those described above have often bedeviled our attempts to scan multi-column magazine articles. As a result, we recommend hand-held OCR scanners only for documents which can be laid flat on a hard surface and which contain only small amounts of text (so you can touch up significant errors quickly). Examples of documents of this type include articles from a newspaper (for a clipping file), small invoices, security reports, airline tickets (for expense records), and similar documents.

  ## Earning a degree in desktop publishing

Since there are few professional degrees of any kind in publishing, learning the skills of desktop publishing in a classroom setting is rarely as easy as signing up for night courses at your local community college. Aldus, Apple, Adobe, Letraset, Xerox, and others either offer courses or training programs themselves or authorize others to do so. Such courses and programs tend to concentrate on specific software and don't give college credit; check the pages of *Publish* for up-to-date information on training programs and training centers.

For a more formal education, a number of university-sponsored programs offer courses or workshops covering many aspects of the publishing industry, including desktop technology. Among them are Stanford's Professional Publishing Course and Communications Workshops, U.C. Berkeley's Certificate Program in Publishing, the impressive Photo Offset Printing program (including a recently proposed Certificate in Electronic Pre-press Publishing) at Kennedy-King College (one of the City Colleges of Chicago), and City University of New York's Education in Publishing Program. You'll find a complete, up-to-date listing of such programs in the "Courses for the Book Trade" section of the standard publishing reference *Literary Market Place*, which should be available at your local library.

Getting files to and from

Sending disks in the mail

Postal employees tell us we're crazy even thinking about mailing 3½-inch disks in standard envelopes; automatic sorting machines, they say, eat unprotected floppy disks for breakfast. But we send and receive disks in letter-size or #10 business envelopes all the time, and so far not one has been dead on arrival (or failed to arrive altogether).

One key to our sterling success rate may be that we always make sure that the disk's sliding metal door is at the bottom of the envelope. This way, the door isn't under the postage cancellation stamp. Although it may be wishful thinking on our part, we believe our precaution reduces the chance that the disk will arrive with a crushed door.

Start communications with two phone lines

The first time you establish telecommunications settings with someone, use two phone lines, one for the humans (to talk over) and the other for the modems (to send data over). Unless both parties are computer engineers or psychics, using only one line makes the task a lot more difficult. Let the more experienced of the two parties guide the less experienced.

Economical and orderly file transmission

To send a publication comprised of several pages of layout, text, and graphic files over a modem, use an archiving utility (such as **Arc** on the PC or **StuffIt** on the Mac) to compress the files and combine them into one large archive. Storing the files in one large archive ensures delivery of all the required files, sending one large file is a lot easier than sending many smaller files, and compression reduces the time required for the transfer and concomitant telephone charges. The person receiving the document must have a copy of the same archiving utility or a compatible de-archiving and decompression program in order to extract the files from the archive; extraction-only utilities are often available at little or no cost from on-line bulletin boards.

Using PC disks and their files on a Mac

If your Macintosh is equipped with an FDHD disk drive (commonly called a "superdrive"), there are several ways you can examine the contents of MS-DOS formatted 3½-inch disks and use the files they contain. The cheapest though not the simplest technique is to use Apple File Exchange—a program you'll find on one of your Macintosh System Software disks. Launch Apple File Exchange first. Then insert the MS-DOS disk in the disk drive. (The order of events is important; if you insert the MS-DOS disk first, the computer will assume that it is an unformatted Macintosh disk and ask if you want to format it.) In the Apple File Exchange window, you'll see the files on the DOS disk displayed in one file list and the contents of your current Mac drive or folder in the other (Figure 9-1). Copy the desired files from the PC disk to a Mac disk using the Translate button to make them available to your Macintosh applications.

A more elegant alternative is to use **DOS Mounter** (Dayna Communications). Once it is installed, DOS Mounter automatically displays MS-DOS formatted disks and files on the desktop alongside standard Macintosh disks and files. Files on MS-DOS disks are represented by standard file icons, DOS subdirectories by folders, and disks by standard disk icons. Except for initializing or erasing an MS-DOS formatted disk, all the standard Macintosh disk and file management procedures apply, such as copying or moving files by dragging, and deleting files via the trash.

Of course, mounting the disk and seeing or copying the desired file solves only part of the problem. To work with a file created in a DOS application, it must be in a format that's compatible with your Macintosh application. All Macintosh word processors and database programs, for example, can work with basic text or ASCII files. And some applications, such as Microsoft Word, can recognize and convert files created by their PC counterparts. In many instances, however, the file will need to be converted to a compatible format in order to be understood by a Mac application; in this situation, we recommend using **MacLinkPlus/Translators** in combination with Apple File Exchange to accomplish the desired conversion.

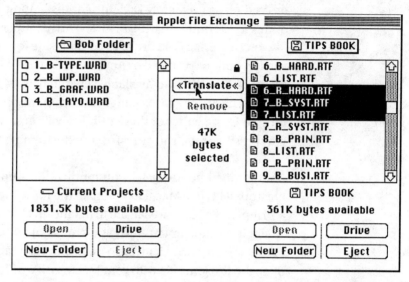

FIGURE 9-1 *Apple File Exchange in combination with an FDHD Super-Drive allows you to copy files from an MS-DOS disk (right) to a Macintosh disk (left).*

  ## Preserving tabs when sending text files

Telecommunicating an ASCII (text-only) file from a PC to a Macintosh is an easy and widespread method of transferring a file from one platform to the other, but the transfer process almost always replaces tabs with spaces. If your documents contain large numbers of tabs—if they contain tables or lists constructed with tabs—there are several ways you can prevent the wholesale loss of tabs during a transfer.

One method is to transfer and convert the file with a utility such as **Apple File Exchange** or **MacLinkPlus/PC**. MacLinkPlus/PC is a complete file transfer and translation kit containing a PC-to-Mac cable,

PC and Mac programs (which work with the direct-connection cable, a modem connection, or disk-to-disk), and over 100 file translators covering a wide variety of format-to-format conversion situations. Apple File Exchange, part of the Macintosh's system software, handles only disk-to-disk transfers and conversions. If the desired file is on an MS-DOS format disk, Apple File Exchange requires a Mac outfitted with an FDHD drive (SuperDrive) or an Apple 5¼-inch external DOS drive. To compensate for the limited file conversion options supplied by Apple, you can use the file translators in MacLinkPlus/PC (also available separately as MacLinkPlus/Translators) with Apple File Exchange to convert the file to a standard Mac format. Using either of these utilities will preserve your tabs—and may preserve much of the rest of your document's formatting as well.

Another method uses a telecommunications program to transfer a file from a PC to a Mac. First prepare the file by performing a search and replace to change each tab to a stand-in character not used elsewhere in the document, such as a pound sign (#), an at sign (@), or a caret (^). Then save it in ASCII (text-only) format. After the transfer, open the text-only file with your Macintosh word processor and perform a "reverse" search and replace, changing each occurrence of the stand-in character back to a tab. Remember that in order to specify a tab in the Find/Change dialog box, you usually need to enter a special code or use a command. In Microsoft Word you enter ^t, for example; in MacWrite you press Command + Tab.

A third method involves one special (but not that uncommon) telecommunications situation in which you can skip all the search and replace tap-dancing. This is when you are telecommunicating a Word for the PC file and intend to use it in Word for the Mac, or when the two word processors involved both comprehend Microsoft's Interchange (RTF) format. In this situation, simply save the file on the PC in RTF format. Send the RTF file in the usual way (RTF files are text-only files; tabs and other formatting have been replaced by the RTF code). Finally, instruct your Macintosh word processor to open the file and convert it from RTF to standard Mac format. Virtually all formatting (including tabs) is preserved using this method.

Locking out viruses

When you give a floppy disk to a service bureau or anyone else, always lock the disk to prevent infection by a computer virus. To lock a 3½-inch Macintosh or PC disk, locate the plastic slide in the upper-left corner of the back side of the disk (Figure 9-2). Push the slide up with a fingernail or pen or pencil point so that you can see through the hole beneath. When the hole is open, the disk is locked. To lock a PC 5¼-inch floppy, locate the write-protect notch on the right-hand edge of the floppy and cover it with one of the adhesive write-protect tabs that often come with 5¼-inch floppies, or use a short piece of opaque tape. When light can't shine through the notch, the diskette is locked.

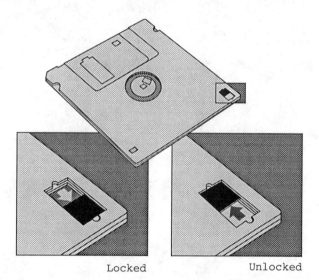

Locked   Unlocked

FIGURE 9-2 *Locking and unlocking a Macintosh floppy disk. (Illustration © Apple Computer, Inc. Used with permission.)*

Unstuffing everything

To unstuff all of the Mac files stored in one StuffIt Classic or StuffIt Deluxe archive in one fell swoop, double-click on the archive in the Finder and then press the Shift Key until the unstuffing procedure begins. (Make sure you double-click first, and then press Shift, not the reverse.) To quickly unstuff all the files in several StuffIt Classic or StuffIt Deluxe archives in a single action, first select all the archives in the Finder (click on the first one, Shift + click on the others). Then choose the OPEN command from the Finder's File menu (or press Command + O) and hold down the Shift Key until the unstuffing procedure begins. (Again, make sure you press Shift after invoking the OPEN command.) In both procedures, a new folder is created for each archive and the unstuffed files are placed within.

Putting It All Together

☞ Writing and editing this book was merely a part of what we three co-authors accomplished. We also directed or performed ourselves every aspect of the book's production up to and including the creation of camera-ready mechanicals. It's a question of putting your mouse where your mouth is, and, in our case, it was only fitting that a practical book on desktop publishing be the product of a desktop shop. By hiring the designer, copy editor, and proofreader ourselves, by implementing the design and laying out the pages, we gained control over every part of the book's creation. In addition, we put ourselves to the test, fortified with the contents of the very book we were working on. And new problems meant new solutions, hence new tips and techniques; necessity, as always, bore us further invention. Thus, in this final chapter, we show you *Desktop Publishing Secrets* in action, publishing an actual book—the one in your hands.

The big picture

Unavoidably, big projects create problems big and small, and *Desktop Publishing Secrets* was certainly no exception. Three different authors, two different computer platforms, a huge mass of material which was at first totally disorganized—these and other factors forced us to think very carefully about what we were doing. On the following pages, we describe many of the problems that arose as we wrote and produced this book. In this section, we describe the more general issues and how we resolved them. In the "Gory Details" section later in the chapter, we explain some of the most interesting technical problems and solutions for those who want to know more.

. . . .

Far-flung correspondents

A long document is headache enough, but coordinating three co-authors who live thousands of miles apart can be a migraine of the first order. Robert was in New York during much of the work, and Bob and Ted live on the West coast. Since we edited each other's work and divided other tasks among us, we needed to be able to exchange files frequently during the writing process. Fortunately, with Federal Express, regular mail, the U. S. Postal Service's Express Mail, and cheap 2400 bps modems, trading files was usually no problem. Straight text was often exchanged over a direct modem-to-modem connection using Kermit transfer protocols. Large numbers of text files, graphics files, and layouts containing graphics were usually sent more economically via Federal Express, regular mail, or Express Mail, depending upon the urgency of the situation, and the time of day (before or after the express delivery drop-off deadline).

The physical exchange of files was only part of the problem, however. Each of us entered a lot of basic formatting—such as text in bold face, italics, or small caps—as we worked, according to the conventions we adopted at the very outset of the project. Having to respecify type during the page layout phase was something we wanted to avoid, so it was essential that text formatting be preserved when we traded word processing files. This would not have been an issue had we all used the same word processor, but we couldn't all use the same program since Robert uses a Mac and Bob and Ted use PCs.

Since we couldn't all use precisely the same program, we instead used two very similar word processors: Microsoft Word for the Macintosh and Microsoft Word for Windows. In theory, these programs should have been able to read each other's native formats perfectly, without conversion of any kind, but that feature proved unreliable for us. Instead, we traded files after converting them to RTF (Rich Text Format), a format which reliably preserves all formatting, including style sheets. Since RTF is ASCII-based (plain text), it's easy to send RTF files over the wires. (We usually did so in the evening, when phone rates are lower.) For RTF files exchanged on 3½-inch disks, we used Apple File Exchange's default translator and the superdrive on Robert's Mac IIx to move RTF files from Mac disks to DOS disks or vice versa.

What's your number?

With three people working on hundreds and hundreds of tips, it was not hard to imagine a slow descent into purgatory. Fortunately, one of us early on suggested that we assign a unique serial number to each tip. The foundation of each serial number was a simple code that specified the source of the tip (whether it was an original tip or, if not, the year and month it appeared in *Publish*) and the origin of the text file (the author's unedited archives, *Publish*'s copy-edited version, or the final—and sometimes heavily cut—printed version). A prefix to the source code indicated the chapter to which the tip was assigned, and a suffix told us whether the tip was not yet edited, in progress, or the final version.

Initially the numbers helped us divide material equally between authors, refer to the original tip files when questions arose, and keep track of each tip. But this strategy paid off later in ways that greatly aided in organizing and laying out the book. Illustrations, for example, were labeled with the tip's serial number so there'd be no confusion about which figure belonged to which tip. The same number was also used to identify the necessary graphics frames, frame anchors, and figure number cross references in Ventura Publisher, as we'll discuss in greater depth in "The Gory Details" below. Ultimately, of course, all serial numbers were either deleted or hidden from the reader.

What's my (out)line?

As mentioned above, early in the writing and editing phase we adopted a set of Microsoft Word formatting conventions which we could all use in our respective versions of the program. One of the most important conventions we adopted was to format tip section heads and titles as level one and level two headline styles. (We redefined these two headline styles so they matched our basic manuscript style. Word's default definitions for these styles are, in any event, so ridiculous and ugly that they are of little use to anyone.) Using Microsoft Word's outlining feature, we could then arrange and rearrange individual tips and entire sections with very little effort.

In Word's outline view, we could see the full document on screen, or we could "collapse" the view, hiding the text so that only the section heads or section heads and tip titles were visible (Figure 10-1). This skeletal view of the document made it easy to evaluate the organization of each chapter. If we felt that a particular tip belonged in a different section, we simply dragged it to a new position—no cutting and pasting was required and the entire tip (both the title and the text and caption underneath) moved as a single object. Similarly, we could rearrange the order of chapter sections simply by dragging section titles from one location to another. Because of our experience

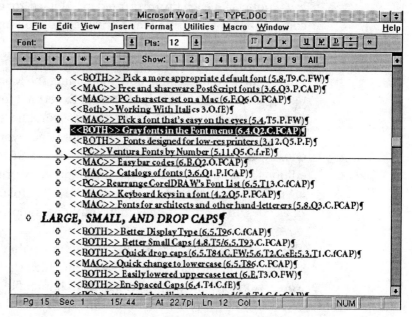

FIGURE 10-1 *Word's outline feature made it easy to reorganize each chapter. In Outline view, we could drag a single tip (as shown above) or an entire section to a new position. The gray horizontal line clearly indicates the new location in the text.*

with this book, we've become real converts to Word's outliner. We recommend it enthusiastically as a powerful (and too often overlooked) writing and editing tool.

. . . .

Hard choices: picking a page layout program

As you have no doubt noticed by now, *Desktop Publishing Secrets* is a highly structured document. A straightforward design makes it easy to pick out important information. Icons indicate whether the tip applies to the Mac, the PC, or both. The steps in a given technique are listed in a numbered sequence. Illustrations are numbered and cross-referenced. In terms of organization, the book is laid out in a clear, hierarchical scheme: Chapters are organized into sections, within which the individual tips are ordered. The tips themselves are further organized into introductory paragraphs, then, in many instances, an ordered list of steps or a bulleted list of options, and so on. Typographic conventions accent important items in the text: the key products for each tip are printed in boldface, for example, menu commands appear in small caps, and menu options appear in italics.

Implementing this structural design posed a number of problems. Among them were creating and positioning the Mac and PC icons, taking advantage of the Adobe Utopia Expert Set font for ligatures and small caps, drawing the dotted lines separating items, and other issues. Having settled upon the PC as our page layout platform, we chose Ventura Publisher's 3.0 (we used both the GEM and Windows editions at various stages) for our layout program primarily because of Ventura's open file structure and use of ASCII (plain text) formatting codes, in combination with its implementation of style sheets.

The advantage of Ventura's open file structure is that it stores graphics and text files separately from its chapter files. (It doesn't, in other words, store text and graphics *inside* the chapter file.) From the very beginning, we suspected that, in many instances, it would be more efficient to bypass our page layout program's menus and make changes to text and graphics files directly. And our experience with this book has amply confirmed our suspicion. With Ventura's open file structure, we could easily edit or otherwise alter our text and graphics after they were placed in the layout, right up to the last minute. We could make global changes in our word processor using its search-and-replace function or custom macros, for example, even after the text had been loaded and formatted in Ventura.

Ventura's style sheets also offered us a highly efficient means of automating the book's formatting. Ventura still has the most comprehensive list of formatting features which can be included in a named style. With style sheets, you simply tag a paragraph with a given style name and that paragraph will automatically reformat itself based on the specifications of the particular style. Once tagged, almost all format changes can be made simply by changing the style specifications. With Ventura's style sheets, we were able to position the PC and Mac icons and adjust their position document-wide, easily assign and alter formats of subheads and text, and by and large avoid tedious page-by-page formatting of the document.

Last but not least, it was Ventura's use of ASCII (plain text) formatting codes that attracted us to the program. Why would we opt to hand-code our book when we had Ventura's handy interactive menu system at our disposal? The answer, as usual, is efficiency. Ventura plain-text formatting codes allowed us to add index entries and cross-references directly into our word processing documents as we wrote and edited them. But even more importantly, in a structured document like this one, page-by-page interactive formatting via menus is much too time consuming. For example, it would have taken us from one to five hours per chapter to work through the 20 to 90 pages of text, mouse in hand, tagging paragraphs. Instead, we used a Microsoft Word macro (which took about an hour to perfect) to apply tag codes to paragraphs in about 45 seconds per chapter. The net savings was several days' work.

As it turned out, in combination with Ventura's plain text formatting codes, Word for Window's Word Basic macro programming language was crucial to this project. Since it is a complete programming environment based on Microsoft QuickBasic, Word Basic dwarfs the macro programming features of competing word processors. Fortunately, some of Bob's misspent youth was consumed writing Basic

454   DESKTOP PUBLISHING SECRETS

utilities for transforming text in volume mail applications. With
Bob's expert hand, Word for Windows was turned into a text processing robot that could analyze our text, copy or move specific paragraphs, add or delete Ventura codes, and so on. Using macros, we
quickly applied tag codes to paragraphs, as described above, and
automatically prepared and saved specialized-purpose files, such as
caption files.

Other operations we decided to automate with macros were far more
complicated. A not-too-complex example is the conversion of
Word's Small Kaps type style (which uses standard uppercase letters
of two different point sizes.[1]) to the required fonts in the Adobe Utopia Expert Set (which contains true-cut small caps). To correctly set
the command PAGE SIZE & LAYOUT in small caps in Ventura, for example, we would have had to select each string of lowercase letters,
like the *age* in *Page*, open the Set Font Attributes dialog box, and
choose the expert set font which contains the true-cut small capital
characters we needed. Thus, for this one command name, we'd have
to select and reformat text three times, once for *age*, once for *ize*, and
once for *ayout*.

How long would this take for a book that includes thousands of command names in small caps? Way too long. Instead we wrote a Word
Basic macro that located each command formatted with Word's
Small Kaps character attribute. It then analyzed the selection and
figured out which strings of letters were small caps and which regular
caps. It inserted the appropriate Ventura font change codes, indicating where the font change to Utopia Expert should occur (by inserting the code <F1008M>), and where Utopia Regular should resume
(by inserting the code <F255D>). After using our small caps macro,
the coded text for PAGE SIZE & LAYOUT would look like this:

---

1 Microsoft Word, like PageMaker, creates small caps by replacing all lowercase letters
with capital letters in a smaller point size. Trouble is, the smaller-size capitals appear
a little on the thin side next to the full-size capital. Compare, for example, these two
commands: PAGE SIZE & LAYOUT using Word's method, and PAGE SIZE & LAYOUT using
the Adobe Expert Set's custom-designed small capitals.

P<F1008M>age <F255D> S<F1008M>ize & <F255D>L<F1008M> ayout<F255D>

For more information about how we used macros to add formatting and other codes to our text files, consult "The Gory Details" section later in the chapter.

. . . .

Hard work: laying out the pages

Our second major page-layout task, in addition to formatting the text, was placing the illustrations and captions. Doing this on a page-by-page basis would have been very time consuming. As much as possible, we wanted to avoid

going through each chapter, locating the items with accompanying illustrations, and creating the appropriate illustration frame (with correct dimensions, margins, padding, caption label, etc.) for each one. We also wanted to avoid either re-entering the caption or cutting caption text from the manuscript and pasting it into the caption frame attached to the illustration. Doing all this by hand for up to 50 illustrations in some chapters would clearly eat up precious time and guarantee errors of one sort or another.

Instead of proceeding page by page, we again took advantage of Ventura's plain text codes and automated the process as much as possible. All illustration frame anchors were specified with plain text codes during the text editing stage.[2] Automatic cross-referencing codes for illustrations were also added at this time.[3] Then, in Ventura, we created the requisite number of empty illustration frames on an extra page at the end of each chapter. Finally, we invoked Ventura's RE-ANCHOR FRAMES command to send all frames automatically to the appropriate pages in the chapter (see "The Gory Details" section at the end of this chapter for more about this technique.)

2 In Ventura, a frame anchor is a marker embedded in the text against which a frame (containing an illustration, for example) will automatically position itself. The frame anchor and the frame itself have the same name, which is how the frame finds its corresponding anchor point.

The serial number assigned to each tip greatly simplified the addition of the frame anchor and cross-reference codes. Remember, we used this serial number in the raw text, for both the tip number and any figure references, and as the name of the corresponding illustration file. Using a Word macro, we could automatically convert the in-text serial number to a Ventura cross-reference code simply by highlighting the serial number in the reference and hitting a macro hot-key. A similar macro generated the frame anchor codes. For example, say the manuscript for tip number 6.5.T56 contains the reference "as illustrated in Figure 4-6.5.T56." In this case, running the macro would generate the automatic cross-reference code <$R[F#,6_5_T56,]1>. Looks scary, but because the macro takes care of everything, we really didn't have to think about it. Of course, Ventura eventually processes the code so that the final reference reads something like "(See Figure 4-17)."

Using Word macros containing some relatively straightforward file manipulation tricks, we were also able to automate the placement of illustration captions. One macro read through the chapter text and moved the captions that appeared there into a new, caption-only file. Another macro converted this list of captions into a file conforming to the relatively simple Ventura caption file format. Finally, we substituted Ventura's caption file (which contained no caption entries) with the one our macros had generated. When we next opened the chapter, Ventura automatically grabbed our caption file and popped the correct caption text beneath each illustration. This technique reduced a day's work to two or three minutes, which was definitely the kind of efficiency we yearned for. (For a step-by-step explanation of this technique, see "The Gory Details.")

. . . .

Printing: direct from desktop to you

It had always been our hope to produce *Desktop Publishing Secrets*, including the final mechanicals, entirely (except for a handful of

---

3 With Ventura's automatic cross-referencing, a figure reference in the text, such as "refer to Figure 4-27," always uses the correct figure number, even if we reorder the figures, since Ventura will automatically renumber them.

illustrations) on our desktops. Therefore, instead of printing on a high-resolution imagesetter at a service bureau, we decided to print proofs and final copy on a desktop plain-paper printer, an 8 page-per-minute LaserMaster TrueTech PostScript compatible. This particular unit prints at up to 1000 by 400 dpi (dots per inch), but uses a patented resolution enhancement known as TurboRes to emulate 1000 by 1000 quality. Numerous manufacturers are now offering something like TurboRes in their printers. We chose the LaserMaster printer because LaserMaster was the first to widely market resolution enhancing printer controllers, and because their printers have worked well for us in the past.

Debate still rages whether the various forms of resolution enhancement, such as TurboRes, are as good as true 1000 by 1000 dot resolution. Thus, one reason we went the desktop, plain-paper route in printing our mechanicals was to demonstrate the current state of plain-paper technology. Some of our colleagues think the LaserMaster type looks great; others are privately scandalized by our choice. Now that you've had the chance to see for yourself, what do you think? How would this quality of type work in your publications?

We recognize, of course, that a key attraction of desktop publishing has been and remains device independence, and our plain-paper experiment is in no way meant to pretend otherwise. Device independence means that you can transport your desktop-created document, with relative ease and without distortion in its format, to a high-end typographic or color-production service bureau for final copy or prepress film. The point is that you're not stuck with your own physical desktop, that you're free to move your document to specialized systems should you require the extra quality. In fact, we had a high resolution imagesetter service bureau print some of our illustrations, primarily the ones containing grayscale images, because plain-paper printed halftones, even on a 1000 dpi printer, too often end up looking dark and murky after an off-set press run. For more thoughts on this subject see "Plain-paper typesetting" in the "The Gory Details" section below.

. . . .

The gory details

Casual readers are forewarned: The following sections contain some pretty technical stuff and are not for the faint-of-heart. If you want step-by-step descriptions of how we accomplished some of the more difficult and/or interesting feats this book required, read on.

. . . .

Picture perfect

We relied on Ventura's frame anchoring feature to speed our placement of graphic illustrations. We created all of a chapter's illustration frames on a blank page, giving each a unique frame anchor name. Ventura Publisher then moved them automatically to the right page (most of the time). To guide us as we created the frames, we used a list of illustration captions (prepared automatically via macro, of course). The captions in this list appear in the same order as the captions in the chapter, and include the serial number of each tip (from which the file name of the corresponding figure can be deduced) and the actual caption text. This is how we created and labeled each graphic frame with the correct anchor name:

1. We first added a new, blank page to the end of the chapter.

2. On the new last page, using the Sizing & Scaling dialog box under the frame menu (see Figure 10-2), we created a frame and set its frame height, frame width, and horizontal and vertical padding for a standard-sized illustration. A rather large horizontal padding value of 7 picas prevented text from wrapping into the left margin of the illustration. (Later, we applied the same horizontal and vertical padding to the smaller caption frame, which is placed below the illustration frame.)

3. Using the ANCHORS & CAPTIONS command under the Frame menu, we chose *Below* as the Caption option. We entered the following codes and text in the Label text box:

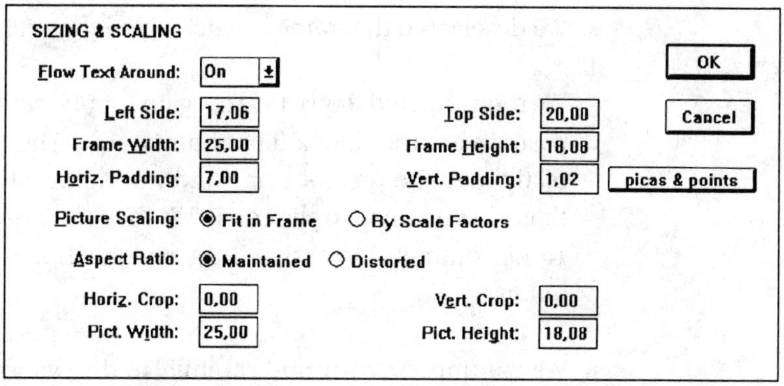

SIZING & SCALING

Flow Text Around:	On ±		OK
Left Side: 17,06		Top Side: 20,00	Cancel
Frame Width: 25,00		Frame Height: 18,08	
Horiz. Padding: 7,00		Vert. Padding: 1,02	picas & points

Picture Scaling: ◉ Fit in Frame   ○ By Scale Factors

Aspect Ratio: ◉ Maintained   ○ Distorted

Horiz. Crop: 0,00	Vert. Crop: 0,00
Pict. Width: 25,00	Pict. Height: 18,08

FIGURE 10-2 *We fine-tuned the dimensions of our standard-size illustration frames using Ventura's Sizing & Scaling dialog box.*

```
<F1008MP010.5>figure [C#]-[F#].
```

(The bracketed code changes the font to the Utopia Regular Expert Set, which contains the true small caps used in the figure label, set at 10.5 points. The [C#] and [F#] represent automatic chapter and figure numbers, respectively.) We purposely left the Anchors text box blank. We then cut the frame to the Clipboard.

4. We pasted a frame back in from the clipboard, using the PASTE FRAME command under the Edit menu (or by pressing the Insert Key). After referring to the printed list of captions, we selected the ANCHORS & CAPTIONS command under the Frame menu and entered the anchor name (based on the caption's serial number) in the Anchor text entry box (see Figure 10-3).

ANCHORS & CAPTIONS

Anchor: 6_5_T16	OK
Caption: Below ±	Cancel
Label: <F1008MP010.5>figure [C#]-[F#]	

Inserts: ○ Table # ◉ Figure # ○ Chapter # ○ Text Attr.

FIGURE 10-3 *Each frame created for an illustration was given a unique anchor name based on the serial number of the tip to which it referred.*

4. We deselected the frame by clicking on the underlying frame.

5. We then selected PASTE FRAME again (or pressed the Insert Key) to paste in another blank illustration frame. The new frame lay directly over the previous one and was automatically selected, so there was no need to click on it. We then used the ANCHORS & CAPTIONS command to assign it the next anchor name indicated by our list.

6. We continued slowly and carefully in this way, proceeding down the printed list of captions, until we had completed a stack of illustration frames for the entire chapter.

The last step was to use the RE-ANCHOR FRAMES command under the Edit menu, selecting the *All Pages* option from the dialog box that appears, thus moving the stack of frames into position within the document.

Capping it off with captions

After we had anchored the illustration frames as described in the previous section and saved the chapter, the Ventura caption (.CAP) file looked something like this:

@Z_CAPTION =

@Z_CAPTION =

@Z_CAPTION =

@Z_CAPTION =

Each of these lines signifies a blank caption entry, since, for the moment, Ventura is unaware that there are any. For a chapter containing 50 illustrations, for example, there are 50 blank caption entries, one for each illustration in the document (provided that you're not using using Box Text, which you should avoid at this stage).

As noted earlier, we used a Word macro to convert the actual list of captions (which we generated from the captions in the manuscript) to the Ventura caption file format. In that relatively uncomplicated format, the actual caption text is bracketed by @Z_CAPTION = on the left end and a carriage return on the right end, with a carriage return separating each caption. For example, a portion of our final Ventura caption file might read something like this:

@Z_CAPTION = When the dot on the i gets in the way, use the dotless i.

@Z_CAPTION = You can use italicized typewriter-style quotes (bottom) as a quick substitute for the Symbol font's prime characters (top).

@Z_CAPTION = WriteFontSize's grid displays the entire character set for the selected font.

@Z_CAPTION = ...etc.

Finally, we used the DOS COPY and RENAME commands to substitute the file we created for the one Ventura created. When renaming the file, we used the name of the corresponding chapter file and added the .CAP extension at the end. A chapter named 1_TYPE.CHP, for example, would have a caption file named 1_TYPE.CAP.

Icon and off

The Mac and PC icons adorning each tip or technique were created using a paint program on the Mac. We then converted them to PC PaintBrush format (.PCX) using DataViz' MacLink Plus Translators on the Mac. We contemplated converting them to PostScript font format (using CorelDRAW's WFN BOSS utility) but opted ultimately to place them as anchored graphics. This proved to be simple and straightforward. Here's how we did it:

1. We touched up the icons using the Image-In image editor and saved each icon as a separate TIFF file. The two files were named named MAC.TIF and PC.TIF.

2. In the blank document which served as the template for each chapter, we created two frames of equal size, one for each icon, and loaded one icon image file into each frame.

3. We selected each frame in turn, and, using the ANCHORS & CAPTIONS command under the Frame menu, we entered MAC in the Anchor text entry box for the Mac icon frame and PC in the Anchor text entry box for the PC icon frame.

4. We saved the template to preserve our changes.

In each chapter's text file, we inserted the anchors for the two frames. In the manuscript we had already placed—according to a convention established early on—temporary labels indicating a tip's orientation: the characters <> preceded all PC-relevant tips, <MAC> preceded all Mac-relevant tips, and <BOTH> preceded all tips applicable to both computers. (The dual brackets (< >) prevented Ventura from interpreting these ad hoc labels as typesetting codes.) We thus created three macros that searched for and automatically converted our temporary labels to properly formatted anchors. Each macro searched for one of three temporary labels and replaced it with one of three different types of anchor code, as follows:

- In one macro, the <PC> label was replaced with a paragraph containing the code @ANCHOR = <$&PC[-]>. For example, a typical title line first appeared in the manuscript like this:

<PC>Budget Bullets.

After running the icon-anchoring macro, the same title line would be split into two paragraphs, each with its own style tag, like this:

@ANCHOR = <$&PC[-]>
@TITLE_TIP = Budget bullets

In the above example, the @ANCHOR = portion is the tag name, and <$&PC[-]> is the code for an anchor point with a anchor name of PC. The [-] indicates that the anchor should use Ventura's *Relative, Automatically at Anchor* option in anchoring the icon frame. This means that Ventura positions the icon frame precisely at the anchor point, wherever it is in the text. Though we entered the frame anchor codes directly in the text, you'd normally insert frame anchors via the *Frame Anchor* option of the INSERT SPECIAL ITEM command under the Edit menu in the GEM Edition or under the Text menu of the Windows Edition (Figure 10-4).

To position the icon correctly in relation to the tip title, we selected *No* as the Line break option for the ANCHOR tag using the BREAKS command under the paragraph menu. Correspondingly, we selected *After* as the Line break option for the TITLE_TIP tag of the title paragraph following the icon(s). This ensures that the line doesn't break between the two paragraphs, and the icon(s) sits on the same line as the tip title.

- In a second macro, the temporary <MAC> label was replaced with the code @ANCHOR = <$&MAC[-]> followed by a properly tagged tip title paragraph. You'll notice that the only difference between this anchor code and the one used for the the PC icon is the change in anchor name from PC to MAC.

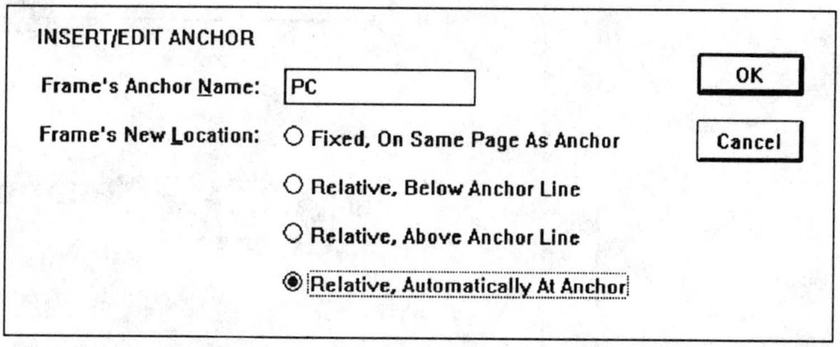

FIGURE 10-4 *A Mac or PC icon appears wherever an anchor point named Mac or PC appears in the text, entered via the* Frame Anchor *option of the* Insert Special Item *command. The actual frames containing the images are also name Mac and PC, respectively, matching the anchor point.*

- The temporary label <BOTH> required that both icons be placed side-by-side. Thus the third macro changed <BOTH> to the code @ANCHORS = <$&MAC[-]>*tab*<$&PC[-]>. (Note that an actual tab character, not the word *tab*, is inserted between the two anchor codes.) We gave the dual-icon paragraph a different style name (@ANCHORS instead of @ANCHOR) so that we could freely modify the line's indent and the icons' spacing independently of the single-icon lines (Figure 10-5). Adjusting the spacing between the Mac and PC icons was easily accomplished by changing the tab stop via the TAB SETTINGS command under the Paragraph menu.

With the icons' anchor points added to the manuscript, and with the Mac and PC icon frames (with anchor names) patiently waiting in our Ventura document, all we had to do was load the coded text file into the chapter, and the anchor styles and frame anchors automatically took care of placing the icons. The tops of the icon frames aligned with the tops of the text lines containing the actual anchor points. Since the icon frames were taller than a single line of text, the extra length of the icon frames extended below the line containing the actual anchor points, which was just what we wanted.

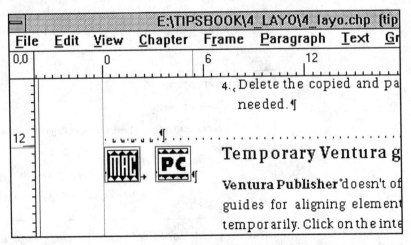

FIGURE 10-5 *A tab (the arrow symbol) placed between the Mac and PC frame anchors made it easy to adjust the spacing between the icons.*

Although we created a single frame only per chapter for each icon, dozens of icon frames appear in each chapter, wherever there's a frame anchor marked with the name MAC or PC. This automatic repetition of frames is an undocumented Ventura feature that's very useful for a structured document like this book. Global changes to the icons are also a snap since any change made to a single frame (scaling and cropping the image within it, for example) automatically takes effect for all frames bearing the same anchor name.

The heartbreak of headless pages

After adding the PC and Mac icons, we noticed an odd Ventura "feature" while printing a sample of the first chapter. For no obvious reason, some pages printed without headers and without any illustration captions. The longer the chapter, the more frequently this occurred; often up to 10 percent of a chapter's pages were so afflicted. After some checking we realized that the problem also showed up on screen, so it wasn't simply a problem at the printer (a PostScript interpretation problem, for example). The headers and captions were consistently missing from precisely the same pages every time we checked the chapter. This problem occurred in the Ventura Publisher 3.0, Windows and GEM Editions, and in a pre-release copy of version 4.0 of the Windows Edition.

Oddly enough, we could get the headers and captions to display and print a page at a time. All we had to do was turn to the problem page, select the HEADERS AND FOOTERS command under the Chapter menu, and then, without making any changes, just click OK when the dialog box opened. This way, at least, we could print the problem pages one-at-a-time while waiting for a return call from Ventura Software technical support.

After several calls back and forth and the examination of a sample file, Ventura Software's technical folks determined that we had run up against a "known problem," not to be confused with a type of insect. It seems that the problem of the missing headers and captions was related to the use of frame anchors employing the *Relative, At Frame Anchor* option. Tech Support people found that removing this type of anchor from a chapter removed the problem with headers and captions; it also, unfortunately, removed our icons. We were told that the problem first appeared in Ventura Publisher 3.0, but hadn't been in Version 2.0. We were also told that a quick fix to Version 3.0 was not in the offing.

Thus, after fretting for awhile, we decided to go all the way back to Ventura Publisher 2.0, with the Professional Extension, at least to print the book. We needed the separately installed Professional Extension for its hyphenation, table and equation formatting, and cross-referencing features, all of which we'd employed in the 3.0 versions. As we'd hoped, the disappearing captions reapeared when we used version 2.0, so we took it out of mothballs for the final production of *Desktop Publishing Secrets*.

Caption label heartburn

As we noted in the previous section, Ventura Publisher 2.0 with the Professional Extension offered us everything that version 3.0 did, minus the problem we had printing headers and captions. But we did run into one problem transferring our Ventura Publisher 3.0 chapters to version 2.0: The caption labels and the page numbers in the headers acquired a spurious set of extra characters.

Here's how a typical caption of ours looked in Ventura Publisher 3.0, as formatted with Ventura's plain text codes:

FIGURE 1-1 *When the dot on the i gets in the way, try using the dotless i.*

But this is what the same caption looked like (again in coded form) after we transferred it to Ventura Publisher 2.0:

1008^m 010.5figure 1-1 *When the dot on the i gets in the way, try using the dotless i.*

We discovered that Ventura Publisher 2.0 Professional Extension hiccuped when it translated Ventura 3.0 header, footer, and caption labels if the items' font attribute entry code specified type at a half-point size increment (10.5 points, for example, instead of 10 points). When Ventura encountered the half-point font attribute code, it printed the font attribute code instead of changing the font size. For example, in our standard caption label code, *<F1008MP010.5>*, the right half of the code, the *P010.5* portion, specified a font size of 10.5 points—hence our trouble.

We got ourselves into this mess, as it happens, in a rather circuitous fashion. Font attribute codes are useful if you intend to use more than one font in a header, footer, or caption label; they allow you to specify a font or point-size other than the default established with the paragraph's style. In the headers of this book, the page numbers are set in a different point-size from the text of the headers, so we prefixed the numerals with a font attribute code which specified the nonstandard (half-point, in this case) font size. For our caption labels, we initially intended to use two different font sizes and embedded one of them, the 10.5-point size, in the attribute code in the label entry, as described in "Picture perfect," above. In the end, however, we decided to use only one font size in the caption label; taking the path of least resistance, we left the existing font attribute code in place since it specified the point-size we wanted. It was this 10.5-point size attribute code, which we really didn't need, that was causing us heartburn in our captions.

Having gotten ourselves in a bind with our half-point font size header and caption codes, we now had to get ourselves out. We thought briefly about using styles to do so. The caption label has a style tag (Ventura generates one called Z_LABEL_FIG), and you can change the default point-size of the caption label by changing the Z_LABEL_FIG style via the Paragraph menu, just as you would with any style. Unfortunately, this doesn't change the font attributes embedded in the caption code. After several other ideas that also lead nowhere, we came to the conclusion that the best way to solve our problem was to specify integer point sizes, not fractional sizes, for our headers and caption labels. We consulted with our designer; fortunately, he felt the change wouldn't significantly alter the appearance of the page.

To switch to integer point sizes, we'd have to change font attribute entries like *<F1008MP010.5>* to *<F1008MP010>*, or delete the font attribute code altogether and let the style tag take charge. It was easy to make this type of change for the header page numbers since we only needed to change two headers (left and right) in the Headers & Footers dialog box for each chapter. But caption labels were quite another matter. To make the change by hand, we'd have to edit or delete the caption label font attribute codes frame by frame; Ventura lacks a global command for such changes. Considering that there are over 200 illustrations in this book, changing them one at a time, via the Anchors & Captions dialog box, would have taken most of a day.

Fortunately, manual reconstitution of caption label codes was not necessary. Instead, we deleted the offending codes by editing each chapter's chapter (.CHP) file and then specifying the desired font size with the caption label style tag. The chapter file is a fairly cryptic file that contains pointers to the files that compose your document and information about frames, anchors, captions, and other aspects of the chapter's organization. After making a backup copy, we opened a chapter file in WordPerfect and searched for the caption information. (We used WordPerfect instead of Word for technical reasons too arcane to get into here.) Here's what a sample portion looked like:

```
#BI 04 0210 01 . 01 0C1C 1C60 1388 0CC3 . * * * * 1103 0CC3 "6_4_T2"
__ * * * * * * * * 138C 0578
__ * * * * * * * * 138C 00E9
__ 0042 * * "Z_LABEL FIG" "<F1008MP010.5>figure [C#]-[F#]"
__ * . . * * *#BC FF 0200 01 . 01 0C1C 2923 1388 02BC . * * 0001 * * * ""
__ * * * * * * * * 138C 0578
```

Now this is pretty cryptic stuff, even for veteran hackers, but a couple of things stand out. The frame anchor name (6_4_T2, in this case) hints that this section refers to one of the illustration frames. Indeed, the line containing the text "Z_LABEL FIG" has just what we're looking for: the caption label, <F1008MP010.5>figure [C#]-[F#], just as we'd entered it in Ventura's Anchors & Captions dialog box. A little snooping through the file revealed that our caption label code reappears many times in the chapter file, once for each illustration. To delete every instance of the problematic font attribute code, all we had to do was use WordPerfect's search-and-replace feature. Here's what we did:

1. With the chapter file loaded into WordPerfect, we positioned the cursor at the start of the document by pressing Home + Home + Up arrow.

2. We pressed Alt + F2 and entered the text to search for, in this case it was <F1008MP010.5>, the troublemaking font code.

3. We pressed F2 again to enter the replacement text. In this case we entered nothing since we wanted to delete the entry.

4. We pressed F2 again to finish the search-and replace-operation. Here's how the example chapter reference looked after the search and replace:

    __ 0042 * * "Z_LABEL FIG" "figure [C#]-[F#]"

5. We saved the chapter file as a DOS text file by pressing Ctrl + F5. We then pressed 1, the *DOS Text* option, pressed 1 again, the *Save* option, and took care to enter the correct name and path for the edited chapter file.

Checking the Anchors & Captions dialog box when we opened the chapter again in Ventura, we saw that the bracketed font codes were indeed gone from the Label text entry box. Since there now weren't any font attribute codes overriding the font and point-size specified by the Z_LABEL_FIG paragraph style, we could change the caption label's font specifications very easily, using the FONT command under the Paragraph menu.

. . . .

Speedier than thou

Although Adobe Type Manager and the moveable menus of Ventura Publisher 3.0 Windows Edition made it easier to work with text on screen, printing turned out to be about two times slower than in

Windows version 2.0 or GEM version 3.0 or 2.0. In both GEM versions, for example, pages two through eleven of Chapter 1 printed in 2 minutes, 24 seconds; the Windows Edition took 5 minutes, 43 seconds to print the same pages. Extrapolating from these numbers, it would require approximately 22 hours to print this book using a GEM version of Ventura, as compared to 51 hours using the Windows version.

Ventura Software technical support maintains that the GEM versions print faster because Ventura wrote the PostScript printer driver for those versions; they were able to optimize printing speed. For Windows, Ventura must rely on the Microsoft or other third-party printer drivers that work with Windows, so they're stuck with the performance those drivers can provide. And, of course, Windows is a more complicated, hence slower executing, operating environment than GEM. Ventura Software did admit to us, though, that there is room for improving the speed with which the Ventura Publisher 3.0 Windows Edition handles the printer interface—something they say they are working on for version 4.0 and beyond.

"When I'm good, I'm very, very good..."

After some discussion, we decided that the quality of the LaserMaster TrueTech 1000 output was perfectly adequate for the type and most of the illustrations in this book. True, the print quality of desktop plain-paper typesetting is not as good as the quality obtainable from washing machine-sized photoimagesetters. Even with the micro-fine toners now coming into use, toner-based printing can't quite match the crisp, sharp edges and finer detail of photoimagesetting. Although we can certainly see the difference, we simply don't feel the difference is as important as do some of our colleagues, who are highly sensitive to the finest nuances in type and design.

Print quality was not the only factor in our decision to use the LaserMaster, however. Plain-paper printing, it turns out, has several advantages over photoimagesetter printing which must be weighed against the issue of quality. The number one advantage is control. For this book, we were our own service bureau. For the most part, we weren't dependent on anyone else's schedule to generate our final type or print last-minute corrections. Instead, we had instant gratification, no one- or two-day turnarounds. Geography also played a part: Semi-rural Ashland, Oregon, where the final pages were produced, lacks a photoimagesetter service bureau.

Advantage number two is economic. Plain-paper typesetters are a far less costly investment than photoimagesetters, so it's more likely you could own your own. Even if you can't justify owning your own, a service bureau equipped with a plain-paper typesetter will probably charge only one or two dollars a page, instead of the $7 to $15 dollars a page typically charged for photoimagesetting. The equipment takes up less space in your work area and doesn't require specially grounded or conditioned electrical circuits. Neither does it require additional space and plumbing for chemical photoprocessing and drying. Plain-paper typesetting print time is faster—3 to 4 mixed type and graphics pages per minute with the RISC-based TrueTech controller versus roughly 1 to 2 minutes per page for high-resolution photoimagesetting. Throw in the time required for photoprocessing of photoimagesetter type, and the efficiency of plain-paper typesetting is obvious to anyone.

All told, we've done some very hard thinking about the quality vs. efficiency issue at stake in plain-paper typesetting, and we're quite comfortable with our decision. We have found LaserMaster True-Tech TurboRes type to be surprisingly crisp and uniform, and the controller itself is fast and reliable. Although the PC-mounted printer controller board uses a Microsoft TrueImage-based PostScript "clone" interpreter, we experienced no PostScript incompatibilities. In fact, due to the large number of fonts used in this book (including an Expert Set font for each Utopia face), we were regularly running out of memory when printing proofs on our PostScript printer (which has 4 MB of memory). As a result, we eventually used the TrueTech AFM 1000—in its 400-by-400 dpi "proof" mode—to print our page proofs as well. The term *AFM* stands for Automatic Font Management. This feature keeps track of all the PostScript fonts installed on your computer's hard drives or connected network drives and those downloaded to the printer. If a font is needed, and isn't already downloaded, AFM automatically downloads the font at high speed to the TrueImage controller. This gave us the kind of convenience offered by those PostScript and compatible printers which allow for hard disk font storage via special SCSI interfaces. As a result we spent almost no time downloading or otherwise fiddling around with fonts.

. . . .

Playing by the (dotted) rules

To create the dotted rule above each tip and section title, we first tried using the RULING LINE ABOVE command under Ventura's Paragraph menu. In doing so, we hoped to be able to insert each rule automatically as part of the title's style tag. For the rule itself, we selected the *Dashes* option and adjusted the Dash Width and Dash Spacing values to get the effect our designer wanted. We also selected *Margin* as the Width option in order to have the rule span the page margins.

But, despite all our good intentions, Ventura Publisher threw us a curve: It created a noticeably longer dash at the far right end of the dashed rule, like the one in the rule below:

. . . . -

We tried adjusting the Dash Width and Dash Spacing values, after some fairly elaborate calculations, to avoid this unsightly and unacceptable artifact. We then employed trial-and-error, brute force, and wishful thinking. Everything failed to remove the final, fat dash. Exasperated, we called Ventura Software's technical support, which informed us, after some testing, that we were experiencing a known feature of the program.

Since it was apparent that we couldn't use the RULING LINE ABOVE command to create our dashed rules, we turned to two other more complicated techniques. The first is a variation on the second technique included in the "Spread the word" tip described in Chapter 1, which employs text justification to evenly spread a string of characters between the left and right margins. We used this technique for the rules above every tip and section title in the main text. Here's what we did:

1. On a page in our Ventura Publisher document, we created a new paragraph style named Periods. Using the ALIGNMENT command under the Paragraph menu, we selected *Justified* as the Horiz. Alignment option.

2. We entered a string of periods as a separate paragraph, with a space character between each period and a single additional space after the last period.

3. After the normal space character following the final period, we entered enough nonbreaking spaces (obtained by pressing Ctrl + Space) to force the fixed spaces to wrap automatically to the next line. The periods then appeared evenly spaced across the line.

This gave us the dotted line we wanted, but we had no desire to manually copy and paste this rule into the hundreds of locations where it was required. Instead, in Word for Windows, we opened the coded text file of our Ventura document and copied the dotted rule paragraph, Ventura tag name and all. Around this copied paragraph we developed a Word macro that automatically inserted the dotted line codes above each tip and section title in the text file. We then ran the dotted line macro in the text file for each chapter; hundreds of now perfect dotted lines were thus inserted in just a few minutes.

For the dotted rules used in the mini-contents overviews at the start of each chapter, we tried a different approach, one that employed dotted tab leaders. Here's what we did:

1. As before, we created a new paragraph style for the dotted line. For the dotted line itself, we entered a tab character only, no string of periods.

2. Using the TAB SETTINGS command under the Paragraph menu we selected *Right* as the Tab Alignment option. We then set the Tab Location at the right margin, so the leader would span the full distance from left to right margins.

3. Also in the Tab Settings dialog box, we clicked on the *Enabled* and *Leadered Tab* Options to select them. We then made sure the *Leader Char.* option was set for a dotted line and that the Leader Spacing was set to 1. Finally, we clicked on the *Auto-Leader* option to select it as well (Figure 10-6.

4. Using the ALIGNMENT command under the Paragraph menu, we selected *Left* as the Horiz. Alignment option.

5. At this point we had ourselves a nicely spaced dotted rule. The only problem was that the first leader dot was slightly indented inside the left margin; as a result, there was a small space at the beginning of the dotted rule. To correct this, we selected *Outdent* as the First Line option in the Alignment dialog box, and entered an In/Outdent Width value of 7 points. The outdent aligned the first leader dot with the left margin, hanging the unwanted space to the left of the left margin. This gave us a dotted rule extending from the left to the right margin.

Having tried both techniques, this last one is the one we now prefer since it inserts only a single character (a tab), not numerous characters (many periods), for each dotted rule. If you're using many such dotted rules, this can reduce your document's file size significantly.

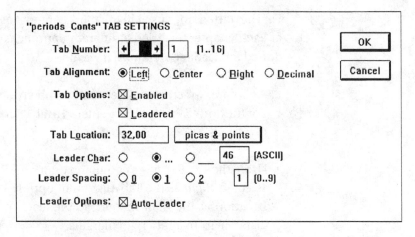

FIGURE 10-6 *The leadered Tab Settings, under Ventura's Paragraph menu, for our dotted rules.*

Buying Guide

Adobe Illustrator for Macintosh, $595;
Adobe Systems; 800/833-6687,
415/961-4400.

Adobe Illustrator for MS-DOS, $495;
Adobe Systems; 800/833-6687,
415/961-4400.

Adobe PhotoShop, $895; Adobe Systems;
800/833-6687, 415/961-4400.

Adobe Streamline, $195; Adobe Systems;
800/833-6687, 415/961-4400.

Adobe Type Guide, Volumes I and II, $20
each; Adobe Systems; 800/833-6687,
415/961-4400.

Adobe Type Reunion, $65; Adobe Sys-
tems; 800/833-6687, 415/961-4400.

Adobe Wood Type, volumes 1 and 2,
$185 each; Adobe Systems; 800/833-
6687, 415/961-4400.

After Dark, $49.95; Berkeley Systems;
800/877-5535.

Aldus FreeHand, $595; Aldus; 800/333-
2538, 206/628-2320.

Aldus PageMaker, $795; Aldus; 800/333-
2538, 206/628-2320.

Aldus Persuasion, $495; Aldus; 800/333-
2538, 206/628-2320.

Alpha Laser Cartridge; 800/999-6167,
213/696-2000.

ArchiText (two of 24 faces in FontSet),
$65; EmDash; 708/441-6699.

Arts & Letters, $695; Computer Support;
214/661-8960.

Bar Code Kit, $179.95; ElseWare;
206/547-9623.

Barbara Sisters fonts, $79.95; Judith Sut-
cliffe: The Electric Typographer;
805/966-7563.

Bill's Box Specials, Bill's Barnhart Ornaments, Bill's DECOrations, Bill's Victorian Ornaments, $29.95 each;
U-Design Type Foundry; 203/278-
3003.

Bitstream Amerigo (six faces), $45 per
face; Bitstream; 800/237-3335,
617/497-6222.

Bitstream Charter (six faces), $45 per
face; Bitstream; 800/237-3335,
617/497-6222.

BlackLightning Iron-On Heat Transfer
Toner, $89.99 (300-copy economy
size) and $247.99 (2,200-copy profes-
sional size); BlackLightning; 800/252-
2599.

Book Marketing Update, $48 per year;
Ad-Lib Publications; 800/669-0773.

Borders & Ornaments, DigitArt Volume
23, $99 (complete DigitArt set on Art-
Room CD ROM, $799); Image Club
Graphics; 800/661-9410, 403/262-
8008.

Borders fonts, $59.95 per package; Alt-
sys; 214/424-4888.

Canned Art: Clip Art for the Macintosh, $29.95; Peachpit Press; 800/283-9444, 415/527-8555.

Capture, $129.95; Mainstay; 818/991-6540.

Chicago Laser (part of Key Caps, Fluent Laser Fonts Volume 29), $130; Casady & Greene; 800/359-4920, 408/484-9228.

ChicagoSymbols, $10 shareware fee; available from most electronic and disk-based shareware software libraries.

ClickArt Color Graphics for Presentations, $169.95 Mac or PC version (second set of EPS format files, $19.95 add'l.); T/Maker; 415/962-0195.

ClickArt EPS Animals & Nature, $129.95; T/Maker; 415/962-0195.

ClickArt Publications, $49.95; T/Maker; 415/962-0195.

Clip Art Masterpieces CD-ROM, $149; Wayzata; 800/735-7321, 218/326-0597.

Color for the Electronic Age, $32.50; Watson-Guptill Publications; 212/764-7300.

ColorStudio, $995; Letraset; 800/343-8973.

Computer Color, $24.95; Chronicle Books; 415/777-7240.

Comstock Desktop Photography CD ROM, Vol. I $199, Vol. II $89, and Vol. III $199; Comstock; 800/225-2727

CorelDRAW, $495; Corel Systems; 613/728-8200.

COSMEP Newsletter, $50 per year, included with membership; COSMEP, The Int'l Assn. of Independent Publishers; 415/922-9490.

Creatures of the Sea; The Wonderful World of Insects; A Treasury of Birds; A Treasury of Large Mammals, $20 each; Sunshine; 512/453-2334.

Darkroom CD ROM, $399; Image Club Graphics; 800/661-9410, 403/262-8008.

Decorative Alphabets and Initials, $6.95; Dover Publications; 516/294-7000.

Designer's Guide to Charts and Graphs, $32.50; Watson-Guptill Publications; 212/764-7300.

DeskPaint (includes DeskDraw), $199.95; Zedcor; 800/482-4567, 602/881-8101.

Desktop Publishing CD ROM, $79.95; Educorp; 800/843-9497, 619/536-9999.

Digital Formats for Typefaces, $44 ($22 for students or for additional copies); URW; 603/ 882-7445.

Disinfectant, free; available from most Macintosh freeware and shareware libraries.

DiskExpress II, $89.95; ALSoft; 713/353-4090.

DiskFit, $99.95; SuperMac Technologies; 408/245-2202.

DiskTop, $99.95; CE Software; 800/523-7638.

DOS Mounter, $89.95; Dayna Communications; 801/531-0600.

Down to Earth CD ROM, $249; Wayzata; 800/735-7321, 218/326-0597.

DRM-600 multi-disk CD ROM drive, $1,295 (PC or Mac SCSI adapter $100 add'l.); Pioneer Communications of America; 201/327-6400.

Drop Caps font, $25; Image Club Graphics; 800/661-9410, 403/262-8008.

DynoPage, $125; Portfolio Systems; 914/876-7744.

Educorp CD ROM, $199 (two disks); Educorp Computer Services; 800/843-9497, 619/536-9999.

Electric Hand I, $45; Judith Sutcliffe: The Electric Typographer; 805/966-7563.

Envisioning Information, $48; Graphics Press; 203/272-9187.

FindPIXymbols, $30 (included free in all Page Studio Graphics font packages); Page Studio Graphics; 602/839-2763.

Fine Print, $45 per year (four issues); Pro Arte Libri; 415/543-4455.

Flags of the USA, Flags of the World, $125 each; Disk Art; 415/820-3734.

FlipTIFF, free; available from user group software libraries and electronic bulletin boards (on Compuserve, it's file FLIPTI.BIN in Library 9 of the Macintosh Design Forum).

Font & Function, free; Adobe Systems; 800/833-6687, 415/961-4400.

Font Special Effects Pack, $295; Soft-Craft; 800/351-0500.

FontMonger, $99.95; Ares Software; 415/578-9090.

Fontographer, $495; Altsys; 214/680-2060.

FontStudio, $595; Letraset; 800/343-8973.

FullWrite Professional, $395; Ashton-Tate; 213/329-9989.

Goudy's Illuminated Initials, $450; Giampa Textware; 604/253-6333.

Graphic Design for the Electronic Age, $24.95; Watson-Guptill Publications; 212/764-7300.

Graphics Master 4, $69.50; Dean Lem Associates; 800/562-2562, 213/478-0092.

HandOff II, $79.95; The HandOff Corporation; 214/727-2329.

Harvard Graphics, $595; Software Publishing; 415/962-8910.

INIT Manager, $59.95; Baseline Publishing; 800/926-9676, 901/682-9676.

INITPicker, $69; Microseeds Publishings; 813/882-8635.

Inkjet printer papers; PaperDirect; 800/272-7377.

Inkjet Ultra DTP paper, $15 per 100 sheets (approx. price at press time); PaperDirect; 800/272-7377.

Inside Santa's Workshop, $22.50; Henry Holt and Co.; 800/247-3912.

InterBridge, $799; Hayes Microcomputer Products; 404/449-8791, 404/441-1617.

Key Caps (Fluent Laser Fonts Volume 29), $130; Casady & Greene; 800/359-4920, 408/484-9228.

Laser printer papers; PaperDirect; 800/272-7377.

LaserTalk, $249 (Mac) and $399 (PC); Adobe Systems; 800/833-6687, 415/961-4400.

Leaves I, $75; Giampa Textware; 604/253-0815.

Leonardo Hand (includes Tagliente and Tagliente Initials), $79.95; Judith Sutcliffe: The Electric Typographer; 805/966-7563.

Lucida and Lucida Sans, $185 each; Lucida Math, $145; Adobe Systems; 800/833-6687, 415/961-4400.

Lutahline, $45; Judith Sutcliffe: The Electric Typographer; 805/966-7563.

Mac the Knife Volume 3 (Mac the Ripper), Volume 5 (People, Places, Things), $49.95 each; Miles Computing; 818/340-6300.

MacDraw II, $199; Claris; 408/727-8227.

Macintosh Repair and Upgrade Secrets, $32.95; MacMillan Publishing Company; 800/257-5755.

MacLinkPlus/PC, $199; DataViz; 203/268-0030.

MacLinkPlus/Translators, $169; DataViz; 800/733-0030, 203/268-0030.

MacroMind Director, $995; MacroMind; 415/442-0200.

MasterJuggler, $89.95; ALSoft; 713/353-4090.

Media Master, $49.95 (DOS or CP/M version); Intersecting Concepts; 818/879-0086.

Megachrome color printing service; ReproCAD; 415/284-0400.

Micrografx Designer, $695; Micrografx; 800/733-3729.

MicroPhone II, $295; Software Ventures; 800/336-6477, 415/644-3232.

Microsoft Word for MS-DOS, $450; Microsoft; 800/426-9400, 206/882-8080.

Microsoft Word for the Macintosh, $395; Microsoft; 800/426-9400, 206/882-8080.

Microsoft Word for Windows, $495; Microsoft; 800/426-9400, 206/882-8080.

MockPackage Plus Utilities, $49.95; CE Software; 800/523-7638, 515/244-1995.

MoreFonts, $149.95; Micrologic Software; 800/888/9078.

NameViewer, $15 shareware fee; AaStar Technologies; available from electronic bulletin boards and user groups.

NEC Photo Gallery, 399; NEC Technologies; 800/826-2255.

Now Utilities, $129; Now Software; 800/237-3611, 503/274-2800.

On Cue, $59.95; Icom Simulations; 312/520-4440.

PaperKit and PaperSelector, $19.95 (free with order of $30 or above); PaperDirect; 800/272-7377.

Papers For Printing, $34.50; Coast to Coast Books; 503/232-9772.

ParaFont, $99; Design Science; 800/827-0685, 213/433-0685.

PICTure This, $99; FGM.; 703/478-9881.

PIXymbols 2000, 2005, 2008, 2011, 2012, 2013, 2014, $145 each ($99 each, direct); Page Studio Graphics; 602/839-2763.

PIXymbols 2107/09 and 2110, $185 each ($125 direct); Page Studio Graphics; 602/839-2763.

PM4 Shortcuts, $10 (shareware); available from CompuServe's DTP Forum and other Macintosh shareware libraries.

PMA Newsletter, $25 per year; Publishers Marketing Assn.; 213/372-2732.

PowerDraw Translator, $275; Engineered Software; 919/299-4843.

PrintBar, $95 (per ImageWriter volume), $225 (per LaserWriter or imagesetter volume), $295 (per combined LaserWriter and imagesetter volume); Bear Rock Technologies; 916/622-4640.

PrintCache, Printer Control Panel, $149 each; LaserTools Corp.; 800/767-8004.

Printer's Ink, free; Thomson Shore; 313/426-3939.

Printer's Ornaments fonts, $59.95; Altsys; 214/424-4888.

Professional Photography Collection, $149; DiscImagery; 212/675-8500.

Prospera (includes Egyptian Bold Condensed), $119; Alphabets.; 708/328-2733, 800/326-4083.

PSPlot, $175; Legend Communications; 800/552-9876.

Pyro!, $39.95; Fifth Generation Systems; 800/873-4384, 504/291-7221.

Quality Artware CD ROM, $279; FM Waves; 800/487-1234, 415/474-7464.

QuarkXPress, $795; Quark; 800/356-9363, 303/934-2211.

QuicKeys 2, $149.95; CE Software; 800/523-7638, 515/224-1995.

QuillScript Flowers (part of ATF Classic Type, Volume 1), $165; Kingsley/ATF Type; 800/289-8973.

Recycled papers for laser and inkjet printers; PaperDirect; 800/272-7377.

Redux, $99; Microseeds Publishing; 813/882-8635.

Rival, $99; Microseeds Publishing; 813/882-8635.

SAM, $99.95; Symantec Corp.; 800/441-7234, 408/253-9600.

SendPS, free; Adobe Systems; available from the Adobe forum on Compu-Serve and most Macintosh freeware and shareware libraries.

Shortcut, $79.95; Aladdin Systems; 408/685-9175.

Signature, free; Griffin Printing; 213/245-3671.

Smart Art, $99; Adobe Systems; 800/833-6687, 415/961-4400.

SmartScrap & The Clipper, $89.95; Solutions; 802/865-9220.

SPECtacular, $79.95; Omega Systems; 916/894-6351.

Step-by-Step Electronic Design, $48 per year; Dynamic Graphics; 800/255-8800.

Stock Photography Handbook, $24; ASMP; 212/889-9144.

Stock Workbook/The National Directory of Stock Photography, $40; Scott & Daughters; 213/856-0008.

Stone Serif, Stone Sans, Stone Informal, $275 each; Adobe Systems; 800/833-6687, 415/961-4400.

Suitcase II, $79; Fifth Generation Systems; 800/873-4384, 504/291-7221.

SUM II, $149.95; Symantec Corp.; 800/441-7234, 408/253-9600.

SuperBoomerang (part of Now Utilities, $129); Now Software; 800/237-3611, 503/274-2800.

Surf Style, $50; Image Club Graphics; 800/661-9410, 403/262-8008.

Tagliente Initials (one of three fonts on Leonardo Hand disk), $79.95; Judith Sutcliffe: The Electric Typographer; 805/966-7563.

Tekton, $185; Adobe Systems; 800/833-6687, 415/961-4400.

Tempo II Plus, $169.95; Affinity Microsystems; 800/367-6771, 303/442-4840.

The Font Catalog, Vols. 1 and 2, $11 each; HyperActive Software; 612/724-1596.

The Macintosh Font Book, Second Edition, $23.95; Peachpit Press; 800/283-9444, 415/527-8555.

The MacTography PostScript Type Sampler, $162.50 (includes update subscription); Publishing Solutions; 301/424-3942.

The Norton Utilities for the Macintosh, $129; Symantec Corp.; 800/441-7234, 408/253-9600.

The Right Images CD ROM, $249.95; Tsunami Press; 800/448-9815, 908/613-0509.

The Self-Publishing Manual, $14.95; Para Publishing; 805/968-7277.

The Visual Display of Quantitative Information, $40; Graphics Press; 203/272-9187.

ThePage, $65 per year; PageWorks; 312/348-1200.

Tiffany Plus, $89; Anderson Consulting & Software; 800/733-9633.

Tom Boy, $45; LetterPerfect; 206/851-5158.

Totem Graphics clip art volumes, animal collections $125 each, general clip art collections $95 each; Totem Graphics; 206/352-1851.

Trade Customs and Printing Contract, $13.45; Printing Industries of America; 703/841-8100.

Treasury of Authentic Art Nouveau Alphabets, Decorative Initials, Monograms, Frames and Ornaments, $6.95; Dover Publications; 516/294-7000.

Troubador (includes Troubador Initials and Abelard), $79.95; Judith Sutcliffe: The Electric Typographer; 805/966-7563.

Troubador (includes Troubador Initials and Abelard), $89.95; Casady and Greene; 800/359 4920, 408/624-8716.

TrueTech AFM 1000, $6,995; LaserMaster Corp.; 612/944-9457.

Type Before Gutenberg I, $145; Adobe Systems; 800/833-6687, 415/961-4400.

Typographers' Ornaments, EPS series $49.50 per disk, TIFF series $25 per disk; The Underground Grammarian; 609/589-6477.

UniForm, $69.95 (DOS or CP/M version); Microsolutions; 815/756-3411.

Using Charts and Graphs, $34.95; R.R. Bowker, 800/521-8110, 212/645-9700.

VDT News, $87 per year (six issues); 212/517-2802.

Ventura Publisher, $795; Ventura Software; 800/822-8221.

Virex, $99.95; Microcom; 919/490-1277.

Wet Paint: Printer's Helpers, $79.95; Dubl Click; 818/700-9525.

WetPaint: Animal Kingdom. $79.95; Dubl-Click; 818/700-9525.

WordPerfect, $495; WordPerfect; 800/451-5151, 801/225-5000.

WriteFontSize, $7 (shareware fee); available from most Macintosh shareware libraries.

XenoCopy-PC, $79.95; Xenosoft; 415/644-9366.

22DISK, $25; SYDEX; 503/683-6033.

386MAX, $130; Qualitas; 301/907-6700.

911 Utilities, $149.95; Microcom; 919/490-1277.

1001 Ways to Market Your Books, $19.95 hardcover, $14.95 paperback; Ad-Lib Publications; 800/669-0773.

Index